The Hashemite
Kingdom of Jordan
and
the West Bank

Publication of this Handbook was made possible by a grant from Mrs. Judith Miller, in memory of her husband, the late Dr. Benjamin F. Miller — scientist, healer, teacher, author, humanist, poet, and a founding member and officer of the American Academic Association for Peace in the Middle East.

The Middle East Confrontation States

THE HASHEMITE KINGDOM OF JORDAN and THE WEST BANK

A Handbook

Edited by

ANNE SINAI and ALLEN POLLACK

American Academic Association for Peace in the Middle East

New York

First printing: April, 1977

Main entry under title:
The Hashemite Kingdom of Jordan and the West Bank
The Middle East Confrontation States.
Bibliography: p. 361
Includes index.
1. Jordan. 2. Jordan (Territory under Israeli occupation, 1967-   )
I. Sinai, Anne. II. Pollack, Allen.
DS153.M53   956.95'04   77-77821

Library of Congress Catalog Number: 77-778-21.

ISBN: 0-917158-01-6

Printed in the United States of America
Composition by Topel Typographic Corp., New York City

Table of Contents

5

III

JORDAN AND ISRAEL

IV

JORDANIAN-ARAB RELATIONS

V

JORDAN IN THE INTERNATIONAL COMMUNITY

VI

THE WEST BANK

VII

VIEWS ON THE FUTURE OF THE WEST BANK

VIII

JERUSALEM

IX

JORDAN: A POLITICAL DIRECTORY

X

APPENDICES

LEBANON
Tyre
SYRIA
IRAQ
Mediterranean
Sea
35°
37°
39°
33°
33°
Acre
Haifa
Lake
Tiberias
Izra
ISRAEL
Dar'ā
Netanya
Jenin
Irbid
Salkhad
Nablus
Ajlūn
Al Mafraq
Tel Aviv-
Yafo
As Salt
Az Zarqā'
Ramla
'AMMĀN
JERUSALEM
Azraq Shishān
Dead Sea
SAUDI   ARABIA
Hebron
Be'ersheba
Al Qatrānah
Al Karak
31°
31°
Al Hasā
ISRAEL
At Tafīlah
Al Jafr
Ma'ān
THE HASHEMITE
KINGDOM OF
JORDAN
Ras an Naqb
∙∙∙∙—∙∙∙∙ INTERNATIONAL
BOUNDARY
■ NATIONAL CAPITAL
WEST BANK
EGYPT
Elat
Al 'Aqabah
0   25   50 Miles
Gulf
of
Aqaba
Al Mudawwarah
0   25   50 Kilometers
35°
37°
39°
29°
SAUDI   ARABIA
29°
n. dlin
Source: Adapted from U.S. State Dept.
1977

Jordan R.

Introduction

The area called Palestine, a name given to it by the Romans when they crushed the last Jewish Kingdom, has undergone many divisions throughout its centuries-long history. From the Mediterranean, the coastal plain, which is modern Israel, is richer in rainfall and cultivation. The green inland slopes and formidable sand hills between the coastal plain and the Jordan River form the area that is known as the West Bank. Across the river, the desert is more in evidence everywhere and the rainfall more sparse, but the same taste of heat, the rolling hills and sudden gushing floods in ancient river beds characterize what is the modern Hashemite Kingdom of Jordan. The hills of Amman, Jordan's pleasant capital, echo gently the flowing hills of Jerusalem, Israel's capital, whose ambience combines the luster of the watered plains and the starkness of the desert. It is but a short ride from Jerusalem to Ramallah on the West Bank, which begins almost on the outskirts of Jerusalem, and from Bethlehem, just below Jerusalem, the main West Bank artery leads through the burning oasis that is Jericho and across the Allenby Bridge into Jordan, where the blazing yellow hills climb up to the pretty gardens of Amman.

Palestine is today a land of two peoples and two national destinies—Arab and Israeli. Its modern division into the states of Jordan and Israel began to be shaped when Britain, which had been assigned the Mandate for Palestine at the San Remo Conference in 1920, entered into a temporary, private arrangement with the Emir 'Abdallah, King Hussein's grandfather. By the time the British Mandate was confirmed by the Council of the League of Nations on July 24, 1922, the area of Palestine across the Jordan River—Transjordan—had been removed from the area provided for the Jewish National Home. It was ultimately transformed into a separate Arab state. For the Arabs and the Jews of Palestine, the international forum of the United Nations determined, in the Partition Resolution of 1947, on the creation of a Palestinian Arab state alongside a Palestinian Jewish state, both to be formed in the area of Palestine west of the Jordan River. The Arab states conducted a war in 1948 for the purpose of preventing the recommendations of the Partition Resolution. During the war, the West Bank—that part of Palestine west of the Jordan River that had been designated as a section of the Arab state—was occupied by the Jordanian Arab Legion. By the will of its leaders, it requested a union with Jordan. This union was by no means an unnatural one. The population of the West Bank had always had close ties of kinship with the population of Transjordan; there had always been economic and social interchange between the two banks. The West Bank population was the more settled and urbanized, but they spoke the same language, had the same mores and the same customs and traditions.

Jordan's annexation of the West Bank in 1950 was formally recognized only by Britain and Pakistan. It was strongly opposed by the Arab League, whose Arab state members refused to accept any solution other than the total annihilation of the State of Israel. A compromise solution was nevertheless achieved, in which the West Bank (so named by Jordan) was placed as "a trust in Jordan's hands until the Palestine case is fully solved in the interests of its inhabitants."

The West Bank-East Bank union worked, although it was not without its problems. Because the West Bank population had a higher economic and cultural level and greater political awareness, West Bank intellectuals found themselves in opposition to government restrictions on the freedom of political organization. They agitated for greater parliamentary control of the executive and also complained that the government favored the development of the East Bank at the West Bank's expense. There was never, however, any West Bank attempt to separate itself from the East Bank. Many West Bankers came to hold important positions in the state, and the West Bank itself became an integral part of the Jordanian economy. It was responsible, in the mid-1960s, for 60 to 85 per cent of the country's agricultural and 48 per cent of its industrial products, thereby furnishing some 35 per cent of the kingdom's GNP, over 40 per cent of the government's revenues and one-third of its foreign currency income.

But the situation in Jordan was intensely complicated by the influx of another group of Palestinians—Arabs who had lived in the area that became the State of Israel and who had fled as refugees to both the East and the West Banks of the Jordan (and to other Arab states) on the eve of the Arab invasion of Israel in 1948. Jordan labored to absorb this new population. The newcomers were granted immediate citizenship — which no other Arab state offered — and began to be absorbed into the economy.

Thousands of these new citizens of Jordan (officially still maintaining their status as refugees) soon left the refugee camps and made use of their skills, talents and education to gain positions in all sectors of the state. Their industry and ability created new suburbs around Jordan's towns, new industrial enterprises, a competent civil service, and a new look almost everywhere in the kingdom. Thousands remained stranded in the tattered refugee camps on both banks run by the United Nations Relief and Works Agency (UNRWA). All had gone through a traumatic experience. Their leaders—and the Arab states—had persuaded them to leave with the promise of a swift return to their former homes and enjoyment of the fruits of Palestinian Jewish enterprise upon the speedy Arab annihilation of the projected Jewish state. Instead, they had only become uprooted. After 1964, the discontented and the disaffected—and their breeding grounds were mainly in the refugee camps—were recruited by a new leadership that offered the promise of a renewed effort to annihilate the State of Israel and also the conquest of all of Palestine, including the Hashemite Kingdom of Jordan.

This new leadership was expressed in the Palestine Liberation Organization, created by Egypt. The PLO has been, since its inception, a loosely-knit umbrella organization of disparate groups engaging in terrorist acts directed mainly against Israel but also against one another on occasion, or against Jordan or other Arab states, their policy depending on the particular Arab state which sponsors and subsidizes them. The man who gained the attention of the international community was the PLO's third chairman, Yasser Arafat, born in Egypt but stemming from the Jerusalem branch of the Husayni family, the clan of Hajj Amin al-Husseini, Grand Mufti of Jerusalem and sworn enemy of King 'Abdallah as well as of a Palestinian-Jewish state prior to partition. Arafat, no friend of King Hussein, created an effective commando group — *al fatah* — and an even more effective propaganda machine. The Palestinian commandos soon became a state within a state in Jordan, openly calling for the overthrow of the King and the Government and for the creation in its place of a Palestinian entity that would soon spread, through war, across the whole of Palestine.

The PLO ambition to begin its hegemony over Palestine by gaining control of Jordan was stopped in Jordan's bloody civil war of 1970. Before that, however, Jordan had lost the West Bank, drawn into the war of 1967 by Arab states' and PLO pressure.

Jordan has often found itself isolated in the Arab world. Its King, who has ruled the country for more than twenty years, has often had to pursue policies, at least temporarily, that may have been distasteful to him, at the prodding of nationalist and radical elements at home and abroad. Hussein has, however, persistently pursued a policy of friendship and close relations with the West, at first with Britain, as Jordan's creator and chief sponsor, and then with the United States. There has been recognition between Jordan and the United States of the mutual benefits of this association. For Jordan, United States aid and support has helped to maintain this state's stability and independence. For the United States, Jordan has proved to be a consistent Arab ally in the uncertain and unstable politics of the Arab Middle East. Jordan is Soviet-backed Syria's southern Arab neighbor, but the Soviet Union has found little ground except that of professed mutual friendship to tread on in this state. King Hussein has taken advantage of President Assad's opening toward the West to achieve a treaty of mutual economic (and a form of possible military) cooperation with Syria—a country long a source of extreme hostility toward him. He has also cemented good relations with Egypt and Saudi Arabia.

The West Bank, severed from Jordan by war, is still closely linked with that state through the Open Bridges across the Jordan River that encourage the flow of produce and trade and commerce between the two banks and by the comings and goings of visiting families and West Bank politicians. West Bank members of the Jordanian Parliament still retain their seats. All West Bankers are still Jordanian citizens, and Jordanian law prevails in this area that is under Israeli military occupation. Since 1967, the Meir and Rabin

Governments in Israel have constantly reiterated the need to find a solution to end the occupation and to take the area out of its political limbo, although with certain modifications which the Israelis demand to guarantee the security of their own state. King Hussein has by no means given up his claim upon this former part of his kingdom. He proposed a plan for a West Bank-East Bank federation in 1972 which was unacceptable to Israel because it did not include any allusion to a peace agreement between Jordan and Israel. Despite the decision taken by the Arab states at Rabat in 1974 to name the PLO as the sole legitimate representative of the Palestinian people, Hussein has nevertheless persistently reiterated his sense of responsibility for the area's welfare and has put this concern into practical effect.

Current West Bank opinion appears to be swinging toward his side, although ostensibly most of its leaders profess to support the PLO—while displaying a wide range of differences with that organization's declared aims and objectives. Many among the new West Bank mayors, some of them PLO adherents, have made fresh contact with King Hussein and are receiving the benefits of Jordanian support for their municipalities.

The PLO, divided and divisive, has not been able to fashion a policy to modify its ambitions or to prepare itself to rule over a separate West Bank state—something it openly regards as only a first step, in any event, in its ultimate objective: the elimination of the two legitimate inheritor states in Palestine, Jordan and Israel. It could not agree, at its last National Council meeting in Cairo in March 1977, to reconsider its National Covenant, which calls for armed struggle to "liberate" Palestine. The organization and its factions have never accepted U.N. Security Council Resolution 242 of 1967 calling for negotiations with Israel and an Israeli withdrawal in a peaceful settlement. In this Hussein, like Egypt, has shown more responsibility. Though hostile to the Jewish state and not unwilling to see it annihilated, he has nevertheless recognized that cold reality would demand a peaceful settlement with it and acknowledgment of its right to coexist with Jordan in Palestine.

The problem of a solution to the West Bank is further complicated by the Jewish historical and religious ties with the area, and by the problem of achieving an accommodation regarding the Holy Places in Jerusalem, the third most sacred city in Islam and the center of Christianity, and the very heartbeat of Judaism. These are not, however, problems that need remain insoluble once a peaceful settlement is genuinely sought.

Clearly, history, geography and demography demonstrate that Palestine, east and west of the Jordan River, remains, as it has for centuries, the homeland of two peoples, its Jews and its Arabs. The Hashemite Kingdom of Jordan, beginning as an artificial creation, has in effect become a Jordanian-Palestinian entity. Whatever its future arrangements with the West Bank area may be, Amman has become the center for this region of Palestine.

I

Jordan: Past and Present

Jordan: Past and Present

Jordan in the Biblical and Classical Periods

That part of historic Palestine which lies on the east bank of the River Jordan and today forms the territory of the Hasemite Kingdom of Jordan has known the imprint of mankind for at least two hundred thousand years. Stone artifacts are to be found here, as in all the other areas of Palestine. Caves and mounds record the succession to each stage of technological and cultural development. In the neolithic period the inhabitants of Transjordan—the land across the river—produced giant stone megaliths, the source of the biblical accounts of the land of the Anakim. Copper was mined and used for tools and weapons. In the Bronze Age, cities and city states grew up, where people practiced agricultural and pastoral skills, arts and crafts, and developed mythology and religions and a syllabic script—the language of this period being the predecessor of the south Canaanite, of which the Hebrew of the Bible was a close relative.

Abraham and his family roamed the Palestinian uplands. Egypt conquered the whole area, as is attested by the Armarna letters of the fifteenth and fourteenth centuries B.C., written by local potentates in Akkadian, the *lingua franca* of the time. Transjordan was occupied in the thirteenth century B.C. by several Semitic-speaking tribes, and these established the kingdoms of Edom, Moab, Ammon and Amori and the kingdom of Bashan in Gilead.

The Hebrew tribes settled on both banks of the River Jordan in the twelfth century B.C., crumbling the walls of Jericho on the West Bank—a city whose first structures are eight thousand years old. The Hebrew patriarchs, all honored as prophets by Muslims, left an indelible impression on later local Arab folklore and belief. Hebron, on the West Bank, is the burial place of Abraham—the town itself is also know as *Halil* (friend, i.e., Abraham, the Friend of God). *Wadi Musa* is associated with the rock struck by Moses to bring forth water to the thirsting Israelites. His tomb is thought by Muslims to be on the northwestern shore of the Dead Sea and Mount Nevo, a shining peak in the distance in the East Bank desert, is confidently displayed by Jordanians as the spot where Moses stood and saw the Promised Land, while mysterious Petra, a desert city built into red rock, is thought to be the burial place of Aaron *(Jebel Harun)*.

These and many more places on both banks of the Jordan River are full of biblical associations, and the West Bank in particular is the scene of Israelite history and the Hebrew kingdoms; this is the land of Judea and Samaria, in which Jews have had a presence, both weighty and minor, throughout the centuries, from biblical to modern times.

The Greeks and the Romans had a presence on the East Bank as well as in the rest of historic Palestine. After Alexander the Great, the area became part of Egypt under the Ptolemies and part of a struggle between them and the Seleucid kings of Syria. Cities were developed on the East Bank and were populated with Greeks. The Greek language and religion was implanted in Ammon (Amman) and other cities. The power of these Greek cities was broken by the kingdom of Judah, and this gave the nomads—the Bedouin—a chance to extort blackmail from the cities in exchange for "protection" and to destroy many of them. In Roman times, the Greek cities formed a federation of which Damascus was a part, and their influence led to the construction of aqueducts (which are still in use on the West Bank hills).

The land of the east bank of the Jordan River was a backwater, but it had always been crossed by important roads. Even in the Iron Age, it was one of the main lines of migration to Syria. The ancient empires of Egypt, Assyria and Persia had tried to protect these arteries of commerce. The Nabateans had established a network of tracks guarded by forts along the roads, which later became Roman garrisons, and when the Nabatean kingdom fell and the province of Arabia was created, the Romans built roads through Jordan which are still evident, defended by a number of permanent forts and posts near centers of cultivation. Among these forts, Philadelphia (Amman) was very important. Under the Romans, also, a new form of agriculture was established. The land passed out of the hands of a few wealthy landlords and became the property of numerous small proprietors, thus bringing a much larger area under cultivation. In religion, the area had became strongly Christian, influenced by events in Jerusalem and the Byzantine rulers who succeeded the Romans. Even sections of the Bedouin tribes felt this influence, although most practiced idol worship.

What decisively molded the modern character of Jordan, however, was its Muslim conquest in 633-636 A.D., and the rapid Islamization of its population. Arabic soon became the language of the land and Islam the religion of the majority of its people. Jordan has become identified with the Arab-Muslim culture introduced from Arabia. So strong was this tradition that the Crusaders' century-long domination over the major parts of Palestine, which extended deep into the East Bank, has come to be regarded as only a brief episode.

The Muslim Conquest

The peoples of Central Arabia—also known as the Nejd—have throughout history moved northwards, through Jordan toward Syria and Iraq, and were absorbed in the local populations in one way or another. There were times when they swept over the area in a storm, following disturbances in the area of the Yemen, but the Muslim conquest brought not only new people but a whole new civilization, religion and culture to the whole Middle East.

The Prophet Muhammad is reputed to have passed through Jordan on a journey at the age of twelve. Thirteen years later, he used the same road on his triumphant drive toward Damascus: this road, still used today, is the great Pilgrim Route to Medina and Mecca.

The newly conquered territory became part of the province of Syria, which extended from the Mediterranean in the west to the Euphrates in the east and from the frontier of the Byzantine Empire in the north to the Sinai in the south. Palestine, Jordan (the East Bank) and Syria were divided into four *Junds* (military districts). The *Jund* of Palestine included both Jaffa and Amman in the north and Rafah and Ma'an in the south. The *Jund* of Urdon (Jordan) had its capital at Tiberias and included the towns of Deraa, Irbid, Beisan, Acre and Sidon. The Caliph Omar introduced laws to ensure the ownership of land for the newly arrived Islamic soldiers settling everywhere and also to protect the settled inhabitants of the conquered territories. He made a journey through Jordan to Jerusalem and expelled the Jews and the Christians from the Nejran, acting, he declared, on the last wish of Muhammad, who had declared that there should be no other religion in all of Arabia but the religion of Islam. The populations of Pella and Jerash remained "foreign," nevertheless, for some two hundred years after the Muslim conquest. The Jews and the Christians of Palestine, east and west, accommodated themselves to Muslim domination.

The Caliphate, suffering from incessant rivalries for the succession, changed its nature through the centuries. The Ummayad dynasty (661-750), forgetting the teachings of the Prophet—of love for the nomadic life and the desert and the simplicity, dignity and virtue this environment engenders (these mores are still the ideal of modern Jordanians today)—loved luxury and ease. Jordan, near Damascus and the desert, became a favorite resort of the Caliphs and their courts, but when the Abbasids who succeeded them moved their capital to Baghdad, Jordan became too far away, and the former castles and pleasure domes of the Ummayads were abandoned and fell into decay. Even the Pilgrim Road became less used; a new road was constructed across the desert from Mesopotamia. From the Fatimids, invading Palestine from Egypt, to the Seljuk Turks, Jordan again was a little-known backwater, subject to disorder and periodic local revolts. This situation was not much improved by the Crusaders, who ravaged northern Jordan in their struggle with Saladin. For both these conquerors, Jordan was only the hinterland from which the rest of Palestine could be ruled.

Saladin and the Ayyubid dynasty he founded were followed by the rule of the Mameluks, a people of principally Circassian origin, who sought to restore order on the east bank of the Jordan River so as to secure their vast dominions against Mongol incursion. They restored the Pilgrim Road but had difficulty subjecting the unruly Bedouin tribes so that the annual pilgrimage could proceed without hindrance from Cairo and Damascus to Mecca.

Throughout their rule, and into the next, Jordan remained an unruly place, full of hidden dangers to the pilgrim caravans.

Jordan Under Ottoman Rule

The Turkish Ottoman Sultan Muhammed (the Conqueror) captured Constantinople on May 29, 1453, bringing an end to the centuries-old struggle between the Muslims and the Eastern Roman Empire. Jordan now became of importance, since the main Pilgrim Route from Constantinople to the Hejaz passed through the middle of the area. In order to stop the Bedouin from molesting the pilgrims, the Turks occupied the area and made the *Wali* of Damascus responsible for it. He set up a government in Kerak and placed a garrison at Shobek—also suppressing a rebellion in Nablus on the West Bank. The new governor of Kerak proved rebellious, however. With the support of local tribes, he declared his independence from Ottoman rule. The Ottomans made no further efforts to re-establish their rule there, and the area ruled itself under a chief Sheik of its own.

The Ottoman system of government was, in general, to maintain a large military garrison and a staff of civil officials in the principal cities such as Damascus or Aleppo. The government maintained full control within five to twenty miles of the town, but beyond that taxes were only fitfully paid, and the roads were unsafe. In areas still further away, tribal chiefs were in control, virtually independent but paying occasional lip service to the authorities. Now and again, when tribal lawlessness passed certain bounds, a military force would be sent out as a punitive measure. If the tribes were defeated—which did not always happen—their villages were burnt and their encampments plundered. The weakness of the central government thus allowed the tribal chiefs to rule much as semi-independent sheiks. The tribes were almost always out of control; the town dwellers relied on the government, and the agricultural population suffered from the exploitation of both the government and the semi-independent tribes. The result was the neglect of the area and the growing disintegration of its agriculture.

Adding to the area's hardships was a new mass influx of tribes from the interior of Arabia, making the history of Jordan from the fall of the Mameluks to the beginning of the nineteenth century one of intertribal wars, incessant raids, disorder and bloodshed.

Ottoman rule had also redivided Palestine as a whole. The Ajlun district was placed under the *mutasarrif* of Nablus, and its northern boundary became the Zarqa River. The Remtha area, cut off from the rest of Ajlun, was included in the *Sanjak* of Hauran (in Syria) and the Ghor came under the governorship of Tiberias.

Palestine had again been administratively overhauled in 1873. Galilee and Samaria became two *sanjaks* (districts) of the *Vilayet* (province) of Beirut (called the *Sanjak* of Acre and the *Sanjak* of Balqa respectively). The rest of Palestine, including Judea and the south down to the Gulf of Aqaba became the independent *Sanjak* (or *Mutessariflik)* of Jerusalem. The East Bank was divided into the districts of Hauran, Jaulan, Amman, Salt, Kerak and Aqaba.

It was in an area suffering periodic incursions, changes of overlordship, frequent battles, denuded by ruthless exploitations and prey to brigandage and violence, recurrent famines, epidemics, petty wars and short-lived uprisings — conditions characteristic of both banks of the Jordan River—and with boundaries ill-defined but constantly changing and divided through the centuries that the modern history of Jordan began.

The Creation of the Emirate of Transjordan

During the whole of the nineteenth century the territory of the East Bank was a stagnant place hardly touched by events west of the Jordan River. Nomadic life continued unchanged, acknowledging no authority except that of the sheik of the tribe. The situation was different on the West Bank, where a considerable part of the population was urban, lived in villages or farmed the land. They had known something of Europe, in the form of the Crusaders, but had regarded them as uncultured barbarians. In the nineteenth century, however, the representatives of the West arriving in the Middle East appeared much more attractive to them, in the light of Ottoman misrule. The British, French and Russians soon made their presence felt in the whole of Palestine. Russian influence was especially strong among the Orthodox Christian population. German engineers built the Hejaz railway through the East Bank, a task completed in 1908. It connected Constantinople with Medina and passed close to the ancient road.

With the onset of the twentieth century, as great power rivalries intensified, the Ottomon Empire cast in its lot with Germany, and soon after the outbreak of World War I Palestine, as Ottoman territory, was drawn into the struggle. The Arab population had little interest in the war at first, but its impact began to be felt when trade became paralyzed and hunger and epidemics spread. Palestine was an Ottoman base, but on the East Bank Arab irregulars, organized and partly led by T.E. Lawrence with Feisal and 'Abdallah, the sons of the Sharif Hussein of Mecca, harassed the Turks across this area and repeatedly disrupted the rail traffic on the Hejaz line.

The participation of the Sharif of Mecca and his sons had been initiated at the recommendation of T.E. Lawrence. Sir Henry McMahon, Britain's chief representative in Egypt, established contact with the Sharif in 1915. This took the form of an exchange of letters. The key letter, written by McMahon on October 24, 1915, accepted Hussein's proposal to establish Arab independence in the Arabian Peninsula and in Syria and Iraq but stipulated certain limitations on complete sovereignty. These were that ''the districts of Mersin and Alexandretta and portions of Syria lying to the west of the districts of Damascus, Homs, Hama and Aleppo, cannot be said to be purely Arab, and must . . . be excepted from the proposed delimitation.'' This gave rise to a later dispute between Britain and the Arab nationalists, who maintained that Palestine was not part of the excluded area, while Britain argued that she had never intended to include Palestine in the area of Arab independence—a stand confirmed by McMahon in a letter to the Colonial Office dated March 12, 1922. But in 1916 it drew the Sharif and his sons into what became known as the ''Arab Revolt'' against the Ottoman Empire.

Sharif Hussein proclaimed himself the ruler of Mecca on June 5, 1916, and King (in Mecca) on November 2, 1916. General Allenby accepted the surrender of Jerusalem on December 9, 1917, captured Jericho in February 1918 and replaced the old wooden bridge across the Jordan River, which had been destroyed by the Ottoman army, with a new steel structure thereafter called the Allenby Bridge. The Ottoman Empire surrendered to the Allies on October 31, 1918.

The British placed Palestine under British administration immediately following its conquest while the coastal area of Syria came under French control (in keeping with the Sykes-Picot Agreement of 1916, whereby Britain, France and Russia had exchanged secret notes about the partitioning of the Ottoman Empire). The East Bank of the Jordan River remained, for the time, ruled by the Emir Feisal (Sharif Hussein's third son) as did the interior of Syria.

The Arabs had dreamed of establishing a huge and unified independent state in the whole Middle East—the Arab nationalists in their way and the Hashemite Sharif Hussein and his sons in their rather different way (they wanted a kingdom ruled by the dynasty). But the Arabs were not the only contenders for independence in the Middle East. There was the issue of Jewish rights to independent statehood in Palestine, as expressed in modern Zionism, which had inspired a movement, beginning in the nineteenth century, that sought to turn the Jewish diaspora back to its original homeland. As has been noted, Jerusalem and Nablus, among other places, had always had a Jewish population—that of Jerusalem was larger in the mid-nineteenth century than the Muslim and Christian populations—and to this Jewish population had been added Zionist pioneers who established settlements and towns all along the coastal plain of Palestine from the 1870s on.

The Palestinian Jewish community had contributed to the Allied war effort in produce, services and soldiers. By 1917, the Zionist movement was important enough to draw, from Britain's Prime Minister Balfour, a letter (dated November 2, 1917) that has come to be called the Balfour Declaration, stating that ''His Majesty's Government view will favor the establishment in Palestine of a national home for the Jewish People, and will use their best endeavors to facilitate the achievement of this object.'' At the Peace Conference in the spring of 1919, the British delegation opened discussions with the representatives of the Zionist Organization on proposals for a draft of the Mandate of Palestine. While the negotiations on the precise wording of the Mandate was going on, rule over the East Bank — now called Transjordan — was temporarily assigned by Britain to the Emir 'Abdallah, second son of Sharif Hussein. 'Abdallah remained in Transjordan with British consent—and an annual British subsidy. The final draft of the Palestine Mandate, therefore, received a new article which gave the Mandatory authorities the right to withhold the application of the Mandate to the territories east of the Jordan River. When the League of Nations approved the Mandate in this form and assigned it to Britain, the legal basis was established for the creation of the Emirate of Transjordan; it was removed from the area allotted for the establishment of the Jewish National Home, as defined by the Balfour Declaration.

Transjordan Under 'Abdallah

The Emir 'Abdallah (with the aid of British troops) succeeded in winning the quiescence of his Transjordanian subjects, a collection of disparate tribes, villagers, townsmen and nomads accustomed to the rule of their sheiks and hostile to any central authority. The new emirate's boundaries were delimited—its southern boundary was finally defined when in March 1922 'Abdallah's father, during a visit to Amman, transferred sovereignty of Ma'an, Aqaba and Tabuk to his son (the British government declared this section to be part of Transjordan in 1925). Transjordanian independence was proclaimed on May 15, 1923, together with an official British announcement in Amman by the British High Commissioner for Palestine that Britain recognized the country's existence.

With his country's status established, 'Abdallah's military force—the Arab Legion—was also created, with a British commanding officer, Captain F.G. Peake, at its head. Its chief task was to exercise some control over the Bedouin tribes (these were not disarmed because they had to defend themselves against the Hejazi tribes south of the border). On February 20, 1928, Britain and Transjordan signed an agreement, followed by an Organic Law (published April 19, 1928) which recognized the Emir 'Abdallah as the head of the state with hereditary rights and declared Islam to be the religion of that state. The Emir agreed "to be guided by the advice of His Britannic Majesty . . . through the High Commissioner for Transjordan . . ." Britain reserved the right to "maintain armed forces in Transjordan" and to raise and control those that it deemed necessary. One of the points in the agreement, the formation of the Transjordan Frontier Force, came into effect the same year. It was a British formation designed to guard the borders.

At this period Transjordan had a population of about 300,000—with only some 130,000 of this number living in towns and villages. A series of

agreements was made to control the movement of the nomads between Trans-
jordan and what became, with the Wahhabi conquest of the Hejaz, Saudi
Arabia. Government business was transacted by an Executive Council of
official members until 1929. At the country's first elections, in 1929, for a
Legislative Council, sixteen members were elected to represent Muslims,
Christians, Circassians and Bedouin. An additional six official members consisted of the Chief Minister, the Minister of Justice, the Chief Secretary, the
Treasurer, the Director of Health and the Director of Education. An addition
to the Organic Law of 1928 granted the representative members complete
freedom of speech during deliberations of the Council—for three months of
the year.

The Emir exacted written guarantees of good behavior from the sheiks of
the Bedouin tribes, set up a railway service between Amman and the rest of
Palestine, organized tribal courts and schools (for boys and girls) and other
government services. In 1928 the towns of Amman, Salt, Irbid, Kerak,
Ma'an, Madaba, Zarqa, Husn, Ajlun, Jerash, Tafile and Aqaba elected
municipal councils. In June 1931, new elections were held for the Legislative
Council. In the spring of 1934, 'Abdallah travelled to Britain, where he
negotiated amendments to the 1928 Anglo-Transjordanian Agreement. A new
British Resident was appointed to Amman, representing the High Commissioner for Palestine and Transjordan. The country was permitted to set up
consular offices in the neighboring Arab states and the Emir undertook to
defray the normal expenses of the civilian government and administration. No
customs barrier was placed between Palestine and Transjordan.

Transjordan in the 1930s

Politically, the population of Transjordan followed ancient and traditional
affiliations in the early years of the Emirate. The nomads and semi-nomads
aligned themselves with the centuries-old *Qays-Yaman* (north-south) tribal
division, in which every individual, family and tribe had its traditional,
genealogically-determined place in one of the two opposing factions. In the
towns family loyalties assumed a political character, and it was there that
political parties, full of the passionate intensity of traditional family rivalries,
first began to grow.

The most prominent of these was the *Istiqlal* (Independence) Party—a
branch of its Syrian and Palestinian Arab tree, and its leadership was made up
of Arab nationalists who came to Transjordan as political exiles from Syria,
Palestine, Egypt and the Hejaz. They preached an Arab federation to be
created by Transjordan, Palestine, Syria and Iraq and were vehement opponents of 'Abdallah and his pro-British policy. Their most powerful supporter
was Hajj Amin al-Husseini, the Grand Mufti of Jerusalem (and the leader of
Arab nationalism in Palestine) and his Palestine Arab Party. The Grand Mufti

became the vociferous enemy of 'Abdallah. The Emir himself supported the *Shaab* (People's) Party, formed in 1927, which became Transjordan's ruling party in 1937 and consisted almost exclusively of native Transjordanians, among them powerful local sheiks. This party had friendly relations with the Palestinian National Defense Party headed by Raghib Bey Nashashibi, the mayor of Jerusalem and no friend of the Mufti's.

In 1936, a plan to partition Palestine into an Arab and a Jewish national canton was promulgated by a former official of the government of Palestine, suggesting that the Arab canton should consist of the Emirate of Transjordan and the mountain areas of Galilee, Samaria and Judea, with an "Arab corridor" to the Mediterranean, including Ramleh, Lydda and Jaffa. The cities of Jerusalem and Bethlehem and the Haifa Bay area were to be placed under the direct administration of the Mandatory power, and the Jewish areas were to consist of two unconnected parts north and south of the Arab corridor.

The plan was rejected by Arabs and Jews alike, but it reflected the growing tension between the two peoples living in the British Mandate area of Palestine. The Emir 'Abdallah began to take an increasing interest in Palestine affairs, for he had ambitions of his own to resuscitate the Islamic Caliphate, to be ruled by his Hashemite dynasty in the form of a "Greater Syria." He made an effort to end the strike and the uprising organized by Palestinian Arabs in protest against Jewish immigration and sale of land to Jews by Arabs in 1936 and urged the rulers of Iraq, Saudi Arabia and Yemen and the Palestine Arab Higher Committee to stop the bloodshed and pin their faith on the good intentions of the British. He figured prominently in the report of the Royal Commission headed by Lord Peel in July 1937. The commission recommended that Palestine be divided into sovereign Arab and Jewish states and a British Mandatory zone. The Arab state was to include Samaria, most of Judea and the entire Negev (Israel's south) and was to be united with Transjordan. Prior to publication of the Peel Commission report, Nashashibi's party formally dissociated itself from the Arab Higher Committee, which was dominated by the Mufti. After publication, it came out against partition. 'Abdallah, for his part, sent an evasive reply to an appeal by the Arab Higher Committee, which wanted him to condemn partition.

When a new British government proposal, the White Paper of 1939, recommended the establishment of a Palestine state in which Jews and Arabs would exercise governmental authority on a joint basis, 'Abdallah did not view it with disfavor, in contrast to the other Arab states. However, it indicated that 'Abdallah—and Transjordan—had become directly involved in the Palestine problem.

In 1939, revisions in the Anglo-Transjordanian treaty gave the government of Transjordan more leeway. Revisions in the constitution turned the Executive Council into a Council of Ministers directly responsible to the Emir, who became commander-in-chief of the armed forces. A new commanding officer of the Arab Legion, Major John Bagot Glubb, succeeded Peake Pasha.

The country benefited by Britain's modernization of the Arab Legion during World War II; it became the most effective of the Arab armies. The British subsidy to Transjordan was increased; the Haifa-Baghdad road was constructed through Transjordanian territory, and the country proved its strategic significance to the Allies.

But the Emir and his policies had become more and more isolated from the other Arab states. King Ibn Saud, who had expelled his father from Mecca, remained an enemy. Syria and the Palestinian Arabs were suspicious of his "Greater Syria" ambitions, and relations with Egypt and Iraq (ruled by another member of the Hashemite family) were tepid. Transjordan was nevertheless one of the signatories of the Arab League, created in 1945.

The Hashemite Kingdom of Jordan

Britain, in 1943-44, promised to grant Transjordan complete independence after the war and notified her intention to the United Nations in 1946. In a new Treaty of Alliance, signed March 22, 1946, this independence was formally recognized. There were provisions for certain British military obligations and for British experts and technicians to be stationed in Transjordan, and British forces were permitted to be stationed at Amman and elsewhere while there were to be consultations between the two countries on matters of foreign policy "which might affect their common interest." On May 25, 1946, the Emir assumed the title of King of the Hashemite Kingdom of Transjordan, both his independence and his crown winning the approval of the other Arab states.

Under the treaty, the British Resident in Amman, Sir Alec S. Kirkbride, continued in office with a new title of British Minister to Transjordan. The state published its new Constitution for Transjordan on February 1, 1947. This provided for a parliament consisting of two houses. The Chamber of Deputies was to have 20 members (12 Muslims, 4 Christians, 2 representing the Bedouin tribes and 2 the Chechen and Circassian communities) to be elected for five years by male suffrage. The second house, the Council of Notables, was to have ten members, appointed by the King. The first elections took place on October 20, 1947. On March 15, 1948, a new treaty with Britain reduced Britain's military prerogatives but enabled her to retain the two air bases (at Amman and Mafrak) and set up a Joint Defense Board responsible for the country's external security.

'Abdallah, not unsympathetic to the Palestinian Jewish presence in Palestine, nevertheless found himself trapped into acceptance of the general Arab opposition to a Palestinian Jewish State—something he did not approve of himself. The United Nations General Assembly voted for the partition of Palestine into an Arab and a Jewish state with an economic union on

November 29, 1947. The Palestinian Jews accepted the resolution. The Palestinian Arabs—and the Arab states—did not. Threats had been made, and openly, that an independent Jewish state would be invaded immediately. The first Arab detachments entered Palestine very quickly. By February 1, 1948, the clashes between Arabs and the Palestinian Jewish community had resulted in over 2,500 casualties.

The British Mandate ended on May 14, 1948. On the same day, the Jewish National Council, meeting in Tel Aviv, announced the creation of the independent State of Israel. Contingents of the regular armies of Syria, Lebanon, Iraq, Egypt, Transjordan and Saudi Arabia moved across the borders. 'Abdallah, sure that the Arab venture would end disastrously, as he makes clear in his memoirs, turned out to have the only truly effective army—the Arab Legion.

The Israel-Transjordan armistice agreement was entered into on April 3, 1949 at Rhodes, with Dr. Ralph Bunche as the acting United Nations mediator. The war had left an area, designated in the Partition Resolution as part of the projected Arab state, going begging—the West Bank of the Jordan River. King 'Abdallah's Arab Legion had occupied the area in the war (and also the Old City of Jerusalem). 'Abdallah declared himself King of Palestine in Jericho on December 1, 1948 but this title was only a temporary one. On April 1, 1949 he annexed the West Bank and became King of Jordan, and included West Bank notables in his Cabinet.

The annexation was strongly opposed by the Arab League and recognized only by Britain and Pakistan, but it was not entirely a unilateral act. The demand had come from the Palestinian National Conference held in Jericho on December 1, 1948, which passed a resolution in support of the unity of the two banks "in appreciation" of 'Abdallah's effort during the Arab-Israel war. The Congress proclaimed 'Abdallah King of all Palestine. On April 24, 1950, the King responded in kind at the opening session of the new Jordanian-Palestinian parliament, which marked the final annexation of the West Bank following general elections.

Jordan, by 1950, felt the impact of its new West Bank population and of the addition of almost a half-million Palestinian refugees. It became the first—and only—Arab state to grant the refugees full citizenship. The West Bankers and the Palestinian refugees were more urbanized and more highly educated than the Transjordanians. They came to be included in Jordanian Cabinets and to let themselves be felt in all walks of the country's life.

The Arab League, so vehemently opposed to the annexation, had threatened to expel Jordan but came to accept it *de facto;* a compromise formula was worked out, whereby the West Bank was to be held temporarily by Jordan in trust. The League thus accepted the annexation—in exchange for 'Abdallah's renunciation of his intended signing of a separate non-aggression treaty with Israel (the draft had been negotiated in February 1950).

Internally, the population of the East Bank had been loyal to 'Abdallah and remained so, but elements among the added population of some 400,000 West Bankers and 200,000 West Bank refugees, plus another 100,000 refugees already in the East Bank, created considerable opposition to the regime. The Palestinians demanded curtailment of the King's power and that the Cabinet be made responsible to parliament. Rumors of the King's secret negotiations with Israel only increased the tension.

The King was assassinated by a Palestinian while entering the al-Aksa Mosque in Jerusalem on July 20, 1951. At his side was his young grandson, Prince Hussein. A bullet had been fired at the fifteen-year-old boy also but was deflected by a medal on his chest.

'Abdallah's son, Talal, succeeded to the throne. He approved a change in the constitution making the Cabinet responsible to parliament (a two-thirds majority was required to dismiss the Cabinet; this was amended in 1954 to a simple majority) and strove for a rapprochement with Egypt and Syria. He was, however, found to be mentally ill and was declared unfit to rule and deposed by parliament. Hussein, his son, was crowned (following a regency until he attained the age of eighteen) in May 1953.

On December 14, 1955 Jordan finally achieved international recognition when it was admitted to the United Nations.

Jordan Under Hussein

Hussein, under twenty years of age, king of a country dependent on Britain, faced one of his greatest tests very soon; he found himself involved in a tussle with President Nasser of Egypt, the most admired man in the Arab world.

The battle centered around Jordan's possible participation in the Baghdad Pact, which Britain wanted and which Hussein's cousin Feisal of Iraq was ready to sign with Turkey. In March 1955, Nasser called on Jordan to join a security pact with Syria, Egypt and Saudi Arabia. Hussein was not enthusiastic — he had evidence by the bushelful that Egypt was instigating trouble in Jordan—and the taking of such a step by Jordan would endanger the British connection.

Hussein leaned toward signing the Baghdad Pact. When that became known, he was blasted by Radio Cairo, the government fell and demonstrations poured out in the streets of most Jordanian towns. Egged on by Egypt, there were riots everywhere, started by crowds of schoolchildren rampaging through the streets armed with slogans provided by their teachers. In this situation, British prime minister Anthony Eden flew several parachute battalions to Cyprus. On December 31, Hussein received six of nineteen Vampire jet fighters promised by Britain. The army restored order, remaining loyal to the King, but Hussein said that Jordan would join no pacts, neither British nor Arab, and Nasser stopped his propaganda attacks.

Hussein's next decision was to fire Glubb, the commanding officer of the Arab Legion. It did not destroy his links with Britain, and it gained him popularity and prestige in the Arab world.

In the spring of 1956 he was again faced by a new call to Arab unity by Nasser, in a new alignment of states. Hussein now faced the radicalized Palestinian refugees at home and Nasser abroad. His own sentiments leaned toward the traditional policies of Iraq, allied at the time with Saudi Arabia against Nasser.

To counterbalance the threat growing from an Arab Legion that was still loyal and manned mostly by Transjordanian Bedouin, but also mixed with technical and administrative Palestinian personnel, he made his uncle, Sharif Nasser, head of a private army of Bedouin to protect the royal palace (this Royal Guard soon became a full brigade). 'Ali Abu Nuwar, seemingly loyal, was appointed to Glubb's former position and the King's cousin, 'Ali al Hiyari, as his deputy. The Arab offer to grant Jordan an annual subsidy to replace the £10,000,000 given by Britain was politely refused. Hussein flew to Iraq, Damascus and Egypt, agreed in vague terms on mutual coordination and defense policies with the radical Arab states and on the establishment of closer economic and cultural links, but expressly excluded any commitment to a unified military command.

The United States refusal in 1956 to finance the Aswan Dam set President Nasser to action again. He nationalized the Suez Canal. Throughout the summer, tension on the Israel-Jordan border increased. Bands of infiltrators raided Israel from Jordan, and Israel retaliated.

The Palestinians clamored for war. Egypt, Iraq and Syria offered troops, but Hussein was highly reluctant to invite the presence of foreign armies on his soil, and especially those from Egypt and Syria. Jordan did not participate in the Suez war, but Hussein found himself forced to invite Saudi, Iraq and Syrian troops to enter the country.

In January 1957 Jordan signed an agreement with Egypt, Syria and Saudi Arabia providing for an annual subsidy of £12,500,000 to cover the country's defense expenditure and thus enable her to abrogate her treaty with Britain. The Anglo-Jordanian Treaty of 1948 was annulled in March 1957, and all British troops were evacuated by July. Parliament recommended acceptance of Soviet aid.

To Hussein, this was anathema, and the Arab subsidy meant a threat to his independence. Taking advantage of the Eisenhower Doctrine promulgated after the Suez war, he asked the United States for aid and began a propaganda campaign against communist infiltration as a threat to the Muslim religion.

The clash between the King and the government, led by Nabulsi, brought the army to the fore again—and again the army proved its allegiance to their king. On the West Bank, the streets filled with demonstrators. The main Jordanian radio station in Jerusalem refused to transmit his speech, the station at Ramallah was beseiged by crowds who interrupted the King's message to his army, a brigade of some 3,000 Syrian troops stood in a state of alert in the north, the army commander, al Hiyari, defected to Syria and Radio Cairo blasted him once more, but Hussein held his ground. The situation was not a little helped by the fact that U.S. Sixth fleet units were moved to the eastern Mediterranean and that the White House declared that it considered the "independence and integrity of Jordan" as vital.

Aged twenty-one, Hussein instituted military rule in Jordan in April 1957. Though the British subsidy was coming to an end, and Jordan's relations with Syria and Egypt had worsened with the fall of the Nabulsi government, the country's internal situation was under control. Jordan's chief problem was economic. The promised Arab subsidy was not coming through—except for the Saudi's share. A plan to harness the Yarmuk River for irrigation and hydroelectric schemes was held up by the prevailing Israeli-Syrian-Jordanian hostility, and Jordan had no oil. The United States offered aid in the form of military equipment—Syria's move toward the Soviet Union had brought the American realization of Jordan's usefulness as an ally. In the Arab arena, Hussein formed an Arab Federation with Iraq (Februrary 14, 1958), and five months later his cousin Feisal was assassinated, and the Iraqi "revolution" brought still another radical regime to Jordan's doorstep. Even the Saudi King Saud failed Hussein. Feisal, his prime minister, wanted relations with Nasser. Jordan was suddenly sealed off and her king threatened with extinction.

In this critical hour of need, oil was flown in by the United States over Israeli airspace, with Israeli approval—a humiliating event for Hussein. People expected his assassination daily. He was again aided by Britain, whose prime minister, Macmillan, sent paratroopers (July 1958)—again via overflights across Israeli territory. Jordan severed relations with the United Arab Republic (of Egypt and Syria, 1958-1961) and lodged a complaint with the U.N. Security Council (on the ground that armed infiltrators had been sent across Jordan's borders). The issue was transferred to a special session of the U.N. General Assembly, which adopted a compromise resolution (drafted by the Arab states) which noted that these states had agreed, in the Arab League Pact, to respect each other's sovereign independence and which welcomed their renewed assurances to observe that commitment and requested that arrangements be made that would "facilitate the early withdrawal of the foreign troops."

The British troops were withdrawn from Jordan by October, and the British intervention had given Hussein his breathing space. A Nasserite plot to overthrow him was uncovered in the spring of 1959, but by the early 1960s political stability was once more established.

Now Hussein engineered the naming of his brother Hassan as crown prince in preference to his second brother, Muhammed, who was judged unfit for the throne. In this period of stability, and with U.S. and British aid, Jordan's industries developed and new industries sprang up. The new Palestinian-Jordanian middle class of industrial workers, managers, businessmen, merchants, teachers and other professional people drew much of its dynamism from the West Bankers and the Palestinians, and prosperous suburbs sprang up around Amman and other Jordanian towns.

The King favored the East Bank, which was a West Bank grievance, but the East Ghor Canal on the east side of the Jordan Valley improved agricultural output vastly, the national income increased at a rapid rate, and the economy was advanced by a competent civil service—mainly Palestinian.

Hussein's reconciliation with Nasser began in 1961; he joined Egypt in a common Arab opposition to Israel's proposal to draw water from the Jordan River to irrigate its Negev desert. (The Johnston Plan of 1955 had allotted 40% of this water to Israel and 60% to Lebanon, Jordan and Syria.) Israel had nearly completed her pipeline from Lake Tiberias, and how to stop Israel's completion of the project became one of the leading topics at the first Arab Summit meeting of January 1964 in Cairo. Jordan's stability was not ensured as a result of the Summit. Her refusal to sign the agreement dividing the Jordan waters—on the common Arab ground that this would imply recognition of Israel—held back her own irrigation projects. The direct consequence of this meeting, however, was the creation of a "Palestinian entity"—the Palestine Liberation Organization (PLO)—with a military force (decided upon at a second Arab Summit conference in Alexandria in September 1964). Jordan rejected proposals to station Arab troops on her territory to protect her from Israel, recognized the PLO only reluctantly and allowed it to open an office in Jerusalem.

War and Civil War

President Nasser—with Jordan's reluctant consent—had created (via the Arab League) the Palestine Liberation Organization. Its most active component was *al fatah,* headed by Yasser Arafat, recruited by him in Kuwait, Egypt and Jordan. Jordan, where the bulk of the refugees were living, was the source of his main strength, and the refugee camps were *fatah*'s training grounds. Hussein was once again trapped by radicals, and this time they were well-armed, heavily subsidized by the various Arab states, well-trained and in his very heartland.

Forming themselves into commando units, the various PLO factions began an intensified series of actions against Israel from Jordanian territory, bringing about at times large-scale Israeli retaliation. Hussein was accused of neglecting the defense of his people—mainly by the Syrians and the PLO, which called on all Jordanians to revolt, while Radio Cairo described the King and his government as "imperialist stooges" with whom cooperation was impossible.

In the spring of 1967, as tension between Egypt and Israel increased and war appeared inevitable, King Hussein flew to Cairo, where he signed a defense agreement with Nasser on May 30, 1967, placing his troops under Egyptian command. On the eve of the Six-Day War, the Israeli government advised the King, via the United Nations, that Israel would not attack Jordan if Jordan remained neutral. Hussein, with the PLO and Egypt on his back—and perhaps believing in an Arab victory—shelled the Israeli sector of Jerusalem. The result of Jordan's participation in the war was the loss of the West Bank and a new influx of refugees—some 200,000 people.

The loss of the West Bank was a heavy blow to Hussein's position and prestige, and the new refugees placed a new burden, for the first several years, on Jordan's economy. Hussein's position was also continuously being undermined by the Palestinian Arab commando organizations which he permitted, step by step, to establish what became virtually a state within a state in Jordan.

Hussein constantly reminded the organizations that Jordan had given the Palestinian refugees vastly greater opportunities than they enjoyed in any other Arab state and that Jordan's development had, because of this, come about with no little difficulty. When he opened the first meeting of the Palestinian National Council in Jerusalem in 1965, he had asked the organizations to guarantee their full support, but later, following differences with Ahmed Shuqaiyri, the PLO head, closed the PLO office in Jerusalem. A battle of words—over Arab states' radios—had followed. It had reached a peak in July 1966, when Shuqaiyri was reminded (by the Jordanian delegate to the summit meeting of Arab heads of state in Cairo) that he himself had declared on occasion: "We must liberate Amman before we liberate Tel Aviv." Shuqaiyri was replaced by Yahia Hamoude in December 1967. The battle of words calmed down for a while, but the battle of arms escalated.

This was expressed in a mushrooming of the PLO organizations in Jordan and a sharp increase in their raids into Israel, usually with the cooperation and backing of Jordanian troops and artillery. When Israel carried out reprisals, the Jordanian army fought side by side with the Palestinian commandos. Hussein complained that control was slipping out of his hands. The organizations, and particularly their most vociferous member, the *Popular Front for the Liberation of Palestine,* openly agitated for his overthrow. Hussein had accepted United Nations Resolution 242 of 1967; this demonstrated, they claimed, that he wanted a peaceful settlement with Israel. The PLO, a collection of terrorist groups with differing ideologies and concepts, were united on one point only: there was to be no peace with Israel, no acceptance of Israel and no recognition of Israel (in the spirit of the Khartoum Resolution of 1967—to which Hussein had been a party).

The organizations moved their bases of operation from the front lines to the major towns in Jordan. Amman became their headquarters. They checked people's identity cards, confiscated cars and interrogated people. Clashes between the Jordanian army and the organizations followed the government's announcement of new security measures on February 10, 1970. The Palestinians resisted all state control, and all the towns of Jordan became battlefields. Hussein himself almost became a victim of assassination when a commando group attacked his car on June 9, 1970.

Arafat, the new head of the PLO, broadcasting from Cairo, denounced the attack, a well-conceived maneuver to bring about a truce, although he had in reality little or no control over any organization except *al fatah*. The organizations clamored for the dismissal of Zayd bin Shakir, the King's cousin and commander of the army division stationed around Amman, Sharif Nasser bin Jamil, the Commander-in-Chief of the Army, Rasul al-Kaylani, the Minister of Interior and Sallah Abou Zeid, the Minister of Information. They assassinated bin Shakir's sister and murdered Robert Perry, the United States military attaché, but Hussein nevertheless dismissed the four men and stopped his army from entering Amman. Abd al-Mun'im al-Rifa'i became head of a new Cabinet of "reconciliation" and in a July 10 agreement the commandos were given freedom of movement—if they pledged to move their bases from Amman.

The agreement proved to be only a piece of paper. Following the hijacking of three commercial airliners in September and a new attempt on the King's life, martial law was declared on September 16, and a new Cabinet was appointed composed of army officers, with the demand that the organization lay down their arms.

The civil war that followed lasted ten days. In the north, the Palestinian commandos had the backing of Syria, which sent troops across the border, but these were pushed back by the army, loyal as ever to the King. The organizations accepted the cease fire of September 25. The next day Hussein appointed a Palestinian, Ahmad Tuqan, to head the government.

Meeting in Cairo, under the auspices of President Nasser, Hussein and Arafat signed a new agreement on September 27. An agreement of October 13 forced the commandos to retire from the Jordanian towns. A new Cabinet was appointed under Wasfi al-Tal. He was assassinated by *Black September,* and further commando-army clashes ushered in the denouement on July 19, 1971—the army's destruction of the commando strongholds between Ajlun and Jerash. The battle of Jerash, the final and extremely bloody clash between Hussein and the organizations, is constantly being brought up by the PLO today.

Hussein, however, issued a Royal Decree of amnesty for those imprisoned in the course of events. On September 7 he announced the formation of the Jordanian National Union—and elections. In 1972, in an effort to reconcile Palestinian and Hashemite positions, he announced his plan for a federal Kingdom, to consist of the East and West Banks. To the PLO it may have been a hint that the King envisaged this as a necessary first stage in the eventual takeover of the whole of Palestine, but neither the PLO nor the Israelis found it acceptable. The PLO regarded the plan as a Hashemite ploy. Israel saw no recognition of its existence mentioned anywhere.

Jordan: 1973-1977

The war of October 1973 took Jordan by surprise. The King's response to Syrian and Egyptian demands for a third front on the Jordan River was to order his army to full alert and to call up his reserves. (Hussein later described his contribution to the war effort as one of pinning down considerable Israeli resources along a static Jordanian border and in this way helping to defend the Syrian army's left flank.) He also, however, deployed one of his best units in Syria—the same brigade he had used three years earlier to repulse the invading fifth Syrian Division in northern Jordan. (The irony was not lost in Damascus, which pointedly neglected to thank him or even acknowledge the move publicly.) The military commitment was accompanied by internal quiet in Jordan. The towns and the refugee camps remained calm, and Hussein toured his army units to explain why a third front was not advisable.

After the war, Syria and Egypt took up the Palestinian issue once again, providing a new challenge to Hussein. Egypt offered the PLO leaders a role in what appeared to be a coming Geneva peace conference with Israel, and recognition by the Arab League of their status as the "sole authorized representatives" of the Palestinian people. For Jordan it indicated a divesting of its own status as a bargaining partner over the future of the West Bank. The King hinted that he might agree to a PLO delegation at the peace conference—as a complement to the Jordanian representation. His position remained that the West Bank had to be returned to Jordanian sovereignty and that only after that could a realization of Palestinian rights of self-determination follow. He had the promise of Dr. Kissinger. it appears, that the Hashemite Kingdom's interests would not be short-changed, and on the West Bank itself, Israel's initiative of an "Open Bridges" policy, accepted by Jordan, had opened the opportunity to maintain links between the two banks. Hussein had many West Bank supporters who wished to reunite the kingdom, and others, though they did not wish to return to Hashemite rule, did not want PLO rule either.

The Jarring Mission of 1973 and the Geneva Conference—both of which Hussein had found acceptable—ended without any solution to the Palestinian problem. The PLO could not bring about the convening of the Palestine National Council, which had to pass the appropriate resolutions enabling the organization to go to Geneva, and Arafat demonstrated once again that he had no control over the radical elements within it.

Apprehensive that an Egyptian-Israeli agreement in negotiation in 1974 might leave Jordan in a precarious position, Hussein, through his prime minister, Rifa'i, demanded that Jordan join the disengagement talks. The

Jordan River, it was argued, was a much less formidable natural barrier than the Suez Canal, and therefore a separation of forces along that border should be effected as well—presumably by an Israeli withdrawal. This idea reportedly led to talks between Jordanian and Israeli representatives in a closing meeting in Geneva. The Israel government viewed the issue favorably, since "separation of forces talks" could lead to a Jordanian-Israeli settlement of wider issues, but opposition from *Likhud,* the opposition bloc, and other parties in the government coalition, found such talks "premature," protesting that this would lead to the creation of a Palestinian state whose only objective, as often stated by the PLO, would be Israel's demise. The idea was also certainly not acceptable to the PLO.

Between February 2 and 7, 1974, a minor crisis made itself apparent in the Jordanian army. Complaints centered around lack of funds and took the form of petitions, road-blocks and verbal confrontations. Jordan's inflation rate was soaring, and the government had granted a 10% salary increment to civilian officials while the military had received only minor increases. Hussein flew back from a trip abroad and personally promised to match the civil servants' increases, and the crisis died down. There was, however, dissatisfaction with the unpopular Chief-of-Staff, bin Shakir and a demand for the acquisition of ground-to-air missiles and tanks from the Soviet Union.

On the West Bank there was talk among some of the notables of establishing a Supreme Palestinian Committee as a permanent representative body for the West Bank and the Gaza Strip. Crown Prince Hassan pressed the King to dissociate himself once and for all from the Palestinian problem and to declare his return to the pre-1948 Kingdom of Transjordan, something the King appeared not willing to contemplate, for relinquishing his claim to the West Bank would amount to giving up half his kingdom. He would become "King of Amman"—as his enemies mockingly called him. In July 1974 he succeeded in mending his fences with Egypt. In a joint communique with President Sadat in Alexandria the two leaders declared that the mandate of the PLO did not include the Palestinians who live in Jordan and that the Egyptians had removed their opposition to Jordanian insistence on a disengagement along the Jordanian-Israeli lines. In November, however, Hussein's chances to reunite the East and West Banks appeared gone forever. The Rabat Arab Summit Conference declared the PLO the sole representative of the Palestinians. Jordan submitted to the decision—at least in its public pronouncements.

The issue is, however, still far from resolved. In December 1976 President Sadat came out in favor of a Jordanian-Palestinian solution. The West Bank mayors—even those professedly PLO—have, in recent months, visited Amman. The PLO itself lacks unity. The radical organizations—the Rejection Front—continue to oppose all notion of recognition of Israel or negotiations with that country, and Arafat, in his pronouncements in the Arab states and to the PLO, is equally adamant. A new Syrian-Jordanian rapprochement has been achieved, with broad plans for cooperation in the economic sphere and Syrian antagonism to the PLO, the result of the events in the Lebanese civil war, has shaken the organization's prestige and has made its value questionable among most of the Arab states.

Inside Jordan, the forty-one-year-old King has benefited from the results of the new prosperity brought about by a shift of Arab funds from Lebanon to Amman. Since 1973, when twenty terrorists tried to seize the Amman council. the country has been peaceful. The November 1976 terrorist attack on the Jordan Inter-Continental Hotel in Amman was quickly subdued.

Hussein still has a formidably large Palestinian citizenry to face (some sources estimate that Palestinians make up 56% of the population of Jordan), but these are not all irredentist or Hussein's enemies. The civil war of 1970-71 has left scars (Palestinian losses were estimated at 4,000 dead and 12,000 wounded by the Palestinian Red Crescent), and Palestinians still do not participate in the making of key decisions but they are among Jordan's top industrialists, merchants, officials and diplomats. Military service has been made compulsory, a new departure designed to move the whole country's youthful population on the road toward full Jordanization. Hussein's goal is evidently the integration of his Palestinian citizenry into all spheres of activity in Jordan.

Great Britain and Jordan, 1918-1956

By BRITON COOPER BUSCH

Britain's connection with Transjordan began in the wake of the collapse of the Turkish war effort in late 1918. This undeveloped and remote corner of the Ottoman Empire had no separate political history in the recent past save as an appendage of Syria, governed from Damascus. Nor, as the least important part of General Allenby's "Occupied Enemy Territory," did it come into any new prominence so long as attention focused upon the problems of Emir Feisal's Arab government further north.

Only sporadic attention could be given to territory east of the Jordan River, but a handful of British officers and agents made their presence felt. The policy of the administration of Palestine in Jerusalem was to encourage local notables in the several Transjordanian towns to establish their own governmental administrations; nothing was yet said about one Transjordanian

Dr. Busch is Professor of History at Colgate University, Hamilton, New York. His books include *Britain, India and the Arabs, 1914-1921*, University of California Press, 1971 and *Mudros to Lausanne: Britain's Frontier in West Asia, 1918-1923*, State University of New York Press, 1976.

state. The area could not be allowed to go by default so long as it dominated possible routes to Iraq (all the more important when France took control of Syria). On a local level, such inexpensive political arrangements might well prove a useful buffer against troublesome tribes. Similarly, if uncontrolled, the area might become a center for propaganda directed against the Palestine administration. As it became clear that Feisal would not survive in Syria, a further motive presented itself: to compensate the Arab national war effort in some way for the loss of Syria. Finally, the more Jewish settlement in Palestine became a Middle Eastern, rather than merely Palestinian, problem, the more desirable it seemed to limit the area of settlement to the west of the Jordan River. On the other hand, no one indigenous authority emerged to dominate Transjordanian politics, and Jerusalem had not abandoned control of the other side of the river.

And so Transjordan might have remained had not Feisal been driven out of Syria by the French and had his brother 'Abdallah not arrived (November 1920) in Ma'an, then still part of the Hejaz, ostensibly to raise forces to restore Feisal.[1] Britain already had problems aplenty both in that part of the Arab world which it administered directly and in its dealings with the French the world around. Specific Middle Eastern problems came under consideration at the Cairo Conference in March, 1921. 'Abdallah, now in Amman and extending his influence, was potentially a serious problem; Winston Churchill, Colonial Secretary, resolved to offer the administration of Jordan to 'Abdallah on certain terms. So long as the Emir agreed to recognize the validity of the Palestine mandate and to restrain his followers from attacking Syria, then 'Abdallah represented the solution to several problems at once, including the future political structure of Transjordan, the debt to the Hashemites, and Britain's reluctance to assume direct administration of the area. An agreement was reached: 'Abdallah would be established as Emir of Transjordan, independent within the framework of guiding advice from the British resident to be posted to Amman. For his cooperation 'Abdallah was to receive a monthly subsidy of £5000 for a six month trial period, regularized before the year was out to an annual sum of £150,000 paid through the resident. Since this sum represented the main predictable source of income, it was clear where the real locus of power lay.

The 1920s saw the steady evolution of the Emirate. After the inter-allied meeting at San Remo, Transjordan was formally part of Britain's Palestine mandate, but equally formally, according to Churchill's famous White Paper of 1922, not subject to the application of the Balfour Declaration. The Emir's — and thus the resident's — main problem in this decade was defense against

---

1. "Whether his bellicose intentions toward Syria had ever existed was a moot point," wrote Sir Alec Kirkbride, *A Crackle of Thorns* (London, 1956), p. 27; but compare A. S. Klieman, *Foundations of British Policy in the Arab World: The Cairo Conference of 1921* (Baltimore, 1970), Chapter 9.

successive Wahhabi incursions from Saudi Arabia to the east. King Saud had little love for Hashemites in general, and none for artificially created states on his frontier. A particular issue was the much-debated Ma'an-Aqaba district, claimed by Ibn Saud as part of the Hejaz he had conquered but included by British fiat in Emir 'Abdallah's territory on the ground that it had been part of the *vilayet* of Damascus. The conflict was only partly eased when Britain reached an agreement with Ibn Saud in the Treaty of Jidda (1927): the Saudis would do no more than temporarily accept the Jordanian status quo.

Because of this issue — as well as occasional clashes with Syria and a certain amount of resistance from Transjordanians to centralized control in and taxes paid to Amman, some military force was required over and above the existing local police. As clashes with the Saudis, most serious in 1922-4, multiplied, Britain agreed to help: the Arab Legion was organized in 1921 (the name dates from 1923); by 1926, it numbered over 1500 men. The force's utility to 'Abdallah was substantial; P. J. Vatikiotis has argued persuasively that the role of the Legion was critical in the formation of the Jordanian state.[2] The Legion's history was not unchequered, however, nor did it function without assistance. The R.A.F. established an air station near Amman in 1921, and henceforth its air power and armored cars were available to support the Legion's operations. The creation in 1926 of a new "Trans-Jordan Frontier Force," responsible for frontier defense, restricted the Legion to police functions; the T.J.F.F., as a British force, was responsible to the High Commissioner in Jerusalem (and the War Office in London), while the Legion, under Lt.-Col. F. W. Peake from its inception until 1939, was the armed force of the Transjordanian government. On the other hand, the creation of a "Desert Mobile Force" in 1930 under Captain (later Lt.-General) John Glubb as an elite Bedouin force within the Legion once again pointed the Legion in the direction of army rather than police, although the immediate motive was to restrain an outbreak of inter-tribal raiding which the R.A.F. and T.J.F.F. had failed to control.

Aside from frontier problems, the administration of Transjordan was relatively uncomplicated through the 1920s, operating as a benevolent paternalism subordinate to, but not directly part of, the Palestinian mandate. The economic position of Transjordan improved, but so too did the costs of government. Britain continued to provide at least one-quarter of the Emir's expenses, allocated primarily to military affairs. Most important governmental posts were held by British officers responsible to the Emir but in practice working closely with British Residents Sir Henry Cox, 1927-39, and his successor Sir Alec Kirkbride, 1939-51, who had been the first British official to greet 'Abdallah upon his arrival in Jordan.

'Abdallah's provisional recognition was made permanent in 1923, but it

2. *Politics and the Military in Jordan: A Study of the Arab Legion, 1921-1957* (New York, 1967).

was not until 1928 that a formal agreement was concluded between Britain and the Emir which clarified Transjordan's international position. This document stipulated that the Emir would continue to administer Transjordan on Britain's behalf on the proviso that all relations with other states would be conducted through the British resident; that all necessary laws and regulations would be made as required for the full discharge of Britain's international responsibilities; that the Emir would be guided by the resident in all important foreign and fiscal affairs which might affect Britain (including budget, currency, customs duties, succession to the throne, military forces, and the like). It was, in short, the establishment of a virtual protectorate, but in return 'Abdallah was promised that Britain would continue to offset budgetary deficits through grants or loans and to provide such armed force as Britain deemed necessary "for the defence of the country and to assist His Highness the Emir in the preservation of peace and order" (Article 10). The 1923 recognition was also conditional upon the establishment of a constitutional regime, and this was satisfied by the preparation of an Organic Law in 1928 which established limited constitutional procedures for the now hereditary Emirate.

The arrangements of 1928 remained in being until the approach of war — and the much nearer problem of Palestine — forced a change. 'Abdallah remained generally aloof from Arab-Jewish-British relations in Palestine; he held pro-Arab views but saw no reason to jeopardize the intimate and necessary connection between his regime and Great Britain over this issue. For the same reason, he did not share in the vocal opposition to the recommendations of the Peel Commission to establish separate Jewish and Arab states in Palestine under a British mandate.

On the other hand, partly to keep a reliable ally friendly, partly as a way of meeting internal criticism of Britain's close tutelage, Britain made several concessions, including looser controls over expenditure and freedom to 'Abdallah to increase his military forces without British consent — a hollow gift, since Britain still controlled military finances in practice. 'Abdallah's loyalty and Britain's scarcity of resources encouraged Whitehall to sponsor the Legion's wartime expansion, however, and the Legion proved useful in the operations in Iraq to topple the pro-Axis government of Rashid Ali (1941) and in the campaign against Vichy French forces in Syria. The Legion proved a good investment and 'Abdallah, Britain's one sure Middle Eastern ally — but the Legion's success also strengthened 'Abdallah's own position.

In 1946, conditions had changed. France had left, and the Arab League had been founded; for Britain it was time to take a hard look at Egyptian, Iraqi, and Transjordanian alliances. Only 'Abdallah was willing to accept London's terms, but only 'Abdallah was in the same financial dependency. The mandate came to an end, and a formal alliance was concluded between Great Britain and Jordan. The alliance was still one of a preferential nature. Although the two states were to consult upon matters of common interest, Britain still preserved the right to station troops in Jordan and to train Jordan's military forces, for which Britain would continue the subsidy, for the twenty-five year life of the treaty. The alliance lasted not twenty-five years, but two, for general Arab reaction to the new arrangement was cool, and Britain's withdrawal from Palestine left Jordan's special relationship rather exposed. For this reason, Britain agreed to bring the Jordanian treaty into line with the (abortive) agreements then being discussed with Egypt and Iraq.

The 1948 agreement governed relationships for the next decade. This new twenty-year treaty was phrased in language chosen to define the two states as equal partners. The principal changes, however, were the restriction of British units to the R.A.F. bases at Amman and Mafraq and the establishment of a joint advisory body to coordinate defense matters. Britain continued to pay, and the Legion continued to expand: by 1950, to 12,000 men at a cost of £6 million a year.

The Legion's expansion was no surprise in view of Britain's Palestine withdrawal and the subsequent war. 'Abdallah wished to occupy at least a portion of Palestine, and Britain certainly preferred him to rule over the proposed Arab state in Palestine if it was to be established at all. The 1948 War cancelled such plans, but the Legion, now commanded by Glubb and some forty British officers, fought well, holding the Old City of Jerusalem and much of the "Arab sector" of Palestine. In December, this territory was officially annexed to Jordan (after April, 1949, the "Hashemite Kingdom of Jordan"). Jordan's growth did not meet with unquestioned international approval, to say the least, particularly in the United States. Britain, however, as eager to spread the burden for Jordan's defense as to withdraw from Palestine, supported a tripartite Anglo-American-French accord in 1950 to plan joint action in case of disruption of the Jordanian-Israeli frontier.

The Palestine War and the Tripartite Agreement were only the beginning of the decline of Britain's position in Jordan. The Legion subsidy was increased, but Jordanian opinion shared the general Arab impression that Britain had considerable responsibility for the establishment of Israel. The assassination of King 'Abdallah in 1951 was a further complication, for it removed a loyal friend of long-standing. His successor King Talal was deposed the next year and had little time to take a decisive stand on the British relationship, although there were signs that he was not immune to anti-British spokesmen (Egypt was at that point renouncing its own British treaty). King Hussein who now came to the throne, knew England well from his own education (Harrow, Sandhurst). But events, and costs, were outstripping the efficacy of an exclusive Anglo-Jordanian financial dependency just as the Palestinian War had altered Jordan's frontiers and responsibilities. As the subsidy rose to £8.5 million in 1954, only just covering military-security expenditures, the United States began to share in the cost, just in time for the major crisis of 1955-6.

In December, 1955, Foreign Minister Macmillan sent Britain's Chief of Staff, Sir Gerald Templar, to Amman to invite Jordan to join the regional defense (Baghdad) pact, the outgrowth of a new Turkish-Iraqi defense agreement. Sir Gerald offered the inducement of an increased subsidy from the then-current £10 million to £16.5 million to pay for further expansion of the Legion (some 25%, which would raise the force to about 25,000). The offer was tempting to Hussein and his advisors, but it could not be accepted. Britain had already declined to pay the subsidy direct to Jordan, and thus to give Hussein direct control over the army, so there were strings attached. A bigger factor was nationalist hostility to any further military pact with a foreign power.

Simple refusal was insufficient, and Hussein reached the decision that Glubb had to go. After twenty-five years of service he was unquestionably a symbol of Britain's tutelage, however loyal he might be personally (and however close to retirement). The direct, and public, causes for his dismissal were his refusal to prepare the Legion for battle with Israel, rather than to maintain it as the all-purpose military force which he envisioned; his belief in long-term professional service, which antagonized those who demanded that the Legion be opened to zealous Arab volunteers; and his opposition to more rapid transfer of command responsibility to Arab officers. But the principal issue was less specific military policies than the natural Jordanian wish to control Jordan's military forces — and perhaps Hussein's desire to steal the thunder of some of his more determined nationalist opponents. Propaganda emanating from Nasser's Egypt was obviously a factor in raising the level of agitation in Jordan, but it was not Hussein's motive.

The final break with Britain did not come until the Suez War. For 1956-7 the subsidy was actually raised to £12.5 million (from a total budget of £23 million, of which £9 million went for military expenditures of all sorts). With Suez, however, the last remaining British officers were dismissed (two dozen stayed on), and Hussein was under considerable pressure to abrogate the Anglo-Jordanian treaty. Fortunately, Britain had reached the same conclusion. "The problem was, how to disengage without taking upon ourselves the responsibility of bringing down in chaos the State which we had so laboriously constructed over the years," as Charles Johnston, the British Minister who had the job of ending the treaty, has explained.[3] Johnston could not let it appear that Britain was eager to withdraw — and thus abandon Iraq, where old friends yet remained in power — or that Britain had been kicked out, so Jordan had to take the initiative and the agreement had to be amicable. After delicate negotiations, in March 1957 Britain promised to withdraw all forces in Jordan within six months, turning over most military installations, buildings and equipment for a Jordanian payment of £4¼ million over six years (in

3. *The Brink of Jordan* (London, 1972), p. 23.

fact, Jordan paid £700,000 and the rest was forgiven). Military subsidies, frontier guarantees, freedom to station troops in Jordan, all now disappeared. Some British funds still went to Jordan as part of a 1953 five-year development program, but Jordan would have to find other sources for its defense and budgetary deficit needs.

After 1956, Jordan looked to the United States, and, increasingly, its wealthier Arab neighbors, for aid, as Britain absorbed the lesson of Suez on its Middle Eastern power role. In 1958, Hussein asked for help, fearful of the backwash of the revolution in Iraq and the crisis in Lebanon. British paratroopers were flown in from Cyprus in response. It seemed like the good old days, but the troops were gone in a few months (the last such British effort in the Middle East except for Kuwait in 1961) — a short epilogue to the longstanding Anglo-Jordanian connection. But Britain had created Jordan, for better or worse, and had done so effectively enough that Jordan, born in a personal conversation between a British Colonial Secretary and a Hejazi Hashemite Prince, lives on despite its accidental, artificial, and foreign antecedents.

The Jordanian Wars

By EDGAR O'BALLANCE

On assuming sovereign power in 1953 on his eighteenth birthday, Hussein found his Hashemite Kingdom of Jordan to be in two distinct parts, separated by the River Jordan, the East Bank being the former Emirate of Transjordan, and the West Bank, formerly part of Palestine, which had been annexed by his grandfather, King 'Abdallah. Of his some two million people, about one-third were West Bankers, who considered themselves to be Palestinians and were not reconciled to his authority, one third were displaced Palestinian refugees housed and fed by UNRWA in camps scattered on both Banks, and the remaining third were East Bankers, predominantly Bedu, upon whom his grandfather had traditionally relied for basic support. Hussein also inherited the British-trained and led Arab Legion, which although small was then probably the most efficient armed force possessed by any Arab country.

After the 1948 War, triumphant Israel set about consolidating, absorbing Jews from the Diaspora and creating a strong defense force, while on the other hand the disunited Arab countries, some still under colonial influence, were divided, disorganized and at varying stages of development. Even though demoralized and leaderless, groups of Palestinians from the refugee camps

Major O'Ballance is a free-lance journalist specializing in military affairs and a member of the International Institute for Strategic Studies (London). His latest book, *No Victor, No Vanquished,* Presidio Press, 1977, deals with Middle Eastern and international terrorism.

made small raids across what was then mostly an open border into Israel, and these gradually increased in number until, for example, the Israelis claimed in 1952 there were "3,742 illegal crossings," resulting in over 60 Israeli deaths and many more wounded. The Israelis in their turn shelled, and sometimes struck at, the Palestinian staging camps near their frontier, a process that spasmodically continued until in 1955 a new type of Palestinian appeared, the *fedayeen*, ("Freedom Fighter") who was encouraged, especially by Egypt, to raid into Israel to undertake terrorist acts that would both alarm the Israelis and undermine their growing confidence. During 1956, the incidents of Palestinian *fedayeen* raids into Israel from Jordan increased, provoking even larger reprisal raids, notably one on Dhariya and another on Qalqiliya, in which Jordanian and Palestinian lives were lost.

1956

During the Anglo-French assault on Egypt in 1956, the Israelis made a thrust into the Sinai towards the Suez Canal, which began on the 29th October, and ended in an Israeli victory that caused, amongst other things, President Nasser of Egypt to disband his Egyptian-sponsored *fedayeen* units, and other Arab Governments to restrict *fedayeen* activities from their territory into Israel as far as they were able. However, the *fedayeen* idea had caught on, and coincided with a surge of youthful restlessness in the Palestinian refugee camps, irked with waiting for Israel to collapse, the policy recommended by their dispirited elders, which found expression in the appearance of several clandestine organizations, whose aim was to cross into Israel to conduct terrorist activities. But they were unstable, shifting and mercurial, and although at one stage they numbered over 40, none were very effective, as they mushroomed, grouped together, regrouped and disappeared, being influenced by the changing policies of Arab Governments and national and factional rivalries.

Israeli development of the Negev depended upon more water, and in 1964, work was begun on the National Water Carrier, designed to syphon off water from the River Jordan for this purpose, a process considered by the Arabs to be sheer riparian rape. In July that year, as a face-saver, the Palestine Liberation Organization (PLO) came into being, largely sponsored by President Nasser. Financed by the Arab League, its first Chairman was a Syrian, Ahmed Shuqaiyri. The PLO was authorized to recruit a military arm, the Palestine Liberation Army (PLA), and small units were formed and armed on conventional lines in both Egypt and Syria. Shuqaiyri wanted to initiate revolutionary warfare inside Israel, and for this purpose established base camps inside Jordan near the Israeli frontier, where he had far more freedom of action than in either Egypt or Syria. He was soon openly quarrelling with King Hussein, who would not allow him to tax Palestinians in refugee camps, or allow PLA units to man the Israel-Jordan frontier posts. In 1965, King

Hussein disbanded his 30,000-strong National Guard, a part-time force, whose task was to guard that border, and which was composed mainly of West Bankers—i.e., Palestinians, because of its unreliability and susceptibility to PLO influence, and replaced them by regular East Bank soldiers.

Meanwhile, impatient of tardy Arab Government action, there arose a clandestine Palestinian organization, whose exact origins are still debatable, called *fatah*, whose object was to carry out terrorist acts inside Israel, in order to provoke massive Israeli reprisals which would in turn cause the Arabs to march against Israel in the war it was thought the Arabs would win. The main sponsor of *fatah* at this stage was Syria, (as, after his 1956 experience, Nasser was more cautious), and its personnel began to cross into Israel from Jordanian territory, Hussein being unable to prevent this (Syria then being hostile to Jordan). The first *fatah* "success" in Israel occurred on the 14th January 1965, when it caused an explosion on the National Water Carrier, and during that year there were at least another 26 such raids from Jordanian territory, which resulted in Israeli reprisal assaults on Qalqiliya and in the Jenin area.

In February 1966, King Hussein, who had given the PLO certain facilities, allowed it to open an office in Amman, but he closed it down again in April, because it was used to foment discontent against his regime, arresting many PLO personnel. This caused Hussein to become the target, almost the priority one, of Shuqaiyri's hate and his propaganda machine. Although he had no control over it at all, Shuqaiyri saw *fatah* as an ally in his personal feud against King Hussein. In turn the Jordanian Government detained *fatah* personnel, but owing to a public outcry in their favor, was compelled to release them again. During 1966, *fatah* carried out a series of incidents inside Israel, a number, in November, close to Jerusalem, which provoked an Israeli reprisal assault near Samu, in which 15 Jordanian soldiers were killed. Usually, after a heavy Israeli reprisal attack, terrorist incidents slackened off for a short while. Friendless and isolated by other Arab States at the time, Jordan was the main springboard for *fatah* incursions into Israel.

Both Egypt and Syria, having received large quantities of Soviet arms, were sabre-rattling against Israel, and the Egypt-Syria Defense Pact came into effect in March 1967. Further spates of *fatah* raids and Israeli reprisals, prompted Nasser, prodded by the Soviet Union, to embark upon a course of brinkmanship which got out of control, and at his surprise request, U Thant, the UN Secretary General, called in the UN Emergency Force manning the frontier observation posts between Israel and Egypt. On the 23rd May, Nasser announced he had blockaded the Straits of Tiran, the Israeli southern naval life-line, even though a UN Resolution of March 1957 had guaranteed freedom of shipping through its waters. Jordan, which had remained at odds with its Arab neighbors had begun to mobilize on the 17th, a process that was completed on the 24th, the day an explosion in a bus at Ramtha, on the

Syrian-Jordanian border, killed 14 people and injured 23 others. Hussein promptly broke off diplomatic relations with Syria, but the following day, anxious senior Jordanian officers persuaded the King to come to an agreement with Nasser to end their country's isolation. On the 30th, Hussein made his sudden, dramatic flight to Cairo to join the Egypt-Syria Defense Pact, to which Iraq adhered on the 3rd June. Nasser's plan was that Syrian, Iraqi and Saudi Arabian troops should move into Jordan, preparatory to a combined attack on Israel on three Fronts.

Meanwhile, Britain, America, France and certain other maritime nations made ineffectual gestures and suggestions for reopening the Straits of Tiran to Israeli and other shipping. This closure was one of the cardinal principles on which the Israeli Government felt it had no option but to resort to war, and on the 24th May, Premier Eshkol warned the Arabs in a broadcast to his nation, explaining that he had tried to resolve the dispute with Egypt by all diplomatic means to ''obviate the necessity of Israel having to use her armed forces in her defense.'' Eshkol firmly stated that the closure of the Straits to Israeli shipping ''constituted an act of aggression against Israel, which has the right to self-defense and will exercise it if necessary,'' but Nasser, and other Arab leaders, ignored this statement of intent.

1967

President Nasser still required a few more days grace to position troops before attacking, when suddenly, on the morning of the 5th June 1967, Israel beat him to it by making an aerial pre-emptive attack, striking at 17 of his main airfields and destroying about 300 combat aircraft, the bulk of the Egyptian air force, in the first hours of the war.

The Israeli Government did not want Jordan to enter the war: it had not done so in 1956, and Premier Eshkol sent a message to Hussein, through the UN Commander in Jerusalem, to the effect that Israel would not initiate hostilities against Jordan, but adding that it would react ''with all our might'' if Jordan attacked Israel.[1] This message did not reach Hussein until after 1100 hours, by which time Jordanian aircraft had already taken off to bomb targets in Israel. The Old City and East Jerusalem were tempting prizes,[2] and as sporadic mortar and small arms fire had begun in the sector, at 1215 hours, the Israeli Air Force struck at the Jordanian one, which consisted of 22 combat aircraft, all of which had returned from their initial mission, but having only 16 trained pilots, and destroyed it.

The Jordanians had four infantry brigades holding the West Bank, with two armored brigades lying back, one at Damiya Bridge over the River Jordan, and the other at Jericho, with other troops on the East Bank, all of which had been placed under the command of General Riad, an Egyptian. On the first day of the war, the 5th, the Israelis generally were hesitant and cautious in their actions against the Jordanians. As the expected Arab reinforcements did not arrive in Jordan, and as there was only a vague offensive plan to cut into Israel in the area of Nathanya, General Riad merely moved one armored brigade up to near Jerusalem and the other to take its place at Jericho.

On the second day (6th) the Israelis made numerous feints and probes along the length of the Front, which they not very successfully tried to turn into deep penetration thrusts. Meanwhile, General Riad reversed his orders to the armored brigades, which had to turn round and retrace their routes, eventually arriving in positions to combat the advancing Israelis, tired and with little fuel. In the Jerusalem area the Israelis fought their way through the sector north of the Old City to reach the dominating Augusta Victoria Ridge, but took heavy casualties. By evening Riad had become pessimistic, and urged Hussein to ask for a cease-fire and to withdraw to the East Bank, which the King resisted. Nevertheless, General Riad ordered a withdrawal to the East Bank, but when Hussein realized what was happening, he insisted on countermanding it, and so his Jordanian soldiers had to retrace their steps, sometimes fighting, and sometimes failing, to regain their former defensive positions. The majority of the unit holding the walled Old City evacuated that night, leaving only a handful of men behind as snipers.

The third day (7th) was one of success for the Israelis, who took the Old City and Jericho, and penetrated to the Jordan River during the afternoon. To the Israelis these gains, especially the prestigious one of the Old City, were an unexpected bonus, as they had anticipated Hussein would remain neutral. Hussein's loyalty to the Arab cause had been costly; in three days he had lost his West Bank. Despite confused orders and needless countermarching, his soldiers had fought well, but without air cover they were outclassed by the Israelis.

1970

King Hussein retired to the East Bank where he collected his forces, set about restoring confidence and consolidating what he had salvaged from defeat, but within months had to contend with a new *fedayeen* movement, now expanded into several virile organizations, that was suddenly wildly popular with the Arab masses, and which settled on his Kingdom like a plague of locusts, ostensibly to conduct guerrilla operations against Israel. Basing themselves in Palestinian refugee camps, the *fedayeen* set up staging camps near the Israeli border, were soon swaggering about the streets of Amman fully armed, and generally ignoring national restraints. This was the heyday of the *fedayeen*, whose arrogant behavior caused friction with the Jordanian armed forces; also the new Chairman of the PLO, Yasser Arafat, had little time for King Hussein.

The *fedayeen*, then nominally controlled by Arafat, had moved into Jordan in force in 1968 and 1969, and had taken over full control of all the Palestinian refugee camps, into which they would not allow Jordanian security personnel to enter. As a next stage, the *fedayeen* began to move on to the streets of Amman and other population centers, openly carrying arms and jostling Jordanian security forces. Arafat mounted a violent propaganda campaign against King Hussein, who was attempting to restrict *fedayeen* movement and subject them to normal national restraints, with the object of toppling the King and establishing a regime in Jordan more in sympathy with *fedayeen* ideals; one that would allow them internal freedom of movement and action. (The *fedayeen* were using Jordanian territory as a springboard for launching raids into Israel, which provoked Israeli retaliation on Jordan.) At a Graduation Ceremony of *fedayeen* recruits, held at the Jebel Wahdat refugee camp near Amman on August 16, 1970, Arafat claimed that King Hussein was moving four of his brigades to crush the *fedayeen* movement in Jordan by force of arms and boasted: ''We shall turn Jordan into a graveyard for plotters.'' By the end of August, there were frequent clashes between the *fedayeen* and the Jordanian Security Forces, and on September 1, the *fedayeen* made an unsuccessful attempt to assassinate Hussein.

The climax came in September 1970, when three airliners were hijacked by members of the *Popular Front for the Liberation of Palestine* (PFLP) and flown to Dawson's Field, a desert airstrip north of Amman, where for three days some 400 people were held hostage before the world television cameras.[3] On the 9th of that month, the three aircraft were blown up and the hostages gradually released, but this incident made Hussein determined to crack down on the *fedayeen* in his country. Action against them developed into civil war, which did not terminate until July 1971, when the last of the *fedayeen* had been either arrested or ejected from the country.[4] In October 1970, Syrian armour had briefly entered northern Jordan to aid the *fedayeen*, to clash indecisively with Jordanian tanks, while an Iraqi division at Zarqa Camp, ostensibly there to ''bolster the Eastern Front,'' and which Hussein ultimately had difficulty in persuading to leave, looked on impassively. For ejecting the *fedayeen* from Jordan, King Hussein was again banished from the Arab fold, and relations between Jordan and Syria were particularly bad.

1973

When it came, the War of October 1973 was a great shock to the Israelis, as it dramatically demonstrated that the Arabs could fight, plan and keep a secret, three things never before thought possible. Acting simultaneously on the 6th October, Egypt and Syria attacked Israel on two Fronts at 1400 hours, and initially drove the Israeli troops back in a disorder that almost amounted to panic at times. Hussein had been vaguely privy to Operation Badr, being only latterly drawn into it to pose a ''Third Front'' threat, and he did not know when the attacks were to be made. He immediately telephoned both Presidents Sadat and Assad, who confirmed that the war had begun, and both asked him to open a Third Front at once. However, the King simply placed his army on a state of alert and waited, his excuse for inaction being that he had few combat aircraft and no "missile" air cover. There were dark suspicions that Hussein was in collusion with the enemy, with the French acting as intermediaries, not to attack, especially as the Israelis had only left three brigades to cover the Jordanian Front, and because he maintained his Open Bridges policy, that allowed movement and trade across the River Jordan.

On the Golan Plateau, after almost reaching the River Jordan, the Syrian divisions were driven back again with huge tank losses, until by the 11th. Israel's Defense Minister Dayan was able to say "The Syrian army is broken." On Soviet advice the Syrians had abandoned their tanks, guns and vehicles, and fallen back to their strong Sasa Defense Line, which held the Israelis. At loggerheads with Iraq, Syria at first had been reluctant to accept the offer of Iraqi troops, but admitted them "in the hour of panic,"[5] the first brigades arriving on a confused battle scene on the 9th. By the 12th, the Iraqis were in position on the southern flank of the Sasa Defense Line, in time to stop an Israeli probing detour thrust.

On the 10th, King Hussein recalled his reservists and released some *fedayeen* prisoners he was holding, and the next day decided to send troops into Syria, his 40th Armored Brigade arriving there on the 14th, to be positioned next to the Iraqis, in time to take part in the combined Syrian-Iraqi-Jordanian attack on the Israelis on the 16th. This was successful in that it stopped the Israelis, but the Arabs did not regain any territory. The Jordanian formation took part in a second similar assault on the 19th, which advanced some way, but had to give ground again by evening.

Another Jordanian formation, the 90th Armored Brigade, arrived in Syria on the 22nd, and was scheduled, together with the 40th, to take part in a projected five-division advance, due to commence at 0300 hours on the 23rd. However, UN Resolution 338, calling for a cease-fire on the 22nd, was accepted by Egypt without prior consultation with Syria, which had, reluctantly, to follow suit. The offensive was called off by Syrian GHQ at 0005 hours on the 23rd, and that virtually ended military land movement on that Front. Jordan accepted the UN Resolution and had withdrawn its two brigades by January 1974, having lost 28 soldiers killed, had 29 wounded (but lost none as prisoners), 18 tanks destroyed and 19 armored vehicles damaged in battle. Lack of positive Arab success on the Golan Plateau was due to poor cooperation between the three national forces, clouded by an atmosphere of mutual suspicion.

Hussein's initial hesitation to enter the fight could perhaps be traced back to his defeat and losses in 1967. In 1973, had he attempted to penetrate the West Bank as urged to do by Sadat and Assad, without air cover he would again have suffered heavy loss, but by waiting and fighting only on Syrian soil, he came out of the war with martial honor satisfied, and his East Bank Kingdom intact. Thinly veiled and painfully muted Syrian hostility during Jordanian participation in the battle showed through again when the Jordanians withdrew. Hussein's motives had been political, and had Iraqi troops not moved into Syria and been positioned adjacent to this northern frontier, he may not have even entered the war at all, because of his distrust of the Syrian intentions. He later stated: "After the war broke out I had an agreement with President Sadat and Syrian President Assad, that Jordan would enter the war and mount an offensive across the River Jordan, once the Syrians had completely liberated the Golan Heights and the Egyptians overran the major desert passes that control Sinai,"[6] but this was not confirmed by either of the two Presidents, or other sources. In both wars, Jordanian soldiers fought well, although in the first one they were badly directed by an Egyptian general, and in the second, were handicapped by unfamiliarity with Syrian and Iraqi procedures and tactics. In both they sadly lacked air cover, and so were at a big disadvantage.

A stark, major fact high-lighted in the October War, was the fantastic rate of material destruction in battle. For example, some 3,000 tanks and 500 aircraft were destroyed in the 23 days fighting; losses no country could stand for long. This has produced the premise that whenever war breaks out, a nation must be prepared to fight with whatever arms and equipment it happens to possess at that moment, because more armaments cannot be automatically guaranteed to arrive, as formerly. In view of this, the U.S. has more than replenished Israeli war losses, and provided stockpiles in Israel that are secretly and nominally under U.S. control. On the other hand, Jordan has not been so fortunate in obtaining corresponding quantities of sufficient arms for its own defense, and in particular, has had difficulty in obtaining US HAWK missiles for air cover, causing Hussein at one stage to try and obtain SAM missiles from Russia.[7] Matched singly against Israel, Jordan would be able to do no more than put up token resistance.

The armories of both Egypt and Syria were replenished by the Soviet Union, and as long as those two countries were in agreement with each other, it was unlikely they would allow Israel to move into Jordan. But Arab alignments are changeable, and in 1974, Syria and Egypt quarrelled because Egypt made the Sinai Accord with Israel, and this rupture caused Syria to draw closer to its old enemy, Jordan, and also to another old adversary, Iraq, in the hope of reactivating the defunct Eastern Front[8] against Israel. If a new Eastern Front materializes its continuous air defense barriers of SAM missiles (and perhaps US HAWK missiles) would be a strong deterrent against any Israeli temptation to advance eastward across the River Jordan to seize and hold the high ground on the other side to make it its "eastern strategic frontier"[9] in any future war.

FOOTNOTES

1. See, Edgar O'Ballance, *The Third Arab-Israeli War,* Archon, 1972. The latest confirmation that there was such a note is given by former Israeli Premier Golda Meir in *My Life,* Dell, 1976, pb. p. 343. She writes: "Although we had sent him (King Hussein) constant messages promising that if he kept out of the war nothing would happen to him (the last of these messages was sent to Hussein by Eshkol through the good offices of the UN Truce Supervisory Organization on the very morning that the war broke out) . . ."

2. The Old City was a tempting prize to both the Israelis and the Jordanians, as it contains several sites regarded as sacred to the three main religions. The Western Wall and the old Jewish Quarter had been overrun by the Jordan Arab Legion in 1948. The Muslims consider the al Aksa Mosque to be the third most holy in Islam. To be Guardian of so many religious sites was far more of a "prestige prize" than a purely strategical or tactical advantage. The Jordanians realized that the Old City was far beyond their capacities to conquer and occupy. Jordan's stated aims were to recover the West Bank and the Gaza Strip (although Jordan had never held the latter). As a matter of interest, it had always been King 'Abdallah's ambition to be King of Palestine as well as Transjordan. Golda Meir, in *My Life, op. cit.,* p. 210, writes of the secret mission she made to him immediately prior to the declaration of Israel's independence. 'Abdallah said: "Drop your demands for free immigration. I will take over the whole country and you will be represented in my parliament. I will treat you very well and there will be no war."

3. The hijacked airliners were later joined by a third, three days later. These hijackings sparked off the civil war.

4. The civil war gave birth to the *Black September* movement which assassinated the Jordanian Premier in Cairo in November, 1971.

5. See, Edgar O'Ballance, *No Victor, No Vanquished,* Presidio Press, 1977.

6. *Daily Mail,* (London), June 4, 1974.

7. The contacts appear to have been serious ones, but Hussein may have balked at the condition of accepting Soviet technicians with Soviet arms. It should be remembered that the King had signed a trade protocol with the Soviet Union on August 28, 1970, which was much an empty letter, but which the Soviet government periodically tried to activate. The U.S. Department of Defense became somewhat alarmed, in case Hussein, perhaps in pique, might be tempted to accept not only SAMs but also other arms he needed, together with Soviet personnel.

8. A front often talked about, formed on Syrian and Jordanian territory, supported perhaps also by Iraq, which would contribute troops and arms. Such a Front could then present a barrier of ground-to-air missiles, being SAMs in the north (in Syria) and HAWKS in Jordan, with perhaps SAMs brought forward by Iraq. It was such a formidable missile barrier (of SAMs) that caused the huge Israeli air losses in the early days of the October 1973 war.

9. In Israel, there is much talk of "Secure Frontiers", meaning strategic ones that are favorable to defense, such as the Litani River in the north. In these terms, the "secure frontier" to the east of Israel is along the crestline of the mountains overlooking the River Jordan, which if the Israelis held, would enable them to control the Jordan Valley.

Jordan and the Palestine Liberation Organization, 1967-1971: A Chronology

Background Note:

Jordan's struggle against the commando groups in her territory began with the creation of the Palestine Liberation Organization by the Arab League and the establishment of a Palestinian commando recruiting office in Jerusalem. Between 1968-1969, as the various commando groups became more deeply entrenched in Jordan, King Hussein, faced with the pressure of the Arab states (and the presence of an Iraqi expeditionary force on Jordanian soil—a residue of the 1967 war) tolerated the groups and permitted his army to cooperate with them in their infiltrations into Israel. Members of *al fatah* and other groups were exempted from military service but appeared freely in the streets of Amman and other Jordanian towns carrying arms and dressed in uniform. Commando bases were permitted near the border with Israel and the commandos were free to open fire all along the border.[1] The Jordanian army also provided information on Israeli troop movements, coordinated the time and places of infiltration, gave covering fire during crossings and returns and treated the wounded. The commandos' headquarters were transferred from Syria to Jordan. Iraq supplied arms, training and, through its 41st commando battalion in Jordan, special support. Hundreds of officers and men of the Palestinian battalions stationed in Syria moved into Jordan to join the commandos. The 141st Palestinian battalion in Egypt was assigned to sabotage activities and underwent special training in army camps near Cairo. It was then transferred to Jordan and was run by the Egyptian embassy in Amman (its actions were credited to other organizations).

On March 21, 1968 following an Israeli raid on Karameh, the "United Fedayeen Forces" displayed a placard in Amman which proclaimed: "The fedayeen, the heroes, members of *al fatah, al-Zaaka*, the *National Sacrifice*, the *Popular Front for the Liberation of Palestine* and the *Liberation Organization*—stand as one with the Jordanian Army . . . Long live the unity of the brave *fedayeen* together with the brave Jordanian Army. Long live the brave Iraqi army . . ." Radio Amman broadcast a statement by King Hussein. He said: ". . . the residents of Karameh fought with courage and it is difficult to tell the difference between the *fedayeen* and the others. We are likely to reach a situation in which we will all be *fedayeen*, and it is possible

Source: The above excerpts are derived from *Political Terrorism*, edited by Lester A. Sobel, *Facts on File, Inc.*, New York, 1975, and are reprinted by permission.

1. Under the terms of the U.N. sponsored cease-fire of June 1967, accepted by all the parties, it was the responsibility of all the governments concerned to prevent all offensive action of any sort or kind to be initiated from their territory.

that this will materialize in the near future.'' The King told a gathering of 150 public figures and senior officers in Amman that he was prepared to cooperate with the organizations although he would not agree to the existence of a ''state within a state.'' *(Eds.)* ▼

Oct. 12, 1967: Israeli police in Jerusalem arrested 24 *al fatah* members and captured large quantities of arms. The terrorists said they had been trained by Syrian and Algerian officers at camps near Damascus and the Syrian-Lebanese border. Trucks of the Palestine Battalion of the Iraqi army, stationed in Jordan, were said to have moved the terrorists from Syria to Jordanian territory near the Jordan River.

Dec. 7, 1967: Israeli forces wiped out a terrorist base in a cave near Nablus, seizing a cache of arms including Soviet and Chinese weapons.

Dec. 21, 1967: The Israeli paper, *Ma'ariv,* reported that 54 captured terrorists had confessed to receiving orders to stir up trouble in East Jerusalem and Bethlehem during Christmas observances.

March 7, 1968: Israeli authorities reported the seizure of 2 suspected *al fatah* commanders—William Naguib Nasser and Kamal Nammer. Nasser had trained terrorists in Algeria and West Germany and was an instructor in Syria. 35 of 50 infiltrators trying to cross the Jordan River were reported killed in 10 days. They carried sabotage equipment and Russian and Chinese submachine guns.[2]

March 21, 1968: A force of about 15,000 Israeli troops carried out a day-long retaliatory raid against alleged Arab terrorist bases used for guerrilla attacks on Israel. Jordanian army troops also entered the fray. Israeli Premier Levi Eshkol said the operations were designed to forestall an expected ''new wave of terror'' against Israel. The U.N. Security Council convened in emergency session March 21 and unanimously adopted on March 24 a resolution condemning Israel. Israel's major assault was directed primarily at a *fedayeen* camp at Karameh, 3 miles east of the Jordan River and at nearby Shune, north of the Dead Sea. Another Israeli force crossed the Jordan River south of the Dead Sea to strike at suspected guerrilla bases in the Jordanian towns of Safi and Dakal. Israeli and Jordanian authorities both claimed victory and gave conflicting versions of the number of casualties and damage inflicted. Israelis claimed 150 saboteurs killed, 23 Israelis killed and 3 missing, 138 terrorists captured and nearly 1,000 weapons, mostly of Soviet and Chinese make seized. One Israeli plane downed by Jordanian gunfire crash-landed in Israeli territory. Before withdrawing, Israeli forces occupied Karameh, searched its houses and blew up several installations. Jordan claimed 20 killed, 65 wounded, 15 Jordanian civilians slain and 30 commandos killed in Karameh, and that Israeli forces suffered more than 100 killed and 100 wounded. Jordan claimed to have destroyed 45 Israeli tanks and downed 5 planes. Israeli premier Eshkol told the Israeli Knesset (parliament): ''The terrorist bases are well known to the Jordanian government. Members of the gangs appeared openly wearing their uniforms and bearing arms . . . a new wave of terror was about to take place. Since political contacts did not bring about cessation of the murders, we had no other choice but to act in self-defense to avert these dangers.''

Eshkol noted that since mid-Feb. 6 Israelis had been killed and 44 injured by terrorists. 2 adults and 28 children had been blown up by a mine in a school bus Mar.

---

2. Other sources cite 20 incidents between February 17 and March 17, 1968 including several involving exchange of fire between Israeli and Jordanian forces. *(Eds.)*

18 in the desert near Eilat. King Hussein declared Mar. 23 that his government was not responsible for the security of Israel and would do nothing to inhibit activities of guerrillas stationed in Jordan (an *al fatah* member captured by Israel told reporters in Tel Aviv Mar. 23 that the Jordanian army gave *al fatah* military intelligence and provided covering fire for river crossings but that the Syrian and Iraqi armies gave *al fatah* most of its help).

March 29, 1968: Israeli and Jordanian forces engaged in a 6-hour artillery duel along 85 miles of the Jordan River, accompanied by Israeli air strikes.

April 8, 1968: Israeli army authorities reported that a few dozen Israeli helicopter-borne soldiers had crossed 18 miles into Jordan to pursue *fedayeen* infiltrators. The Israeli raid followed the killing Apr. 8 of 2 Israeli soldiers and a Bedouin scout. Jordan claimed its troops had repelled the Israeli invaders.

April 12, 1968: A report from Cairo said the UAR had begun to help guerrillas attacking Israel by giving them arms, training and intelligence information. In its first broadcast, *al fatah* said May 11 that its objective was to free all of Palestine and not only to terminate Israeli occupation of the areas seized in June 1967.

April 28, 1968: An Israeli patrol killed 13 infiltrators on the West Bank. The clash occurred several miles north of Jericho. (The Israeli government Apr. 26 issued one of its sternest warnings to Jordan about retaliation for continued incursions.)

June 4, 1968: Israeli and Jordanian forces engaged in an all-day clash along the Jordan River near the sea of Galilee. The fighting was marked by Israeli air attacks. Israeli authorities blamed Jordan for starting the fighting by shelling the Israeli settlement of Kfar Ruppin in the Beit Shaan Valley on June 3-4. Jordanian UN representative filed a complaint with the UN Security Council, claiming Israel had carried out a "surprise attack" and shelled Jordanian villages and the city of Irbid.

June 22, 1968: Israel reported its forces had killed 11 of an *al fatah* unit near Jericho.

July 17-18, 1968: Israel reported killing 13 terrorists in a brief engagement northwest of the Dead Sea. They had crossed the Jordan River from the east bank and carried Soviet assault rifles, bazookas, grenades and explosives.

July 22, 1968: All 6 of a terrorist force were killed in a clash with an Israeli patrol between the Damiya and Allenby bridges. This brought to 59 the number of terrorists killed since the beginning of June. 2 Israelis were killed and 10 wounded.

July 26, 1968: 7 members of *al fatah* were killed in a 2-hour clash with Israeli troops near Jericho. 2 Israeli officers were killed.

July 28, 1968: An Israeli patrol killed 2 as it repulsed a guerrilla unit that crossed the Jordan River. Jordanian army guns opened fire to provide cover for the retreating infiltration force.

August 4, 1968: Israeli planes carried out a heavy raid on guerrilla bases 10 miles inside Jordan. The air strike was followed by an Israeli ground incursion Aug. 6 by troops pursuing a band of terrorists. The Jordanian communique said Israeli planes bombed positions in the vicinity of Salt, killing 23 civilians and 5 soldiers and wounding 76 civilians and 6 soldiers. During the 3-hour strike, Jordanian and Israeli tanks and artillery exchanged fire across the Jordan River. Gen. Haim Bar Lev, Israeli chief of staff (said): ". . . I hope this will help the authorities in Jordan to finally realize that violations of the cease fire will bring unpleasant consequences." The Israeli army said *al fatah* had chosen the area around Salt as "a substitute for Karameh." About 12 bases had been shifted there, with the southern sector serving as *al fatah's* command center. According to an Israeli army report, the terrorists had carried out 98 forays against Israeli territory in July. The PFLP threatened reprisals against Israeli civilians. It claimed to have set off an explosion in a bar in Jerusalem in retaliation for the Israeli attack on Salt.

Nov. 3, 1968: Tension between Jordan and a commando group based in Jordan erupted into an open clash in and around Amman. 25 civilians and 5 soldiers were killed; 70 persons arrested. The commando unit was identified as *Kataeb al Nasr* (Contingents for Victory), also called *al-Sa'iqa*. King Hussein assailed "phony elements" among the commandos in Jordan and charged in a broadcast that their target was "not occupied territory but the east bank itself." The two largest commando groups in Jordan—the PLO and *al fatah*—agreed to government demands to submit to official checkpoints; to abolish their own checkpoints and to keep their armed followers out of Amman. The PFLP rejected the government demand. At a meeting of the commando groups in Cairo Nov. 5 Jordan was accused of attempting to break up the guerrilla forces and make peace with Israel.

Nov. 16, 1968: A 7-point agreement governing the relations between Jordan and the commando groups operating from Jordan was reached. Terms of the agreement (some of which formalized previous government-commando understandings) were: (1) commandos were forbidden to carry arms or wear uniforms in Jordanian towns; (2) commandos had no right to search civilian cars; (3) commando vehicles were to carry Jordanian license plates; (4) commandos were to carry identity cards of their organizations; (5) a crime committed by a commando was to be investigated by Jordanian authorities in the presence of a representative of the guerrilla's organization; (6) commandos were forbidden to enlist Jordanians subject to conscription or deserters from Jordan's armed forces; (7) commando-Jordanian government disputes were to be handled by a council made up of 4 major commando groups based at the Amman headquarters of the PLO.

Nov. 22, 1968: A bomb explosion in the Jewish section of Jerusalem killed 12 and injured 55. The blast ripped through Jerusalem's Mahane Yehuda market. The PFLP announced its members were responsible.

Dec. 1, 1968: An Israeli commando attack centered on targets east of Sodom at the southern end of the Dead Sea. The Israelis, UPI reported, had destroyed a highway bridge 60 miles north of Ma'an and a Hejaz railway bridge. An Israeli army spokesman said it was in retaliation for 50 infiltration attacks since the signing of the Jordanian-Palestinian commando pact of Nov. 16. In a simultaneous engagement, Israeli and Jordanian forces traded artillery fire to the north—the heaviest since 1967, with an Israeli air attack on Irbid. Commandos fired rockets into the Degania "A" settlement.

Dec. 1, 1968: Israeli commandos attacked targets 37 miles inside Jordan and destroyed 2 bridges. The raid precipitated heavy Israel-Jordanian artillery and aerial bombardments, continuing through Dec. 3. Iraqi troops stationed in Jordan were involved. The Israeli army spokesman said the raid was in retaliation for 50 Arab infiltration attacks against Israel since Nov. 16. The incident included bazooka and rocket attacks on Israeli civilian settlements and industrial facilities.

▼

Israeli sources reported that between June 6, 1967 and Dec. 31, 1968, Israel had been subjected to 1,288 acts of sabotage and border incidents—920 in the Jordan-Israel sector.

▼

Feb. 3, 1969: Yasser Arafat was elected Chairman of a newly formed PLO Executive Committee.

Feb. 6, 1969: Yasser Arafat of *al fatah* and chairman of the PLO announced plans to shift a large part of his guerrilla force from Egypt and Syria to Jordan, according to Cairo's *Al Ahram*. The force was said to consist of 3 battalions: 3,800 men in Egypt, 3,000 in Syria and 1,200 attached to an Iraqi division in Jordan. Arafat had his first meeting with Hussein in Amman Feb. 16.

Feb. 18, 1969: An Israeli El Al Boeing 720 commercial airliner with 17 passengers and 10 crewmen was attacked by 4 Arab terrorists with submachine guns as it was about to take off at Zurich, Switzerland. A statement issued Feb. 18 by the PFLP at its headquarters in Amman claimed responsibility for the attack. The statement said the raid was in accordance with PFLP policy to track down and strike the El Al fleet, which it called a military arm of Israel. Switzerland sent notes Feb. 28 to Jordan, Syria and Lebanon, protesting against the attack on the Israeli plane. A Swiss Foreign Ministry communique issued in Berne said the 3 surviving Arab raiders had told Swiss investigators they had been "trained in Jordan and some of them left Syria to carry out their attack in Zurich."

Feb. 21, 1969: A bomb exploded in a crowded Jerusalem supermarket, killing 2 and wounding 9. The PFLP claimed responsibility.

Feb. 25, 1969: A bomb heavily damaged the British consulate in East Jerusalem. The PFLP claimed responsibility, alleging a British decision to supply Israel with tanks as the reason. A bomb exploded in Lydda, injuring 1.

March 5, 1969: 80 Arabs were arrested on charges of conducting an extensive guerrilla operation. Most were suspected PFLP members. The group were said to have operated from Jerusalem, the West Bank and the Gaza Strip and received instructions from the Egyptian embassy in Amman.

March 6, 1969: A bomb exploded in the cafeteria of the Hebrew University in Jerusalem, wounding 29 students. In Beirut, the PDFLP and the PFLP claimed credit for the attack. Israeli security forces destroyed 5 Arab houses in East Jerusalem that had been found to contain arms, explosives and other terrorist equipment. The Israelis had discontinued the practice previously.

April 17, 1969: The Lebanese Communist newspaper *Al Nida* reported that Iraq had curbed the activities of the commandos operating there. The secretary of Iraq's ruling Revolutionary Command Council, in a note dated March 31, had ordered the PLO to work through a new Iraqi-controlled *Arab Liberation Front,* accused them of establishing contacts with "certain political organizations" and suggested the PLO establish training camps at al Rutbah, on the Jordanian border.

June 20, 1969: 3 bombs exploded on a street leading to the Wailing Wall in Jerusalem. 1 Arab was killed, 5 others wounded, including two American tourists and an Israeli soldier. 20 suspects were arrested. The PFLP in Amman claimed responsibility, stating this was "to remind the world and tourists of the Zionists' barbaric and Nazi-like acts and to warn the enemy to stop these actions."

Aug. 29, 1969: PFLP leader George Habbash warned in Amman that Jewish-owned firms in London faced assaults similar to a bomb explosion Aug. 25 in the London office of Zim, the Israeli shipping company.

Sept. 8, 1969: Arab youths hurled bombs at the Israeli El Al Airlines office in Brussels, Belgium and tossed hand grenades at the Israeli embassies in The Hague. Netherlands, and in Bonn, West Germany. The PFLP in Amman claimed responsibility and said the attacks were carried out by teenage members of the "Young Tigers" of the "Ho Chi Minh Section" of the PFLP. A PFLP spokesman said Sept. 9 that its forces planned an all-out war against Israeli commercial interests around the world and warned travelers not to use Israeli planes or ships.

Nov. 27, 1969: 2 Jordanian members of an Arab commando group tossed a hand grenade into Israel's El Al Airline office in Athens, wounding 15 and causing heavy damage. One of the injured was a 2-year-old Greek boy who died Nov. 29. The Amman-based PFLP claimed responsibility.

Dec. 21, 1969: Greek police arrested 3 Arabs, including 1 woman, suspected of planning to hijack a U.S. TWA plane in Athens. They were seized as they were about to board the plane bound from Tel Aviv for Rome and New York. The trio possessed guns, hand grenades and mimeographed announcements that the hijackers were PFLP members.

Feb. 10, 1969: 3 Arab terrorists killed 1 Israeli and wounded 11 others in a grenade attack on a bus and lounge at an airport in Munich, West Germany. Police identified the assailants as an Egyptian and 2 Jordanians.

Feb. 10-12, 1970: At least 30 were killed or wounded in clashes between Jordanian troops and Palestinian guerrillas in the Amman area. The fighting was precipitated by commando violation of a government decree restricting their activities. It barred them from carrying arms in towns and gave them two weeks to turn in weapons, banned demonstrations and unauthorized publications and outlawed political party activity. *Al fatah* called this a U.S.-supported attempt to disarm the Palestinians in preparation for a settlement with Israel. A government-commando accord Feb. 22 said that Jordan would permit the commandos to exercise their own discipline but they must refrain from carrying arms or appearing in uniform in public in the main cities.

Feb. 21, 1970: A Swissair passenger plane bound from Zurich to Israel crashed after takeoff, killing all 47 persons aboard. An Arab guerrilla group first claimed responsibility but later denied Arab involvement. The Swiss government officially cited sabotage Feb. 22. Another Swiss plane en route to Tel Aviv crashed. The denial of an Arab connection was announced Feb. 23 by the unified command of Palestinian guerrilla organizations, which comprise 10 groups based in Jordan.

Feb. 28, 1970: Maj. Gen. Mohammed Rassoul Kilani, who reportedly advocated a tough policy against the commandos, was removed as Jordanian interior minister.

June 6-10, 1970: About 200 persons were killed and 500 wounded in clashes between the Jordanian army troops and Palestinian guerrillas in and around Amman. King Hussein yielded to commando demands that he oust two top army officers accused by the commandos of plotting with the U.S. against the Palestinian cause. Syria proclaimed its support of the Palestinian commandos against the Jordanian government. The underlying cause of the violence remained commando opposition to Jordanian government attempts to restrain their operations against Israel.

June 9, 1970: King Hussein was the target of an assassination attempt in a small town west of Amman. A truce pact was reached in negotiations between Hussein and Arafat. It called for the return of all guerrilla forces to their barracks, the establishment of joint controls and checkpoints, the release of prisoners and the formation of two committees to investigate the cause of the clashes and to prevent their recurrence. The PFLP rejected the truce agreement and demanded instead the abolition of what it called the government's anti-commando organizations and the dismissal of officials believed to be hostile to the commandos. Following further talks with Arafat June 11 Hussein yielded to PFLP demands and dismissed his uncle, Maj. Gen. Nasser Ben-Jamil as commander in chief and Maj. Gen. Zayd bin-Shakir as commander of the Third Armored Division which surrounded Amman. Commandos killed U.S. military attache in Amman, Robert Perry, and kidnapped the head of the embassy's political division. 60 foreigners were held hostage in 2 Amman hotels for three days, most of them Americans and Britons. A PFLP spokesman had said June 10 that they were being held to force the Jordanian army to halt the shelling of guerrilla positions in refugee camps.

June 9, 1970: A new 27-man Central Committee of the 10 Palestinian commando organizations was formed at an emergency meeting of all the groups in the *Palestine Armed Struggle Command* in Jordan. Arafat was elected commander in chief of all Palestinian forces. The Supreme Military Council, composed of the 10 commando groups, divided Jordan into several military zones and appointed a separate command for guerrillas operating from each zone. The 10 commando groups were: *al Sa'iqa* (sponsored by the Syrian *Ba'th* party); the *Popular Front for the Liberation of Palestine;* the *Popular Democratic Front for the Liberation of Palestine;* the *Popular Front for the Liberation of Palestine–General Command,* and the *Palestine Arab Organization* (the last 3 had broken away from the PFLP); the *Action Group for the Liberation of Palestine,* (an offshoot of *al fatah); the Arab Liberation Front,* sponsored by the Iraqi *Ba'th* party; the *Popular Liberation Forces* (the military branch of the PLO), and the *Popular Struggle Front.* Only 4 of these—*Sa'iqa, fatah,* the PDFLP and the PLF were represented on the PLO executive committee. The Palestine National Council also established a joint committee of commandos and leftist organizations in Jordan and Lebanon.

July 10, 1970: Jordan and the commandos signed an agreement in Amman worked out by representatives of Egypt, Libya, Sudan and Algeria. The accord reasserted most of the terms of the agreement reached the previous February. Its principal points: the commandos would remove their forces from Amman and other major towns but a civilian militia would be permitted to remain under supervision of a joint government-commando committee; the commandos would refrain from carrying arms in public places, using unlicensed vehicles, military training with live ammunition, storing heavy weapons and explosives in populated centers and maintaining bases in towns; the commandos would obey Jordanian statutes, hand over law violators and refuse to accept recruits liable for service in the Jordanian army. The Amman government pledged to support the Palestinian guerrilla movement and to bar any government body from carrying out acts detrimental to the commandos.

Aug. 27-28, 1970: Following clashes between commandos and Jordanian troops Aug. 26-30 in Amman, the guerrillas called for a continued military struggle against Israel at a meeting of the Palestine National Council in Amman. Resolutions adopted denounced a U.S. peace initiative that had brought about negotiations between Israel,

Jordan and Egypt. The council said anyone opposed to the campaign to destroy Israel "is a traitor to his cause and the revolution and deserves severe punishment."

Sept. 1, 1970: King Hussein escaped injury when a would-be assassin fired on his motorcade in Amman. The incident was followed by an exchange of gunfire between the army and the commandos in and around Amman. A government communique declared: "The Jordanian government assures the Jordanian people . . . that the situation in the capital and the kingdom is under full control. Any rumors by the army of a crackdown on the commandos are completely untrue and the aim of these rumors is to create confusion."

Sept. 6, 1970: Members of the PFLP hijacked 3 airliners bound for New York from Europe and diverted them to the Middle East. The attempted seizure of a fourth, an El Al plane bound from Amsterdam, was thwarted by security guards aboard the aircraft, who killed one hijacker and wounded the other. The plane made an unscheduled landing in London where the wounded hijacker was identified by British police as Leila Khaled. The planes seized included a Swissair DC8 bound from Zurich with 155 on board; a TWA from Frankfurt with 151 and a Pan American World Airways jumbo jet bound from Amsterdam with 152 passengers. The Swissair and TWA planes were flown to "revolution airport" in the desert at Zarqa in Jordan. The Pan Am plane was first flown to Beirut, then to Cairo, where the aircraft was blown up. The PFLP held the occupants of the 2 planes in Jordan as hostages for imprisoned commandos in Israel, Britain, Switzerland and West Germany. It warned the two planes with its passengers would be blown up if the guerrillas jailed for attacks involving planes were not freed. The 127 passengers from the two planes in Jordan, mostly women and children, were housed in 2 Amman hotels. The planes were surrounded by the commandos and by an outer ring of Jordanian army troops, including more than 50 tanks and armored cars. A PFLP spokesman in Beirut said Sept. 6 that the planes had been seized "to give the Americans a lesson after they supported Israel all these years," and in retaliation for the U.S. peace initiative in the Middle East; and the Swiss plane was hijacked in reprisal for the sentencing of 3 terrorists for their 1969 attack on a plane in Zurich.

Sept. 9, 1970: A BOAC jet was hijacked after takeoff from Bahrein with 105 passengers and ordered to land at Beirut to pick up a woman commando. The plane was flown to the desert airstrip near Amman. The PFLP announced the passengers would be hostages for the release of Leila Khaled, jailed in London. The TWA, Swissair and BOAC planes were blown up by the terrorists on Sept. 12, at the end of a week of international efforts to secure release of the more than 300 passengers and crewmen. These efforts were complicated by the renewal of fighting between Jordanian troops and the commandos. Most of the passengers were allowed to leave. Some 54 remained in commando hands as hostages Sept. 15. Passengers reported that after the planes had been blown up, Jordanian armored units surrounding the airstrip had moved to circle the passengers and their commando escorts. The troops withdrew when the guerrillas warned the passengers would die with them. The PLO Central Committee suspended the PFLP from membership Sept. 12 for destroying the aircraft. The remaining hostages were freed by the guerrillas in separate groups Sept. 25, 26, 29 as part of a deal for the release of terrorists held in Europe.

Sept. 16, 1970: Two weeks of sporadic but heavy fighting between commandos and Jordanian troops led to the installation of a military government by King Hussein. The prior government was reported dismissed when Hussein learned the terms of a truce agreement negotiated with the commandos, which reportedly would have turned control of Jordan's major cities over to the guerrilla leaders. The fighting broke out following the assassination attempt on the King. The fourth truce was worked out with the aid of Arab League mediators and was signed Sept. 15. The truce agreement called for replacing army guards by police units throughout Amman, reductions in army strength near the capital and the evacuation of all new positions by both sides. The commandos were to remove roadblocks and stop all interception, interrogation and arrest procedures. The Army agreed not to intercept commandos. The post office, power plant and water stations would continue to be guarded by units of both sides. The King reportedly declared that he "had been betrayed" when presented with the agreement by Premier Rifa'i.

The new military cabinet was headed by Brig. Muhammed Da'ud as premier and included 5 generals, 2 colonels and 3 majors. Field Marshal Habes al-Majali replaced Maj. Gen. Mashur Haditha as commander in chief of the army and military governor of Jordan. Real authority was believed to be in his hands. Hussein's letter appointing Daoud ordered him to implement the cease fire agreement negotiated with commando leaders by Rifa'i. Government spokesman said Sept. 16 that the military leaders were aiming at a "Lebanese" solution[3] which would concentrate the commandos in border areas adjacent to Israel. An *al fatah* spokesman said the commandos would not leave their strongholds in the cities of northern Jordan. The PLO Central Committee rejected the military government as the product of a "fascist military coup." It ordered commandos to hold their positions and fortify them. Its statements broadcast that day by the commando radio in Baghdad and Damascus said the PFLP had been readmitted to the committee and that all guerrilla units were now under Arafat.

Sept. 17, 1970: The committee called for a general strike to help topple the government. Baghdad and Damascus radios backed the commandos. Columns of tanks and troops under orders of the new military government entered Amman at dawn and immediately engaged guerrillas emplaced in buildings throughout the city. The fighting quickly spread to other parts of the country. The fiercest fighting was in the capital, where Jordanian tanks and infantry units surrounded and attacked the Al-Husseini and Wahdat refugee camps, sites of commando operational headquarters. The government charged in a broadcast that the guerrillas began the fighting by firing on the army's general staff headquarters shortly before dawn. By 5 p.m. Amman radio announced that government troops were in command of the city except for scattered pockets of resistance. As the fighting ebbed in the capital at sunset, clashes in the north increased in intensity. At Zarqa government forces overran a guerrilla redoubt that had once been a staging area for commando forays into Israel.

Sept. 18, 1970: Fierce house-to-house fighting continued in Amman.

Sept. 21, 1970: A large guerrilla force, fighting from behind a column of Syrian tanks, routed Hussein's forces in northern Jordan. The guerrilla radio reported that all the cities in the north except Amman had fallen to the commandos.

Sept. 23, 1970: Jordanian tanks pushed back a guerrilla force that had driven a wedge between government forces in the north and south. Syrian tanks spearheading the guerrilla advance were chased back across the border into Syria after constant

---

3. i.e., accords reached between the commandos and the government in Lebanon. *(Eds.)*

pounding from a squadron of Jordan jets. Field Marshal Majali announced a cease-fire
order in Amman. The order was ignored as both sides continued to exchange small-
arms fire throughout the city. Hussein noted an agreement between his government
and four captured commando chiefs. This was repudiated in a broadcast from Damascus by Arafat, who called it a "conspiracy."

Sept. 24, 1970: The level of fighting ebbed as Arafat announced he would meet
with 4 envoys representing the Arab chiefs of state meeeing in Cairo to seek an end to
the civil war.

Sept. 25, 1970: King Hussein's government and the Arab commando leadership
jointly ordered an immediate nationwide cease-fire. At the time, Jordanian forces
controlled nearly all of Amman and had pushed north to encircle guerrilla forces
holding Irbid, Ramtha and Jerash.

Sept. 26, 1970: Hussein appointed a new civilian-military government of "national
reconciliation." The military retained the key defense and interior ministries in the
new government. The commandos assailed the new cabinet in Damascus, stating that
it "does not change our attitude in the least. Nor will it make any change in the
situation, as long as the royal regime exists and the real criminals, first and foremost
King Hussein, are in power."

Jan. 8, 1971: Jordanian troops launched a major attack against Palestinian commando bases north of Amman. Fighting continued in the area and in the capital itself
until Jan. 13 when a truce was agreed to by both sides. The fighting broke out around
the towns of Jerash, Salt and Ruseifa. The government said the clashes in the Jerash
area followed the kidnaping Jan. 7 by commandos of two noncommissioned army
officers and the killing of a Jordanian soldier. *Al fatah* claimed that a hospital at el
Rumman had been shelled and that the al Baqaa refugee camp had been bombed. A
clash in Amman resulted in the deaths of three civilians and a policeman. Ibrahim
Bakr, a member of the Central Committee, the coordinating group of the 10 guerrilla
organizations, said Jan. 11 that the latest Jordanian attack had paralyzed the commando movement and made it impossible for them to mount raids against the Israelis.
A 13 point agreement that went into effect Jan. 14 reportedly contained nothing new
except a timetable to implement the unfulfilled pledges outlined in the pact that had
ended the September 1970 fighting. The latest treaty called on the guerrillas to withdraw to bases outside the cities and towns and for both sides to release all prisoners by
Jan. 20.

March 26-April 6, 1971: Jordanian troops and Palestinian commandos engaged in
sharp fighting in Amman and in the northern sector around Irbid. Fighting broke out
for the first time along the border with Syria from which some guerrilla units were
believed to have moved into Jordan. The commando forces . . . initiated offensive
actions and widespread acts of sabotage. Fighting spread to Amman March 28 as
government troops fired on a crowd of demonstrating women, killing three of them. A
guerrilla announcement, April 2 declared that the *fedayeen* were fighting to force King
Hussein to replace Wasfi Tal as premier and to oust the high-ranking officers whom
they regarded as responsible for starting the latest round of fighting. It was charged
that he and some army officers were planning to "finish off the commando movement
once and for all." Amman reports April 5 told of a meeting of commando leaders in
the town of Dera, Syria April 1, in which they had decided on a "scorched earth"
policy to force Hussein to accede to their demands for freedom of action and move-

ment in Jordan. Syria was reported April 4 to have warned Jordan that the 6,000 regular troops of the PLO stationed south of Damascus would be permitted to move into Jordan "unless harassment of guerrillas was quickly stopped."

June 2, 1971: Hussein gave orders for a "final crackdown" against the Palestinian commandos, whom he charged with attempting "to establish a separate Palestinian state and destroy the unity of the Jordanian and Palestinian people." Hussein's directive, given to Premier Wasfi Tal, demanded "bold, decisive action against the handful of professional criminals and conspirators who use the commando movement to disguise their treasonable plots." A statement issued by the central committee of the PLO in Beirut June 1 had accused Jordan of mounting an offensive against commando bases in Jordan "in a conspiracy against the Palestine revolution."

June 5, 1971: Seven commando groups called for the overthrow of King Hussein's government and the formation of a national union government. A joint statement broadcast by Baghdad radio said "this is the only way to prevent a unilateral peace agreement between Jordan and Israel." The statement was signed by *al fatah*, the PFLP, the PDF, the *Popular Front-General Command*, the PLO, the *Arab Liberation Front* and the *Popular Struggle Liberation Front*. The Jordanian army began an all-out attack against the commandos in northern Jordan July 13. After several days of heavy fighting, the government claimed the guerrillas had been crushed and that more than 2,000 of them were captives. The government announced July 14 that it had launched the assault to oust the guerrillas from inhabited areas, following attacks they had made on Jordanian troops in the Jerash area. The fighting was centered in the Ajlun-Jerash area, 25 miles north of Amman, stronghold of the commando movement. The main Palestinian resistance was reported quelled by July 15. Palestinian sources reported July 18 that scores of commandos had fled across the Jordan River into Israel-occupied territory to escape capture by the Jordanian forces. Israeli officials, confirming the unprecedented development, reported July 19 that 72 guerrillas had crossed into the occupied west bank July 17-19 and surrendered to Israeli authorities.

July 21, 1971: A government announcement said 2,000 captured Arab commandos had been released. An Amman spokesman said several hundred had left for Iraq and Syria . . . most of the others would remain in Jordan, having agreed to surrender their weapons and return to civilian life. Authorities July 20 had freed 831 guerrillas in Amman and in Irbid. Another 500 were set free in Amman July 21.

Nov. 28, 1971: Premier Wasfi Tal of Jordan was shot to death by three Palestinians while entering a hotel in Cairo. In Beirut, the PFLP claimed responsibility for his death. The gunmen described themselves as members of a Palestinian commando faction called the *Black September*[4] organization. It had been formed in July to avenge the slaying of Palestinian guerrillas in the Jordan civil war in Sept. 1970.

---

4. *Black September* is the overseas terrorist military wing of *al fatah* and directly controlled by Arafat. *(Eds.)*

II

Geography, Economy, Government and Population

Geography of Jordan

Between 1950-1967, the territory of the Hashemite Kingdom of Jordan totalled some 35,000 square miles, some 6% of which was on the west bank of the Jordan River. Jordan's only outlet is along the Gulf of Aqaba, which provides its access to the Red Sea. The country's dominant feature is a great north-south geological rift, forming the depression of the Jordan River Valley (which extends through Lake Tiberias in Israel and the Dead Sea (whose banks are divided between Jordan and Israel). The depression is hot and the landscape forbidding. It has served as a barrier, throughout history, between the lands of the east and those bordering the Mediterranean.

Distribution of rainfall continues to determine the pattern of settlement in Jordan. The majority of the population lives in the north, where rainfall is sufficient to support cultivation. Some 82% of the East Bank is sparsely populated desert. The population is concentrated in the north-western corner, near the Jordan River system, where the major towns are located.

Arable land is Jordan's most valued resource. The East Ghor Canal, completed in 1963, has brought much of the northern Jordan Valley under irrigation. New plans for projects in the Jordan Valley, itself the site of major development efforts since 1973, provide for further land reclamation, the greater exploitation of water resources and the construction of roads, bridges, dams and electrical plants.

Jordan's borders do not follow well-defined or natural features of the terrain, but were established by various international agreements. Its border with Israel (excluding the West Bank) are based on the Armistice Demarcation line agreed upon in April 1949 by Israel and Transjordan, following negotiations under the auspices of the United Nations mediator. Until 1967, the demarcation line divided the city of Jerusalem between the two states. Jordan occupied the Old City and most of the Holy Places while the newer areas on the west were part of Israel.

Jordan's borders with Syria, Iraq and Saudi Arabia were drawn across the deserts around Transjordan after World War I. Agreements with these states recognize, for the few remaining nomadic tribes in the area, the principle of freedom of grazing and provide for a continuation of their migratory practices, subject to certain regulations. Jordan's border with Saudi Arabia was defined in a series of agreements made by Great Britain. The first was the Hadda Agreement of 1925. This and other agreements resulted in a more or less stabilized border until 1965, when the two states concluded a bilateral agreement. In an exchange of territory, Jordan's coastline on the Gulf of Aqaba was extended by some twelve miles. This border, which passes through arid and almost rainless and unpopulated desert or semi-desert, also established a zone where the two countries would share petroleum revenues on an equal basis if oil is discovered in the area.

Administratively, the East Bank is divided into five major divisions known as governorates *(alwiya* pl. *liwa* sing.): Amman, al Balqaa, Ma'an, Irbid and al Kerak (the West Bank is divided by Jordan into the three governorates of al Quds, Nabulus and al Khalil). Each governorate is centered around a major town which has long been the political and economic hub of the surrounding area.

Jordan has few mountainous areas, but consists of a fairly high plateau divided into ridges by valleys or gorges. This has been the scene of repeated earthquakes and the rubble of temples and other buildings of antiquity can frequently be found. In the north, flowing to the Syrian border, there are wide fields of broken lava and basaltic rock. The greater part of the country east of the rift depression is desert and arid; most of the land is part of the great Syrian or north Arabian desert, consisting of broad expanses of sand and dunes, particularly in the far south, and of salt flats.

The rolling hills and the low mountains support a meager and stunted vegetation. Toward the depression in the western part of the East Bank, there is a rise in the desert, which evolves into the Jordanian highlands, a steppe of high limestone plateaus and an area of wadis (ravines or water courses which are dry except in the short winter rainy season). The lowland area south of the Yarmuk River (at the northern end of the Dead Sea) is intensely cultivated, irrigated from the East Ghor Canal, which runs parallel to the Jordan River. Cereals, maize (corn), tobacco, groundnuts (peanuts) and fruit are the chief crops in this area. The market furnished by the neighboring oil-producing states has stimulated the cultivation of cash crops, including tomatoes, citrus fruit, artichokes and potatoes. Government sponsored agricultural extension work to prevent soil erosion and flash flooding has also stimulated agricultural production and the development of dams and outlets for tributary streams from the plateau has also significantly increased the region's agricultural potential.

The Jordan River flows through sources on Mount Hermon in the north to its mouth at the Dead Sea. Its principal tributary is the Yarmuk River which, near its junction, forms the border between Israel on the north west, Syria on the north east and Jordan on the south. The Az Zarqa River, the Jordan's second main tributary, rises and empties entirely inside the East Bank. It has been developed, since 1973, to provide irrigation for the lower eastern Jordan Valley. South of the Dead Sea is the Wadi al Arabah, which rises gradually through a region of barren desert to reach sea level halfway to the Gulf of Aqaba.

Jordan has a rainy season (November to March) and a hot, dry summer, made not unpleasant by cool evening breezes. The greater part of the East Bank receives less than five inches of rainfall per year. It is an area of strong, dry, dust-cloud winds—the *khamsin*—swirling in from the desert before or after the summer season, but it enjoys, on the whole, a Mediterranean climate.

The country is poor in mineral fuels and metallic ores and oil has not been discovered in any commercially feasible quantity. The manganese ore in the Dead Sea area has a high copper content and there are copper deposits near the port of Aqaba. Phosphate rock, located at Wadi al Hasa, ninety miles south of Amman, is Jordan's most important mineral resource.

Jordan's only rail line is the narrow-gauge, single track Hejaz railway, built in the early 1900s to accommodate pilgrim traffic between Damascus and Medina. It was largely destroyed during World War I but sectors have been reconstructed (by agreements among Syria, Jordan and Saudi Arabia) to carry some 500,000 pilgrims annually to and from Mecca. A branch extends to the port of Aqaba.

Jordan's main highway connecting the East and West Banks runs from Amman to Jerusalem across the Jordan River at the Allenby Bridge. Another major highway crosses the river farther north, at the Damiyah Bridge and continues to the West Bank town of Nablus. The Trans-Arabian pipeline (tapline) crosses Jordan from Saudi Arabia to Sidon in Lebanon. Jordan's major international airport is near Amman.

Jordan on the Gulf of Aqaba

By ALEXANDER MELAMID

The Kingdom of Jordan has today a shoreline of about 12 miles at the head of the Gulf of Aqaba which includes the town and port of the same name. This attachment of territory on this Gulf to a state located to its north has been throughout history an infrequent and usually tenuous feature of political geography. Although the Gulf of Aqaba is an arm of the Red Sea and is thus connected to the world's oceans, it was, in the age of sail, only very rarely used by ships. Strong northerly winds blow there most of the year, usually on over 350 days, and northbound sailing on the narrow Gulf with its many reefs was therefore extremely slow, tortuous and dangerous. History records only two doubtful voyages in Solomonic days, about 1,000 B.C. and one in the 13th Century C.E. by the Crusader Renald de Chatillon whose ship did not make the return trip. As a result there were no permanent ports and port cities on this Gulf in the days of sail and there was little inducement for states to

Dr. Melamid is Professor of Economics at New York University. He has contributed numerous articles to scholarly journals, among them, ''The Evolution of Economic Regions in Iran,'' *Geographical Review*, October, 1975.

incorporate its desert shores into their territory. Instead Turks, Arabs, Byzantines, Romans, Nabateans and probably their predecessors used ports and territory on the open Red Sea for their maritime trade with the South and East. As edible fish are also relatively rare in the Gulf, there were also no fishing settlements, and competent explorers and archeologists such as Baron de Laborde (1836), T.E. Lawrence (1914), Sir Mortimer Wheeler (1954) and others comment on the absence even of boats. Due to the absence of boats, Laborde, Lawrence and others had to construct their own rafts from palm trunks to reach islands near the head of the Gulf.

As a result of the absence of maritime trade and fishing, the town of Aqaba with its good wells and whose main grazing areas were to the south and east, was nothing but an agricultural center with date gardens that catered only to the trading needs of neighboring Bedouin. During the Ottoman Empire Aqaba was therefore administratively part of the *vilayet* or province of the Hejaz which encompassed Mecca and Medina and thus the western Arabian peninsula rather than part of the *vilayet* of Syria which was geographically closer and included the area of the Dead Sea. However, during most of the 12th century, the town of Aqaba and its immediate vicinity was held by the Crusader kingdom of Jerusalem as part of its fief, the Duchy of Oultre-Jourdan. The crusaders placed a small garrison in the town and made it a bishopric (the title "Bishop of Aqaba" has survived in the Roman Catholic Church). The purpose of this occupation was to divide militarily the Muslims of Egypt from those of Arabia; otherwise the town was of no significance to the Crusaders and they left there very few architectural relics. During the 19th century Aqaba became part of Egypt. After the Egyptians constructed a road across Sinai during the 1830s and 40s, Aqaba became an Egyptian staging and boundary point on the pilgrim route from Egypt to Mecca. Improvements of navigation on the Red Sea after 1840 soon reduced the significance of the land route via Aqaba and Egypt abandoned the town and the head of the Gulf of Aqaba to the Ottoman Empire without regrets when the boundary between these two states was demarcated across the Sinai Peninsula in 1906. (This boundary is today the boundary between Israel and Israeli occupied Sinai Peninsula.)

Thereafter, Aqaba remained a sleepy oasis until 1917 when the British began using the area for a supply route in their military offensive against the Ottoman Empire. Steamers began calling at Aqaba and in the absence of any port facilities discharged their cargoes on beaches. From there these supplies reached the fighting fronts by camels, mules and a few automobiles. When Chaim Weitzmann (later President of Israel), visited the area in 1918 he travelled via Aqaba. With gradual removal of enemy ships and especially submarines from the eastern Mediterranean, and later the end of the war, Aqaba ceased to be used by ships and reverted to its previous status. Visitors again commented on the absence of ships and boats (see Scherti [1936], for example).

After the end of World War I, Great Britain received a mandate for Palestine which included the modern states of Israel and Jordan. However, the southern boundary of this mandate was not defined. Politicians of the Arabian peninsula believed that this boundary was located 20 to 50 miles north of the town of Aqaba as this had been the approximate boundary of the former Ottoman *vilayet* of Hejaz. This would have allotted the southernmost part of Jordan, as well as the vicinity of the modern Israeli town of Eilat, to the Kingdom of Hejaz, which in 1925 became part of Saudi Arabia. Indeed, the last King of Hejaz made his last stand against the incorporation of his kingdom into Saudi Arabia in the town of Aqaba.

Subsequently, the British Government arranged for a series of treaties with Saudi Arabia which established eastern boundaries for its mandate. However, no southern boundary was agreed upon and Britain delimited unilaterally a boundary with Saudi Arabia which ran approximately east-south-east from a point on the Gulf just south of the town of Aqaba. This gave about five miles of shoreline to what later became the Kingdom of Jordan between a boundary point with Palestine (now Israel) demarcated only in 1946 and the beginning of Saudi Arabian territory. The unilateral British action was not accepted by Saudi Arabia which, however, agreed to maintain the status quo thus established pending a solution of this dispute. This boundary was never demarcated on the ground and some detailed maps of the area indicated the boundary with the legend "end of Saudi Arabian administration."

With the brief exception of 1917-18, the territory that became Jordan used Haifa and Jaffa on the Mediterranean as its ports. With the establishment of the State of Israel in 1948, access to these ports was cut. Although the port of Beirut in Lebanon was usually accessible to Jordan, freight rates to Beirut are very high, the route is tortuous and inconvenient, and traffic was several times interrupted due to conflicts with Syria and between Syria and Lebanon. In the 1950s Jordan therefore began developing a port at Aqaba which had already been connected by a paved road to the terminal of Jordanian railroad (formerly called Hejaz railroad) at Ma'an in 1936. Use of this port increased with the development of Jordanian phosphate and potash exports. External piers projecting in the Gulf were constructed and dry cargo shipments at Aqaba almost immediately exceeded the volume of dry cargoes of the equally new Israeli port of Eilat; however Eilat handles a significantly larger volume of liquid cargoes, mainly crude oil. Due to the steepness of the land, no extension of the railway from Ma'an to Aqaba was built. With the growth of traffic, there was soon insufficient land for port development and ancillary installations within Jordanian territory at Aqaba. A treaty with Saudi Arabia in 1965 finally provided a solution both of the 40-year old boundary dispute with Saudi Arabia and the land requirements of the port of Aqaba. In exchange for about 4,000 square miles of Jordanian territory in the desert interior (roughly in the extreme south-eastern corner of the state), Jordan obtained about six miles of additional coastline south of the previous (undemarcated) boundary point on the Gulf, together another approximately 3,000 square miles of desert in the interior. The new boundary point on the Gulf of Aqaba is 330 yards north of the Saudi Arabian police post of Al Durra. The additional Jordanian territory has permitted expansion of both port and urban facilities, as well as development of beach resort areas, at Aqaba besides settling a frequently acrimonious, if nonviolent, boundary dispute. A similar boundary rectification between the Belgian Congo (now Zaire) and Portuguese Angola (now Angola) involved an exchange of a quarter of a square mile of potential port area near the Congo port of Banana for 25,000 square miles of land in the interior.

Under normal conditions of peace, it would be cheaper for Jordan as well as Israel to handle most of their traffic through Mediterranean ports rather than through the Gulf. Land freight rates to the Gulf, now partly government subsidized, are extremely high and are not offset by relatively high Suez Canal charges. Since the opening of the Suez Canal to Israeli cargoes in 1975 much cargo formerly handled through Eilat has already been diverted to Israeli Mediterranean ports. Peace and restoration of free access to Mediterranean ports in the Middle East can therefore be expected to transfer much traffic away from Aqaba, except perhaps for bulk mineral exports to Indian and Pacific Ocean areas. As bulk mineral handling in ports does not require much labor, a significant population decline in Aqaba can then be anticipated. As at Eilat, the significant recreation use of Aqaba can be expected to continue.

MAJOR REFERENCES

Lawrence, T.E. *Wilderness of Zin*. London, 1915.

Melamid, Alexander. "Political Geography of the Gulf of Aqaba." *Annals of the Association of American Geographers,* Vol. 47 (1957), 231-40.

———. "Legal Status of the Gulf of Aqaba." *American Journal of International Law,* Vol. 53 (1959), 412-13.

Runciman, Sir Stephen. *A History of the Crusades*. Cambridge, 1952.

U.S. Department of State, Bureau of Intelligence and Research. *Jordan-Saudi Arabia Boundary, 1965*. International Boundary Studies #60, 1965.

Wheeler, Sir Mortimer. *Rome Beyond Imperial Frontiers*. London, 1954.

Constitution and Government

The Hashemite Kingdom of Jordan *(Al Mamlaka al Urduniya al Hashemiyah)* is a constitutional monarchy. At its head is His Majesty King Hussein. The Crown Prince, appointed 1 April, 1965, is the King's young brother, Prince Hassan. The official religion of Jordan is Islam and the official language is Arabic.

Great Britain recognized Transjordan as a sovereign independent state by a treaty signed in London on 22 March 1946. The Emir 'Abdallah, King Hussein's grandfather, assumed the title of King on 25 May 1946. On 17 June 1946, upon ratification of the Anglo-Jordanian treaty, the name of the territory was changed to that of The Hashemite Kingdom of Transjordan.

The Constitution[1] provides that there be no discrimination on account of race, religion or language among Jordanian citizens and that there be equal opportunities in work and education. It provides for individual freedom, a free press, for schools to be established freely, provided they follow a recognized curriculum and educational policy, and free and compulsory elementary education.

Legislative power is vested in the National Assembly and the King. The National Assembly consists of two houses: a) the Senate, and b) the House of Representatives. The House of Representatives has 60 members, elected by universal suffrage (of men only, by secret ballot). Thirty of these members come from the East Bank ("East Jordan") and 30 are from the West Bank ("West Jordan"). These members are elected for a 4-year term of office.

The Senate consists of 30 members, who are nominated by the King. Senators must not be related to the King, must be over 40 years of age and are chosen from present and former prime ministers, other ministers and past ambassadors, and from members of the civil and *shari'a* courts, or may be retired army generals or former members of the House of Representatives. Senators are appointed for 4 years and may be reappointed.

The King approves laws and promulgates them. He declares war, concludes peace and signs treaties (which must be approved by the National Assembly). He orders the holding of elections, convenes, adjourns and prorogues the House of Representatives and appoints the Prime Minister and the President of the Senate as well as the Senators.

The Council of Ministers, consisting of the Prime Minister, President of the Council, and his Ministers, conducts all affairs of state both internal and external.

The Constitution provides that the Cabinet be responsible to Parliament.

Amendments to the Constitution approved on 9 November 1974 by both Houses of Parliament empower the King to dissolve Parliament and to delay calling elections for a period of twelve months.

Jordan's last elections were held on 16 April, 1967.

1. See pp. 343-348 for excerpts.

Political Parties

Political parties have not become rooted in Jordan, although the Parliament's increasing powers have encouraged their formation. In September 1971 King Hussein announced the formation of a *Jordanian National Union*. In March 1972 the organization was renamed the *Arab National Union*. It has an estimated membership of 100,000. Other political parties which have appeared in Jordan are:

- *The National Socialist Party*—headed by Sulayman al-Nabulsi, who was Jordan's Prime Minister, October 29, 1956-April 10, 1957 and who was replaced by a military government. Several members of the party are in the present Parliament.

- *The Ba'th ("Resurrection") Party*—Jordanian branch—headed by 'Abdullah al-Rimawi, initially stood for union with Iraq and later became pro-Nasserist. The party is proscribed in Jordan, despite this country's present relations with Syria, whose ruling party is the Ba'th—Syrian branch.

- *Hiz al-Tahrir ("Liberation") Party*—is an extremist right-wing party similar to the *Muslim Brotherhood*. Accused of plots and attempted coups, the party was outlawed in Jordan.

- *The Communist Party*—is underground and outlawed in Jordan.

Economic Development in Jordan Since 1967

By ELIYAHU KANOVSKY

Any attempt to analyze economic development in Transjordan since 1967 is fraught with numerous obstacles. The many external and internal "shocks" [it has endured] make it difficult to detect the underlying economic trends. In the case of Jordan, the sharp annual fluctuations in rainfall, and hence in agricultural production, have always had a great impact on the economy as a whole. Between 1950 and 1966 these fluctuations had a decreasing effect, both because of increasing irrigation, and the diminishing *relative* importance of agriculture in the Jordanian economy. Nonetheless, the effect of drought or abundant rainfall on the Jordanian economy in the mid-1960s was still considerable. As for the East Bank economy, where other sectors were generally far more developed, and where the bulk of the irrigated area is concentrated, the effects of the erratic rainfall pattern are of lesser importance, but they remain, nonetheless, significant. While official estimates of agricultural production in the East Bank are provided for the post-1967 period[1] no overall index is compiled. Separate agricultural production figures for the East Bank in the pre-1967 period are not available. In addition to the man-made disturbances to production in 1968-71 . . . the drought in 1968, and the even more severe drought and very adverse weather conditions of 1970 and 1973, make it difficult to detect the basic trends.

The national income accounts since 1967 continue to be, *officially,* for both the West Bank and the East Bank combined. There is a presumption that the *changes* in the national income figures reflect, primarily, changes in East Bank economic activity. An additional problem is the inflation since 1969. The national accounts, both before and since 1967, have been in current prices. However, until 1969 there appears to have been a relatively high degree of price stability, and the current data could be taken as reasonable approximations of real developments. Since 1967 the government has been

Dr. Kanovsky is the author of, among others, *The Economic Impact of the Six Day War,* Praeger, 1970 and numerous articles.

The above forms Chapter Three, entitled "Economic Development in the East Bank (Transjordan) Since 1967," of *Economic Development of Jordan,* a book prepared by Dr. Kanovsky within the framework of a comprehensive study directed by Professor Z.Y. Hershlag on *The Economic Implications of Peace in the Middle East,* at the David Horowitz Institute for the Research of Developing Countries, Tel Aviv, Israel, and published by University Publishing Projects, Tel Aviv. Reprinted by permission.

compiling a cost of living index for Amman and Zarqa. No wholesale price index has been calculated, nor a GNP price deflator.

As a result of all these problems, our analysis of developments in the East Bank economy will be based on various partial indicators which are available, such as the index of industrial production in the East Bank, construction activity, in terms of area, in the main cities in the East Bank, and other indicators of this nature, as well as broad changes in the national accounts.

Agriculture

Agriculture in Transjordan consists of three regions: 1. The Ghor (valley) region has a total cultivable area of almost 100 thousand acres. The whole area is below sea level, and water for irrigation is available. More than one crop can be produced annually, and as a result of the climate, early crops can be produced. Commercial farming, mainly fruits and vegetables, typify this area. 2. The Highland region, which is mainly dependent on very erratic rainfall. Farm practices in this region are far more primitive. The main crops are wheat, barley, legumes, and tobacco. Terracing and planting of some fruit trees started quite recently in this region. Land holdings are fragmented and small, and as a result of poor farming practices, soil erosion is a major problem. Afforestation programs have been instituted to combat soil erosion. Some scattered springs and ground water are used for irrigation. 3. The Badia (desert) region is by far the largest in terms of area, and is used mainly for the grazing of cattle. As a result of poor farming practices this land has steadily lost much of its economic importance. Hydrological research which has been carried out, thus far, shows that ground water is available to irrigate about 48 thousand acres, of which about one sixth is being utilized.

Describing the characteristics and problems of East Bank agriculture the authors of the Three Year Development Plan 1973-75, noted the following (in 1972): 1. The fragmentation and small size of farms increases costs of production, limits investment, and reduces output. 2. The prevalence of "traditional" cropping patterns reduces soil fertility. 3. Erosion, and the lack of sound soil and water conservation practices. 4. The planting of cereals in marginal areas. 5. Disorganized grazing which has contributed to aridity, and "mass cattle destruction" in dry seasons. 6. The areas planted with forest and fruit trees are very small. 7. Inefficient marketing services and facilities. 8. Poor and insufficient credit facilities.[2]

In the development of agriculture, the Jordanian authorities have put the greatest emphasis on irrigation projects. Of these, the major one is the Jordan Valley Development project.[3] Work on this project commenced in 1958 specifically the East Ghor Canal, which was completed in 1963. Work was continued to raise the sides of this canal, in order to increase its capacity. This, as well as some other dam projects in the East Bank were completed in early 1967. Additional projects (also in the East Bank) were completed in 1968 and

1970. One major project was not completed since Israel had occupied one bank of the Yarmuk, in the 1967 war. It has been estimated that the East Ghor canal project accounted for almost two percentage points of Jordan's 7% average annual growth rate of value added in agriculture, between 1959/60 and 1965/66. A study made by the U.S. Agency for International Development, shortly before the Six Day War, indicated a number of projects which would provide irrigation for an additional 127 thousand acres in the East Bank, eight thousand acres in the West Bank, and one project that would provide irrigation for an additional eight thousand acres on both sides of the Jordan. These were in addition to the 30 thousand acres already irrigated by the East Ghor Canal.[4] According to the Ministry of Agriculture, the total irrigated area in Transjordan in 1971 was about 62 thousand acres, of which over three fourths was in the frost-free Jordan Valley. The latter is ideally suited for high-value, off-season vegetables, and there are indications that this development is proceeding rapidly. The U.S. Department of Agriculture, in a 1972 publication (dealing with agriculture in both Banks) gives a much higher estimate for the irrigated area in the East Bank—81,500 acres and 17,300 acres in the West Bank.[5] The discrepancy between the two estimates may be due to the latter's inclusion of partially-irrigated areas. The 1973-5 Plan calls for the continued rapid expansion of the irrigated area by over 27 thousand acres. About one half of this expansion was to take place in the Jordan Valley.[6]

In 1972 the Planning Council prepared a major development project for the Jordan Valley—a large area, stretching from the Syrian border, along the Jordan river, the eastern shore of the Dead Sea, and southward to Ghor Al-Safi, a valley about midway between the Dead Sea and the Red Sea. The comprehensive plan includes the development of water resources, roads, dams and bridges, electric power, and the construction of 38 new villages with the necessary infrastructure, to settle 137 thousand people, including a large number of Palestinian refugees. Financial as well as technical aid is being provided mainly by the US, West Germany, and the World Bank. This project is likely to have a major impact on Transjordan's economic development.[7]

Though the irrigated areas constitute but a small fraction of the cultivated area, they account for an increasing share of farm production. However, since most of agricultural production is still dependent on a very erratic pattern of rainfall, and Jordanian progress in dry farming has been rather slow (as compared with developments in irrigated farming) total farm production continues to be subject to very wide annual fluctuations. In the accompanying Table No. 1, the sharp annual changes in crop production are especially evident in the cereal and other field crops, largely unirrigated, as was the case before 1967. However, most of the fruit and vegetable crops were adversely affected by the post 1967 fighting along the Israeli-Jordanian cease-fire lines;

the Israeli destruction of the East Ghor Canal; the severe civil war; and the post-civil war embargo imposed, especially by Syria. What made matters worse was that Jordan's markets in Saudi Arabia, Kuwait and the Persian Gulf area were adversely affected by a rather rapid development in agriculture, especially in Saudi Arabia. Jordan's tomato crop had become a mainstay of its farm economy, accounting in 1966-68 for about one half of the country's farm exports. Between 1966 and 1969 export prices of Jordanian tomatoes more than doubled. Subsequently they dropped sharply, with 1972 prices 35% below their peak 1969 levels.[8]

The sharp annual fluctuations in wheat, barley and other field crops, which are largely unirrigated, are due to the rainfall patterns. 1970 was a particularly bad year in terms of weather conditions.[9] Fruit and vegetable crops were affected to a far lesser extent by weather conditions. The hostilities and the boycott imposed, especially by Syria, had a significant impact on these crops. Nonetheless it is note-worthy that even during this period yields of the irrigated crops tended to increase. The disturbances also affected some new fruit plantations, though new olive and vine plantations continued to increase rapidly during the 1967-71 period.[10] These are generally in the drylands which were largely unaffected by the fighting. Olive trees occupied about three fourths of the total area of fruit trees in the East Bank in 1971, and grapes an additional 10%.[11] Other positive developments include the increased use of tractors and of inorganic fertilizers, especially since 1971.[12] Modern poultry and dairy farms have been established and many farmers have adopted the system of growing vegetables under plastic coverings. The 1973-75 Plan call[ed] for investment of JD 14.6 million in irrigation projects—one fifth of planned public sector investments. The plan call[ed] for an additional JD 8.9 million in public sector investments in agriculture, and for JD 4.1 million by the private sector. Most of the funds [were] for a large expansion in the area of fruit trees in the drylands; various livestock projects; and the improvement of dryland farming.[13] The goal [was] a rather modest average annual increase of 6.4% in agricultural production . . . The abundant rainfall in 1974, and the internal peace in Transjordan — despite the October war — were reflected in major increases in farm production.

Table No. 1

AGRICULTURAL PRODUCTION
Thousands of Metric Tons

Product	1965	1966	1967	1968
Wheat	277.9	101.1	196.1	95.1
Barley	94.8	22.8	63.4	19.7
Other field crops	62.4	23.8	37.7	15.4
Tomatoes	188.9	179.0	216.3	127.3
Other Vegetables	234.1	232.2	164.5	52.0
Melons	160.0	47.7	58.3	36.4
Olives	37.4	32.7	22.2	12.6
Grapes	79.2	61.9	28.1	7.6
Citrus fruits	47.0	48.9	29.0	17.6
Other fruits	60.4	54.3	33.5	10.2
Tobacco	1.1	1.6	1.7	1.8

SOURCES: The Hashemite Kingdom of Jordan, Department of Statistics *Statistical Yearbook 1971* pp. 113-118; Central Bank of Jordan *Annual Reports* and *Monthly Statistical Bulletin* various issues.

Industry

As noted earlier, since over 80% of the value added in the manufacturing and mining sectors had been concentrated in the East Bank before the Six Day War, and current and planned investments in industry, at that time, were also in that region, the Israeli occupation of the West Bank in 1967 had but a minor effect on this sector. The recovery of this sector began in 1968 and continued until mid-1970. The civil war during the latter half of 1970, had a particularly depressing effect on this sector. The index of industrial production in 1969 was 11% above the 1966 level. The uptrend continued during the first eight months of 1970, but for 1970 as a whole, the index of industrial production was down over 13%.[14] Despite the intermittent hostilities within Transjordan during the first half of 1971, industrial production was rising rapidly. The index of industrial production in June 1971 reached 135.1 (1966 equals 100) as compared with 95.9 for 1970. The Syrian closure of its borders in July 1971 had a particularly adverse effect on the major phosphate industry, as well as on some other industries which were dependent on raw material imports through Syria.[15] For 1971, as a whole, the index of industrial production was 113.7 or 18.6% above 1970—a noteworthy achievement, in view of the internal and external problems in that year.[16] The gradual relaxation of the Syrian border restrictions in 1972, and their removal in December 1972, as well as internal tranquility, occasioned a sharp increase in industrial production. For 1972, as a whole, the index of industrial production was 139.1, or 22.3% above 1971. The uptrend continued through 1975, with industrial production 28% above 1972.[17]

Kingdom of Jordan and East Bank

1965-66—Kingdom of Jordan:			1967-74—East Bank		
1969	**1970**	**1971**	**1972**	**1973**	**1974**
159.3	54.1	168.1	211.4	50.4	244.5
42.4	5.5	26.2	34.0	5.9	40.2
31.3	11.4	35.9	36.3	13.9	51.6
150.1	137.4	137.0	152.7	83.1	133.5
69.1	70.2	89.8	93.4	65.0	141.3
53.2	22.8	27.1	63.0	56.1	45.8
23.9	3.0	18.5	35.0	5.2	40.1
14.2	6.4	18.6	18.2	22.1	17.8
24.3	48.9	41.2	20.9	15.4	33.9
27.7	22.5	14.5	15.8	5.2	17.5
2.0	1.2	1.1	0.7	1.1	0.9

NOTE: The government of Jordan does not publish an index of agricultural production.

In 1970 East Bank industries employed 20,800 workers, and mining and quarrying an additional 3,400 workers. The industrial sector employed about 6-7% of the East Bank labor force and accounted for 14% of its gross domestic product. Over 90% of the enterprises were very small, employing fewer than five workers, accounting for less than 50% of total industrial employment, and a much smaller share of the value added. In the mining and quarrying sector the large Jordan Phosphate Co. was dominant, employing about 1200 workers. In manufacturing there were 15 large firms employing 10 or more workers, accounting for 19% of total manufacturing employment, and 60 firms employing between 25 and 99 workers each, accounting for 12% of total manufacturing employment. The larger firms were the cement plant, oil refinery, cigarettes, pharmaceuticals, and the iron works. These are far more capital intensive, with a far higher than average value added per employed person.

Government policies favor and encourage the development of private enterprise, both domestic and foreign. However, foreign private investment has been insignificant. The government has provided financial aid to the larger and more rapidly expanding industries both through loans and equity participation. In the industrial sector the government has a controlling share in the phosphate, cement, and paper companies, and minority shares in others. High tariff protection, or a virtual ban on competing imports, is the rule for these larger industries, affording them a position of monopoly in the domestic market. The effects on efficiency and quality are obvious. The Industrial Development Bank established in 1965, with one third government participation, has been an increasingly important source of long-term capital. Between

1967 and 1973, outstanding loans of the bank (including loans to the tourist industry) increased by 122%, and rise an additional 55% by mid-1975.

Phosphates continued to be Jordan's main commodity export, but were severely restricted as a result of the Syrian border closure, and the Indian boycott. Though the Syrian embargo was not completely removed until December 1972, Jordan's phosphate exports increased sharply in that year— 46% above the 1970-71 level, though still 13% below 1968, which had been the peak year. In 1974 phosphate exports rose sharply, and were 43% above the 1968 level.18 The main manufactured goods have been cement, batteries, cigarettes, and some processed foods, mainly to the neighboring Arab countries. Some of the more recently established industries such as pharmaceuticals and paper products have become important in terms of the country's exports. The export of manufactured products has shown the most rapid rate of growth in recent years. In 1973 they were over 3.5 times the average 1964-66 level of exports, and almost doubled in 1974 . . . The export of manufactured products constituted 18% of total commodity exports in 1966—the remainder being mainly fresh fruits and vegetables, and phosphates. By 1974 manufactures rose to 26% of total export earnings (which were 4.5 times the 1966 level).

The authors of the 1973-75 Plan note some of the characteristics and problems of Jordanian industry: 1. The large majority of enterprises are very small. These are under capitalized, and the value added per employed person is but a fraction of that in the large industries. 2. The limited size of the domestic market makes it essential to expand exports. This is, of course, a problem faced by all small countries. However, one might add that while other small countries—as well as large ones—engage in devaluation or export subsidies to encourage exports, the Jordanian Government has not devalued its currency since the British devaluation in 1949. It maintained the dollar-Jordanian Dinar exchange rate between 1949 and 1972, and *revalued* its currency by 11% in February 1973, from the equivalent of $2.80 to $3.11. The abundance of foreign aid has permitted the government to pursue this policy. 3. Most industries operate at under capacity level. The authors of the Plan do not explain, but it may be due, in part, to the liberal import policy, and the lack of adequate encouragement for manufactured exports. 4. There is a shortage of semi-skilled labor, and since most establishments are small family-owned and managed, the management tends to be conservative, in terms of innovation and risk-taking, and is averse to engaging entrepreneurial skills. 5. Inter-industry integration is weak, such as in the utilization of agricultural products by industry. 6. Industrial enterprises are overwhelmingly concentrated in the Amman-Zarqa district. 7. Quality control is poor, and hence the consumer preference for competing imported products. 8. Prices of some locally manufactured products are high because of monopoly privileges granted to some (the larger) enterprises. 9. Domestic capital is inclined to invest in commercial or real estate ventures, which offer the prospects of a quick return, rather than in industry. Foreign investment—almost exclusively by Arabs of other countries—has been meagre and been confined to shareholding in existing industrial enterprises. 10. The cost of petroleum and of electric power is high (this was *before* the major increases in the prices of crude oil since 1973).19 While the educational levels of the labor force are higher than in most other Arab countries, the availability of high-paying employment in Kuwait, Saudi Arabia, and other oil-rich Arab countries, has raised skilled wage rates in Jordan significantly.

The 1973-75 Plan for industry and mining [was] quite ambitious, but appear[ed] feasible. Planned investment [was] JD 26.1 million, or 15.6% of planned total investment in the economy. Over three fourths of investment in this sector [was] to be by the private sector. The extent of planned investment in Transjordanian manufacturing (excluding mining) in 1973-75 is readily apparent when comparing the planned investment of JD 19.5 million in *three* years, to the previous *Seven* Year Plan (1964-70) which called for JD 11.1 million in investment in the Kingdom of Jordan.20 The main manufacturing projects envisioned by the 1973-5 Plan include[d] a phosphoric acid plant utilizing some of the low-grade phosphates. At a later stage this would be developed and expanded for the production of fertilizers. Another important project [was] a plant for the production of ceramics. Recent discoveries of excellent kaolin deposits are the basis for this industry. Recent discoveries of very large reserves of good quality silica sands are the basis for the projected glass factory. The oil refinery is to be expanded from a capacity of 780,000 tons a year to 2.5 million tons. In the mining sector the main investment was to be in expanding and up-grading the production of phosphates. Recent discoveries of various minerals include iron ore, sulphur, feldspar, manganese, copper, and others. The 1973-5 Plan provide[d] funds for technical and economic feasibility studies.[21]

Reports from Jordan in 1973 and 1974 indicated that the prospects for implementation of the industrialization program were good. In addition to a large number of smaller plants, work was being started on the establishment of larger factories for the production of paper, ceramics, food processing, detergents, shoes, woolen cloth, steel tubes, an additional cement plant, cotton textiles, a large chemical fertilizer plant, a vehicle assembly plant, and others. Additional prospecting indicated that the phosphate, copper and manganese deposits are far larger than had been envisioned earlier.[22] Most of the financing is from various Western and Arab sources, and technical aid is being provided by Western firms and governments, as well as international organizations.

The Three Year Plan aimed at an annual average growth rate of 14% for the industrial sector. This would be achieved through utilization of unused capacity (estimated at 25-30% in 1972) and through the new investment program.

This rate of growth approximates that which was achieved in 1959-66. Barring unforeseen external or internal "shocks" the prospects for achieving this goal appeared to be favorable.

Other Economic Sectors

During the 1950s and especially the 1960s, the government laid great emphasis on the development of a modern transportation sector. Highway construction was even more extensive than that envisioned in the 1964-70 Plan. Aqaba port was developed and the figures on tonnage—both exports and imports—reflect this growth. Exports through Aqaba were mainly phosphates. However, in order to reduce its dependence on imports through Syria and Lebanon, the government provided special inducements for the use of Aqaba port. The closure of the Suez Canal had an adverse effect on Aqaba, since most of the country's imports were from Western Europe and the U.S. Imports through Aqaba (in thousands of metric tons) declined from 590 in 1966 to 161 in 1968. Thereafter there was an almost steady uptrend to 519 in 1972. On the other hand, exports rose from 657 in 1966 to 695 in 1968. The Indian political ban on phosphate imports from Jordan, noted earlier, was apparently the prime factor in the subsequent sharp decline to 186 in 1970. However, 1972 exports through Aqaba were 705, or 7% above the previous peak level reached in 1966, the uptrend continued in the following two years with exports in 1974, 58% above the 1972 level.[23]

The 1973-75 Plan provided for the largest allocation to investment in transportation—20% of total planned investments, of which over three fourths would be by the public sector. Put differently, 28% of planned government investment was to be allocated to transportation. The main projects included an extension of the railway to Aqaba—to reduce the cost of phosphate exports, and incidentally of imports, via the country's only port. A West German loan was the main source of finance. A new international airport is to be built near Amman, also with West German aid. An even more ambitious road construction program is planned, as well as other projects.[24]

Except for 1970 when much of the economy was paralyzed during the months of the civil war, electric power production has been rising rapidly. The average annual rate of growth was 11.6% between 1967 and 1972.[25] In 1973 the increase was 14.8% followed by an increase of 17.6% in 1974. However, this growth rate has been insufficient, and industrial production has been hampered by the inadequacy of the power supply. The 1973-75 Plan included a number of projects for the expansion of the power supply, of which the major one is the construction of the Zarqa power station, and additional capacity in the Amman and Irbid areas. The latter projects were initiated in 1971 and 1972 with British financial and technical aid. The Zarqa station was initiated in 1973 with aid from the International Development Association, and from Kuwait. Other projects were included for the southern region of Transjordan.[26]

Political-military disturbances have, as one might expect, a sharp effect on construction, both residential and other. The Six Day War had a temporary negative effect, but in 1968 the area of construction (in thousands of square meters) was 392 in the East Bank, as compared with 316 in the Kingdom of Jordan in 1966. In 1969 it rose sharply to 492. Almost all of the housing construction is undertaken by the private sector. The large number of refugees was instrumental in the construction boom, adding to the pressures of the long-term rural-urban trend, and a large rise in marriages at that time.[27] The civil unrest in 1970 and 1971 brought about a sharp decline to 327 and 256, respectively, followed by sharp increases to 502 and 603, in 1972 and 1973. Data for Amman and Zarqa—the main population centers—indicate that there was a sharp revival in construction permits issued since 1972.[28] The Three Year Plan calls for a larger role on the part of the government, especially in providing low and middle class housing, as well as in the large Jordan Valley project. Three fourths of planned investment in housing is still expected to be by the private sector. Total planned investment in housing and non-residential construction in the East Bank in 1973-5, greatly exceeds that of the pre-1967 period in the Kingdom of Jordan. The sharp uptrend in building permits issued since 1972 seems to indicate that the goals of the Plan will be reached or exceeded—barring the unforeseen.

Tourism

As noted earlier, income from tourism declined sharply as a result of Israel's occupation of the West Bank in 1967. In 1968 gross income from tourism was estimated at JD 4.6 million as compared with JD 11.3 million in 1966, which had been the peak year for this industry. 1969 income was 27% higher than in 1968, despite the internal strife as well as hostilities along the Israel-Jordan "cease fire" lines. During the first half of 1970 the uptrend continued, but the civil war during the last months of 1970, lowered tourist income (for 1970) to JD 4.9 million. The Syrian blockade in 1971-72 further depressed tourism, and added significantly to the price of passenger fares from Beirut to Amman. According to the managing director of Jordan's national airline, the Syrian blockade had caused a 30% drop in passengers from Beirut, the airline's principal route. In order to reach Beirut from Amman, without entering Syrian air space, the airline had to take a circuitous route, which involved 1400 miles, as compared with 200 miles, via the direct route. Flying time was increased from 45 minutes to four hours. The rerouting caused a loss of 300 thousand dollars per month. Passenger fares were doubled and, in addition, the government provided a 100% subsidy for every ticket sold by the airline.[29] Despite all these problems, tourist income increased by 31% in 1971 and again in 1972. With the removal of the Syrian blockade in September 1972, and a continuation of internal tranquility, tourist expenditures rose sharply during the first half of 1973—as compared with the comparable period in 1972. The October War, though it did not involve any hostilities within Jordan, depressed its tourist industry. Nonetheless tourist income increased by 29% in 1973, and by 61% in 1974, exceeding the 1966 level by 53%.

Though the West Bank was the mainspring of the tourist industry in pre-1967 Jordan, there was an increasing recognition on the part of the authorities, at that time, that the various touristic sites, and the potential of the East Bank, were being neglected. According to official data, during 1963-66 and the first quarter of 1967, 30-40% of the visits to historic sites were in the East Bank. Undoubtedly many of those who had visited East Bank sites, may never have visited Jordan were it not for the attraction of Jerusalem and other West Bank historic sites. One Western observer, I.W.J. Hopkins, assessing the East Bank and the West Bank, stated: "The East Bank has two main assets, i.e., agriculture and tourism . . . the fertile soils of the plateau of Transjordan and the spectacular scenery and ruins (with Biblical connections) which provide the base for a tourist industry . . . Already the area beyond the Jordan (the East Bank) attracts as many visitors as Jerusalem and its shrines."[31] The Seven Year Plan, 1964-70, implicitly recognized this, and allocated larger sums for these sites in the East Bank.[32] Already in 1966 the government contracted with a Greek firm to make a study of the tourist potential of the Aqaba area. The report was very favorable and recommended a major development program costing JD 21.5 million. The 1973-75 Plan provides for the development of tourism in this area, as well as in the Amman, Petra and other areas. The planners' projections for tourist income appear to have been conservative, anticipating that gross tourist income would rise to JD 10 million in 1975, approaching the JD 11.3 million earned in 1966.[33] It had already reached JD 17.3 million in 1974. Tourism is most susceptible to even the "smell" of trouble, and the possibilities of realizing these goals are crucially dependent not only on tranquility within Jordan, but in the region as a whole.

Reports from Jordan indicate that some of these projects have been, or are being implemented. These include the completion of a new airport at Aqaba in 1971, a highway to the Saudi Arabian border, and new hotel facilities. A major American firm had contracted in January 1973, to build a 200 room hotel in Amman, and a 110 room hotel in Aqaba.[34] Work on the new international airport near Amman was scheduled to begin in mid-1974, with West German aid. Other tourist facilities had also been initiated.

The authors of the 1973-75 Plan considered it important to stem the major increase in Jordanian travel abroad. These expenditures had been rising very rapidly both before and since the Six Day War. Between 1960 and 1966 these expenditures rose from JD 2.2 million to JD 5.2 million, an average annual rate of growth of 15.4%. By 1972 they had reached JD 11.3 million, an average annual rate of growth of 13.6% in the 1966-72 period. Not all of the Jordanian expenditures for travel abroad reflect tourist spending. They include expenditures by Jordanian students, businessmen, as well as emigrants. However, the authors of the 1973-75 Plan believed that a good part of it was for recreational purposes, and that the development of tourist facilities in the country would succeed in stemming the rising outlays of Jordanians abroad, as well as in attracting foreign visitors.[35] In 1974 expenditures by Jordanians for travel abroad rose sharply from the previous year's level, to JD 17.4 million, equaling income from tourism.

FOOTNOTES

1. See Table No. 1.

2. The Hashemite Kingdom of Jordan *Three Year Development Plan 1973-75* pp. 55-62. This publication will be referred to as the *Three Year Plan*.

3. M. Clawson, H.H. Landsberg & L.T. Alexander, *The Agricultural Potential of the Middle East,* American Elsevier, N.Y. 1971, p. 33, 134.

4. *Three Year Plan* pp. 93-95.

5. U.S. Department of Agriculture *Jordan's Agricultural Economy in Brief* 1972, p. 4.

6. *Three Year Plan* pp. 97-8.

7. *Middle East Economic Digest* March 3, 1972, p. 244; Sept. 7, 1973, p. 1036; Oct. 19, 1973, p. 1219.

8. International Monetary Fund *International Financial Statistics* January 1974, p. 214.

9. See Table No. 1.

10. *Statistical Yearbook 1971* p. 117.

11. *Three Year Plan* p. 74.

12. Hashemite Kingdom of Jordan, *Statistical Yearbook 1971* p. 122, 131.

13. *Three Year Plan* pp. 36, 92.

14. Central Bank of Jordan *Seventh Annual Report* 1970 p. 7.

15. Central Bank of Jordan *Eighth Annual Report 1971* p. 10.

16. See Table No. 3. (In *Economic Development of Jordan.*)

17. Central Bank of Jordan *Monthly Statistical Bulletin* Nov. 1975 Table No. 36, and earlier issues.

18. International Monetary Fund *International Fiancial Statistics* Dec. 1975, pp. 224-5.

19. *Three Year Plan* pp. 111-3.

20. Three Year Plan, p. 136; The Hashemite Kingdom of Jordan *Seven Year Program for Economic Development of Jordan 1964-70* p. 201.

21. *Three Year Plan* pp. 122-135.

22. Economist Intelligence Unit *Quarterly Economic Review—Saudi Arabia/Jordan* No. 1, 1974, p. 17; No. 4, 1973, p. 20; No. 3, 1973, p. 20.

23. Central Bank of Jordan *Monthly Statistical Bulletin* Nov. 1975, Table No. 27 and earlier issues.

24. *Three Year Plan,* p. 36, 160-190.

25. See Table No. 3.

26. *Three Year Plan* pp. 152-9; Economist Intelligence Unit *Quarterly Economic Review—Saudi Arabia/Jordan* No. 1, 1974, p. 17; *Middle East Economic Digest* January 12, 1973, p. 41.

27. *Three Year Plan* p. 279; The Hashemite Kingdom of Jordan *Statistical Yearbook* 1973, p. 271.

28. Central Bank of Jordan *Monthly Statistical Bulletin* Nov. 1975, Table No. 38, and earlier issues. It should be noted that these figures should be taken as no more than indicators of trends. The *Statistical Yearbook 1971* refers to its data as the area of construction in reporting municipalities, and only with respect to Amman does it refer to building permits issued by the municipality, rather than actual current construction. The Central Bank of Jordan, *Monthly Statistical Bulletin* apparently refers to the area of building permits. In any case, the large number of permits issued in 1972 and even more so in 1973, presage a building boom of far larger proportions than before 1967.

29. *New York Times*, Dec. 26, 1971, p. 46.

30. Central Bank of Jordan *Monthly Statistical Bulletin* Nov. 1975, Table No. 15, and earlier issues.

31. I.W.J. Hopkins "The Hashemite Kingdom of Jordan—What is its Future?" *Contemporary Review*, Feb. 1968, pp. 78-9.

32. The Hashemite Kingdom of Jordan *Seven Year Program for Economic Development of Jordan 1964-70*, p. 185.

33. *Three Year Plan* pp. 139-147.

34. *Middle East Economic Digest* Feb. 2, 1973, p. 125.

35. *Three Year Plan* pp. 138-9.

FOREIGN AID TO JORDAN

Preliminary estimates indicate that foreign aid received during [1973-1975] was considerably more than anticipated, JD 222.5 million, of which JD 184.2 million was in the form of grants from other governments.[1] Kuwait resumed its aid in October 1973 following its suspension by Libya and Kuwait as a result of the war between the Jordanian army and the *fedayeen* in 1970-71. Libya did not resume its aid, but this was more than offset by increased aid from the U.S., Saudi Arabia, West Germany, the U.K., Denmark, the Gulf States, and others.

. . . The plethora of forcign aid has permitted the authorities to further liberalize imports since the spring of 1974. Furthermore it permitted a resumption of the payment of salaries to 6,000 civil service employees in the West Bank. These payments had been suspended in 1971 when Libya and Kuwait had cut off their aid to Jordan.[2] In almost all cases these are employees of the [Israeli] Military Administration and municipalities in the West Bank, by whom they have been paid since the Six Day War . . . the extra expenditures incurred by the Jordanian government, regardless of the motives, indicate that its financial position appears to be sound and that it anticipates no difficulties in meeting both current and investment expenditures in the East Bank.

Source: Economic Development of Jordan by Eliyahu Kanovsky, p. 119.

FOOTNOTES

1. *Middle East Economic Digest* April 23, 1976, p. 22. In dollar terms the increase was even greater since the Jordanian Dinar was revalued in February 1973. These figures exclude transfers by UNWRA for the refugees.

2. *Middle East Economic Digest* April 12, 1974, p. 425; May 3, 1974, p. 513.

Jordan's Five Year Plan 1976-1980

*Excerpts:**

THE THREE YEAR PLAN

The Jordan economy had achieved in the decade preceding the 1967 Middle East War outstanding rates of socio-economic progress. During that period per capita income increased in real terms at an average rate of 5% annually and school enrollment doubled with the number of students reaching by 1966 about one fifth of total population. The 1967 War prematurely interrupted this rapid process of development. With the reinstatement of law and order the Three Year Plan was launched in 1973 to reactivate the economy and resume its previous development momentum. Despite the outbreak of the fourth Middle East War in 1973 and the occurence of severe drought conditions in both 1973 and 1975, the objectives of the Plan have been largely achieved.

·   ·   ·

GDP & Sectoral Average Annual Compound Rates of Growth in Real Terms

Period	Agriculture %	Industry %	Services %	Total GDP %
1954-1961	2	14	13	10
1962-1966	6	15	5	7
1967-1972	-2	-1	1	0
1973-1975	-1	23	3	6
Five Year Plan	7	20	9	12

Capital Formation:

Investment reached record levels during the Plan with its ratio to GDP reaching 31%. In absolute terms 96% of the investment target of the Plan was achieved.

Balance of Payments:

The import content of investments during the Plan, coupled with the rise in agricultural imports precipitated by agricultural failures, resulted in the expansion of the trade gap despite the rapid rise of exports. Exports in fact trebled during this period reaching a record level of 16% of GDP compared

Source: *The Economic Development of Jordan,* Published by The Hashemite Kingdom of Jordan, November 1975.

* The above excerpts were selected by Professor Oded Remba, The College of Staten Island (C.U.N.Y.).

with their historical level of 6%. This can be regarded as a major achievement of far reaching implications for the Jordan economy. The increase in the receipts from current transfers to the Government and in remittances from Jordanians abroad together with development grants and loans however were sufficient to finance the trade gap.

Public Finance:

The Government managed during the Plan to reduce its reliance on foreign revenues reducing their contribution to total revenues from 57% prior to the Plan to 50%. Revenues from direct taxes nearly doubled during this period. Government capital expenditures increased from their historical level of about 20% of total expenditures to 24%.

FIVE YEAR PLAN: RATIONALE

The Five Year Plan aims at achieving a basic structural change in the Jordan economy through capitalizing on the achievements of the Three Year Plan. The magnitude of the Plan and its implications are fully appreciated by Jordan. The selection of targets is based on the challenges that lie ahead, and on an appreciation of the potentialities and difficulties of meeting these challenges, rather than on any lack of realism. The Jordan economy is in fact at a turning point in its history which presents a real opportunity for breaking-through the major constraints that have surrounded it since its emergence a quarter of a century ago.

The burdens that will be imposed by this programme on the administrative and managerial capacities in both the public and mixed sectors are fully appreciated. In fact one of the main instruments of the Plan is a programme for increasing the administrative capacity and efficiency within the economy to a level commensurate with the requirements of the investment programme.

Economic Structure:

A heavy concentration of services in terms of both production and employment has persisted in the Jordan economy throughout its previous phases of growth. The origins of this structural imbalance can be traced to the heavy burdens imposed on the economy by the events of 1948 and 1967. The previously limited possiblities for developing the non-services sectors have been fundamentally changed by a combination of factors which have imparted a significantly enhanced potential to the existing mineral and agricultural resources of the country. Accordingly the larger part of the capital formation under the Plan is directed towards the agricultural and mineral sectors together with the necessary supporting infra-structure for these sectors. The 'enclave' nature of the mining projects increases the capacity of the economy to absorb a seemingly high level of investments in these sectors.

•   •   •

Guiding Principles:

—All elements of development to be undertaken within the next five years are integrated by the Plan within a system of priorities aiming at maximum utilization of resources.

—The citizen is the centre and objective of development. The Plan aims at the active participation of the population in development and their sharing in its gains and benefits within the framework of an equitable and just distribution of income. Fiscal and monetary policies will be coupled with social organizational measures supporting farmers associations, cooperatives, labour organizations, small scale and handicraft industries, labour training and rehabilitation, strengthening of local government and popular participation in social and voluntary work.

—The absorptive capacity of the economy must be commensurate with the magnitude of the Plan. In both the public and mixed sectors administrative and organizational reforms are part and parcel of the Plan. The Government's role will continue to be regulatory, providing the infrastructure and incentives necessary for the fullest possible participation of the private sector.

—Education and manpower training policies must be tailored to suit the requirements of development. Wider participation of women will further mobilize the required manpower and skills to help face the competition for human resources within the region.

FIVE YEAR PLAN: TARGETS AND IMPLICATIONS

Targets:

—12% annual growth rate of GDP
—Equitable distribution of the gains of development
—Increasing the reliance of the budget on domestic revenues
—Reducing the trade deficit

·   ·   ·

The National Government:
Processes and Forces

By URIEL DANN

Jordan is no self-evident entity like Egypt, or even like Syria or Iraq. Yet the state, created by Churchill and the Sharif 'Abdallah for their common convenience, has by now existed for two generations—time enough to set a socio-political pattern. One should, therefore, regard with caution the easy commonplace that Jordan is "artificial"; that its raison d'être is self-perpetuation in the interest of the king and a handful of his supporters, protected by a "Bedouin army"; and that this interest is opposed to the interest and wishes of the majority of the population, and the more progressive and better educated majority at that . . .

The "image of Jordan" can be defined . . .; as follows: A kingdom, hereditary in the Hashemite family, successor to the British-mandated Emirate of Transjordan, and heir, as far as possible, to the Emirate's political, social, and psychological values; hence, the king as linchpin of the political machine; the trappings of monarchy possessing real significance; an establishment jealous for the independence of the state and fearful of "liberated" pan-Arabism, whatever the origin of its appeals; determined to lean on the West and dependent on its aid; a professional army in the background, to be called out on comparatively slight provocation and used ruthlessly if need be. The disappearance of any of the components would mean a fundamentally different Jordan—provided it survived at all—posing a fundamentally different challenge to the observer and to the world at large.

The population of Jordan within the country's de facto boundaries is about 1.5 million; . . . Of this number the "political public" is certainly a small percentage, if the criteria applicable to the West are taken as the sole yardstick. However, it will be shown that on occasion "the masses" exerted an influence in contexts which are not devoid of a genuine political rationale. Also, it must be kept in mind that the political public of today's West Bank is much involved, emotionally at least, in East Bank politics. . . .

Once the "image of Jordan" as delineated above is accepted, the first

Dr. Dann is a member of the Department of Middle Eastern and African History at Tel Aviv University, and Research Associate of its Shiloah Center for Middle Eastern and African Studies. His publications include *Iraq Under Qassem: A Political History, 1958-1963*, Jerusalem University Press, 1969.

The above is excerpted from a chapter entitled "Regime and Opposition in Jordan Since 1949," by Uriel Dann, which appears in *Society and Political Structure in the Arab World*, edited by Menahem Milson. The Van Leer Jerusalem Foundation Series, Humanities Press, N.Y., 1973, by permission.

sector demanding attention is the population native to the East Bank, the Transjordanians proper—rather less than one half of the population. However, some qualifications are necessary. For one, the nomad and seminomad population, the Bedouin proper, must be bracketed out. Their way of life, their needs, values, and history under the Emirate, establish them as a sector to be assessed separately. Secondly, the term "native" cannot be taken literally. At the least, hundreds of families originating in Palestine, and to a lesser degree in Syria and the Hejaz, settled in Transjordan between 1921 and 1949. They came to play an important part in the administration and economy of the Emirate. On purely pragmatic grounds, they must be considered "Transjordanians" in our context. Thirdly, though the inhabitants of Transjordan are in their vast majority Sunni Muslims who think of themselves as Arabs, there are two minority groups important enough to be considered here: the one is the Circassians, Sunni Muslims who originally emigrated from their native Caucasia to Transjordan and other frontier regions of the Ottoman Empire during the last quarter of the nineteenth century. They settled as farmers, with Amman, Wadi al-Sir, and Jerash as their main concentrations in Transjordan. With a language of their own, vividly conscious of their national distinctiveness, socially and economically ahead of their neighbors, the Circassians have played so far, as individuals and as a group, a part in the history of the country far greater than their modest number of about fifteen thousand would warrant. There are signs that the younger generation tends toward assimilation among the "Arabs," but for the time being the community must still be considered a factor in any political assessment. The other minority group, though larger by far in numbers, has played a less impressive role. These are the Christians native to Transjordan, most of them Greek Orthodox, rather less than ten percent of the population in 1948; their main communities are at Salt, Kerak, and Madaba. In line with their traditional role in the Ottoman Empire, they have not made themselves conspicuous in extra-communal affairs; . . .

An important subdivision of the "Transjordanian" population for the purpose of political analysis runs along regional lines. Climate, topography—the lateral cleavage of the settled country by a number of deep canyons—and one instance of near chance—'Abdallah's choice of Amman as his capital in 1921—account for at least three distinct regions, each with its own traditions, loyalties, and aversions. The north centers about Irbid, the second city of the kingdom, and Jerash. It has a compact agricultural population, sedentary since times immemorial. There is a tradition of self-reliance that goes back to closely knit associations for local defense, *Nahiyas,* which still did duty two generations ago and which have survived in the attitude of the population toward outside interference. Further south lies al-Balqa around Salt, long the most important town of the East Bank; it has a tradition of hostility to Irbid, family ties with Nablus, and distrusts the central administration in Amman— the upstart rival which has displaced Salt from its relative eminence within living memory. Amman, the young metropolis, shelters one-third of the country's population. However, its mushroom growth—fifteenfold over the last thirty years—has so far precluded the emergence of the "Ammani" as a meaningful category of political citizen. In contrast, the countryside south of Amman definitely constitutes a recognizable unit in this sense. Its comparative remoteness from the centers of social and political unrest in the contemporary Arab world, its closeness to the conservative Hejaz, the paucity of prospects for economic advancement, and, most important, a kinship system which preserves tribal identifications and values give this region a peculiar significance relative to the "image of Jordan."

The second primary sector are the Palestinians, for our purposes the inhabitants of Jordan born in Palestine under the mandate . . . The Palestinians were about two-thirds of the population when 'Abdallah took possession of the West Bank. Their part in the population of the East Bank has grown steadily ever since, and today they constitute half of the population of Jordan in its post-1967 frontiers. The position of the Palestinians in Jordan, their attitudes, advantages, and handicaps, has too often been described to justify repetition. Yet a few points must be made. The Palestinians have been citizens of Jordan in the full legal sense since 1949-50. It is an impermissible generalization that they were, because of their background, "more progressive" politically than the Transjordanians; in advanced administrative experience, they lagged behind Transjordanians of comparable status. Lastly, although . . . many Palestinians were entrusted with high office, these cases bear on the theme of this study only when the officeholders were invested with a share in high-level decision making or decision enforcing. The subject will come up later on.

It is meaningful to subdivide the Palestinians into three subsectors: (a) natives of the Jordanian West Bank, including those who moved their homes to the East Bank between 1949 and 1967; (b) refugees in the wider sense, i.e., Palestinians born in what was by 1949 Israel, whatever their circumstances at the stage under survey; (c) refugees in the narrower sense, i.e., inhabitants of refugee camps.

The Bedouin have been important in the history of the state since the establishment of the Emirate. Their notables had been on terms of intimacy—not necessarily of friendship—with the Hashemite ruler from the first. Since the 1930s they have provided the core of the fighting units of the army. The number of "pure" Bedouin—tent-dwelling, camel and sheep-raising nomads with only marginal recourse to agriculture—has been steadily diminishing for decades. But it is established that Bedouin *mores* keep alive for a generation or more after a community becomes sedentary, and thus the term "Bedouin" must comprise for the present purpose more than nomads proper. It is therefore difficult to arrive at even an approximation of their number: 100,000 may be near the mark for the wider interpretation. It is further advisable to distinguish between the two chief tribal groups, the Beni

Sakhr and Huwaitat, in view of the rivalry between them for political influence and royal favor. As each of the two groups has a periphery of client tribes, they have been loosely referred to below as "northern" and "southern" Bedouin, respectively.

The Jordanian army, still popularly known as the Arab Legion, has been identified with the established order in the state to an extent that few armies have achieved anywhere, whenever the regime was not outright military in nature. There were stages when active disloyalty was not uncommon among individual officers. They have never succeeded, so far, in inspiring a movement in the army which became a serious threat to the regime. Since its inception as a fighting force the army has never, as an institution, disappointed the trust which the rulers of the state put in it. Its very reputation for loyalty has probably deterred would-be plotters in more cases than will ever be known. The instances when it took action against domestic enemies of the regime must be numbered in scores. The causes for this devotion are reasonably clear: long-term service under excellent material conditions; a carefully nurtured ésprit de corps and good leadership from the throne downward; fear for its position under a regime which rejects the "image of Jordan." The widely accepted explanation of a Bedouin army alienated from a *hadari* population is too simple, though it contains some truth, especially with regard to the rank and file. The following may serve to introduce some differentiation. Apart from the rare eruption of the rank and file as a primary political factor, three aspects of the role of the army will be probed: the communal background of its chiefs, on the one hand; that of defectors and conspirators, on the other; the part senior officers have played on occasion in the councils of the ruler outside their substantive appointments.

The last sector is undoubtedly the smallest, but not the least significant. Few royal families can nowadays be as closely knit as the Hashemites, descendants in the male line of the Prophet's daughter. All three kings of Jordan were the offspring of marriages between cousins: Hussein himself took a kinswoman as his first wife. It is only to be expected that members of the family should occupy positions of political importance, official and otherwise . . .

The "establishment," for the purposes of this enquiry, has been narrowly defined. It comprises the high-level decision makers and the high-level decision enforcers; the manipulators, but not the manipulated. It does not comprise holders even of exalted office—if it can be fairly shown that the office, or the appointment, conferred administrative responsibility, wealth, or prestige, but no primary political power.

The first place, according to the "image of Jordan" as defined, goes to the King. From among the Cabinet, only the Prime Minister, the Deputy Prime Minister, the Minister of the Interior, and, since the inception of his office, the Minister of Information always belong to this group. (The Nabulsi cabinet of 1956-57 is an anomaly, in this respect as in others.) But it is important to realize that the Foreign Minister and the Minister of Defense as such never did: the former is expected to interpret the King's day-to-day policy to the outside world and to supervise the diplomatic staff for the same purpose; the latter executes some of the functions of a director-general at his ministry, with far less responsibility and elbow-room than career directors-general at the Ministry of Defense enjoy in most countries.

The heads of the army inside the "establishment" are: the Commander-in-Chief and his deputy; the Chief of the General Staff and his assistant for operations; the commanders of the top formations, brigades until the mid-sixties and divisions afterwards; the Director of Military Intelligence; and, finally, the Director of Public Security, the Chief of Police.

Outside these functional categories, there is a circle of "King's friends" who may or may not hold official appointments, but who have the King's ear and who are apt to be entrusted with missions of political importance. Among the former are the Chief of the Royal Cabinet and the senior Aide-de-Camp; the latter are usually identified by common report.

The "anti-establishment elements," that part of the political public which essentially rejects the "image of Jordan," for long fell into two categories: civilian politicians who generally owed what weight they had to their membership in the House of Representatives; and army officers engaged in conspiracy or other acts of fundamental protest. Both categories were opposed to much or all that Jordan represented, but they had no clearly considered concept to replace the Jordanian entity as such, or even a strong motivation to do so. Thus, with all their enmity to the regime, often deeply felt and sometimes dangerous, they remained members of the body politic in whose framework they struggled. Within the Palestinian organizations, a different category of "anti-establishment elements" emerged . . .

•

When 'Abdallah annexed the West Bank to his kingdom, he furthered an ambition which he had nursed since his first establishment in Amman: that of becoming, in the fullness of time, ruler of a Greater Syria extending over the mandated territories of Syria, Lebanon, Palestine, and Transjordan . . . Britain considered 'Abdallah's plan the best, and nascent Israel considered it the least obnoxious, of all possibilities for Arab Palestine; the anti-Hashemite front among the Arab states, Egypt, Syria, and Saudi Arabia, was incapable of effective action. The complex array of allies and clients which 'Abdallah had managed to set up over the years within the chaos and turmoil of Palestinian politics served its purpose: the Palestinians, thrown into the depth of despair, were readily turned toward the only protector in sight. When the Armistice with Israel was signed on 3 April 1949 all seemed over but the shouting, and the actual integration a matter of formalities to be carried out at leisure.

•

One point which tends to get blurred with the passage of time is the extent to which the attitudes of the preceding decades determined the relations between 'Abdallah and the Palestinian political public: most of the high appointments 'Abdallah made for the West Bank were *Mu'aridun* — Nashashibis, their allies, and followers — and were appointed for that reason. A substantial case can also be made out 'Abdallah's murder was more of a last link in his feud with the Husaynis than punishment for his readiness to come to an arrangement with Israel. This important aspect of the "Palestinians' problem" in its beginnings still awaits research . . .

•

Talal's brief reign is often regarded as an interlude, in the sense that it eliminated, while it lasted, the "image of Jordan" as defined here . . . He was rumored to hate the British and to be uncompromising toward Israel . . . Talal's concept of Arab nationalism was believed to be more in accord with modern strands of opinion. He joined the Arab League Defense pact and demonstrated his wish to bury the feud with Ibn Saud. Domestically, Talal as a prince was reputed to be anti-authoritarian and "democratic." As king his grant of a new constitution, which for the first time accepted the principle of ministerial responsibility to Parliament, and some relatively progressive social legislation tended to confirm this reputation . . .

. . . As king, Talal showed in one or two cases that he could be vindictive and tyrannical in vengeance of personal slights. The constitution was hardly his own inspiration: 'Abdallah had already promised ministerial responsibility and died before he could be fairly accused of bad faith. In any case, the two-thirds majority required from the Chamber of Deputies for a vote of nonconfidence made parliamentary supremacy illusory in practice. Talal kept his father's Transjordanian ménage intact with insignificant exceptions; Glubb and his British subordinates remained as firmly in charge as ever. No attempt to dislodge either is known, and together they certainly conserved the principles of 'Abdallah's rule . . .

•

At the time of Talal's deposition, the heir apparent, Emir Hussein, was a minor, and a regency became necessary until his coming of age nine months hence. For the first time, and until now for the only time, the state had to cope with the protracted absence of a Hashemite ruler, physical as well as constitutional.

The establishment did not change in personnel. The temporary rulers attempted to combine conciliation of "the modern spirit" evoked by Talal with firmness wherever the established principles of government were called into question, and on the whole they were successful. It was then, to give an example, that the time-honored titles of pasha and bey were abolished. Also under the regency, attempts of the *Ba'th* and *Tahrir* parties to achieve recognition, supposedly guaranteed by the new constitution, were put down with a firmness that had lost nothing for 'Abdallah's exit.

. . . The essentials of the 1952-53 situation included Glubb and his array of British commanders, detested by the opposition, but with a fearful prestige for readiness to crush all physical challenges to the regime . . .

•

The last months of 1955 brought the sharpest confrontation of Western and neutralist concepts which Jordan has ever faced . . . [*The Eden government in Britain wanted Jordan to join the Baghdad Pact, which Nasser opposed*] . . . Hussein's attitude was decidedly favorable. Young as he was, his conviction that his fate and the well-being of his country were tied up with the West was as firmly rooted as his grandfather's had been. This being so, the political, diplomatic, and monetary advantages promised to Jordan in case of her adherence were a neat bonus; he had no experience as yet of 'Abd al-Nasser's anger and the rage of a hysterical "street." Hussein's established advisers were in their majority fair-weather supporters: they did not object to the principle; appreciated the bargaining position it gave Jordan opposite Britain; were fearful of domestic trouble from the start; and did not consider the issue worth running unusual risks for. A visit of the Turkish president, Bayar, put the public on the alert. When the British Chief of the Imperial General Staff, General Templer, arrived in Amman on 6 December 1955 to clinch the deal, tension neared the explosion point.

The prime minister, Sa'id· al-Mufti soon thought it prudent to resign in view of the atmosphere. His resignation, and the appointment as his successor of Hazza' al-Majali, reputedly the most determined of the Baghdad Pact supporters, taught the opponents of the pact a double lesson: that time was short and that pressure paid. Within a day, Amman and every town on the West Bank erupted in riots which have never had their equal in Jordan in violence and extent. They were certainly fanned from Cairo and, in no small measure, managed by Egyptian personnel within Jordan. But this point should not be overrated. The passion was genuine . . .

The establishment—king, army, inner cabinet—reacted feebly . . . After four days of pandemonium, . . . Majali resigned in turn, and, though no positive statement was made the public knew that the Baghdad Pact was out. Undoubtedly, mass action had deflected the regime from a major policy. Yet one reason for this outcome was that the stakes were unequally distributed. Once the establishment realized what it was up against, the game was no longer worth the candle . . . A month later violent riots broke out again. The Baghdad Pact issue being practically dead, anti-establishment slogans as such came much more to the fore. This time the authorities reacted forcefully, and the riots petered out.   •

The Nabulsi government is a singular phenomenon in the history of Jordan. It was a cabinet, the senior members of which rejected the "image of Jordan"—consciously and publicly—point by point. The Hashemite tradition was nothing to them; the king, if permitted to reign, should certainly not rule. Arab nationalism meant alignment with Egypt and Syria under 'Abd al-Nasser's leadership. "Positive neutralism" was accepted in its full implication of hostility to the West and friendliness to the Communist bloc. The army was to be weaned from its traditional values through its least tradition-bound sector, the urban officer.

. . . The sudden need to replace an entire leadership put to the fore what had so far been the second rank with few chances of promotion. It was a dazzling vista that opened all of a sudden and, it must be realized, it was a situation which was then almost without parallel in the Arab world. Above all, it affected the officer who was in any case less likely to value the "image of Jordan"—the young, the well educated, the adaptable, the ambitious, the officer with an eye for the political chance. This type of officer knew, of course, to what forces he owed this boon. It is little wonder then that throughout 1956 the most active elements of the officers' corps saw their fortune tied to the civilian anti-establishment sector. It was apparently the combined pressure of the new command group, headed by the new Chief of the General Staff, 'Ali Abu Nuwar, which ensured the holding of new elections for the Chamber of Deputies on party lines, with guarantees for honest scrutiny without army intervention. In the prevailing atmosphere an anti-establishment majority was a foregone conclusion, and it is worth stressing that the establishment candidates fared better than might have been expected.

The elections took place on 21 October 1956. The anti-establishment parties were (with the number of successful candidates in a House of forty): the National Socialist party, 11; the Communists, in the guise of a National Front, 3; the *Ba'th*, 2; the Muslim Brethren, 4; the *Tahrir* party, 1. The Muslim Brethren by then hated 'Abd al-Nasser too much to be effective against Hussein. The Islamic-fundamentalist *Tahrir* party, though uncompromisingly hostile to the establishment, had nothing positive in common with the secular opposition. The first three parties mentioned here shared, however, the characteristics outlined at the head of this chapter, and to that extent they had a common positive policy. Accordingly, the leader of the National Socialist party, Sulayman al-Nabulsi, found no difficulty in forming a coalition government with the other two.

Yet the National Socialist party occupied its own place among the opposition. It was "historical" within the terms of the country: its past went back to the National Congress, the first opposition party, however rudimentary, under the Organic Law of 1928. Its leaders, as a rule, were not pushing newcomers, but respectable citizens whose families were sometimes of older standing in the country than the Hashemites and conscious of the fact. They were little interested in social questions. And for all their identification with Nasserite nationalism—accepted by the public as genuine—they had no affiliations abroad. It is therefore not surprising that alone among the coalition parties, the National Socialists gained seats on the East Bank. That they should also have gained so great an advantage over their coalition partners suggests that even in its oppositional moods, at a time when 'Abd al-Nasser's prestige was nearing its zenith, the electorate did not lack a certain soil-bound stolidity. The National Socialists certainly owed nothing to the authorities.

[*The anti-establishment Nabulsi Cabinet lasted six months. Although it had the support of articulate public opinion, and of Egypt and Syria, the King realized that it was rapidly dissolving the "image of Jordan" and his own position. The King had a good hold on the army and showed courage and determination in the crisis.*]

. . . When first dismissed on 10 April 1957 Nabulsi correctly assumed that the king would not find a cabinet representing the establishment; when the king refused to appoint Nabulsi's nominees instead, Abu Nuwar made a pitifully inept attempt to coerce the king by sending up to the palace a Bedouin regiment from Zarqa recently put under the command of a personal friend. The Bedouin, suitably enlightened by the king's uncle and others, went berserk. Hussein appeared in their midst, carrying with him Abu Nuwar, by now shaking with fright. The Bedouin wept for joy and were dissuaded from lynching Abu Nuwar. The latter disappeared over the Syrian frontier, followed within three days by his friend and successor, 'Ali al Hiyari. The peak of the crisis was over. In the meanwhile, Hussein had appointed a colorless interim Cabinet headed by the elderly Husayn Fakhri al-Khalidi, one of the three West Bankers ever to serve as prime ministers, all ephemeral. Nabulsi himself accepted the Foreign Ministry—perhaps because he interpreted the "interim" in his favor, more probably because by now he was frightened and saw the summons as a pardon. When the interim government could not prevent riots on the West Bank, it resigned, or was dismissed, on 24 April.

•

On 25 April 1957 Hussein appointed a Cabinet dominated by the Old Guard. The same day emergency regulations put the country under the rule of a military Governor General. The emergency regulations stayed in force for a year and a half, until 1 December 1958. This period gave the "image of Jordan"—in essence as old as the state—the specific turn-out which has stuck to it till now. It is a turn-out which largely centers about Hussein's person: . . .

. . . The excitement engendered by the nationalist tide under Nabulsi, the crash that followed, the open substitution of the United States for Britain as protector and guarantor of the regime, the union of Egypt and Syria, the

Lebanese civil war [of 1958] and the revolution in Iraq—all made a strong
hand imperative. Within days the army stamped out disorder. So far as we
know, its rank and file were enthusiastic. The combination of urban politician
and urban officer aspiring to supremacy in the state had evidently shocked
them beyond anything the challengers foresaw. It was a constellation which,
in different circumstances, returned after thirteen years with comparable results.

Once the immediate danger from violence was past, arrests, purges, and
censorship, all vigorously applied, did the rest. The "opposition"—
yesterday's government coalition—virtually disappeared from the Chamber
of Deputies through resignation, flight, or expulsion.

So far as it is possible to assess "atmosphere," these nineteen months held
less tension than might at first be imagined. There was no doubt where the
power lay. It was exercised resolutely and consistently, brutally on occasion,
but not vengefully. Here, too, Hussein took after his grandfather. A number
of incipient plots among would-be Free Officers were nipped with ease. The
West Bank was quiet for once. By the end of 1958 Hussein felt sure enough of
his position to restore civil liberties—for what they were worth.

•

The nine years that passed between the forced settlement of 1957-58 and
the catastrophe of 1967 are no void in the history of Jordan . . .

. . . the establishment kept its character and continuity throughout the
period—political, environmental, and to a large extent personal. If there was
a change, it was one of stress: the importance of the king's role increased until
it assumed an overall significance which even 'Abdallah—under British
tutelage—had never possessed. With the anti-establishment forces the case
lies differently. Here the historical change is the appearance, since about
1964, of a frame which, in the Palestine Liberation Organization, presumed to
represent "the Palestinians" in a positive sense, as a nation prepared to take
charge of its own destiny; a nation no longer content with appearing as
petitioners or protesters making demands, however violent at times, on the
decision processes of mightier friends. It is outside the purpose of this study to
describe the genesis of the PLO, or to analyze the relation between its pre-
sumptions and its achievement. It is, however, relevant here that the PLO
succeeded to no mean degree in being accepted by the Arab world at its own
evaluation. Paradoxically, at first sight, this changed the character of the
anti-establishment forces in Jordan in a way which was not entirely to the
disadvantage of the regime. Alongside the PLO, other opposition moulds lost
much of their relevance and attraction. Yet those older moulds—clans and
families traditionally hostile to the regime, political parties, Free Officers, or
just fleeting combinations of malcontents—had worked from within and had
placed before the establishment a challenge difficult to assess and con-

sequently uncertain and, in the view of the moment, dangerous. The PLO, however, claiming to represent a people of equal status with others inside the Arab community, and assuming as many of the trappings of statehood as circumstances would permit, made it easy for the Jordanian regime to bring to bear its enormous preponderance in material resources. By the same token, the PLO could not afford to reject out of hand overtures which the regime found it politic to make, though obviously a show of coexistence gave the regime an alibi and made the PLO more vulnerable whenever open hostilities broke out afresh. It also worked in favor of the regime that the PLO, by its nature, had many tasks to consider, even if its rejection of the "image of Jordan" was fundamental and unwavering.

For these reasons, the personal background of the PLO leaders is of little interest to our study. Suffice it here to state that Ahmed al-Shuqaiyri, the chairman, and Wajih al-Madani, commander of the PLO armed forces, were both refugees in the wider sense . . .; of the eleven members of the PLO Executive (excluding Shuqaiyri) formed in July 1966, nine were refugees, and one a West Banker.

•

Among the results of the Six Day War, the one which concerns us most is that which has turned Jordan back into "Transjordan" in more respects than the territorial. It is not a result the regime has acknowledged, or which it is likely to acknowledge in the foreseeable future. It is also a result which was not realized in its full implications until recently, with more than three years' delay.

There was an attempt after 1967 to revive an opposition which still accepted the frame of a Jordanian state, though not the traditional image or the establishment which embodied it. This was the *al-Tajammu' al-watani,* the National Grouping (chaired by Sulayman al-Nabulsi), essentially a continuation of the National Socialist party in ideas, background, and membership. For some time, the National Grouping endeavored—without much encouragement from either side—to form a bridge between the regime and the Palestinian organizations, with a decided bias in favor of the latter. When Hussein appointed a new Cabinet in June 1970, at the height of the Palestinian tide, he included about eight members of the Grouping. What was probably meant as no more than a sop to prevailing trends turned out as a political success of the first order. The Grouping, which had so far "explained" the organizations to the regime, promptly reversed its attitude. Since the September 1970 crisis, the National Grouping as such has not been heard of, though its members have not apparently been harassed by the authorities. It is a mistake to attribute this drying-up merely, or mainly, to opportunism. The last four years have seen the acceleration of a process which started even earlier, and the September crisis acted as the catalyst which crystallized the opposing fronts. Today there is no room for anti-establishment forces which reject the traditional "image of Jordan," but accept the state as a desirable, or at least a workable, framework of political existence. The pull of the polarized forces—the regime, on the one hand, and the Palestinian organizations, on the other—has left a no-man's land in between. And it is natural that yesterday's opposition—with a stake in the country as it grew over the last fifty years— should find itself arraigned on the side of the regime, not merely as the smaller evil, but as the side with which it holds more in common.

Whatever turn the fortunes of the Palestinian organizations may yet take, they have ceased to be part of the "public in Jordan" in any meaningful sense. Their leaders' refusal to attempt a takeover of the state—at a time when the chances of success were rated high—may not have been based merely on considerations of utility. It was alien territory, and so long as it did duty as a base there was little temptation to push on. It was the leaders' misfortune that they could not coerce their followers into respecting the coexistence which the regime was then only too willing to accept. It is noteworthy that one major Palestinian organization, which positively urged the immediate overturn of the established state and which deliberately started the chain reaction that led to the confrontation of September 1970, was led by one of the few Transjordanians prominent among the organizations, Nayef Hawatmeh, leader of the *Popular Democratic Front for the Liberation of Palestine* (PDFLP).

On the other side, this "homelessness" . . . led—for the first time since 1949—to fairly general outbursts of physical hostility against the Palestinians throughout the Transjordanian countryside. No doubt these outbursts were not unwelcome—putting it mildly—to the regime, and they are directly connected with the arrogance and ruthlessness which the guerrillas showed in their day of glory. But part of the explanation must lie with the image of the Palestinian organizations as strangers to their host country; many reports show that the villagers of the East Bank tended to regard the guerrillas . . . as intruders undeserving of sympathy . . .

•

The commonly accepted view that Jordan is governed by East Bankers is demonstrated to a startling degree . . . [The] . . . West Bankers figure hardly at all in the "establishment" . . .; refugees, even in the wider sense, are entirely absent. Among the Transjordanians there is a marked, but not an overwhelming, preponderance of southerners over northerners; this is also no surprise. Christians are absent. Whatever their merits in the eyes of the regime—and as a group they have certainly not been characterized by disloyalty—capacity for rule is not one of them. Circassians and the less known Chechens play a prominent role—again a recognized fact. However, it is not generally realized that the "sharifian" origins of the regime are still noticeable in sensitive appointments, though plain Hejazis have no longer a special claim to be admitted to the king's counsel, as they had under 'Abdallah. Bedouin officers [have filled] the majority of the highest army appointments—*of late*.

Much more rewarding is a search for trends. The point is that *there is no trend*. The king and his family retainers, the Kerak and Ma'an notables, the sharifs and the Circassians make up the bulk of the establishment as they did twenty years ago; if anything, more so. This phenomenon cannot be put aside as fossilized immobility. The establishment has been exposed to incessant challenges of different description and in permanently changing circumstances. It has found the proper response to them all so far, without changing its character. Its evident success in the struggle for survival entitles it to be regarded as a living political organism, well-adjusted to its surroundings. It is a verdict valid for the present, whatever the future may bring.

The astonishing number of one-time rebels returned to favor and position is further testimony to the vitality of the establishment. When they strayed from the fold, the rebels broke a pattern; they restored it when they returned.

No socio-political formula works without blemish. 'Akif al-Fa'iz, the Beni Sakhr chief who sympathizes with the Palestinian organizations; 'Abd al-Qadir Tash, the Ammani Circassian who has ever been a faithful supporter of Nabulsi; Mahmud al-Mu'ayta, the Kerak officer of ancient family and leader of *as-Sa'iqa* — they are all genuine exceptions to the pattern. But they *are* exceptions, and the tag that the exception proves the rule may be fairly applied to so complex an equation as the recent history of Jordan sets to the observer.

It will have been noted that Bedouin officers have only recently appeared among the highest army appointments, much later than their comrades of *hadari* background. However, this is no change in trend. It merely took the Bedouin longer to master the requirements which a modern army makes on its command. That the Bedouin officer belonged to the "establishment" long before he was appointed to top positions is proven by the Zarqa incident mentioned above.

Among the "anti-establishment elements" the almost total and continued absence of southern East Bankers, ethnic minorities, and Bedouin leaps to the eye. The constituents of the "anti-establishment"—West Bankers, refugees, and northern East Bankers, mainly from Salt and Irbid—fall into two distinct patterns. The political groups which reject the set "image of Jordan" without putting up an alternative to the Jordanian entity, are represented by West Bankers and northern East Bankers—the latter also playing a considerable role in the establishment, the former next to none. These groups, as described earlier, have been replaced in recent years by others in whose concepts Jordan takes no positive part at all; here refugees predominate, after many years of absence from the leading ranks even of the anti-establishment.

Cabinet Formation in Jordan

By CLINTON BAILEY

Jordan has had forty-nine Cabinets in the twenty-seven years between April 1950, when King 'Abdallah annexed the West Bank, and early 1977. The longest of these Cabinets lasted only twenty-two months; the shortest, five days. Twenty-four Cabinets expired within six months. Only seven survived for over one year. The outstanding feature of this quick succession of Cabinets was that it seldom entailed a change-over of ministers of significantly different political persuasions. The successive ministers have predominantly been supporters of the monarchy. They were "rotated" as part of the fiction that the Cabinet is the policy-making body in Jordan, which pays for unpopular policies or ineffective administration by being dismissed.

According to the Constitution, which was promulgated in January, 1953, the King, with only minor limitations, is fully empowered to appoint and dismiss the Cabinet. By other of its provisions, however, the Constitution strongly implies that each Cabinet makes its own policies, because (1) it enjoins each to present these policies to the House of Representatives and request its confidence, and (2) it states that the ministers are responsible for administering "the affairs of state" (which cover broad categories), specifying that no orders of the King can absolve them of their duties. The role of Cabinets in Jordan was thereby established: to appear to make major decisions, which were really made in the palace, and to represent the policies of the regime as their own. Because policies that are advantageous to the regime are often unpopular with a majority of the population, it remains for the King to appoint ministers upon whom he can depend to bear, or at least share, the responsibility for them. He must also see to it that his candidates have sufficiently different "faces," so as to justify their constant rotation in successive Cabinets.

Eighteen men have held the post of Prime Minister between April 1950 and early 1977. With the exception of Sulayman al-Nabulsi, all prime ministers have felt bound to the monarchy by dint of their personal careers or their membership in families and communities with strong vested interests in the maintenance of the regime. In the 1950s three major prime ministers—Tawfiq Abu al-Huda (five Cabinets), Samir al-Rifa'i (four Cabinets), and Ibrahim Hashim (three Cabinets)—were political careerists, Palestinians by birth, who

Dr. Bailey is a member of the Department of Middle Eastern and African History at Tel Aviv University.

The above, entitled "Cabinet Formation in Jordan, 1950-1970" appeared in *New Outlook*, Vol. 13:8 (118), November 1970, and has been updated by the author. Reprinted by permission.

had come to Transjordan. They monopolized the office of Chief Minister, from 1933 until 1950. Despite their origin, the personal success that each enjoyed under King 'Abdallah put them firmly on the side of the regime in its lingering post-annexation conflict with the Palestinian nationalists.

Sa'id al-Mufti (four Cabinets) was the leader of Jordan's small, but loyal and important Circassian community, whose economic and political welfare has been tied directly to the creation and continuation of the Hashemite regime, as is that of the large, semi-Bedouin Majali tribe of Kerak, from which hailed the young, successful careerist, Hazza' al-Majali (two Cabinets). Majali, a protegé of 'Abdallah, often boasted of having been, at the age of 33, the youngest minister in the country's history. Another young man who enjoyed a brilliant political career was Fawzi al-Mulqi (one Cabinet). At the age of 37 he was Jordan's Foreign Minister, and soon thereafter, he became Defense Minister and Ambassador to the Court of St. James, successively.

The prime ministers of the 1960s carried similar credentials. Most were men in their forties who had established their loyalty in the palace service and as diplomats in important and often difficult posts. Bahjat al-Talhuni (six Cabinets), hailing from Ma'an in the royalist south, belonged to a family with large financial interests in Amman. Previous to his first appointment to the prime ministership, in 1960, he had been close to Hussein as Chief of the Royal Diwan for more than six years. Wasfi al-Tal (six Cabinets), on the other hand, came from an Irbid family of dubious loyalty. Personally, however, he proved sufficiently dedicated to the monarchy to have served variously as Royal Chief of Protocol, Chief Censor, and in the delicate post of Jordan's first Ambassador to Iraq following the coup of 1958, before becoming prime minister. Sa'd Jum'ah (two Cabinets), from the southern town of Tafilah had also been Chief Censor and Ambassador to the United States; and Abd al-Mun'im al-Rifa'i (two Cabinets), a younger brother of Samir al-Rifa'i, had been Ambassador to the United Nations. Sharif Husayn ibn Nasir (three Cabinets), the king's grand-uncle, in addition to serving as diplomat and as Chief of the Royal Diwan, naturally shared the royal family's interest in retaining the crown. In the 1970s, the three main Prime Ministers, Ahmad al-Lawzi, Zayd al-Rifa'i (the son of Samir al-Rifa'i), and Mudar Badran had all earned their credentials in the palace service.

Only three of Jordan's eighteen prime ministers came from the West Bank: Dr. Husayn Fakhri al-Khalidi, a prominent Jerusalemite; General Muhammad Da'ud who headed the single military Cabinet in 1970; and Ahmad Tuqan, a former Mandatory official from Nablus. The prime ministerships of the three West Bankers had two things in common. First they were all short-lived; nine days, eight days, and one month respectively.

Second, all three Palestinians were chosen in the hope of placating the Palestinian population at junctures when it had been particularly alienated.

Al-Khalidi was appointed, in 1957, to soothe Palestinian sensibilities after the popular nationalist prime minister, Sulayman al-Nabulsi, had been dismissed. General Muhammad Da'ud was called to office in September 1970, in order to disguise the very reason for forming a military Cabinet—namely, to curb the Palestinian *fedayeen*. A week later, Ahmad Tuqan was called upon to head a civilian government because the suppression of the *fedayeen* under the military Cabinet had been bloodier than anticipated.

Sulayman al-Nabulsi, the only anti-regime prime minister, was himself not a Palestinian, but rather an East Banker born in Salt. Nevertheless, the Palestinians' choice of an East Banker to lead their first anti-monarchy Cabinet (after the first three parliamentary elections, in October 1956) was politically significant. It highlighted the fact that there were also Transjordanians in the anti-regime movement.

In recruiting East Bank contingents for the Cabinet the regime naturally turns to the most loyal sections of the former Transjordanian population: the southern East Bankers, the Bedouin, the Circassians, wealthy Christians, and relatives and personal friends of the royal family. The southern East Bank, for example, has been represented in all but two short-lived Cabinets by either one or two ministers, and after the Rabat Conference in October 1974, by four or five. The town of Kerak itself has provided ministers for all but five Cabinets. The town's most prominent clan, the Majalis, have been represented in twenty-four Cabinets. Even Nabulsi included a Majali in his anti-regime Cabinet, hoping to win over or at least neutralize this powerful clan. Ministers are also regularly drawn from Ma'an and Tafilah, and from the southern Bedouin tribes—especially the Beni Sakhr and Huwaitat. After 1957, when Bedouin soldiers from the Beni Sakhr confederation foiled the military coup d'etat, their paramount chief, 'Akif al-Fa'iz, was appointed to ten Cabinets.

Following the precedent set by King 'Abdallah in the Mandatory period, one Circassian and one prominent Christian receive positions in almost every Jordanian Cabinet. The Circassian community's leader, Sa'id al-Mufti, who was Prime Minister four times, was also Deputy Prime Minister in seven Cabinets. The Christian notables who received ministerial positions in the 1950s were generally personal friends of 'Abdallah, like Sulayman Sukar (of Salt) and Saba al-Akashah (of Kerak), or others who had served him as officials. Owing to the Christian community's active role in the East Bank economy, Christians often head the Ministries of Finance, Economy, and Commerce.

The East Bank contingent in the Cabinet nearly always includes one or more Muslim personal friends of the ruling family from either Amman or one of the northern towns. In the 1950s, they were mainly older companions of 'Abdallah who took an interest in watching over the monarchy after his death. Such were Dr. Jamil al-Tutunji, who served in twelve Cabinets, Abd al-

Rahman Khalifah and Sheik Muhammad al-Shanqiti who had come from Mecca with the King. Members of formerly Bedouin clans of the northern East Bank whom the regime considers dependable are also utilized as ministers. These are the young officials from the Hindawi, Muflih, Kayid, and Lawzi clans. East Bank contingents also comprise individuals whose career interests and talents alone render them desirable ministers, such as Salah Abu Zeid and Fadl al-Dalqamuni. Finally, there are the king's relatives such as Sharif Abd al-Hamid Sharaf and Sharif Husayn ibn Nasir, whose interest in the welfare of the monarchy is through family ties.

It was clear to the regime, immediately upon its annexation of the West Bank, that it would have to integrate Palestinians into the administration of the country. They would provide trained manpower for a quickly expanded state and also serve to demonstrate that Palestinians were participating in the government of Jordan. The problem of how to recruit loyal Palestinian Cabinet ministers was settled during King 'Abdallah's lifetime. He drew Palestinians from two main sources.

The first comprised the various enemies and rivals of the former Mufti of Jerusalem, Hajj Amin al-Husseini. Husseini had always resented 'Abdallah's cooperation with the British, and the two were bitter foes. Moreover, 'Abdallah had supported the Husayni family's main rivals in Palestine, the Nashashibis, whose political activity, like his own, was based on their cooperation with the mandatory authorities. When 'Abdallah annexed the West Bank, therefore, he naturally looked for support to the Nashashibi family of Jerusalem and the several influential families throughout Palestine who were associated with it, like the Tuqan of Nablus, the Jiyyusi of Tulkarm, and the Khayri of Ramlah. These and other Nashashibi associates endorsed the annexation. In return, several of their number became Cabinet members.

The Tuqan clan, for example, was represented by various of its sons in seven of the first eight Cabinets. Hashim al-Jiyyusi served in fourteen Cabinets, Khulusi al-Khayri in ten, and various Nashashibis in nine. Similarly, the chair reserved for a Palestinian Christian was filled in thirteen Cabinets by Anastas Hananya, also a Nashashibi partisan. In the 1960s and 1970s too, the most recurrent Palestinian ministers have come from the former Nashashibi camp: Dr. Subhi Amin Amru of Hebron (sixteen Cabinets), Hatim al-Zu'bi, originally from Nazareth (seven Cabinets), Ahmad Tuqan (seven Cabinets), and members of the Dajani clan of Jerusalem (six Cabinets).

The second source of dependable Palestinian ministers, until the 1970s, were men who had served in the Palestine Civil Service under the Mandate. While useful to the regime as disciplined and often experienced administrators, their political merits resided in their affinity for the British and in their ability to work for an unpopular government, as they had under the Mandate. In 1955, for example, when Sa'id al-Mufti formed a Cabinet with directives to bring Jordan into the highly unpopular, British-sponsored Baghdad Pact, he composed his Palestinian contingent entirely of former civil servants. In 1967—the period between the war and the Khartoum Conference—when Jordan still considered the possibility of concluding a separate agreement with Israel, the Palestinian contingent in Sa'd Jum'ah's new Cabinet comprised four Mandatory civil servants and three men formerly associated with the Nashashibi camp—men who could, presumably, withstand the public outcry of their fellow countrymen.

By and large, East Bank ministers, Jordan has found, are more dependable than Palestinian ministers, even when the latter are individuals who support the regime. East Bankers tend more easily to feel that the monarchy is the legitimate regime for them, just as it was before 1950; also, they stem from communities that regard support for the monarchy as the right political behavior. Palestinian ministers, on the other hand, are always subject to accusations of selling out by at least some of their countrymen, which limits the amount of overt support they can give to the King.

This state of affairs has been reflected in two ways. First, Transjordanians have outnumbered Palestinians by at least two ministers in most of Jordan's forty-nine Cabinets; and since the Rabat Conference of October 1974, which officially divested Jordan of its jurisdiction over the West Bank, over three-fourths of all ministers have been Transjordanians. In fact, ever since 1950, Palestinians have constituted a majority in only two Cabinets, despite the fact that, until the 1967 war, they comprised two-thirds of the population.

Second, Transjordanians hold the key ministries. They have virtual monopolies on the Prime Ministership and the Ministry of the Interior. The latter, which is responsible for domestic security, has been held by Circassians in nine Cabinets, by natives of Kerak in thirteen Cabinets, and by other intimates of the regime in the rest. During the various crises of the 1950s it was held by the "hatchet-men" Umar Matar (of Ma'an) and Falah al-Madadhah (of Kerak). Only four Palestinians ever headed Interior, three of whose credentials were exceptionally good. Kamal al-Dajani, who held the post twice under Wasfi al-Tal, belonged to a pro-regime family in Jerusalem, and as a judge, had demonstrated his regard for law and order. He was also well-known to Tal, with whom he had served on the Board of the Constructive Scheme of Mussa al-'Alami.[1] Another incumbent, Hasan al-Katib, although a Palestinian of long residence, was originally from Mecca, and therefore trusted by the Hashemite family, itself of Meccan origin. Hashim al-Jiyyusi, the third incumbent, had a record that spoke for itself when he became Minister of the Interior; he had already served in more Cabinets than any other Jordanian politician.

1. A prominent Jerusalem-born lawyer who represented the Palestinian Arabs in the Arab League and founded the "Constructive Scheme" to buy land in Palestine in order to prevent its sale to Palestinian Jews, and to develop the Arab village as a basis of nationalist struggle. After 1948 he created an agricultural training farm for orphaned youth near Jericho. (Eds.)

The Ministry of Information, charged with the difficult task of creating a favorable image of the regime, was until 1970, headed by persons close to the royal family: Salah Abu Zeid, Dhuqan al-Hindawi, and Sharif Abd al-Hamid Sharaf, all East Bankers. Since 1970, however, a West Bank intimate of the palace, Adnan Abu Awdah, was given the post in nine Cabinets, in order to "sell" the regime to his fellow Palestinians more effectively.

The Ministry of Defense, too, although more an administrative agency for the army than the body which determines military policy, is yet deemed safer in the hands of Transjordanians. Therefore, Transjordanians have held the post of Minister of Defense in forty Cabinets, the incumbents coming mainly from the elements that constitute a majority of the army: the Bedouin and the southern East Bankers. Foreign Affairs, on the other hand, if not held by the Prime Minister, is generally allotted to a Palestinian. This is done to allay the fears of the Palestinians that the regime is operating against their interests in the international arena.

In order to maintain the fiction that Cabinets make their own policies and rise and fall according to their merits, the successive ministers, and especially the prime ministers, have to appear to be different enough from their predecessors to warrant their new appointments. This does not mean that there are no true differences and rivalries among political figures. The animosities between Abu al-Huda and Samir al-Rifa'i; Rifa'i and Hazza' al-Majali; and Talhuni and Wasfi al-Tal, were as real as they were well known. Such rivalries, however, are all horizontal; they do not interfere with the politician's basic understanding that the prime consideration is the welfare of the regime.

The regime also utilizes the various reputations that the ministers acquire. In the 1950s, for example, Tawfiq Abu al-Huda, Samir al-Rifa'i and Ibrahim Hashim were disliked by the Palestinians whereas Sa'id al-Mufti and Fawzi al-Mulqi were relatively popular. Abu al-Huda was resented for his ruthless rejection of repeated Palestinian demands for a political union with Iraq, a tougher response to Israeli border raids, and the relaxation of restrictions on Palestinian political activity. Rifa'i and Hashim were disliked as iron-fisted premiers, ever willing to assume office to crush public disorder.

Sa'id al-Mufti had a better reputation. First, it was assumed that as a Circassian, he would not jeopardize his community by persisting in policies that proved unacceptable to the Palestinians. Second, he had himself dabbled in anti-regime politics in the 1930s and it was felt that he was responsive to public opinion. Therefore, in an attempt to appease anti-annexation feeling among the Palestinians in 1950, King 'Abdallah made Mufti the first post-annexation prime minister, replacing Abu al-Huda, whom the Palestinians held responsible for the much resented Rhodes Armistice Agreement of 1949. In office, Mufti earned the further good will of the Palestinians when he evidently rejected 'Abdallah's directives to work out a peace treaty with

Israel. King Hussein therefore called him to office on two subsequent occasions when a popular prime minister was required; once to replace the unpopular Samir al-Rifa'i; once to take Jordan into the unpopular Baghdad Pact.

Another attempt to weaken Palestinian feelings of estrangement from the regime on the important occasion of King Hussein's accession to the throne, was the appointment of Fawzi al-Mulqi to replace Abu al-Huda as prime minister. The anti-regime leaders from the East Bank felt that they had a rapport with Mulqi. Sulayman al-Nabulsi had once been a teacher colleague of his in Kerak, and Shafiq al-Rushaydat had been his pupil at the high-school in Salt.

Hazza' al-Majali, despite his known status as a protegé of the palace, was also liked by the Transjordanian oppositionists, once his youthful companions, with whom he had founded the leading opposition party, the National Socialist Party, in 1954. Majali maintained good relations with the anti-regime forces even after he had proved to be the only person who would attempt to take Jordan into the Baghdad Pact during his five-day Cabinet in 1955. Therefore, his appointment to replace the tough Rifa'i, in 1959, was considered a good-will gesture to the opposition. It was only then, however, that his strong personal hostility to the United Arab Republic earned him the disdain of the Palestinians, and ultimately led to his assassination, in 1960.

Like Majali, Wasfi al-Tal also went from the good to the bad graces of the Palestinians. Initially, they welcomed his appointment to the prime ministership because of the personal service he had given in the Palestine cause (he had worked in the Arab Information Office in Jerusalem in 1945, and had fought in the Palestine War). The Palestinians' disillusionment with Tal occurred only after he had acquired a reputation for being anti-Egyptian. Ironically, Tal was first appointed prime minister with instructions to improve Amman's relations with Cairo; diplomatic ties had been broken when Jordan recognized Syria upon its secession from the UAR in 1961. Tal's tenure of office, however, soon suffered from a new Egyptian policy of defaming the Arab monarchies, and from the violent disorders in Jordan that accompanied the first steps in Egypt's formation of a new Arab union with Iraq and Syria in 1963. Tal had little opportunity, therefore, to demonstrate anything but antipathy for Cairo.

Bahjat al-Talhuni's relationship with the Palestinians was ironic in the reverse sense. Initially, Talhuni did not appear to be pro-Egyptian. He took office upon the assassination of Hazza' al-Majali, in which the UAR was implicated, and still held office at the time of Syria's secession from the UAR, a step in which Egypt claimed he was implicated. To mend relations with Cairo, as stated, he was thus replaced by Wasfi al-Tal. Talhuni's third Cabinet, on the other hand, coincided with Egypt's desire for inter-Arab conciliation following the Cairo Summit Conference of January, 1964. Given this period in which to deal amicably with Egypt, Talhuni developed a reputation for being the ''establishment'' politician in Jordan who most sympathized with Egyptian aims.

Consequently the regime utilized Talhuni's good reputation whenever it was expedient to appear to be cooperating with Cairo. Thus, after the Khartoum Conference, of September 1967, which re-elevated Egypt to the leading position in inter-Arab affairs, Talhuni was reappointed prime minister in an attempt to convince the Palestinians that Jordan sincerely intended to comply with the Khartoum decisions; in particular, not to make a separate settlement with Israel.

By the same token, the regime was careful to preserve Talhuni's reputation. When it was necessary to pursue major, possibly unpopular policies, it removed him from office. In February 1965, for example, when the demands of the Egyptian-sponsored Palestine Liberation Organization posed a challenge to Jordan's sovereignty over the West Bank, the King had Talhuni resign ''for health reasons,'' appointing Wasfi al-Tal, already unpopular, to deal with the problem. Again in the spring of 1969, before King Hussein visited the United States, where he planned to offer Israel separate *de facto* recognition in return for an Israeli withdrawal from the West Bank, he replaced Talhuni with Abd al-Mun'im al-Rifa'i.

In the delicate internal situation prevailing after the Six Day War, the appointment of Tal to head a Cabinet was considered impolitic. Loyal functionaries with no history of open clash with the Palestinians, such as Sa'id Jum'ah or Abd al-Mun'im al-Rifa'i, were thought preferable. On the other hand, when the King finally decided to rid Jordan of the *fedayeen*, Tal was the most suitable politican for this task.

Sometimes, if seldom, the regime chooses ministers from among the anti-regime camp, in the hope that this too will placate the Palestinians for a while. For their part, the Palestinians have believed, particularly in the early 1950s, that the presence of such elements in the Cabinet would lead to the retraction or alteration of policies inimical to their cause. In 1950, for example, Anwar al-Khatib and Sulayman al-Nabulsi asked to be included in Samir al-Rifa'i's Cabinet to ensure that it would not discuss the conclusion of a separate peace treaty with Israel. Khatib had just organized West Bank notables to dissuade Sa'id al-Mufti from such a course, and feared lest Mufti's successor take up the task again. In 1952, Tawfiq Abu al-Huda brought Anwar Nusaybah and Musa Nasir into his Cabinet in order to calm the storm being raised over his restrained border policy with Israel.

In the relatively calm years of the early and mid-1960s, several former leaders of the anti-regime movement were brought into Cabinets. Rashid al-Khatib, who had been sentenced to a year's imprisonment for his part in the disturbances of 1957, was taken into the three Cabinets of Sharif Husayn. Abd al-Qadir Salih, a former leader of the leftist National Front, was appointed Minister for Prime Minister's Affairs, and Qadri Tuqan and Musa

Nasir became Foreign Ministers. By the same token, relaxed conditions led to the ending of old feuds, whereby members of the ex-Mufti's family, the Husaynis received ministries, as did their allies, the Anabtawis. Actually, however, for all these former rebels, opposition to the regime was a thing of the past. Most had despaired of finding a better alternative to the monarchy for Jordan, and therefore decided to join it. The regime, for its part, was glad to have them in its camp. It felt that it gained credibility among the Palestinians through the collaboration of its former opponents.

The Palestinian nationalists have always understood that a change in Cabinets could not enhance their cause very much. They needed a radical change in the regime, whose interests were quite opposed to theirs. While the regime has concentrated on remaining in power, they have concentrated on regaining Palestine. Therefore, policies that have been advantageous to the King have been deemed detrimental to them, such as association with the West, agreement with Israel, the limitation on Palestinian recruitment to the army, and the maintenance of Jordan as a separate political entity. Nevertheless, the Palestinians have had to tolerate the regime since no viable alternative has come along; and so long as this remains the case they must accept the Cabinet system as well. To justify this acceptance, they feel that, as the system reacts to their signals, it gives them a degree of control over policy.

When alternatives seem to present themselves, however, the Palestinians cease to be appeased by Cabinet changes. In 1955, for example, they considered that Nasser was this alternative and were determined to see him rule over Jordan. Thus, when they rioted against Jordan's joining the Baghdad Pact, order could only be restored by the use of the army, under tough emergency Cabinets formed by Ibrahim Hashim and Samir al-Rifa'i. With order restored, the regime sought to appease the Palestinians with the popular Sa'id al-Mufti, but the Palestinians rejected him vociferously, demanding new elections to Parliament. These elections gained them the anti-regime Cabinet of Nabulsi, which the King, however, was ultimately constrained to dismiss. To appease the Palestinians again, the regime appointed a West Bank Prime Minister, Dr. Khalidi, but he was also rejected in the midst of widespread rioting which could only be suppressed by further strong-man Cabinets, under Hashim and Rifa'i, who governed with the aid of the army for an extended period.

In 1963, the planned union of Egypt, Iraq and Syria was thought to be another alternative to the monarchy, and widespread riots were organized with demands that Jordan, too, join the union. As in 1955, the Palestinians were implacable, and Samir al-Rifa'i was again called upon to form an emergency Cabinet. This time however, the oppositionists rejected Rifa'i by organizing their first successful "vote of no-confidence" in the House of Representatives. Rifa'i's successor, Sharif Husayn, was also prepared to take stern action, but was relieved of the crisis when plans for the new UAR collapsed of themselves.

Lack of power has been the other Palestinian problem. Even when an alternative has presented itself, the Palestinians have had no power to overthrow the regime; they could not contend with a determined and loyal army. Only the army itself could effect a revolution; and the closest the Palestinians came to changing the regime, in fact, was when they managed to subvert Ali Abu Nuwar, the Chief of Staff in 1956-57. The regime, on the other hand, has always been loathe to use force against the Palestinians. Every show of force against them is seen as a setback in its quest for legitimacy; its quest for acceptance by the majority section of the population. In place of force, the regime has sought to use the Cabinet system: the Cabinet serves as a safety valve which can be changed before the regime's relations with the Palestinians reach the breaking point.

After the Six Day War the Cabinet system continued much as it had in the past. Ministers were still drawn from dependable elements of the population, there being few cases in which even former anti-regime figures, such as Salih al-Mu'asher or Amil al-Ghuri, were appointed. The context in which the system operated, however, changed. Palestinian guerrilla organizations now appeared on the scene, equipped with what the Palestinians had lacked in the past: a possible alternative to the regime, and military might. The power at their disposal was perhaps not sufficient to defeat the loyal Bedouin army, but it was sufficient to make the army reluctant to act in suppression of Palestinian political activity.

The alternative that the Palestinian organizations provided was also more potential than actual, for they themselves decided that to assume the responsibilities of government was inconsistent with the strategy they believed should be employed against Israel. Instead of outright revolution, therefore, they put their efforts into trying to attain as much freedom of operation as they could get, and to that end, to weaken the King. One way was to remove from power those of his supporters who were hostile to them, such as General Muhammad Rasul al-Kaylani, Sharif Nasir ibn Jamil, and Sharif Zayd ibn Shakir. In this they succeeded.

It was, of course, intolerable to the King that this situation continue indefinitely. He could not, however, afford to launch a major offensive against the *fedayeen*, because his Palestinian subjects so unanimously supported them. Therefore, Hussein bided his time, losing ground politically, but trying to keep firm control over the army and security forces. The Rogers Plan of June 1970 finally provided the chance he had been waiting for. When the Plan was announced, significant sections of the Palestinian population suddenly became divorced from the *fedayeen*. Whereas the average Palestinian welcomed the opportunity offered by the Plan to regain the West Bank, the PLO rejected it. If the King was ever to strike at the organizations with minimal political risk, it was now.

Shortly after the announcement of the Rogers Plan, the King appointed a new Cabinet under Abd al-Mun'im al Rifa'i which comprised more anti-regime elements than any Cabinet since that of Nabulsi in 1957. Most outstanding was the appointment of the Palestinian, Sulayman al-Hadidi, (a Ba'thist and close friend of guerrilla leaders Kamal Nasir and Bahjat Abu Gharbiyah), as Minister of the Interior. The King's action, however, did not reflect a new trend in Cabinet formation. He simply needed a nationalist Cabinet to endorse him in the event that peace negotiations with Israel would result from the Jarring mission.

Throughout the summer of 1970 the *fedayeen* intensified their activities against the King, attempting to demonstrate that he had lost effective control over the country. If this could be established, he would forfeit his ability to be a binding party to the Jarring peace talks, and the Rogers Plan would fall through. To the King, the failure of the Rogers Plan meant that he would lose this perhaps unique opportunity to keep his Palestinian subjects divorced from the guerrilla organizations and get rid of the latter. He therefore had to establish his authority. In mid-September, taking advantage of the bad publicity the *fedayeen* had received when they hijacked four airliners earlier that month, Hussein finally ordered the long-awaited showdown.

Even under such favorable circumstances, however, a total war on the *fedayeen* involved considerable political risks which few civilian politicians could allow themselves to take. Therefore, on September 16, 1970, the King dismissed the civilian Cabinet and formed a military one. The military Cabinet too, however, was composed of officers who reflected the regional balance of power in the Kingdom no less than had their civilian predecessors. This merely confirmed the fundamental fact that in Jordan, still a semi-feudal society, the King's rule is based on the manipulation of, and appeal to, tribal, ethnic and regional groups, rather than the individual citizen.

JORDANIAN CABINETS, 1950-1977

1. Sa'id al-Mufti (b. Amman)
   (Apr. 12, 1950-Oct. 14, 1950)
2. Sa'id al-Mufti
   (Oct. 14, 1950-Dec. 3, 1950)
3. Samir al-Rifa'i (b. Safed)
   (Dec. 4, 1950-July 25, 1951)
4. Tawfiq Abu al-Huda (b. Acre)
   (July 25, 1951-Sept. 7, 1951)

5. Tawfiq Abu al-Huda
   (Sept. 7, 1951-Sept. 28, 1952)
6. Tawfiq Abu al-Huda
   (Sept. 30, 1952-May 5, 1953)
7. Fawzi al-Mulqi (b. Irbid)
   (May 6, 1953-May 2, 1954)
8. Tawfiq Abu al-Huda
   (May 3, 1954-Oct. 21, 1954)

9. Tawfiq Abu al-Huda
   (Oct. 21, 1954-May 29, 1955)
10. Sa'id al-Mufti
    (May 30, 1955-Dec. 14, 1955)
11. Hazza' al-Majali (b. Kerak)
    (Dec. 15, 1955-Dec. 20, 1955)
12. Ibrahim Hashim (b. Nablus)
    (Dec. 21, 1955-Jan. 7, 1956)
13. Samir al-Rifa'i
    (Jan. 9, 1956-May 20, 1956)
14. Sa'id al-Mufti
    (May 22, 1956-June 30, 1956)
15. Ibrahim Hashim
    (July 1, 1956-Oct. 27, 1956)
16. Sulayman al-Nabulsi (b. Salt)
    (Oct. 29, 1956-Apr. 10, 1957)
17. Husayn Fakhri al-Khalidi (b. Jerusalem)
    (Apr. 15, 1957-Apr. 24, 1957)
18. Ibrahim Hashim
    (Apr. 25, 1957-May 18, 1958)
19. Samir al-Rifa'i
    (May 18, 1958-May 5, 1959)
20. Hazza' al-Majali
    (May 5, 1959-Aug. 28, 1960)
21. Bahjat al-Talhuni (b. Ma'an)
    (Aug. 29, 1960-June 28, 1961)
22. Bahjat al-Talhuni
    (June 28, 1961-Jan. 27, 1962)
23. Wasfi al-Tal (b. Irbid)
    (Jan. 27, 1962-Dec. 2, 1962)
24. Wasfi al-Tal
    (Dec. 2, 1962-Mar. 27, 1963)
25. Samir al-Rifa'i
    (Mar. 27, 1963-Apr. 20, 1963)
26. Sharif Husayn ibn Nasir (b. Mecca)
    (Apr. 21, 1963-July 10, 1963)
27. Sharif Husayn ibn Nasir
    (July 10, 1963-July 6, 1964)
28. Bahjat al-Talhuni
    (July 7, 1964-Feb. 13, 1965)

29. Wasfi al-Tal
    (Feb. 13, 1965-Dec. 22, 1966)
30. Wasfi al-Tal
    (Dec. 22, 1966-Mar. 4, 1967)
31. Sharif Husayn ibn Nasir
    (Mar. 4, 1967-Apr. 23, 1967)
32. Sa'd Jum'ah (b. Tafilah)
    (Apr. 23, 1967-Aug. 2, 1967)
33. Sa'd Jum'ah
    (Aug. 2, 1967-Oct. 7, 1967)
34. Bahjat al-Talhuni
    (Oct. 7, 1967-Mar. 24, 1969)
35. Abd al-Mun'im al-Rifa'i (b. Safed)
    (Mar. 24, 1969-Aug. 12, 1969)
36. Bahjat al-Talhuni
    (Aug. 12, 1969-Apr. 19, 1970)
37. Bahjat al-Talhuni
    (Apr. 19, 1970-June 27, 1970)
38. Abd al-Mun'im al-Rifa'i
    (June 27, 1970-Sept. 15, 1970)
39. General Muhammad Da'ud (b. Jerusalem)
    (Sept. 16, 1970-Sept. 24, 1970)
40. Ahmad Tuqan (b. Nablus)
    (Sept. 26, 1970-Oct. 28, 1970)
41. Wasfi al-Tal
    (Oct. 28, 1970-May 22, 1971)
42. Wasfi al-Tal
    (May 22, 1971-Nov. 28, 1971)
43. Ahmad al-Lawzi (b. Swaylih)
    (Nov. 29, 1971-Aug. 21, 1972)
44. Ahmad al-Lawzi
    (Aug. 21, 1972-May 26, 1973)
45. Zayd al-Rifa'i (b. Amman)
    (May 26, 1973-Nov. 23, 1974)
46. Zayd al-Rifa'i
    (Nov. 23, 1974-Feb. 8, 1976)
47. Zayd al-Rifa'i
    (Feb. 8, 1976-July 13, 1976)
48. Mudar Badran (b. Salt)
    (July 13, 1976-Nov. 28, 1976)
49. Mudar Badran
    Nov. 28, 1976-

Population

Population:	*Circa* 2,000,000
Major Cities:	Amman (*circa* 520,700)
	Zarqa (*circa* 225,000)
	Irbid (*circa* 115,000)
Population Growth:	3.4% (U.N. estimate, 1970-73)
	Most of the population is under 15 years of age.
Ethnic Composition:	Majority are Arabs
Religion:	*Circa* 90% are Sunni Muslim. There are also Christians and Shi'ite Muslims.
Language:	Official language is Arabic.
Education:	Free and compulsory; two universities.

The origins of many of the oldest groups in the population of Jordan are difficult and often impossible to trace. The original Jordanians (Transjordan) are members of several hundred tribes and clans who have lived in the area since time immemorial, or who came to settle as soldiers and followers of the armies of Islam, or who wandered into the land across the River Jordan, or who were pushed into it by internecine wars from the north or the south. Those who trace their origins back into antiquity do so through the poetry of the local village bard or the legends related around the campfire, but these story-tellers themselves are losing ground to the radio and TV program. Islam produced a large number of historiographers but these writers paid scant attention to the area of Transjordan. It is known that a great deal of movement of tribes occurred and that land ownership frequently changed hands, either through conquest or raids. Blood feuds broke up some of the tribes and scattered them elsewhere. Some tribes were settled on land granted to them by the Ottoman Sultan. Others purchased their land from him or from land-owners.

In the main, however, it can be said that several of the tribes are thought to be the original inhabitants of the area while others trace their origins back to the Hejaz, home of the Prophet Muhammad, or to the Syrian province of Hauran and to Damascus, or to Iraq, or Lebanon, or the Yemen, or to Egypt or the West Bank or parts of Israel. Some have lived in the area for six hundred years, others for two hundred and still others for only fifty or seventy years.

The population is overwhelmingly Sunni Muslim and basically Jordan can be said to be the home of the ethnically "Arab" — the Bedouin.[1]

Jordan's Christian population is also divided into tribal groupings. In the main, the Christians are the descendants of the early Christian converts in the area and of the Greeks, the Romans and the Crusaders who ruled it (the *Ahl al-Nahiya*'s main stock, for example, is thought to be Crusader; their name is said to be derived from the Greek word for "diocese"). Some trace their origins to Syria or Lebanon, others to Nazareth or the West Bank or Egypt. The Christian denominations are: Greek Orthodox, Greek and Latin Catholic and Protestant. Among the Christians is a small community of Armenians.

The Circassians came to Jordan from the Caucasus. Jordan has a small community of Turcomans. Several Bahai families settled in Jordan in 1910, coming from Persia to dwell on land purchased by Sir Abdul Baha Abbas, head of the Bahai faith, in 1879.

Believed to be descendants of the Hebrews but Muslim in religion are two small tribes, the *Layathna* of Wadi Musa and the *al Bdul* in the hills around Petra, who have many Jewish customs.

Well over 50% of Jordan's population consists of Palestinians, who entered Jordan (the East Bank) via the West Bank following the Arab-Israel wars of 1948 and 1967. Most of them were accommodated in refugee camps administered under the auspices of the United Nations Relief and Works Agency for Palestine Refugees in the Near East (UNRWA), set up in 1949. Many still live in these camps, as wards of UNRWA; all were granted Jordanian citizenship. The Palestinians have ties of kinship with many of the Jordanian tribes. They are the more urbanized of Jordan's population.

Jordan regards the West Bank as an integral part of the country. All West Bankers are Jordanian citizens.

The Bedouin

"My father lived in a tent!" is still a popular expression of pride for many Jordanians. It is the Bedouin virtues and values that the Jordanians feel are part of their character—the freedom of the isolated desert, a sense of honor, pride in noble blood, bravery, generosity, hospitality, protection of the weak, vengefulness and forgiveness, the importance of the family. The Bedouin of Jordan are still nomads, but most are in the transitional stage of becoming what, in the scale of Bedouin values, is invariably the lowest: settled villagers. It has been difficult for the various regimes in the area to induce the Bedouin tribes to settle down to agriculture and several of these tribes are still

1. As defined by Philip K. Hitti, in *The Arabs, A Short History* (New York: St. Martin's Press, 1968), the Bedouin is the "original Arab." He is a man of the desert, moving with his flock, coming from the Arabian desert. This would describe the historical roots of a basic segment of Jordan's population.

nomadic or semi-nomadic. The camps of the nomads are found mainly in an area some 248 miles long and 155 miles wide east of the railway line. Settlements of seminomads exist near the Qaal Jafr and Azraq ash Shishan oases. The former is the site of a government-sponsored agricultural project. A similar settlement has been established near Al Hasa, the center of the phosphate industry. In Jordan, a Bedouin may be seen to pitch his black tent and graze his flock in a plush new suburb in Amman or in the burning desert of the south or the hills of the north. For these last nomads, life continues much in the rhythm it has had for centuries.

Loyal to King Hussein, Bedouin make up a substantial percentage of the Jordanian army.

The following are among the main Bedouin tribes in Jordan:[1]

—The *Beni Attiya,* who wandered gradually into Transjordan from the Hejaz and whose members began to settle more or less permanently in the Kerak district as *fellahin* (peasants) in the 1950s, when they began applying for grants of land from the government;

—The *al Hajaya,* who came to the Kerak district to take refuge after a quarrel within the tribe, or after a raid on a pilgrimage caravan, *circa* 1759;

—The *al Huwaitat,* who inhabit southern Jordan and claim descent from the Prophet through his daughter Fatimah, but who may also be descendants of the Nabataeans;

—The *al Isa,* who claim to be an offshoot of a large tribe near the Euphrates;

—The *Beni Khalid,* who claim relationship with a tribe of southern Iraq and who moved into Jordan some one hundred years ago;

—The *Beni Sakhr,* who claim descent from tribes in the Hejaz and the Nejd and who came to Jordan in the nineteenth century;

—The *al Sirhan,* an ancient tribe said to originate in the Hauran, where they had established a semi-autonomous state which was overthrown by tribes swarming northward from the Hejaz.

1. *A History of Jordan and its Tribes,* by Lt. Col. F. G. Peake (Coral Gables, Florida: University of Miami Press, 1958.)

The Circassians

The non-Arab, Sunni Muslim minority known as the Circassians (Arabic: *Sharakisah)* were settled in Transjordan in the last part of the nineteenth century. They claim kinship with the Mameluk rulers of Egypt[1] and trace their ancestry to two Indo-European Muslim tribal groups, the warrior Iassi and the Kossogs of the Caucasus.

The Russian conquest of the Caucasus began in the tenth century and was only completed in the nineteenth century. Following in its wake was a slow migration southwards of various Caucasian Muslim tribal groups. After the Congress of Berlin in 1878,[2] the Ottoman Sultan Abdul Hamid, as the traditional protector of all Muslims, settled large numbers of Circassian refugees on land which is now in Turkey, Syria and Jordan. The first Circassian community reached Amman in 1878; others were settled in Jerash, Naur and Wadi-Syr. The Middle East today has the largest Circassian communities outside Russia and these Middle Eastern communities still maintain links. Of these, the Jordanian community is the most important economically. There is also a Circassian community in the United States.

In Jordan, the collection of tribes which make up the Circassians are known as the *Adigah.* The *Adigah,* however, consist of several tribal groups (the Kabardian tribes in Amman and Jerash; the Bzadugh and the Abzakh in Naur and Wadi-Syr) which have various fine distinctions among themselves that have not altogether been lost. A related tribal group, the Chechens (also, Shishans) are politically and socially identified with the Circassians in Jordan but speak an entirely different language. Chechen settlements exist in Suwaylih, Rusayfa, Zarqa, Sukhne and Azraq. The community numbers less than 5,000, while the *Adigah* numbers some 20,000-25,000. One of the two seats allotted to the Circassians in the Jordanian Parliament is always occupied by a member of the Chechen community, the other by an Adigah. With no common tribal language, the Chechens and the Adigah communicate in Arabic. The latter, for certain historical reasons, are more economically advanced than the former.

The Circassians are traditionally loyal to the monarchy. Settled in Transjordan for strategic as well as humane reasons, they served the Ottoman ruler's need for loyal and effective soldiers who could be used to hold the unruly Bedouin tribes of the area in check. The early Circassian refugees fought fiercely against the surrounding Bedouin tribes who contested their right to settle on land which had for generations been used as pasture and

---

1. The Mameluk Sultanate, composed of Turks and later Circassians, which came to power in Egypt in the thirteenth century.
2. Following the Russian-Turkish war of 1877.

118

which the Bedouin regarded as their own. This land was, however, mainly government owned and had never been farmed or taxed. Circassian settlement enjoyed the support of the Sultan but the community was also subject to the Sultan's "divide and rule" policy which played one group off against the other, and which, finally, led to the erosion of Circassian loyalty to the Ottoman ruler.

The Circassians nevertheless reestablished the almost abandoned town of Amman and helped to create the first stable government and police force known in the area of Transjordan for centuries. Their introduction of a system of settled agriculture helped to act as an influence on the surrounding area. Their support of the British facilitated the creation of the Hashemite kingdom of Transjordan and their integration into the new country's economic life helped to merge the old tribal structures into the new kingdom.

The Circassians are, in modern Jordan, predominantly agricultural and urban landlords, high government officials and top ranking army and air-force officers. The Adigah representative to parliament has served as Secretary of Agriculture, of Defense and of the Interior in various Jordanian cabinets. One of their number, Sa'id al-Mufti, was a prime minister and a prominent member of the Senate. A Chechen has been the Imman of the Zarqa mosque; another, mayor of Zarqa.

Firmly loyal to Hussein, they are not politically active as a minority group. Their social and cultural life centers in the Circassian Charitable Association located in Amman and the predominantly Circassian Ahli Club, which has produced most of Jordan's finest athletes.

The traditional tribal hierarchy, which consisted of an aristocracy and re-tainers, is fading away (people speak of a Circassian "elite" rather than a "chief") but it is still an important factor in marriage. While endogamous marriages are still preferred, however, the transformation of the Circassians from an agrarian to an urbanized and Arabized community has led to an increasing tendency toward intermarriage with Arab Jordanians. This generally takes place between Circassian women and Arab men, and the offspring of the union become identified as Arab.

The Palestinians of Jordan: Refugees and Citizens

The various studies that have been made of the refugee populations of the East and West Banks reach much the same conclusion: it is difficult to come by an exact estimate of the number of persons coming under this category. The number of refugees fleeing from the West Bank to the East Bank in the months following the war of 1967 has been as much the subject of controversy as has been the number of refugees resulting from the war of 1948. The London-based *Economist Intelligence Unit, Syria, Lebanon, Jordan, Annual Supplement, 1968* estimated that there were at least 250,000 West Bank refugees on the East Bank at that time. UNRWA's figure for West Bank refugees on the East Bank was 289,000 (50,000 families) for 1967 (the number of refugees from the Gaza Strip was given as 177,000, making a total of 467,000). *The New York Times* correspondent in Amman, January 2, 1969, suggested that many refugees had been counted twice in the scramble for U.N. rations and other benefits, and that therefore "experts on the question estimate the true total of refugees in Jordan now at 371,000." Peter Dodd and Halim Barakat, in their study, *River Without Bridges* (Institute for Palestine Studies, Beirut, 1968) cite the UNRWA report for 1966-1967 to the effect that the "new" (1967) refugees constituted some 200,000 persons.

Analyzing the reasons for their flight, Dodd and Barakat come to some interesting conclusions. They point out that the 1967 exodus was sudden, while the 1948 exodus had continued over an entire year, beginning in November 1947. The plight and condition of the 1948 refugees was known throughout Jordan and the Arab world, yet people were still prepared to uproot themselves in 1967. The reason for this, they write, was the panic that had swept over the West Bank population at the suddenness and unexpectedness of events. Another explanation cited as held in some Arab quarters — that these people were "riffraff" who were already refugees living in UNRWA camps on the West Bank before the war and who had left because they feared they would not continue to receive UNRWA rations under the Israeli occupation was shown as incorrect, since the "old" refugees numbered less than half of those who were "new" refugees — people who had never been dependent on UNRWA. A theory that these were people with a "nomadic mentality" was also rejected. The authors' study of 100 families in the Zeezya refugee camp showed that 40% of the "new" refugees had been farmers (as compared with 24% of the "old" refugees); 84% had owned their own house and 34% had owned over 21 dunams of land, while 26% had earned an income of up to 20 dinars (49% were illiterate and 22% had owned no land).

They were thus, the authors concluded, people fleeing from foreign rule; from the unknown and the feared.

A crucial consideration was the issue of *al 'ird* (dishonor). These were people who understood the traditional Muslim modes of warfare and knew what was expected of Muslim warriors, who would be aware of the consequences of any untoward incidents which could lead to years of revenge and blood feuds, while the Israelis could not be expected to understand these behavior norms or to follow the limitations these imposed. A man had therefore constantly to be with his womenfolk in order to protect them. One of the informants told the authors that he had decided to flee when an Israeli soldier asked him the ages of his daughters. Since girls work in the fields and men in the town in the normal course of the day, the only way to protect his daughters, this man apparently reasoned, was to flee with them.

Fear of the unknown, of the rule of people from a society which was alien to their own, of the major threat this represented to their traditional mode of life — and, no doubt, of the terrible things they had heard about the Israelis who, in the absence of contact had become the stuff of myth, folktales and horror stories — appeared thus to have been a basic reason for their flight. Other reasons cited by Dodd and Barakat were: fear of Israeli planes — 57%; "psychological pressure" — 21%; "eviction and destruction of the village" — 19%. (30% gave *al 'ird* as their reason. Some had left an older man behind in charge of their property.)

Despite all this, as the authors point out, only 20% of the West Bank population had fled while 80% remained. Asked whether these new refugees wanted to return home, 82% responded "definitely yes" while only 2% said "no" (64% of the "old" refugees said "yes" and 15% said "no"). Some 14,000 West Bank refugees had been permitted to return to their homes by 1968 (44,000 by 1975).

The direct cost of providing for all the refugees has been borne by UN-RWA, by various international aid programs and also by various governments and international welfare agencies. The Jordanian budget, although it made no specific allocations, increased its expenditure for the Ministries of Education; Health and Social Affairs, Labor; Information, and Development and Reconstruction. By 1955, the World Bank Mission had already noted some of the impact the 1948 refugees had made on the Jordanian economy. By 1969 unemployment in Jordan was lower than it had been before the June 1967 war, despite the influx of the "new" refugees. This can partly be explained by the fact that the Jordanian armed forces had recruited 10,000 men, but it was mainly due to the expansion of the economy.

Uprooted from their homes and villages for no good reason other than the promised sweets of reward in 1948 and fear and panic in 1967, the Palestinian refugees, from their squalid and wretched camp cities of tents and mud and tin shacks exploded into Jordan's economy, and set the country on the path toward urbanization. The town of Amman experienced a construction boom of unprecedented proportions in 1968 and 1969, and most of the new dwellings constructed were purchased by refugees in this and other urban centers. The East Bank had been benefiting from migration from the West Bank for several years prior to 1967. Amman's population had increased from some 250,000 in 1961 to 350,000 prior to the war — migration from the West to the East Bank had been continuous between 1948 and May 1967: in fact, the West Bank's share of Jordan's total population fell from 62% in 1948 to 56% in 1952 to 47% in 1961 — and by 1967 the West Bank had accounted for only some 38% of Jordan's labor force, while the East Bank had accounted for 62%.

From the outset, no distinctions were made in official Jordanian statistics or in official Jordanian policy statements between the settled population and the newcomers. Jordan gave all the refugees immediate citizenship; the state has offered the Palestinian refugees greater opportunities for assimilating into its political and economic life than has any other Arab state. They have been granted the same political rights as other citizens; they may purchase or rent homes or farms outside the camps and may engage in business and all forms of employment. Palestinians today hold dominant positions in industry, commerce, finance, the civil service, the educational and health services and in other sectors of the economy; it is only in agriculture, such as in the East Ghor Rural Development Project, that they tend to be the sharecroppers and to have lower incomes and living standards than do the other farmers.

Between 1952 and 1961, the rate of population growth in Jordan (East and West Banks) averaged 2.8% annually.[1] Although the natural rate of increase was somewhat higher, the population growth rate was held down by emigration, and this emigration was overwhelmingly Palestinian — of the 62,863 Jordanians abroad, according to the 1961 census, 80% were from the West Bank and 20% from the East Bank.

The total number of Palestinians in Jordan is difficult to estimate. The PLO figure is 900,000. Nabeel Shaath gave this estimate for 1968-69.[2] Naseer H. Aruri estimates that the Palestinians constitute two-thirds of the East Bank population.[3] The *Economist* (London), suggested the same figure in 1974.[4] Clearly, the Palestinians make up a highly significant section of the population of the kingdom.

The number of Palestinian refugees still living in the UNRWA camps is estimated at about 40% of the Palestinian population of the East Bank.[5] Those outside the camps live in the towns and the rural areas, but continue to receive some aid from UNRWA. Even in the camps, most of the men appear to have at least part-time employment outside; many do not report the full extent of their employment and earnings in order to retain their UNRWA benefits.

As was reported by *The New York Times* correspondent in Amman in 1975:

> . . . Jordan cannot live without her Palestinians, who fill technical positions in the army and the bureaucracy and who dominate the commerce of Amman — the largest Palestinian city in the world.[6]

FOOTNOTES

1. Hashemite Kingdom of Jordan, Department of Statistics, *First Census of Population and Housing,* Vol. 1, April 1964, p. 34.

2. Nabeel Shaath, ''High Level Palestinian Manpower,'' *Journal of Palestine Studies,* Vol. 1, No. 2, Winter, 1972, pp. 80-95.

3. Naseer H. Aruri, ''Jordan and the Palestinians,'' paper prepared for delivery at the 9th Annual Convention of the Association of Arab-American University Graduates, October 1-3, 1976.

4. *The Economist,* (London), June 1, 1974.

5. *The New York Times,* reported, February 26, 1974, quoting official sources, that 208,000 persons were living in refugee camps on the East Bank.

6. *The New York Times,* August 3, 1975.

III

Jordan and Israel

Jordan and the War of 1948

By TERENCE PRITTIE

There is a widely held view that the Kingdom of Jordan, formerly the Emirate of Transjordan, has somehow been desperately unlucky in the course of the long Middle East conflict. This view is especially prevalent in Britain, for a number of reasons.

Transjordan and Jordan, were traditionally allied with Britain; the very creation of the Emirate involved its detachment from the rest of the British Mandate of Palestine and was effected with British encouragement and connivance. Transjordan's regular armed force, the Arab Legion, was built up, armed, trained and even officered by the British protecting power. Britain and Jordan were bound together by treaty and, in the mid-1950s, Jordan was very nearly brought into the Baghdad Pact. In addition, both the Emir (later King) 'Abdallah and the grandson who succeeded him, King Hussein, were friends of Britain. As a result, there has always been instinctive and solidly based sympathy for Jordan in Britain.

It may be because of this sympathy that the Jordanian role in the 1948 war in the Middle East has tended to be misted over by sentiment. A popular view has been that the Jordanians were drawn into that war against their inclinations and better judgment, and that alone among the principal participants they were not to blame for war breaking out. This may be an over-simplification, based on the supposition that Jordan was under an obligation to join forces with other Arab states, and with the Palestinians, against the "intruder" State of Israel. In retrospect, it seems probable that Jordan had a policy of its own, one which contributed both to the inception and outcome of the 1948 war. There are several reasons for saying this.

First, there were the two secret meetings between the Emir 'Abdallah and Mrs. Golda Meir (then Myerson), of November 1947 and May 1948. In the first meeting, at Naharayim on the River Jordan, 'Abdallah plainly indicated that his desert state had territorial designs of a far-reaching kind on Palestine. He proposed the establishment of semi-autonomous Jewish provinces, under Jordanian sovereignty. The enlarged Jordanian state would stretch from the Arabian desert to the Mediterranean, although 'Abdallah hinted that Jewish autonomy could be granted—if territorial concessions were made in return.

The Hon. Terence Prittie is a noted British journalist, broadcaster and author. He has been chief correspondent for the *Manchester Guardian* and diplomatic correspondent for *The Guardian* and is the Director of *Britain and Israel*, a Newsletter (London). He has published studies on Britain, Germany and Israel, and biographies of international leaders, his latest being *Willy Brandt, Portrait of a Statesman*, Schocken Books, 1974.

This subject was never explored; what 'Abdallah may have had in mind was Jewish evacuation of Eastern Galilee and Jewish support for the extension of Jordanian sovereignty over Jerusalem.

At the second meeting, 'Abdallah again proposed some kind of local autonomy for the Jews in an enlarged Jordanian state. But while he appeared in the role of negotiator in the first talks, he was seeking to enforce terms in the second. Full-scale war was only four days away, and 'Abdallah's view was that, failing virtual Jewish capitulation, his country would have to go to war—his phrase was "Then (in November) I was alone, but now I am one of five" (the other four were Egypt, Iraq, Syria and the Lebanon). On this, as on other occasions, 'Abdallah's saving grace was his courtliness of manner. But his policy was clear enough. He was not prepared to accept the United Nations Partition Plan and its corollary, the setting up of a Jewish State. He wanted, if not the whole of Palestine, then the major part of it. This, in turn, meant that he was opposed to the creation of an Arab State in roughly 50 percent of what remained of the original Palestine Mandate.[1]

In between his two meetings with Mrs. Meir, 'Abdallah sent his Foreign Minister, Tawfiq Pasha, to London to discuss the situation with the British Foreign Secretary, Mr. Ernest Bevin. In this interview Tawfiq pointed out that the Palestinian-Arab State which was envisaged would be politically and economically unviable, and that it would fall under the control of the anti-British Grand Mufti of Jerusalem, Hajj Amin al-Husseini. Tawfiq proposed that the Arab Legion should occupy the "East Arab area"—in fact, what is called the West Bank today, plus the "triangle" of mainly Arab-settled land round Lod and Ramleh. Bevin allegedly replied: "It seems the obvious thing to do," and added "Don't invade the areas allotted to the Jews." Tawfiq was not concerned with the fate of Western Galilee and the Gaza Strip, the other two areas allotted to the proposed Arab state under the U.N. Partition Plan.

This conversation is exactly confirmed by John Bagot Glubb (later General Sir John), the military adviser to 'Abdallah and the commander of the 7,000-8,000 strong Arab Legion.[2] Tawfiq's policy seems, indeed, to have been inspired by this British regular army officer, who had been "lent" to the Emirate of Transjordan. Glubb, moreover, had worked out a "solution" of the Palestinian problem in greater detail than emerged in the Bevin-Tawfiq talks; broad solutions were his speciality. He believed that the Gaza Strip and the Negev Desert should be annexed by Egypt, and Western Galilee by Lebanon, while British garrisons should remain in Haifa and Jerusalem to supervise the implementation of his private peace plan. Glubb was, in fact, totally opposed to the creation of an Arab mini-Palestinian state—and one should note that it would have been larger than the mini-Palestine under discussion in the mid-1970s.[3]

It seems likely that Glubb played a key role in British-Jordanian cooperation in 1948. A naturally modest man, he has played this role down in the various books which he has written about the Middle East conflict. But he was uniquely placed, in that he had the ear of the governments in both London and Amman, where he was liked and trusted. The men of the Arab Legion adored him and Jordan's only regular armed force was halfway to becoming a private army. Glubb, moreover, had ideas which went beyond the carving-up of the proposed Palestinian Arab state; he was utterly opposed to its counterpart, the Jewish state which became Israel.

All his writings show him to have been strongly anti-Zionist, opposed to all Jewish immigration into the area, deeply resentful that the United States and Britain allowed this immigration to continue while not accepting Jewish refugees into their own countries in large numbers, and highly suspicious of the "unholy" alliance of the U.S. and the Soviet Union—both supported the U.N. Partition Plan and both were persistently and carpingly critical of Britain. Glubb believed that the Partition Plan was unacceptable and unworkable, as well as being contrary to Britain's interest in the Middle East as a whole. His fear was that the goodwill gained by Britain in Iraq, Syria, Lebanon, Jordan and Saudi Arabia would be swept away by indecisiveness over Palestine.[4]

According to one historian, the role of the Arab Legion commanded by Glubb was a strange one—"The Arab Legion was in Palestine under odd and unclear conditions."[5] For the Legion remained in areas designated to both the Arab and Jewish states almost up to the outbreak of the 1948 war. Units of the Legion guarded British arms and supply depots, and were given sundry other duties (one company was detached to guard the Iraqi Consulate in Jerusalem). Glubb himself admits that "the greater part of the military units of the Arab Legion were already in Palestine before the British Mandate came to an end."[6] British pressure for them to be withdrawn east of the River Jordan only began in April, and the main but not total withdrawal was completed only by May 14, when the State of Israel came into being.

Even then, most of the Legion withdrew only a short way east of the river. The anomaly of its status was clearly illustrated when Glubb sent a personal signal to the British Commander-in-Chief, Middle East, demanding the immediate dispatch to Aqaba of a ship carrying specified ammunition for the Jordanian infantry and their eight 25-pounder guns. Somewhat ingenuously, Glubb adds in his book, "The C-in-C rose to the occasion and the ship was duly loaded."[7] The sequel was ludicrous—the Egyptians seized and impounded the ammunition, and the ship never sailed. The British Army in Palestine, however, stepped into the breach and, like a maverick uncle, bequeathed all of its surplus ammunition to the Legion.[8]

The Legion was poised to carry out military intervention in Palestine which was expected to be decisive. Glubb himself has (after the event) been at pains to prove that Jewish military forces were far superior to Arab in the war which was to follow. He estimated Jewish armed forces at over 60,000 (in one of his books he estimated total Arab armed strength at 21,500, in another at only 17,500).[9] Jews under arms were, to him, soldiers; armed Palestinian Arabs are conveniently left out of the reckoning, although Glubb and other pro-Arab historians never fail—for political reasons—to stress how many more Arabs than Jews there were in the area.

It may well be that the British Government could have averted Jordan's entry into the war which followed the proclamation of the State of Israel. It seems clear that it made no serious attempt to do so. In the House of Commons a Government spokesman said: "recognition of Israel now would be a positive act of intervening in favor of one side."[10]

Foreign Minister Ernest Bevin urged the British Dominions not to recognize Israel, and instructed the Foreign Office in Whitehall to refer only to a "Jewish National Home."[11] This appears to have been not so much casuistry as plain indecisiveness; the British Government was waiting to see how the fighting would go, and the country's greatest soldier, Field-Marshal Lord Montgomery, gave it as his opinion that "the Arabs will hit the Jews for six" (an expression which denotes a hit over the boundary-ropes at cricket). Glubb has since claimed that the Arab Legion was not allowed to enter the city of Jerusalem, from May 15 to May 19, when it could have done so.[12] This order came, ostensibly, from the Government of Jordan; the implication is that it was either given in deference to Britain, or was British-instigated.

Jerusalem was designated as an International Zone under the terms of the U.N. Partition Plan. Glubb has repeatedly stated, in all of his books about the Middle East, that the Legion only entered "the Arab State"—which, he considered, had already been invaded by the Jews. This was true only at the outset of the fighting; the battle for Jerusalem became the Legion's main preoccupation. Piecing together various accounts of the Legion's activities, this picture of its operations emerges:

Prior to the official outbreak of war, the Legion helped to attack and destroy the four Jewish settlements of the Etzion Bloc (between Bethlehem and Hebron). The attack began on May 4, and units of the Legion, along with four British tanks, quickly joined in it.[13] By May 13 the Legion was in control of Etzion and took survivors prisoner, following the massacre of many of the defenders by the villagers of Hebron (Glubb produces the cold-blooded statement that "These colonies had been so aggressive that they had deliberately compelled Arab retaliation"!)[14]

From May 14 to May 18 the Legion moved into various parts of what is now known as the West Bank. They overran two Jewish settlements, (Atarot and Neve Yaakov) and pushed toward the sea north and south of Jerusalem. Units of the Legion undoubtedly entered Jerusalem by May 16, when it became clear that the Jews were failing in their effort to defend their isolated Quarter of the Old City.

From May 18 onwards the battle for Jerusalem moved into its crucial stage.

Here, the Legion won two successes. It forced the defenders of the Jewish Quarter to surrender by May 28, and it recaptured the Sheikh Jarrah district which became the hub of Arab Jerusalem, outside the walls of the Old City. But the Legion failed to achieve its other objectives—the key strategic area around the Notre Dame convent, Mount Zion, and Mount Scopus. Indeed, the final objective was the capture of the whole of Jerusalem, and this explains the major effort made by the Legion to hold Latrun, dominating the main road from Jerusalem to the sea. The Legion was successful at Latrun, but Jewish Jerusalem's communications with the coastal plain were restored by the building of the so-called "Burma Road," parallel to the main road and to its south.

The Legion failed to hold the "Triangle" of Arab settlement round Lod and Ramleh. Glubb has suggested that this would in no event have been possible—the Legion was too thin on the ground for such an operation. Nevertheless, the Legion reached both places and continued to hold them up to the First Truce.[15] They were lost when fighting began again on July 9. Glubb, for one, fully admits that it was the Arabs who decided to break the truce—he pins the blame on the Egyptian Prime Minister, Nokrashy Pasha.[16] The Egyptians were also chiefly to blame for the breaking of the second truce, which lasted from July 19 until October. The subsequent fighting led to the total ejection of the Egyptian Army from Palestine. On the West Bank, Arab positions were held—mainly because the Legion was concentrated in the southern half of the area and fought a purely defensive battle, while the Iraqi Army desisted from its efforts to reach the coast and held the northern half of the West Bank, centered on Nablus and Jenin.

Considering the whole campaign in retrospect, Glubb is bitter over what he saw as Britain's failure to honor her treaty with Jordan. At one stage he asked for intervention by the British Royal Air Force. It is not clear whether Jordanian appeals for help were responsible for the sole British air-sweep which resulted in several planes being shot down by an Israeli unit. Glubb certainly protested against the withdrawal of British officers seconded to the Legion on May 30. He was also angered by the British failure to send ammunition in the latter stages of the fighting. His criticism of the British Government was based throughout on the argument that the Legion was essentially defending Arab territory in 1948, and that the Anglo-Jordanian treaty provided for mutual aid under these circumstances.

Where the conduct of his campaign was concerned, Glubb emerges with credit. He secured Arab control of over one-third of Jerusalem, including the Old City and most of the Holy Places. He helped to stabilize a military situation which looked at one stage like deteriorating very badly indeed. He may have been luckier than he realized, for Israel's Prime Minister, David Ben Gurion, was only barely overruled by a majority of his Cabinet when he proposed essaying a final push, designed to drive the Legion out of the whole West Bank. Glubb, moreover, won the West Bank for his Jordanian masters, and this—as has already been indicated—was the Legion's principal objective.

The Legion fought well and, in the main, chivalrously—this was in keeping with the character of their commander.

Glubb received little gratitude. The men of the Legion were stoned and spat at in the streets of Ramallah and other West Bank towns. Glubb was himself accused of treachery by members of the Jordanian Cabinet.[18] Less than a decade later this man, who had shown total loyalty to the Hashemite rulers of Jordan, was ignominiously dismissed from his post and barely given time to pack his bags and to steal silently out of Amman, a victim of the machinations of President Nasser of Egypt, who was determined to destroy the young King Hussein's close relationship with Britain. However capricious an historian, Glubb was an able, courageous and honorable soldier.

It could be argued that Jordan, alone among existing Arab states, gained material benefit and prestige from the War, in the shape of the annexed West Bank and East Jerusalem. The country's performance was in stark contrast to what resulted from its disastrous participation in the war of 1967. If there is a political lesson to be drawn from the earlier intervention it must be that the Hashemites embarked on a policy which they have never jettisoned since. King Hussein has, indeed, paid lip-service to the ideal of Palestinian Arab independence and self-determination. But his own plan for turning Jordan into a "federal" state, with the Palestinians enjoying only local autonomy on the West Bank and Gaza Strip, was a reminder that the Jordanian claim to the area has never been truly abandoned. 'Abdallah believed a mini-Palestine to be unviable. His grandson, Hussein, must know in his heart that this is still so. Glubb, for his part, has never doubted this for a moment; it is the principal fact emerging from his account of the war of 1948.

FOOTNOTES

1. Christopher Sykes, *Cross-Roads to Israel*, Collins, 1965, and Bernard Postal and Henry W. Levy, *And the Hills Shouted for Joy*, David McKay, 1973.

2. Sir John Glubb, *A Soldier With the Arabs*, Hodder & Stoughton, 1957.

3. *Ibid.*; see also, Sir John Glubb, *Peace in the Holy Land*, Hodder & Stoughton, 1971, in which he produces a detailed plan for a solution of the Middle East conflict based on the post-1967 situation.

4. Sir John Glubb, *A Soldier With the Arabs, op. cit.*

5. Christopher Sykes, *op. cit.*

6. Sir John Glubb, *A Soldier With the Arabs, op. cit.*

7. Sir John Glubb, *Ibid.*

8. *Ibid.*

9. Sir John Glubb, *Peace in the Holy Land, op. cit.*

10. Bernard Postal and Henry W. Levy, *op. cit.*

11. *Ibid.*

12. Sir John Glubb, *Peace in the Holy Land, op. cit.*

13. Nataniel Lorch, in *One Long War: Arab vs. Jew Since 1920* (New York: Herzl Press, 1976).

14. Sir John Glubb, *A Soldier With the Arabs, op. cit.*

15. Yigal Allon, *Shield of David*, Weidenfeld & Nicolson, 1970.

16. Sir John Glubb, *A Soldier With the Arabs, op. cit.*

17. David Ben Gurion, *Ma'ariv* (Israel Daily), October, 1968.

18. Sir John Glubb, *A Soldier With the Arabs, op cit.*

King Hussein's Plan for a Federal Kingdom

Statement by King Hussein to correspondents and Jordanian officials and notables broadcast on Amman Home Service, 15 March 1972.

Excerpts:

. . . When the Arab armies entered Palestine in 1948, the Jordanian army . . . was able to save from Palestine that area which extends from Jenin in the north to Hebron in the south and from the Jordan river in the east to a point not more than 15 km from the coast in the west. It was also able to save the entire Holy City of Jerusalem and other areas outside the city walls — . . . which later became known as Arab Jerusalem . . .

After a short period of temporary administration in the West Bank, a group of leaders, notables and elders representing Palestinian Arabs who had emigrated from the occupied territories, considered joining the East Bank a patriotic and nationalist demand and a guarantee against Israeli dangers. They held two great historic meetings. The first was in Jericho on 1 December 1948 and the second in Nablus on 28 December 1948. These meetings were attended by the representatives of all the people — leader, thinkers, youth, the aged, workers and farmers — and their organizations.

Those present adopted resolutions calling on the late King 'Abdallah bin al-Hussein to take immediate steps to unify and merge the two banks in a single state under his leadership. The venerable king responded to the nation's call . . .

On 24 April 1950, the new Jordanian National Assembly — . . . — representing the two banks held an historic meeting which marked the first real step in modern Arab history towards Arab unity, . . . The meeting announced the unity and merger of the two banks in a single independent Arab state, a parliamentary monarchy known as the Hashemite Kingdom of Jordan.

•   •   •

The primary fact, the unity of the two banks represented day after day has been that the people on both banks are one and not two peoples . . .   In the sea of suffering the June [1967] catastrophe left behind, the objectives of the Jordanian State in the post-war era have been summarized as (1) valiant steadfastness in the face of the unabating and unending aggressions against the East Bank and (2) confident resolve to liberate the land, the people and the brothers in the West Bank . . .

But suddenly Jordan found itself face to face with a new catastrophe whose inevitable result, if it had been destined to come true, would have been the loss of the East Bank and the establishment of the situation needed to liquidate the Palestine issue once and for all on the ruins of the East Bank . . .*

Naturally Jordan had to stand up and deal with the imminent catastrophe . . . The dissension was crushed on the solid rock of national unity . . .

Throughout all this, since the June 1967 war and perhaps even before then, the Jordanian leaders have been thinking and planning for the future of the state . . .

Jordan understood the magnitude of the catastrophe which had befallen the Palestinian people. When the Zionist plot dispersed them, the sons of this people could not find in any country, Arab or non-Arab, the honorable and dignified life found by those who came to Jordan for shelter in 1948 and afterwards. Under the unity of the two banks in Jordan, the real Palestinian regrouping, the vast majority of the people, came to live on the two banks of the immortal river. The Palestinian found the sound framework within which he could work and move and found the real springboard for the desire of liberation and for the great hopes.

.   .   .

The first inevitable result of all the conditions prevailing in the Arab world — the dispersed ranks, scattered efforts, non-existent coordination, rivalry in establishing axes and camps, abandonment of the essence of the issue and its prerequisite, paying lip service to the issue once and exploiting it several times, . . . — has been the continued Israeli occupation of the West Bank of Jordan and other precious Arab territories. The second inevitable result has been a further intensification of the Palestinian people's suffering . . .

. . . it has been decided to move the country into a new phase which basically centers on liberation and which in essence responds to the aspirations and expectations of man in our country and incorporates his faith in the unity of his nation and his affinity for it. Furthermore, it is based on absolute adherence to the legitimate rights of the Palestinian people and aims at leading the Palestinian people to the point which will enable them to regain and safeguard these rights.

.   .   .

* The reference is to the 1970 Palestinian commandos' challenge to Jordan. *(Eds.)*

We wish to declare here that planning for the new phase has come as a blessed result of a long series of uninterrupted discussions and continued consultations which we have had with people's representatives, personalities, leaders and thinkers of both banks . . .

We are happy to declare that the bases of the proposed formula for the new phase are as follows:

(1) The Hashemite Kingdom of Jordan will become a united Arab Kingdom and will bear this name.

(2) The United Arab Kingdom will consist of two regions: (a) The Palestine region which will consist of the West Bank and any other Palestinian territories which are liberated and whose inhabitants desire to join it. (b) The Jordan region which will consist of the East Bank.

(3) Amman will be the central capital of the kingdom as well as capital of the Jordan region.

(4) Jerusalem will be the capital of the Palestine region.

(5) The Head of State will be the King, who will assume the central executive authority with the help of a central cabinet. The central legislative authority will be vested in the King and an assembly to be known as the National Assembly. Members of this assembly will be elected by direct secret ballot. Both regions will be equally represented in this assembly.

(6) The central judicial authority will be vested in a central supreme court.

(7) The Kingdom will have unified armed forces whose supreme commander is the King.

(8) The responsibilities of the central executive authority will be confined to affairs connected with the Kingdom as an international entity to guarantee the Kingdom's security, stability and prosperity.

(9) The executive authority in each region will be assumed by a governor-general from among its sons and a regional cabinet also from among its sons.

(10) Legislative authority in each region will be assumed by a council to be called the People's Council. It will be elected by a direct secret ballot. This council will elect the region's governor-general.

(11) The judicial authority in the region will be in the hands of the region's courts and nobody will have power over them.

(12) The executive authority in each region will assume responsibility for all the affairs of the region except such affairs as the constitution defines as coming under the jurisdiction of the central executive authority.

Naturally, the implementation of this formula and its bases must be according to the constitutional principles in force. It will be referred to the (Jordanian) National Assembly to adopt the necessary measures to prepare a new constitution.

The new phase which we look forward to will guarantee the reorganization of the Jordanian-Palestinian house in a manner which will provide it with more intrinsic power and ability to work to attain its ambition and aspirations .

Every attempt to cast doubt on any of this or discredit it is treason against the unity of the Kingdom, the cause, the people and the homeland . . .

The armed forces, which from the very beginning marched under the banner of the great Arab revolution and which included and will always include in its ranks the best sons of the people in both banks, will always be prepared to welcome more sons of both banks . . .

This Arab country is the country of the cause, just as it is from the Arabs and for all the Arabs . . . this country will continue on the path of sacrifice with strength and hope until it and its nation regain their rights and achieve their objectives.

This Arab country belongs to all, Jordanians and Palestinians alike. When we say Palestinians we mean every Palestinian throughout the world, provided he is Palestinian by loyalty and affinity . . .

Statement by Israel's Prime Minister Golda Meir in the Israel Knesset on the Hussein Plan, 16 March 1972.

Excerpts:

We have heard the speech of the King of Jordan. It does not bring tidings of peace, it is not founded on the principle of agreement and does not display readiness for negotiations . . .

In all this detailed plan, the term *peace* is not even mentioned and it is not based on the concept of agreement . . .

.   .   .

. . . Hussein announces the establishment of a United Arab Kingdom to consist of Jordan and Palestine. Of what does Palestine, according to him, consist? Palestine consists of the West Bank and of any Arab land that may be liberated . . . King Hussein makes no mention at all of the State of Israel as a country with which settlement and agreement have to be reached. The State of Israel, according to this conception, is nothing more than the result of a Zionist plot to dominate Palestine, and the task of Jordan and the Arabs is to liberate the soil of Palestine from this plot. He tries to give this goal of liberation historic dimension by recalling that as early as 1921, after the Balfour Declaration, it was Jordan's task "to save the West Bank from Zionist plots," and again, in 1948 "to save a large part of it and also succeeded in conquering the sacred place in the Old City of Jerusalem, thereafter known as Arab Jerusalem."

.   .   .

Had the King of Jordan seen fit to change the designation of the Kingdom of Jordan and to call it by the name of Palestine, the United Arab Kingdom or any other name, had he seen fit to introduce changes in the internal structure of his kingdom, if, after negotiations between us, we were to reach agreement, including the territorial issue — it would not then have been our concern to take a stand on internal matters which are within Jordan's sovereign competence and we would not have interfered in them . . . In the present case, however, the King is treating as his own property territories which are not his and are not under his control . . .

Resolution of the Israel Knesset on the Hussein Plan, 16 March 1972.

The Knesset has duly noted the Prime Minister's statement of 16 March 1972, regarding the speech made by the King of Jordan on 15 March 1972.

The Knesset has determined that the historic right of the Jewish people to the Land of Israel is beyond challenge.

The Knesset authorizes the Government of Israel to continue its policy in accordance with its basic principles, as approved by the Knesset on 15 December 1969, according to which: 'The government will steadfastly strive to achieve a durable peace with Israel's neighbors founded on peace treaties achieved by direct negotiations between the parties. Agreed, secure and recognized borders will be laid down in the peace treaties.

The peace treaties will assure [by] cooperation and mutual aid, the solution of any problem that might be a stumbling-block in the path to peace, and the avoidance of any aggression, direct or indirect.

Israel will continue to be willing to negotiate — without prior conditions from either side — with any of the neighboring states for the conclusion of a peace treaty. Without a peace treaty, Israel will continue to maintain in full the situation as established by the cease-fire and will consolidate its position in accordance with the vital requirements of its security and development.

The Knesset supports the Government in its endeavors to further peace by negotiating with the Arab states according to the resolutions of the Knesset.

Israel Government Statement on Negotiations with Jordan, 21 July 1974.

The Government will work towards negotiations for a peace agreement with Jordan.

The peace will be founded on the existence of two independent states only — Israel, with United Jerusalem as her capital, and a Jordanian-Palestinian Arab State, east of Israel, within borders to be determined in negotiations between Israel and Jordan. In this State, the specific identity of the Jordanians and the Palestinians will find expression in peace and good-neighborliness with Israel.

[We] have made it clear on more than one occasion in the Knesset that the Government of Israel will conduct negotiations with Jordan and adopt decisions at every stage of the negotiations, but will not conclude a peace agreement with Jordan that involves territorial concessions of parts of Judea and Samaria before we consult the nation in new elections, should one of the coalition factions demand this. This promise holds good and remains valid.

The Government of Israel has not taken any decision on the subject of an interim settlement with Jordan.

We shall continue — as we have done so far — to shoulder the responsibility of guaranteeing the normal life of the population of Judea and Samaria and the Gaza Strip. We shall continue to maintain the open-bridges policy. We shall not allow the emissaries of the terrorist organizations to gain a foothold among the population of the administered territories. We continue to regard Jordan as our natural neighboring partner in negotiations for peace on our Eastern border.

IV

Jordanian-Arab Relations

King 'Abdallah's Concept of a "Greater Syria"

By ISRAEL GERSHUNI

A NOTE: The idea of creating a "Greater Syria" – an entity that would include Syria, Lebanon, Jordan and Palestine, had its origins in the ambitions of the Hashemite dynasty of what was once the Kingdom of Hejaz. When the Sharif Hussein of Mecca, King of Hejaz and his three sons, 'Ali, Feisal and 'Abdallah, threw their support to the British against the Ottoman empire in what is known as the "Arab Revolt" of 1916, they considered this the opportunity to carve a vast Arab empire, whose units would be divided among themselves, out of the former Ottoman provinces. The idea of a unitary Muslim state extending across the Middle East, as existed in the time of the first Islamic caliphates, has been basic to Arab nationalist thinking in the twentieth century. The radical Ba'th (Resurrection) party envisages this state as a republic made up of local party branches (i.e. the various Arab states) closely linked together under a central body. The present ruling Syrian Ba'th party (branch) under President Assad has been contending to place Damascus (seat of the first Islamic caliphate) at the head of this future unitary Arab state. Iraq, whose leader, Nuri Sa'id had proposed his "Fertile Crescent" scheme – i.e., a union of Iraq, Syria, Lebanon, Palestine – in 1942-3, is currently ruled by the Iraqi Ba'th party (branch), which is challenging Syria's leadership. President Nasser of Egypt, although not a Ba'thist, considered that hegemony over the Middle East should be centered in Cairo. The announcement, on December 21, 1976 of a proposed merger of sorts between Syria and Egypt reflects, in some measure, the revival of the unsuccessful United Arab Republic (of Egypt and Syria) of 1958-61. King Hussein, for his part, has constantly reiterated his belief that the whole of Palestine is an integral part of "the Arab homeland."
                                                              Eds.

King 'Abdallah's plan for the creation of a "Greater Syria" was essentially political, intended as a Hashemite response—'Abdallah style—to the political conditions arising out of World War II.[1] It had a fully developed ideological base, but the plan itself was not a new one; it was merely a late political expression of an ideological approach that had crystallized in 'Abdallah's thinking since the end of the Arab Revolt. It found its first political expression in his futile attempt to restore a Hashemite government in Damascus to

Dr. Gershuni is a lecturer in the Department of Middle Eastern History at the University of Haifa.

replace that of his brother, Feisal, which collapsed in 1920.[2] However, 'Abdallah's concept of a ''Greater Syria'' clearly indicates that it was not confined to a particular time-span and it was not solely based upon favorable political conditions. It reflected, above all, his pragmatic political solution to the problem of the future of the Arab world, the ''Fertile Crescent'' and the Hashemite family. For 'Abdallah, his ''Greater Syria'' plan was an area of fulfillment, destined to concretize his whole complex of concepts and approaches and to translate them into political reality. His aim was to create a political framework for his basic approach to the image and nature of the Arab world in modern times, a framework that would forge a practical and concrete core for an already developed ideology; one that was waiting to become transformed from the potential into reality.

In his writings, 'Abdallah assigns to ''Greater Syria'' *(Suriah al Kubra)* the central and most important role in the Arab nation *(al-Ummah al- 'Arabiyah)*. Greater Syria is, to him, the historic and territorial center of the Arab people, with Damascus as its capital and seat of government. Restoration of Arab sovereignty to Syria and to Damascus is, he considers, the ultimate fulfillment of Arab nationalist aspirations and the crown of the modern Hashemite dream.

'Abdallah drew his idea of Greater Syria as a territorial concept from both history and the Arab Revolt. It had the historical boundaries that existed, 'Abdallah claims, when in Arab history Palestine, Transjordan, Syria and Lebanon comprised a single territorial entity *(Bilad al-Sham)* whose political and spiritual center was Damascus. Dismemberment of this entity therefore constituted a capricious act; a deviation that was antithetical to the desires of its population, its nature and its history.[3] To 'Abdallah, Greater Syria's natural boundaries gain additional legitimacy from the historical framework of *al-Sham,* and he identifies Greater Syria as the twentieth century version (mostly his own) of the old historic territorial framework. ''By the term Greater Syria,'' he writes, ''I refer to Syria in its natural boundaries *(Bilad al-Sham, sic),* considering the fact that Syria constitutes a single geographic, historical and national unit and is therefore a single Arab country, like Iraq for example.''[4] The inhabitants of Greater Syria were, in his view, the *Ahl al-Sham,* the people of the towns and the deserts of an area ranging from the Gulf of Aqaba to the Mediterranean Sea and from there to the Upper Euphrates.[5] Thus 'Abdallah gives Greater Syria *(Suriyah a-Kubra)* both a natural dimension (i.e., natural Syria *(Suriyah al-Tabi'iyah)* and a geographical dimension (geographical Syria—*Suriyah al-Jaghrafiyah)* as well as an historical dimension (characterized by the name *Bilad al-Sham).* All these terms appear in 'Abdallah's writings and speeches as synonyms for Greater Syria and their main thrust is to emphasize the unity of Greater Syria as a natural, accepted territorial unit.

To 'Abdallah, Greater Syria, under renewed Arab sovereignty, had been the main territorial objective of the Arab Revolt.[6] This Hashemite territorial concept had been crystallized by his contacts with the Syrian nationalists and the British before and during World War I. 'Abdallah writes that his father, King Hussein, had been ready to give up important parts of Iraq, which he had recognized as vital to the British, and also to recognize the right to independence of large areas of the Arabian Peninsula, but that he had always categorically refused to accept any compromise on the boundaries of Greater Syria, which he had envisioned as the vital nucleus for the creation of an independent Arab state with its center in Damascus.[7] The realization of a Greater Syria was thus the nub of Hashemite ambitions in the Arab Revolt. To relinquish this dream would, he felt, be tantamount to abandoning the Revolt's main territorial objective. 'Abdallah claims that the Revolt had succeeded (albeit only temporarily) in its territorial ambition. Greater Syria had earned the seal of legitimacy from the Syrian delegates at the National Syrian Congress of 1919.[8] Hence his often-made claim in the 1940s that "we came out of the Hejaz for the sake of Syria, Transjordan, Palestine and Lebanon, which are one entity—Greater Syria . . ."[9]

'Abdallah also constantly stressed the idea that the creation of a Greater Syria would serve to redress an historical injustice. It would restore, to Syria, its natural character and image which had been despoiled, for Syria was not Syria unless it consisted of the natural Greater Syria. "There is no such thing as Greater Syria or Lesser Syria," 'Abdallah declares "there is only one country, whose border on the west is the Mediterranean Sea; on the north—Turkey; on the east—Iraq, and on the south—Hejaz; and that country is Syria."[10] Syria in its current state was divided in its very essence; it is "a dismembered country,"[11] he complains, "and there is not the shadow of a doubt that this condition is abnormal and unnatural."[12]

This situation he asserts must be the concern of the entire Arab world and not of the Syrians alone. He sees the sorry state of the Arabs as a direct result of Syria's unnatural condition. It would end only with the "unification of all parts of Syria, which will bind up the wounds of all the Arab states."[13] "Arab society will feel itself secure only after the citizens of Syria decide to take the right path to fulfill their hopes, namely: unification of all parts of Syria . . ."[14] He speaks of the strong bond between Syria's condition and that of the Arab nation[15] and sees in the creation of Greater Syria a first stage in the solution of the Arab problem as a whole—a necessary stage prior to the realization of Arab national aspirations.[16]

By imposing an Arab nationalist dimension on his Greater Syria concept 'Abdallah transformed it into a national mandate which had to be sanctified by all the members of the Arab nation.[17] Its realization, he writes, had to be accompanied by a condemnation of every manifestation of separatism. Any division would prevent the fulfillment of pan-Arab national objectives. Throughout his life, 'Abdallah constantly attacked the regional separatist trends *(Iklimiyah)* prevalent in parts of Syria.[18] National, all-Syrian loyalty was always placed above local patriotism in his view of the spirit of the Arab Revolt. He writes:

> My father, Hussein, fought not for Lebanese independence, not for Syrian independence and not for Transjordanian independence. He fought for the Arab countries as one . . . His political program was clear: I want a state that will include Syria, Transjordan, Palestine and Lebanon.[19]

Syria, in its modern boundaries had no right to exist. 'Abdallah always referred to it as "northern Syria."[20]

'Abdallah's special relationship to Syria also had a strong emotional basis. He made a distinction between loyalty to the Arab nation *(qawm)* and a sense of belonging to the Syrian homeland *(watan)*. He regarded himself as a Syrian in every respect and therefore as entitled to struggle to mold the image of Syria.[21] For him Syria involved a deep emotional commitment. At the root of this emotional commitment was the perception of injustice, the result of the sad plight the homeland (i.e. Syria) found itself in. There was pain over the division of Syria and its subjugation by foreigners. There was the tragedy of political conditions, which had decreed Syria's dismemberment and had forced him to belong to but a limited segment of the Greater Syrian homeland.[22] 'Abdallah viewed this homeland's subjugation and its lack of political independence as tragic. "How can Syria achieve independence when it is dismembered?" he asks.[23] By its very nature, he felt, the current division prevented the realization of the homeland's independence.[24] To him this division was "the source of all evil." "Syria has no right to exist, divided,"[25] he claims, because "the life of the separatist is short, while the life of the [united] nation is eternal . . ."[26] 'Abdallah contrasts this condition with the stability of the other states in the Arab world, which, he argues, achieved their independence through their territorial completeness. He writes:

> In the aftermath of the Arab Revolt Iraq, Hejaz, the Nejd and Yemen acquired whole territories and as a result became independent. They did not remain dismembered and torn. But regions of al-Sham (al Diyar al-Shamiyah) remained fragmented, which denied them their natural unity in one homeland in a single territory maintaining in one region national, geographic and historical unity, assuring [al-Sham] its independence . . .[27]

Thus the creation of Greater Syria would necessarily relieve and eliminate the injustice of its irresponsible dismemberment.

'Abdallah's emotional tie to Syria also reveals an important ideological aspect of the Greater Syria concept. Syria's political independence and its very reason for existence, is conditional upon the elimination of its current dismemberment.

'Abdallah thus derived legitimacy for the Greater Syria concept from five basic sources: the need to restore Syria's historic image *(Bilad al-Sham);* realization of the Arab Revolt's territorial objectives; reunification of all the "natural segments"; fulfillment of the national pan-Arab goal and the need to redress the injustice perpetrated upon the Syrian homeland.

All his arguments were accompanied by a constantly reiterated claim to be Greater Syria's leader.

He had always regarded his departure from the Hejaz in 1920 as a commitment to restore Syria's honor, which had been diminished by the French conquest.[28] It was his duty, as a Hashemite, to restore Hashemite rule in Damascus. France and Britain had prevented him from attaining his goal in the 1920s but he never relinquished his dream of a return of Hashemite rule over all of Syria. Because he had fought for Greater Syria (in his view, his was the only such struggle in the Arab world), he felt he was the most worthy to be its leader.[29]

He always insisted that Transjordan was an indivisible part of Syria and that Syria was the Transjordanians' homeland, and that they identified themselves only with Syria. It was that part of the homeland which combined redemption, liberation and unification. Transjordan had opened its doors to the Syrian nationalists who fled from Syria following the French conquest in the 1920s. The (Jordanian) Arab Legion had actively assisted the Allies in the liberation of Syria from Vichy rule in World War II. Jordan did not accept its own right to exist, 'Abdallah maintained, except as a part of the Syrian homeland, devotedly nursing the dream of a return to Greater Syria.[30] Jordan was ready to relinquish its status as a separate political entity and to be absorbed into the Great Homeland when this Homeland was liberated and restored to independence. Because of Jordan's unique status in the Syrian homeland, its own leader was, inevitably, entitled to be the leader of the homeland.[31]

Interestingly enough, 'Abdallah argued that the British had promised him the leadership of Syria at his meeting with Churchill in March 1921 in Jerusalem. Churchill, he claims, had assured him that, with patience and avoidance of damage to French interests, he was destined to return to Damascus and to set up an Arab government there. "[Churchill] told me that France would not encourage Feisal's return to Syria. But if you manage your affairs properly and remain here [i.e. in Transjordan] and do not march into Syria, we are hopeful that France will drop its objection, will respond to the claims of justice and will, within a matter of months, return *Bilad al-Sham* to you . . ."[32] This constituted, 'Abdallah claims, his international sanction to be the head of Greater Syria.

'Abdallah's central claim to Greater Syria's leadership rested on the resolutions of the National Syrian Congresses of July 2, 1919 and March 8, 1920.[33] He felt that these two resolutions had established two principles which every loyal Syrian had to respect. They had specifically defined Syria's

natural boundaries as the sole legitimate boundaries of Greater Syria[34] and
they had elected his brother Feisal, as a Hashemite, to be the legal king of
Greater Syria.[35] 'Abdallah maintains that these resolutions had been democratically accepted by all the Syrian delegates[36] and had therefore to be honored; that they gave expression to the authentic wishes of the Syrian people.
The wanton French conquest alone had prevented the Syrian people from
carrying out the resolutions, whose implementation was only postponed to a
more propitious time. With Syria liberated from the yoke of foreign conquest
(i.e., once the British conquered Syria in World War II), the Syrian people
had to carry out the Congress resolutions. Rule had to be restored to a
descendent of the Hashemites: the only legitimate candidate being 'Abdallah.[37] His right to rule Syria therefore derived from the will of the Syrian
people, who were as ready to recognize him as their legitimate king[38] as they
had been to recognize a Hashemite king in the past.

His unswerving support for the Allies in World War II and the aid the
(Jordanian) Arab Legion had given to the British army in the course of their
conquest of Syria from Vichy France had earned him, 'Abdallah claimed, his
right to rule over "liberated" Syria. At a time when some of the Arab leaders
were facing both ways (i.e., were neutral) and some supported Nazi Germany
and Fascist Italy, he had consistently stood by the Allies in general and Britain
in particular—an added reason to support his claim to the leadership of
Greater Syria.

The Zionist threat to the Palestinian segment of Greater Syria gave added
strength to his claim. He always regarded the unification of Syria as a barrier
to the Zionist endeavor in Palestine. As the leader of Transjordan, Palestine's
neighbor, and as the spokesman for the Arabs of Palestine,[39] 'Abdallah was
more familiar with the Palestine problem than was any other Syrian leader. It
qualified him, he felt, to stand at the head of the unified Syrian state which,
among its other goals, would swallow up Zionism and strengthen the Arabs of
Palestine—the natives of Greater Syria.[40]

'Abdallah thus saw himself as the central (and perhaps the only) figure in
the struggle for Greater Syria. His right to its leadership was an essential
ingredient of its very creation, since both derived from identical sources. To
'Abdallah, then, Greater Syria was destined to be the necessary first stage in
the process of the realization of the ultimate goal of Arab unity (al Wahdah
al-'Arabiyah). His selection of Syria as the primary arena for the realization
of pan-Arab unity sprang from his nationalist view of what constituted the
historical area of al-Sham, the heart and soul of the Arab nation.

Although the concept of Greater Syria came into being immediately following the Arab Revolt and was used by 'Abdallah to justify the existence of such
an entity, and to give legitimacy to his claim to its leadership, it was, basically, a concept that developed during the political struggles of the 1940s.
'Abdallah's scheme conflicted, in many respects, with the original Hashemite

concept of the creation of a single, unified Arab state under Hashemite rule and from this conflict sprang many of the contradictions in 'Abdallah's thinking. He ignored the local national entities—the Syrians, the Lebanese, the Palestinians and even the Jordanians. His scheme also conflicted, in the final analysis, with an important premise he believed in — the overall unity of the Arab nation. For pan-Arab unity is a concept which negates the existence of all particularist tendencies and is irreconcilable with the creation of a separate Arab state such as Transjordan, for which 'Abdallah himself was responsible.

Few of the Hashemite's supporters in the Fertile Crescent—particularly in Jordan, Syria and Palestine—openly supported 'Abdallah's Greater Syria scheme. Most of the Arab states were decidedly opposed to it. Lebanon categorically refused to be absorbed into a giant Muslim state. The leaders of the Nationalist bloc who ruled Syria at the time refused to transform their state into a province of a great state whose center would be Amman. The Egyptians were opposed to any subversive program that would strengthen the Hashemite bloc in the Arab world. The Saudis were opposed to anything that might serve to strengthen their traditional enemies, the Hashemites—who might not yet have abandoned their hopes of reconquering the Hejaz and restoring it to Hashemite rule. Even the Hashemites in Iraq, under the leadership of premier Nuri al-Sa'id (who was developing an Iraqi-Hashemite plan for a federative union of the Arab world) remained aloof. The Arab League and its Secretary, 'Abd al-Rahman Azzam, publicly expressed their unequivocal opposition. Britain, 'Abdallah's ally and main supporter, was unenthusiastic, fearing a hostile reaction from France and anxious to avoid a confrontation with the Arab League. As a result of his bitter conflict with the other members of the Arab League over the Palestine issue during 1948-1950, 'Abdallah lost his appeal to large segments of the Arab nationalist movement. His plan for the creation of a Greater Syria died with his assassination in 1951.

FOOTNOTES

1. These changed conditions included the Eden Declaration of May 29, 1941 to the effect that Britain was ready to help unite the Arab world and the Roosevelt-Churchill Atlantic Charter. These declarations convinced 'Abdallah that Britain would support him if he presented a political program which backed the British interests in the area.

2. See, 'Abdallah, *al-Takmilah min Mudhakkirat hadrat Sahib al-Jalalah al-Hashemiyah 'Abd Allah ibn al-Husayn*, (Amman, 1951), p. 39.

3. *Ibid.*, pp. 33-43; Khayr al-Din al-Zarkali, *'Aaman fi Amman* (Cairo, 1925), pp. 19, 28; *Suriyah al-Kubra al-Kitab al-U'rduni al-Abyad (White Book)*, (Amman, 1947), pp. 75-9; 'Abd Allah, *Mudhakkirati* (Jerusalem, 1945), pp. 251-4.

4. *White Book*, p. 252.

5. *Ibid.*, p. 75.

6. *White Book*, pp. 75-8; E. Wright, "The Greater Syria Project in Arab Politics," *World Affairs*, July, 1951, pp. 318-21; also the *Economist* (London), Jan. 21, 1950, p. 142.

7. 'Abdallah, *Memoirs*, pp. 101-2; 'Abd Allah, *Takmilah*, pp. 37-41.

8. See below.

9. 'Abd Allah, *Takmilah*, pp. 38-9.

10. Patrick Seale, *The Struggle for Syria*, (London, 1965), p. 13.

11. *White Book*, p. 252.

12. *al-Hayat*, (Lebanon), Feb. 18, 1958. Muhammad Shukeir, aide to Lebanese premier Riad al-Sulh reported on secret conversations conducted between 'Abdallah and al-Sulh in Amman, July 14-15, 1951. 'Abdallah tried to convince al-Sulh to support his plans for an inter-Arab federation. An English translation of the *al-Hayat* article is in the *Jewish Observer and Middle East Review* (London), July 25, 1958. Cf. A.H.H. Abidi, *Jordan—A Political Study, 1948-1957* (London, 1965), p. 79.

13. 'Abd Allah, *Takmilah*, pp. 34-5.

14. *Ibid.*, p. 33.

15. *al-Hayat*, Feb. 18, 1958.

16. See, "Islam, Arabism and King 'Abdallah of Jordan's Unity Plan" in Kemal H. Karpat, ed., *Political and Social Thought in the Contemporary Middle East*, (London, 1968), pp. 250-4.

17. *al-Hayat, op. cit.*

18. *al-Zarkali*, p. 19.

19. Patrick Seale, p. 13.

20. *White Book*, p. 253.

21. 'Abdallah's attitude to Syria as his homeland was forcibly expressed in all his writings.

22. *Takmilah*, pp. 33-4.

23. *Memoirs*, p. 256.

24. *Ibid.* pp. 256-7.

25. *Ibid.*

26. *Ibid.*, p. 256.

27. *White Book*, p. 76.

28. *Takmilah*, pp. 33-9.

29. *White Book*, pp. 53, 64-5, 239; *al-Zarkali*, p. 15. All the arguments were accepted as basic principles in Transjordanian diplomacy in the 1940s. They were confirmed by the Jordanian parliament (see, *White Book*, pp. 64-70).

30. *White Book*, pp. 99-100; *Takmilah*, pp. 19, 49; also, B. Toukan, "Transjordan, Past, Present and Future," in *Royal Central Asian Journal*, January 1944, Vol. 31, p. 253.

31. *White Book*, pp. 64-70, 84, 239, 252; *Memoirs*, pp. 168-70; *Takmilah*, pp. 39-41.

32. *Takmilah*, p. 39; *White Book*, p. 64-6, 76. This claim has no historical justification.

33. The 2 July, 1919 resolution was transmitted to the King-Crane Commission. The 7-8 March, 1920 resolution was a declaration of Syria's independence. For the text see, Sati' al-Husri, *Yawm Maysalun* (Beirut, 1947), pp. 246-8, 261-5.

34. 'Abdallah's delineation of Syria's boundaries are those cited in the first resolution. See Sati' al-Husri, p. 246.

35. This is also accurate. See resolution of March 8, 1920. *Ibid.*, p. 264.

36. 'Abdallah quotes the two resolutions correctly.

37. Here 'Abdallah ignores the central issue of the resolution. Feisal was selected as a Hashemite but the resolution also states that the Congress chose him for his deeds above his lineage. See, Sati' al-Husri, p. 264.

38. *White Book*, pp. 64-6, 234-5. 'Abdallah's statement is unfounded. The Syrian, Lebanese and Palestinian nationalists were implacably opposed to his ruling over Syria. See, M. Khalil, *The Arab States and the Arab League* (Beirut, 1962), Vol. 11, pp. 28-41. Syria and Lebanon opposed him actively within the framework of the Arab League, but 'Abdallah always insisted

that his plan did not conflict with the existence of the Arab League but on the contrary, aimed at rallying and unifying the Arab world. (See, *White Book,* pp. 234-6).

39. 'Abdallah saw the solution to the Zionist problem within the framework of Greater Syria. He proposed granting autonomy to the Jewish minority in Palestine within this framework. The autonomous Jewish minority would, he felt, carry little weight indeed within the large Arab majority (the populations of Lebanon, Syria, Jordan and Palestine). Greater Syria would overwhelm any Zionist ambitions.

40. *White Book,* p. 252.

Jordan's Place in the Arab World

By DANIEL DISHON

The basic theme that runs through Jordan's relations with the rest of the Arab world was set long before Jordan (and most of the other Arab countries)· became independent: it is the tension between the desire to uphold the traditional posture and image of the Hashemite dynasty, dating back to World War I, and yet to "belong" among, and be accepted by, the Arab regimes formed after World War II as no less patriotic and nationalist than they are.

The elements of Hashemite tradition which were later to have a bearing on Jordan's place in inter-Arab politics may be listed as follows:

• A traditional world view stressing the belief system and values of Islam (as is befitting to the dynasty so long entrusted with the custodianship of Mecca), and the paternalistic nature of authority and power.

• A firm belief that the real roots of Arab nationalism are to be found in the Great Arab Revolt launched in 1916 at the initiative of the Hashemite dynasty;[1] an equally firm belief that the area this dynasty was destined to rule (i.e. "The Arab Kingdom") encompassed the entire "Fertile Crescent" (and, in the original conception, at least part of what is now Saudi Arabia); the unshaken conviction that the heritage of the Great Revolt remains as valid and relevant today as it was at any time since 1916.

• Stemming from the above, the view that the issue of Palestine was a special, immediate and direct concern of the Hashemites—more so than of any other Arab regime.

• Reliance on the West (first Britain, later the United States) as the outside power most likely to be in sympathy with Hashemite domestic and Arab policies.

On many occasions, both 'Abdallah and Hussein came perilously close to compromising one or the other of the above components of the Hashemite image in order to make themselves more "acceptable" in the Arab world, to avoid the *malaise* of isolation and, often, to allay the domestic pressures

Dr. Dishon is a Senior Research Associate at Tel Aviv University's Shiloah Center for Middle Eastern and African Studies, and the editor of *Middle East Record,* the Center's Yearbook.

resulting from flying in the face of fashionable Arab trends. But in each instance, they reverted to the traditional Hashemite policy before their deviation from it threatened to become irreversible.

During and immediately after World War II, the Hashemite view, as reformulated to suit the circumstances of the day, was that the dynasty's post-war objective should be to draw Syria into the Hashemite orbit and make Damascus the Hashemite capital. This was viewed as an act of restoration, rather than a new departure—a restoration, that is, of the shortlived (1918-1920) Hashemite rule in Syria, rudely (but only "temporarily") interrupted by the French mandate. Hashemite restoration in Syria was to be complemented by the inclusion of, or overlordship over, Lebanon and Palestine.

As these concepts evolved in the 1940s, a certain rivalry developed between the Iraqi and the Jordanian branch of the Hashemite dynasty. (King 'Abdallah's brother Feisal had been compensated for the loss of Damascus in 1920 by the gift of the Iraqi throne.) The Iraqi branch, advised (indeed, guided) by the energetic soldier-politician, Nuri Sa'id, proposed the "Fertile Crescent" scheme which was to unite Iraq with Jordan, Syria, Lebanon and Palestine. King 'Abdallah of Jordan promoted the idea of a "Greater Syria" (a "natural," or "geographical Syria") covering the same area but excluding Iraq (with which a loose form of union was envisaged for a later stage).

Both schemes envisaged Hashemite rule for the entire northern Arab areas rather than the establishment of separate states in Syria and Lebanon.

It is against this background that the political front lines in Jordan's inter-Arab relations were drawn at the inception of the post-war era. On the one side, there were the two Hashemite monarchies, each bent on expansion, competing with each other but, by and large, remaining united against the rest of the Arab world. Ranged against them were two other Arab dynasties, that of the Saudis and of King Farouk's in Egypt, each acting from motives of its own but both equally determined to deny the Hashemites any aggrandizement, enhanced standing or added strength. The Saudis were at that time, primarily motivated by the memories of the wars of the twenties, when they had driven the Hashemites out of their ancestral domain in Hejaz and formed what is present-day Saudi Arabia. It was Hashemite *revanchisme* which they still feared, twenty odd years later. Farouk of Egypt, for his part, felt that the consolidation of a Hashemite bloc across the entire area of the "Fertile Crescent" would bar his country from exercising any influence in the Asian part of the Arab world. Though pan-Arabism became Egypt's proclaimed policy (almost its obsession) only in 1952, after Farouk's deposition by Nasser, Farouk was not unmoved by the pan-Arab view and, during World War II, began envisaging a much broader role for Egypt in all-Arab affairs. Hashemite ambitions therefore clashed with his own.

The articles of the Arab League (first worked out in 1944 and finalized in 1945) constituted, in some measure, a compromise between the Hashemites and their adversaries. They were meant to—and they did—ensure the sovereignty and independence of Syria and Lebanon against Hashemite claims. But they did not entirely bar the Hashemites from attempting to draw Syria—once it became independent—into a union, for they contained a clause to the effect that "those Arab states desirous of . . . stronger ties than those specified by this covenant, have a right to conclude such agreements between themselves . . . as they desire" (Article 9).

In the years between the creation of the Arab League and the establishment of the State of Israel (1945-1948), the achievement of "Greater Syria" remained the principal objective of Jordan's inter-Arab policy, and was forcefully reiterated by 'Abdallah in 1946 and 1947. In the meantime, however, Syria was consolidating its own sovereign entity and its institutions, with the support of both Egypt and Saudi Arabia.

'Abdallah's attitude toward Palestine was part and parcel of his concept of "geographical Syria". In the 1930s he had demanded that all of Palestine should come under Jordanian rule, with "safeguards" for the Jewish settlers. Later the prospect of aggrandizement made him tacitly approve of the Palestine partition scheme, provided that the Arab area of Palestine became part of Jordan. When it did, in 1948, the fury of almost the entire Arab world was unleashed against Jordan. Not only had Jordan—and Jordan alone—gained from what became known in Arab writing, as "the Palestine catastrophe"; not only had Jordan ridden roughshod over "the decisions of the Palestinian people," but it had also, in an underhand sort of way, acquired a somewhat broader base from which to launch the eventual, and still hoped for, realization of "Greater Syria." Indeed, in 1950 and 1951, 'Abdallah made new personal attempts to win over the leaders of Syria and Lebanon to his concept. Both approaches failed.

For a while, the Arab League considered the expulsion of Jordan. Gradually, as established facts on the West Bank became recognized as such, and the domestic political upheavals in Lebanon, Jordan and Egypt (1949-1952) deflected all-Arab opinion from the Palestine issue, the furor died down. By then, 'Abdallah was no longer alive. His successors were not to revive the "Greater Syria" idea as an active element in their inter-Arab program. However, for another twenty years, relations with Syria remained tense at most times, and distrustful throughout.

Hussein was proclaimed King in August 1952, within several weeks after the coup d'état by which Nasser ended royal rule in Egypt. The upsurge of Nasserist ideology, the dangers of Nasserist subversion and the drive of Nasser's Arab policies were to be the main challenges to Hussein's rule both domestically and in Jordan's inter-Arab standing until the Six Day War in 1967. For the entire period, Jordan's Arab politics were essentially defensive: a combination of defiance in upholding the traditional Hashemite concepts, and of somewhat apologetic attempts to demonstrate that Jordan's brand of

Arabism was no less Arab, no less modern and no less patriotic and nationalist than that of any regime following the Nasserist pattern.

The Baghdad Pact crisis, the Egyptian-Syrian Union and the period of Arab division into "progressives" and "reactionaries" (1966 and early 1967) were peaks of inter-Arab tension for Jordan, as Hussein tried to avert, or at least survive, the thrust of Nasserism.

In inter-Arab terms (i.e., disregarding, here, its global implications) the Baghdad Pact assumed the significance of a struggle for ascendancy in the Arab world between "revolutionary," anti-Western Egypt and conservative, pro-Western Iraq. The traditional anti-Hashemites—Syria and Saudi Arabia—sided with Egypt. When Jordan gave signs of wishing to join the Pact, not only was it completely isolated from all other Arab states except fellow-Hashemite Iraq, but it also faced, at the end of 1955 and the beginning of 1956, a grave domestic crisis fanned (by overt and covert means) by Egypt and Syria.

Under these pressures, Jordan abandoned the idea of joining the Baghdad Pact and professed re-alignment with the other major Arab states, but evaded a move (in 1956) by Egypt, Syria and Saudi Arabia to be drawn into an "Arab Covenant" with them. Hussein countered by proposing a meeting of *all* Arab heads of state, i.e. including Iraq, now a member of the Pact which was named after its capital city, and Lebanon, known as neutral between the pro-Western and pro-Nasserist camps. In such a forum, Jordan would not be isolated. As Hussein had probably foreseen, the meeting never convened, and Jordan was able to claim credit for an attempt to further the all-Arab cause without having to compromise its basic positions. (As was so often the case before and after, the proclaimed *rationale* of both schemes was to "form a single Arab line of defense" against Israel.) By means of a series of bilateral understandings of studiedly vague content concluded separately with Syria, Egypt, Lebanon, Iraq and Saudi Arabia during the spring of 1956, Hussein demonstrated his ostensible preference for Arab—rather than Western—ties. He projected an image of not siding with any Arab party in particular, and did not commit Jordan to any binding obligation.

The 1956 Suez crisis and, later, the Suez war and the accompanying wave of nationalist and anti-Western feeling, forced on Hussein a further retreat from earlier positions. He had to resign himself to letting Nabulsi assume the premiership. In January 1957, Jordan signed the so-called "Arab Solidarity Pact" with Syria, Saudi Arabia and Egypt and in the belief that it had thus secured an alternative source to replace the British subsidy, abrogated the Anglo-Jordanian Treaty in March.

But the same year witnessed two reversals in the opposite direction. With the dismissal of the Nabulsi government in April and the suppression of disloyal elements in the army, Hussein resumed—and thereafter kept—personal control of the government. Saudi Arabia developed that suspicion of

Nasser's aims, policies and methods which remained central to its inter-Arab policies as long as Nasser was alive, and became Jordan's ally. Thus, Hussein's reassertion of the traditional Hashemite course in 1957, while condemned by Egypt and Syria, was applauded by both Saudi Arabia and Iraq.

In the following year, events in Arab countries other than Jordan again placed Jordan's regime in supreme danger. The union between Syria and Egypt, in February 1958, was seen as the triumph of Nasserism not only in the two countries now constituting the United Arab Republic (UAR), but in the Arab world at large. It gave rise to a wave of messianic pan-Arab expectations which flooded the principal Arab countries and did not stop at Jordan's border. Hussein's immediate reaction was to fall back on Hashemite solidarity. A scheme for a federal union between Jordan and Iraq was hastily devised. Before either side could do much more than proclaim it, the Hashemite monarchy in Iraq was overthrown by Abd al-Karim Qàssem (July 1958) who was at first—in the emotion-laden atmosphere of that year—expected to join the UAR. Jordan now seemed surrounded by enemies on all sides (except in the direction of Saudi Arabia) and the Nasserites confidently predicted that the fall of the Hashemites in Iraq would bring down Hussein as well. British troops were called in to shore up Hashemite rule. Their presence did indeed help Hussein to survive but also made conspicuous to what extent Jordan was then sailing against the prevailing winds.

The British units were not needed for long. By one of the ironic turns so characteristic of inter-Arab politics, it was Iraq's new ruler, Qassem, who emerged as Nasser's great rival and adversary. As a result, both Qassem and Nasser avoided attitudes which might have pushed Hussein into the other's camp and Jordan was, on the whole, able to "sit out"—more quietly than the anxieties of 1958 seemed to presage—the period of the Egyptian-Syrian union until its break-up in 1961. Even the assassination of Jordan's Prime Minister Hazza' al-Majali in August 1960, engineered from Damascus by anti-Hashemite Jordanian exiles collaborating with UAR intelligence operatives in Syria, did not have the destabilizing effect its planners had hoped to effect. It did, however, during the remainder of 1960, produce one of the peaks of Syrian-Jordanian tension, with Jordanian troops concentrating on the Syrian border and a spate of mutual propaganda warfare pouring forth of particular acerbity. Tension died down after a while. In mid-1961, Jordan's participation in an inter-Arab force, formed to protect newly independent Kuwait against Iraqi claims to her territory showed that a measure of "respectability" had been accorded to Jordan at that time.

The break-up of the UAR was welcomed by Jordan as a "blessed up-surge." Hussein was the first Arab ruler to accord recognition to the reconstituted Syrian government (a haste for which he paid by Egypt's severance of diplomatic relations with Jordan for a while). However, Jordan was not now alone: Iraq, Saudi Arabia, and Lebanon (as well as a number of more peripheral Arab countries) followed suit. Nasserism was at one of its low points and Jordan, breathing more freely, found itself, for once, aligned with the majority of Arab League member states. Hussein felt that the policies he had so tenaciously clung to had been vindicated. In the ongoing propaganda battle with Nasser, it was now Jordan which was on the offensive and Nasser—here as elsewhere—who was on the defensive. Yet, at this juncture, too, Hussein was careful to leave open the prospect of a reconciliation with Nasser.

A new period in inter-Arab affairs came in late in 1963. Nasser resumed the initiative, making a determined bid to reassert his ascendancy. The outward sign was the first Arab summit conference ("the meeting of Kings and Presidents") in Cairo in January 1964. Under the slogan, "unity of ranks rather than unity of aims," the new Nasserist approach was to make it possible for the Arabs to "close ranks" even though the political and ideological "aims" of each regime might remain different and indeed divergent. Such a concept made it possible for Jordan to take its place alongside regimes of a different character. Though inter-Arab controversies were not altogether stilled by the "summit spirit" Jordan, at this juncture, fitted into the general pattern.[4]

Late in 1965, however, Nasser reverted to true form. Only "the Arab *revolutionary* force," he said in a major speech, was capable of the "ultimate achievement of Arab hopes." A period of polarization set in, during which the self-styled "progressive" regimes dissociated themselves with increasing emphasis from those whom they called "reactionary." While Egypt, Syria, Iraq, Algeria and Republican Yemen[5] formed the "progressive" camp, Jordan and Saudi Arabia constituted the core of the opposing conservative bloc. The "progressives" made Jordan the symbol of outworn forms of government and, more particularly, of servility to Imperialism. "Britain's son-in-law," and "the agent King" were the two most common epithets used with reference to Hussein[6] in the media of the "progressive" countries. The PLO, led at that time by Ahmed Shuqaiyri but actually under Egyptian tutelage, was used by Nasser as an instrument of his anti-Jordanian policy (both in fomenting domestic unrest and in fostering anti-Hashemite sentiment in other Arab countries). Jordan and Saudi Arabia drew closer together—Jordan now identified more closely with the latter over the issues of the Yemeni civil war and the Arabian Peninsula in general, and both had the overt, or covert, sympathy of countries like Tunisia, Kuwait, Morocco, Sudan and (pre-Qadhafi) Libya.

The division into two camps threatened to split the Arab League into rival bodies. Before this could happen, the Six Day War shattered the pattern with one blow. During the weeks of crisis preceding the outbreak of hostilities, Hussein had, by May 30, 1967, effected a public reconciliation with Nasser and Shuqaiyri. On June 5, he joined the war, impelled by the drive to afford ultimate proof of Hashemite patriotism, trustworthiness and Arabdom. It cost him the West Bank — but it placed Jordan back in the Arab fold. Until Nasser's death in September 1970, Hussein remained his closest Arab ally. For these three years, Egyptian and Jordanian policies were carefully aligned over such issues as U.N. Security Council Resolution 242, the Jarring Mission, the Rogers Plan, and the U.S. initiative which led to the Suez Canal cease fire of August 1970. The latter, however, triggered (though it did not cause) the Jordanian civil war of September of that year. The "agent king" now became "the butcher of the Palestinians" and Jordan became the outlaw of the Arab world. Syria had invaded northern Jordan to intervene on the side of the *fedayeen*, but withdrew before the fire of Jordanian tanks, the visible threat of an Israeli counter-concentration, and the implied threat of United States intervention.[7] Libya and Kuwait discontinued the financial subsidies they had undertaken to pay to Jordan in the wake of the Six Day War. Saudi Arabia, for its part, continued to pay its share, but Saudi political support of Jordan was noticeably qualified during this period.

While the remaining strongholds of the *fedayeen* were slowly being ground into dust in 1971, Jordan went through one of its worst periods of isolation. But Hussein viewed the struggle as one for the very survival of Hashemite rule in its own heartland and would not let consideration of his country's inter-Arab standing deter him until the business in hand was completed.

When it was, and Jordan began to emerge from the political wilderness it was, surprisingly enough, the old arch-foe—Syria—which drew Jordan to his side. The Syrian-Jordanian border, closed in 1971, was reopened in 1972; diplomatic relations were resumed the following year. The muted, unpublicized *rapprochement* burst on the scene in the 1973 war. Jordan had been Egypt's principal partner in the 1967 war (during which the Syrians had assumed a largely passive stance and had been unwilling, even in war-time, to cooperate with Jordan). In 1973, however, Syria was Egypt's major ally while Jordan was a minor participant—and it participated on the *Syrian* front, rather than on its own.

Since then the deepening of the special Syrian-Jordanian relationship has been the central feature of Hussein's inter-Arab policies.[8] In most ways, it must be regarded as a response to Syrian initiatives. President Assad has been active, since the 1973 war, in extending Syrian influence into the neighboring countries of Lebanon and Jordan (and also of Palestine, symbolized, for him, by the PLO). Assad has pursued, that is, a policy of "Greater Syria in reverse," i.e. of putting together a sphere of influence coinciding with the old "Greater Syria" group of countries but now to be directed *from* Damascus (instead of *at* Damascus from the outside, as in the past).

The question is, however, why Hussein cooperates in a scheme which, at least by implication, makes both Palestine and Jordan appear as southern Syria. Several answers come to mind. There is the common Syrian-Jordanian disappointment with Egypt's post-1973 policy which both Hussein and Assad have interpreted as being narrowly Egyptian and unmindful of all-Arab interests. There is the strong bond of common strategic interests vis-à-vis Israel,[9] which has existed all along but had not been translated into action in earlier years because of the prevailing political tension. There is, reportedly, a good personal *rapport* between Hussein and Assad—and in two so highly personalized regimes this is a factor that must be taken into account. There is the constant feature of Jordanian Arab policy of avoiding isolation, if and when possible, and therefore of grabbing whatever hand is extended. But beyond all these factors there was (apparently since 1973) the expectation[10] that Syria might be instrumental in limiting the aspirations and capabilities of the PLO and in reinstating Jordan as a claimant to the West Bank.[11]

Today, Jordan and Syria speak in terms of "one country, one people, one army," and of moves, "as soon as possible" toward a "higher level of integration." A multitude of joint committees has sprung up, dealing with trade, industry, transportation, the unification of textbooks and syllabuses etc., presided over by a Joint Leadership Council consisting of Hussein and Assad themselves. It should be noted, however, that all these have coordinative functions; none of them has supra-national authority. It is obvious that so far at least, there has been a clear limit—set by Hussein—to the Syrian-Jordanian "integration." Nothing is to be done that would constitute an erosion of ultimate Jordanian sovereignty. Nothing should take place which would make "integration" irreversible.

In other words, the essential elements of "Hashemite tradition" listed at the beginning of this article are being guarded as jealously today as they were when independent Jordan first set forth on its path—precarious and marked by so many dramatic turns—through the intricacies of inter-Arab politics.

FOOTNOTES

1. The fact that Britain had a part in it is today being played down as much as possible, by those setting forth the Hashemite view.

2. These are King Farouk's words; in present day parlance this would be termed "the rights of the Palestinians."

3. Talal's reign was too brief to constitute a period of its own in Jordan's inter-Arab relations. It is noteworthy only for an ineffective attempt by the Iraqi Hashemites to unite the two crowns.

4. An anti-Jordanian time-bomb was, however, also planted at that period: the establishment, in 1964, of the PLO at the behest of the summit conference.

5. This was the period of the civil war in Yemen.

6. Then still married to British-born Princess Muna.

7. President Assad, then Syria's Defense Minister, was opposed to the invasion. In the wake of its failure, he took over supreme power in Syria in November 1970. His known opposition to the invasion may later have helped to achieve the Syrian-Jordanian *rapprochement* of 1972.

8. Another important feature of the last three years has been the strengthening of Jordan's ties with all the minor Arab principalities on the Persian Gulf shore, from Kuwait to Oman.

9. Topography makes it apparent that any Israel war-time thrust along the line of the Syrian-Jordanian border could with equal ease be turned into either an outflanking movement into the Damascus area or into northern Jordan.

10. Possibly even implicit or explicit promises—but this we do not know and may not know for a long time.

11. It must be remembered that even though the *formal* recognition of the PLO as "sole legitimate representative of the Palestinians" was only resolved at Rabat in October 1974, it had been accepted almost a year before, at the Algiers summit conference of 1973, and Hussein had read the writing on the wall in time.

V

Jordan in the International Community

Jordan's Relations with the United States

By ROBERT W. STOOKEY

The Hashemite Kingdom of Jordan became independent in March 1946, and simultaneously concluded a treaty of alliance with Great Britain. When King 'Abdallah bin Hussein, who had ruled Transjordan since 1922 under British mandate, requested United States recognition of his new regime no prompt response was forthcoming. America had no material interests in the country, and considered that it remained a British area of responsibility. The matter was moreover bound up with the future of the Palestine Mandate, over which America and Britain had contrasting views. One current of Zionism demanded the opening of Transjordan to Jewish settlement, an opinion that received some support on the floor of the Senate.[1] Only after the Arab-Israel War of 1948 and the seizure of the West Bank territory by Jordan's forces did the United States open formal relations with the expanded State. An American legation was opened in Amman in February 1948, although a minister was not appointed until a full year later; the mission was raised to Embassy status in August 1952.

The relationship thus cautiously embarked upon developed slowly into an important one for the United States and a vital one for Jordan's rulers. It has passed through several distinct phases. Until 1957 the United States contributed modestly to the economic progress of the Kingdom, while leaving to Britain the protection of Western political and strategic interests. During the ensuing decade America served as Jordan's principal source of political, economic and military support, in the interest both of preserving the fragile peace in the Middle East and of deterring the spread of communism and Soviet influence in the region. Since 1967 the survival of Jordan's monarchy has continued to be an objective of American policy, and relations between the two countries have remained sufficiently close to withstand severe tests.

Since the early 1950s Jordan's army, then financed, trained and commanded by the British, has been an essential factor in preserving the Hashemite regime against the revolutionary currents sweeping the Arab East. Incorporation of the West Bank in the Kingdom and the granting of full Jordanian citizenship both to its native residents and to refugees from other parts of Palestine, tripled the country's small population and introduced a politically

Dr. Stookey is Research Associate at the Center for Middle Eastern Studies at the University of Texas at Austin. He was a member of the United States Foreign Service, 1946-1968 and has contributed articles to numerous scholarly publications. His books include *America and the Arab States: An Uneasy Encounter*, John Wiley, 1975. He is preparing a book on *The Yemen Arab Republic: Growth of a Political Culture*, and an English translation of *Langages arabes du présent*, by Jacques Berque, for the University of Texas Press.

volatile component differing sharply from the East Bankers, who were mainly villagers and Bedouin strongly attached to the royal house. West Bank political leaders were receptive to the anti-imperialist, pan-Arab and socialist ideologies preached from Damascus, Cairo, and later from Baghdad. Many tended to accept the thesis that Jordan of itself was not a viable state and should be merged with her Arab neighbors, at the sacrifice of the Hashemite dynasty, in a broad Arab entity strong enough to face up to Israel. King 'Abdallah had consistently pursued the aim of a Greater Syria under his crown, composed of the Syrian Republic, Transjordan, and the Arab portions of Palestine. As a tactic toward this goal he was initially willing to reach some modus vivendi with the State of Israel. This ambition was distasteful to general Arab opinion and particularly to the Palestinians, one of whom murdered the King at the door of al-Aksa Mosque in Jerusalem on July 20, 1951.

'Abdallah's son, Talal, who succeeded to the throne, chafed at Jordan's increasingly unpopular dependence upon Britain, which covered the country's chronic deficit. He endeavored to respond to the new coloration of opinion in his country's expanded population by replacing his father's patriarchal style of rule with more liberal parliamentary forms, and attempting to mend relations with other Arab states. Incurably afflicted with mental illness, he reigned less than a year. A regency council exercised the royal prerogatives until his son Hussein reached his majority at age seventeen and was sworn in as King on May 2, 1953.

The young king's prospects were bleak. His poverty-stricken country had no direct outlet to the Mediterranean; its only port, Aqaba, was isolated from normal sea lanes and lacked modern communication with the major centers of population. The market for the country's agricultural cash crop had disappeared with the formation of Israel. His armed forces were far too small to man the 400-mile border with Israel, across which raids and counter-raids were increasing. Jordan's weakness dictated a moderate posture toward Israel so as not to invite an overwhelming retaliation. Much of Arab opinion regarded this forbearance as traitorous to the Arab cause, and blamed it both upon the British and upon Hussein as their tool. Even before Hussein's accession the Hashemite regime had moved to restrict propaganda and subversion by the local communist party. It had to move more cautiously with respect to regional political movements — socialist, Ba'thist and later Nasserist — which shared some communist objectives including the replacement of monarchical institutions by republican ones, and elimination of British and other Western influence from the area.

The Eisenhower Administration attached importance to preservation of the Hashemite regime despite its obvious debility. Either Jordan's absorption by neighboring Syria or Iraq, or the rise of a militant Arab nationalist government there, appeared likely to provoke Israeli occupation of the West Bank and to precipitate war between Israel and the Arab states. The principle that

Jordan's monarchy was essential to peace in the Near East became a fixed assumption of American policy. The United States was moreover increasingly preoccupied with the spread of communism and Soviet influence in the region, and made little distinction between the local communist parties and the regional movements that were pursuing similar tactical objectives. The American concern was given concrete expression in military assistance to Jordan which began on a small scale in 1950, and in economic aid instituted with a technical assistance agreement of somewhat less than $2 million signed in April 1953. The United States was a passive, if sympathetic, observer of the ill-fated British attempt in 1955 to draw Jordan into the Baghdad Pact.

Hussein had favored association with the Pact as a means of expanding his army. He was unable to defy the violent opposition of both domestic and general Arab opinion, however, and the incident underscored the extent to which Jordan's British connection was becoming a threat to the King's domestic position. It exasperated the Palestinians, who looked more and more for leadership to Egypt's President Nasser as the latter achieved British withdrawal from the Suez Canal, asserted Arab independence by procuring arms from the Soviet Union, and posed as the future liberator of all Palestine. The Arab Legion, Jordan's army, had increasingly to be used to maintain civil order; its failure to protect border towns against Israeli incursions such as those at Qibya (October 1953), Nahhalin (March 1954) and Qalqiliya (October 1956) was attributed to treachery on the part of the British and of the King as well. Even within the Legion the loyalty of Arab officers was undermined by anti-royalist ideologies, and by frustration at finding promotion blocked by the presence of British officers in the higher ranks. At length Hussein found it expedient to dismiss the Legion's British commander, Glubb Pasha, and other British officers in March 1956: a popular act, but one which helped to bring on the Suez War at the end of October the same year. In the wake of that conflict, Hussein found himself virtually isolated within the Arab world; his policies were challenged by a left-wing, pan-Arabist government resulting from Jordan's first free elections, held in October 1956. Syrian and Saudi forces were stationed on Jordanian soil, apparently awaiting the collapse of his regime and the dismemberment of his country. On the basis of empty Syrian and Egyptian promises to replace the British subsidy, the King authorized his ministers to negotiate termination of the 1948 Treaty with Britain and the closure of British bases in Jordan. The British subsidy ceased, and when Egypt and Syria defaulted the task of sustaining Hussein's regime devolved mainly upon the United States.

In January 1957 President Eisenhower and Secretary of State John Foster Dulles proposed to Congress passage of a joint resolution declaring that the independence and integrity of the Middle Eastern countries was vital to the American national interest and to world peace, and promising economic and military aid to those requesting it for the purpose of defending themselves against international communism. This was precisely what Hussein perceived himself threatened by, in the shape of his own cabinet, headed by a socialist Premier, Sulayman Nabulsi, which, with the active support of Egypt and Syria, had relaxed restrictions against communist propaganda, allowed free rein to incitement of street mobs by communist agitators, and publicly stated its goals of opening relations with the USSR, recognition of the People's Republic of China, and a federal union of Jordan with other Arab states. The King promptly expressed interest in American aid, if it were provided without political strings. He furthermore published on February 2 a letter to Nabulsi warning of the destructive aims of communism and the speciousness of its support of Arab nationalism. The Prime Minister, backed by Foreign Minister Abdullah Rimawi, a *Ba'thist,* and by the Commander in Chief of the Army, Ali Abu Nuwar, boldly accused the King of exceeding his constitutional powers in trying to dictate the government's policy. Hussein meanwhile received increasingly circumstantial intelligence of a conspiracy to depose him, and by mid-April troop dispositions ordered by Abu Nuwar appeared to indicate an impending coup attempt.[2] Reacting to the crisis, Secretary Dulles stated in a press conference on April 23 that the United States desired to "hold up the hands of King Hussein," and the White House asserted the next day that the United States "regarded the independence and integrity of Jordan as vital." Units of the Sixth Fleet were ordered from Italy to Beirut. Hussein was assured of an initial sum of $10 million in financial aid. Fortified by this support, the King was able to assert authority over his armed forces and discharge disloyal officers. He dismissed the Nabulsi government and ruled under martial law through trusted East Bank politicians.

Hussein's acceptance of the role of American client intensified the hostility of the revolutionary Arab states toward his regime. The union of Egypt and Syria in February 1958 as the United Arab Republic appeared to be the prelude to an Arab unity in which Jordanian independence would be extinguished. Hussein responded by joining with Iraq, then also under Hashemite rule, in a federation named the Arab Union. This hasty arrangement collapsed with the Iraqi revolution of July 1958, leaving Jordan hemmed in by neighbors actively seeking to destroy its monarchy. The United States sent armed forces into Lebanon, whose government felt similarly threatened, and it was Britain which sent troops to Jordan to bolster King Hussein. An American airlift of fuel, however, made an important contribution to the preservation of his throne. Aside from repeated plots against the King's life instigated from the neighboring Arab states, Jordan was for the next few years spared further direct threat to its integrity.

Hussein worked diligently and effectively to cement his relationship with the United States. In 1959 he paid the first of what were to become annual visits to America. In addition to conferring with the President and other high officials he toured extensively, addressing numerous groups of citizens. His personal courage was widely known and admired, and his firm stand against communism appealed to American attitudes; he soon became one of the best known, and certainly the most popular, of Arab leaders in the eyes of the American public.

Besides budget support, the United States contributed to the development of many sectors of the Jordanian economy: roads, electricity generating capacity, education, technical training, public health, etc. The most important single project, begun in 1959, was the East Ghor Canal, by which water from the Yarmuk River is diverted to irrigate agricultural land along the east bank of the Jordan.[3] The country's gross domestic product rose annually by nearly 8%, progress which permitted a sharp reduction in United States assistance by the late 1960s.

A distinctly smaller contribution of American military aid, totaling $67.4 million through Fiscal Year 1967, made it possible for Jordan to double the strength of its army, to 45,000 men.[4]

In the sequence of events leading to the third Arab-Israel war some had far-reaching consequences. Despite their deep ideological differences the Arab leaders felt the need for some coordinated policy vis-à-vis Israel, and sought to formulate one in a series of summit conferences beginning in January 1964. The first meeting resulted in the founding of the Palestine Liberation Organization, intended to mobilize the Palestine refugees for the recovery of their homeland. The PLO in Jordan rapidly developed into a rival to Hussein's government, which was obliged to use armed force against its activities. Commando formations sponsored by Syria, Iraq, and Egypt were encouraged to make forays into Israel through Jordan, which bore the brunt of retaliation. Hussein's regime was exposed to propaganda of unprecedented violence from the left-wing Arab capitals. When President Nasser instituted the series of provocations that led to the Israeli attack of June 5, 1967, Hussein felt compelled to close ranks with his fellow-Arabs. He made his peace with Nasser, joined the Syro-Egyptian Defense Pact, placed his armed forces under Egyptian command, and re-admitted PLO leader Ahmed Shuqaiyri to Jordan.[5] While these measures helped to restore the King's popularity, they made inevitable both Jordan's entry into the approaching hostilities and its defeat on the battlefield. In the resulting debacle Jordan lost the entire West Bank, including Jerusalem, the Kingdom's second capital, and became host to an additional 150,000 Palestine refugees.

The June War placed considerable strain on Jordan-American relations. Official and public revulsion in the United States against the Arabs made little discrimination between moderates and revolutionaries. Jordan incurred particular odium since King Hussein, deceived by Nasser respecting the tactical situation on the first day of hostilities and misreading his own intelligence reports, publicly accused the United States and Britain of participating in the air attack against the Arab states. American military aid ceased, and remained suspended for the next three years, (except for a small-State-side training program) notwithstanding Hussein's threat, strongly encouraged by other Arab states, to seek arms from the Soviet Union.

Throughout his reign Hussein had recognized not only the need for some accommodation with Israel, but also that it would be suicidal for him to enter into one unilaterally. He was now able to agree with Nasser to use diplomatic channels, rather than military force, in the effort to recover the occupied Arab territories. This principle was incorporated in the resolutions of the truncated Khartoum Summit Conference of August-September 1967.[7] The Conference communique, at the same time, made clear that the contemplated diplomatic effort was to be made through international and third-party channels, as it excluded the possibility of formal peace with, or recognition of, Israel. Both Jordan and Egypt consented to Resolution 242 adopted by the U.N. Security Council in November 1967. King Hussein worked vigorously to improve Arab relations with the United States, and the West generally, and to win support for Israeli evacuation of Arab territory. In a speech before the National Press Club in Washington on April 10, 1969 he insisted that he and Nasser were prepared to abandon all belligerency, to respect the sovereignty, territorial integrity and political independence of all states in the area, to guarantee freedom of navigation through the Gulf of Aqaba and the Suez Canal, and to accept a just settlement of the refugee problem, in return for the withdrawal of Israeli forces from all territories occupied in the June War. Efforts extending over several years by U.N. Mediator Gunnar Jarring failed, however, to break an impasse in which Israel insisted that direct negotiations with the Arab states precede evacuation of any territory, while the Arab states refused negotiations of any sort before all occupied territory was evacuated. The United States joined in condemning the Israeli annexation of the Old City of Jerusalem, but opposed the Arab contention that all territory seized must be returned.

At the Khartoum Conference the conservative oil-producing Arab states (Saudi Arabia, Kuwait, and Libya) undertook to pay annual subsidies to Jordan totaling $112 million until the "effects" of the War were corrected, i.e., until Jordan's lost territory was recovered. While only Saudi Arabia has consistently met this obligation, this support partially relieved Jordan of its exclusive dependence upon the United States to cover its budget shortfall.

After the disaster that befell Jordan, Syria and Egypt in the June War the Palestinian commando forces appeared to be the only effective Arab weapon against Israel. They rapidly became a major political force in the region, supplanted civilian politicians in the PLO, and were generously financed by the wealthier Arab states. Their strength in Jordan was built up substantially. As early as March 1968 an Israeli retaliatory raid demolished the *fatah* headquarters at Karameh, in the Jordan valley. Under relentless pressure from across the border the guerrillas gradually transferred their activities to Amman and other Jordanian urban centers where, under a divided but increasingly extremist leadership, they formed an autonomous government whose barely concealed aim was to destroy Hussein's regime and its commitment to a policy which would deny them their ultimate aim of liberating all Palestine. By the late summer of 1970 Jordan was in the throes of civil war, with the overwhelming weight of Arab world opinion on the side of the commandos against the King. On September 20 most of Jordan's army was absorbed in an attempt to free Amman, much of which was occupied by the commandos; Jordan furthermore faced a massive invasion by Syrian armored forces in support of the Palestinians. Hussein appealed to the United States for help.[7]

The Nixon Administration, convinced that the fall of Hussein would upset the balance of power in the Middle East and was likely to precipitate a general war, had watched the situation with growing alarm and was ready to act decisively. American forces in Germany were ostentatiously moved to airports; units of the Sixth Fleet were ordered to the eastern Mediterranean; Israel was persuaded to plan a military operation to expel the Syrian forces from Jordan; and the USSR was sternly warned that both the United States and Israel would intervene by force unless it ordered its Syrian clients to withdraw.[9] These measures had the calculated effect, and the external threat to Jordan disappeared with the Syrian retreat. Despite peace-making efforts by various Arab states, Hussein undertook a dogged campaign against the commando formations; lasting until August 1971, it left the King undisputed master in his own house.

This effort brought down upon Hussein the indignant condemnation of nearly all Arab states. Kuwait suspended its subsidy temporarily, Libya permanently; only Saudi Arabia continued to fulfill its financial engagement. Jordan's economy, not yet rehabilitated from the 1967 War, had suffered further damage. The United States stepped into the breach by resuming both economic and military aid on an enhanced scale. Together with the gradually resumed generosity of the moderate oil-producing Arab countries, American assistance has made possible spectacular progress of the Jordanian economy toward viability and self-sustaining growth.

The confrontation had far-reaching regional consequences. The Palestinian commandos moved their base of operations to Lebanon, the only Arab country too weak to keep their activities under control. They mounted successive challenges to the authority of the Lebanese government, and contributed to the eruption of the 1975-76 civil war. Hussein lost the credibility he had previously enjoyed as spokesman for the Palestinians by virtue of the fact that Jordan alone, in addition to harboring the largest number of Palestinians, accorded them full citizenship rights. Henceforth they spoke for themselves through the PLO, which was acknowledged as the sole representative of the Palestinians by the Arab chiefs of state at the Rabat Conference in October 1974, and was admitted to observer status at the UN the following year. The

United States has not adapted its policy to this altered situation by opening communications with the PLO.

Jordan-American relations were spared renewed stress during the war of October 1973 when Jordan kept prudently aloof from the attempt of Egypt and Syria to recover territory occupied by Israel. King Hussein's role in Secretary Kissinger's efforts to negotiate disengagement agreements between Israel and her Egyptian and Syrian neighbors was helpful, if marginal. Meanwhile, American economic and commercial relations with Jordan have continued to develop. U.S. exports to Jordan rose from $35 million in 1973 to $76 million in 1975. (The United States imports little or no Jordanian merchandise.) Opportunities for export of American goods and technology should arise as Jordan's new Five Year Plan (1976-1980), calling for an investment of two billion dollars in the economy, gets under way. Twenty-odd American firms responded to the attractive terms offered under Jordanian legislation enacted in November 1975 to encourage the establishment of regional headquarters in Amman.[10]

The growing assertiveness of Congress in foreign policy introduced a disturbing factor into United States-Jordan relations in 1975, when Jordan sought to purchase from America a sorely needed air defense system, to be financed by Saudi Arabia. Rejecting the executive branch's justification of the sale, a majority of the House Committee on International Relations withheld approval unless it were drastically reduced in size, basing its decision on the judgment that it would upset the Middle East balance of power, and on the syllogism that, the Government of Jordan having given its lack of an air defense capability as its reason for not participating in the October 1973 War, acquisition of such a system might encourage its participation in future hostilities.[11] By Autumn Congressional opposition had relaxed, in part as a result of King Hussein's persuasive letters to members of both houses.[12] Jordan had meanwhile added elements to the transaction raising its estimated cost to $713 million, from an original $350 million, and the Saudi government questioned this substantial increase. Deeply concerned at his country's vulnerability, Hussein decided to turn to the USSR, which welcomed the prospect of rehabilitating its declining political position in the Arab world. Financing, it appeared, might be available from Libya. A Russian air force mission arrived in Amman in June 1976 to discuss the contemplated deal, and the King visited Moscow shortly afterward. He drew back from this reversal of policy when the Saudi-American transaction was reinstated in July. This came at the price of Hussein's dismissal of his Premier and Defense Minister, Zayd Rifa'i, his staunch friend of long standing, who had counseled the approach to Moscow and had offended both Americans and Saudis by complaining publicly that the United States had raised the price of its air defense system and that the Saudis were unwilling to pay the increased cost.[13]

While thus not entirely free of irritants, Jordan-American relations rest on a solid basis of perceived mutual interests. This coincidence depends to a large extent upon the political orientation of a single man: the present King. Hussein has repeatedly shown the ability to assert his policies over formidable opposition. The outlook appears to be for continued stability and cooperation between his regime and the United States.

FOOTNOTES

1. Mohammad Ibrahim Faddah, *The Middle East in Transition* (New York: Asia Publishing House, 1974), p. 268, fn. 1.

2. Peter Snow, *Hussein: A Biography* (London: Barrie & Jenkins, 1972), p. 101 ff.; King Hussein I, *Uneasy Lies the Head* (New York: Random House, 1962), p. 155 ff.

3. Claud R. Sutcliffe, "The East Ghor Canal Project: A Case Study of Refugee Resettlement," *Middle East Journal*, Vol. 27 no. 4 (Autumn 1973), pp. 471-482.

4. George Kent, "Congress and American Middle East Policy," in Willard A. Beling, ed., *The Middle East: Quest for an American Policy* (Albany: State University of New York Press, 1973), p. 298; J. C. Hurewitz, *Middle East Politics: The Military Dimension* (New York: Frederick A. Praeger, 1969), p. 325.

5. Snow, *op. cit.*, pp. 172-193.

6. Boycotted by Algeria and Syria.

7. Reprinted in *Congressional Record*, April 14, 1969; E 2850.

8. Snow, *op. cit.*, pp. 223-229.

9. Marvin Kalb and Bernard Kalb, *Kissinger* (Boston: Little, Brown, 1974), pp. 198-209.

10. American Embassy, Amman, *Foreign Economic Trends: Jordan*, June 1976, released by U.S. Department of Commerce.

11. 94th Congress, 1st Session, House of Representatives *Report No. 94-392*, July 24, 1975.

12. *New York Times*, September 5, 1975.

13. *Ibid.*, August 1, 1976.

U.S. Military Assistance to Jordan

Approximate value in millions of U.S. dollars

U.S. Fiscal Year:

	1950 through 1974	1975	1976 (est.)
Grant Aid	196	70	100
Sales Credits	69	30	75
Cash Sales	254	74	50
Total:	519	174	225

U.S. ECONOMIC ASSISTANCE TO JORDAN*

(millions of dollars)

U.S. Fiscal Years

	1950–1970	1971	1972	1973	1974	1975	1976 (est.)
AID Loans	16.0			10.0	7.4	18.6	17.0
Export-Import Bank Loans	10.1			5.9			
Public Law 480:							
Title I	8.5	1.2	1.7	5.8	8.2	6.8	6.1**
Title II	94.6	9.6	2.1	4.2	3.1	1.8	2.9
Budget Support	368.8		55.0	50.0	45.0	67.5	70.75
AID Project Assistance	111.6	1.0	0.6	1.0	1.2	1.5	3.48
Other	1.3	10.0***					
Totals:	610.9	21.8	59.4	76.9	64.9	96.2	100.23

Historical total (est.): $1,030.33

* Figures compiled by U.S. Embassy Amman, provided by courtesy of U.S. Department of Commerce.
** A Title I agreement valued at $5.5 million was signed on November 29, 1976 (*New York Times*, Nov. 30, 1976).
*** Funds for repairing Jordan's 1970 civil war damage.

NOTE: Under Title I of Public Law 480 Jordan purchases agricultural products (mostly wheat and wheat derivatives). Under Title II the U.S. donates food commodities to Jordan, primarily through the World Food program and through U.S. voluntary relief agencies.

United States Arms Aid to Jordan

By HAROLD CHASE

Until the end of World War II, the British supplied most of Jordan's military equipment and training. In the period 1949-1961, Britain herself was receiving military assistance from the United States at the level of one billion dollars. Britain's ability to supply other states was undoubtedly determined in part by what it received from the United States. In this sense, U.S. aid to Jordan dates back to the end of World War II, and as the accompanying chart demonstrates, it was not long before the United States was giving direct arms aid to Jordan.

With United States aid, Jordan had an Army, by 1973, of some 62,000, organized into one armored division, one mechanized division and two infantry divisions,[1] and some 500 tanks, the majority of which were American M-60s, M-47s and M-48s; 250 armored cars and 500 Armored Personnel Carriers; 130 light artillery pieces (105mm) and several bigger pieces (155mm and 203mm). The Army had 70,000 trained reservists. In addition to the Army, Jordan in 1973 had an Air Force of 2,000 with 35 combat and 42 other aircraft. Its Navy consisted of 250 personnel, operating 8 patrol craft.

The level of U.S. support took a quantum jump in 1975 and after, for which the following explanation was offered by Lieutenant General H.M. Fish, USAF, Director, Defense Security Assistance Agency, before the Committee on International Relations, House of Representatives, November 12, 1975:

> . . . Jordan, historically a long-standing friend of the United States, has embarked upon a major military reorganization and modernization program. To the extent that we aid the Jordanian army, we strengthen the ability of King Hussein to maintain stability in his country. We are asking, therefore, for $100 million in military assistance; $800,000 in training funds; and $75 million in military credit sales.[2]

In 1976 Jordan's effort to acquire batteries of the American Hawk missile met with success. The U.S. State Department and the Defense Department were at odds over the number of batteries which should be supplied; State would have provided 21; the Defense Department 8.[3] They ultimately com-

Dr. Chase is Professor Political Science at the University of Minnesota. His latest publication is *Constitutional Interpretation: A Casebook* (West Publishing Co., 1976). A Major General in the U.S. Marine Corps Reserves, he served as Civilian Professor at the National War College in 1964.

JORDAN
(U.S. Fiscal Years - Millions of Dollars)
U.S. OVERSEAS LOANS AND GRANTS - OBLIGATIONS AND LOAN AUTHORIZATIONS

Program	Post-War Relief Period 1946-1948	Marshall Plan Period 1949-1952	Mutual Security Act Period 1953-61	FOREIGN ASSISTANCE ACT PERIOD 1962-1965	1966	1967	1968	1969	1970
I. Economic Assistance—Total	—	5.2	275.4	194.6	45.6	45.5	19.0	11.6	3.9
Loans	—	—	4.7	1.6	8.5	6.6	1.8	1.3	—
Grants	—	5.2	270.7	193.0	37.1	38.9	17.2	10.3	3.9
a. A.I.D. and Predecessor Agencies	—	4.7	227.5	167.8	43.5	37.7	12.2	1.5	1.5
Loans	—	—	4.7	1.6	7.9	1.8	—	—	—
Grants	—	4.7	222.8	166.2	35.6	35.9	12.2	1.5	1.5
(Security Supporting Assistance)	(—)	(—)	(—)	(140.0)	(32.0)	(32.0)	(10.2)	(—)	(—)
b. Food for Peace (PL 480)	—	0.4	46.7	26.8	2.1	7.8	6.8	10.1	2.4
Loans	—	—	—	—	0.6	4.8	1.8	1.3	—
Grants	—	0.4	46.7	26.8	1.5	3.0	5.0	8.8	2.4
Title I Total	—	—	—	—	0.6	4.8	1.8	1.3	—
Repayable in U.S. Dollars—Loans									
Payable Foreign Currency Planned for Country Use	—	—	—	—	—	1.7	1.8	1.3	—
Title II					0.6	3.1			
Total Grants	—	0.4	46.7	26.8	1.5	3.0	5.0	8.8	2.4
Emergency Relief Econ. Development & World Food Program	—	—	34.8	21.7	*	2.1	3.2	6.6	0.6
Voluntary Relief Agencies	—	0.4	11.9	5.1	1.5	0.9	1.8	2.2	1.8

c. Other Economic Assistance	0.1	1.2	—	—	—	—	—	—
Loans	—	—	—	—	—	—	—	—
Grants	—	—	—	—	—	—	—	—
Peace Corps	—	—	—	—	—	—	—	—
Other	0.1	1.2	—	—	—	—	—	—
II. Military Assistance—Total	—	16.2	27.2	22.4	14.4	0.4	14.2	0.2
Credits or Loans	—	—	—	15.0	14.4	—	14.0	—
Grants	—	16.2	27.2	7.4	—	0.4	0.2	0.2
a. MAP Grants	—	15.5	20.2	4.3	—	0.4	0.2	0.2
b. Credit Sales Under FMS	—	—	—	15.0	12.5	—	14.0	—
c. Military Assistance Service-funded (MASF) Grants	—	—	—	—	—	—	—	—
d. Transfers from Excess Stocks	—	0.7	7.0	3.1	1.9	—	—	—
e. Other Grants	—	—	—	—	—	—	—	—
III. Total Economic and Military Assistance	5.2	291.6	221.6	68.0	59.9	19.4	25.8	4.1
Loans	—	4.7	1.6	23.5	6.6	1.8	15.3	—
Grants	5.2	286.9	220.0	44.5	53.3	17.6	10.5	4.1
Other U.S. Government Loans and Grants	NO PROGRAMS PRIOR TO FY 1962		1.6	—	—	—	0.2	8.3
a. Export-import Bank Loans			1.6	—	—	—	0.2	8.3
b. All Other Loans			—	—	—	—	—	—

*Less than $50,000.

Source: "U.S. Overseas Loans and Grants and Assistance From International Organizations." 1975, Statistics and Reports Division. Office of Financial Management, Agency for International Development. U.S. Department of State, Washington, D.C.

JORDAN (Continued)

FOREIGN ASSISTANCE ACT PERIOD

Program	1971	1972	1973	1974	1975	Total FAA Period 1962-1975	Total Loans and Grants 1946-1975	Repayments and Interest 1946-1975	Total Less Repayments and Interest
I. Economic Assistance—Total	16.8	59.4	71.1	64.5	99.3	631.3	899.5	8.4	891.1
Loans	1.2	1.7	15.9	15.6	25.0	79.2	78.6	8.4	70.2
Grants	15.6	57.7	55.2	48.9	74.3	552.1	820.8	—	820.8
a. A.I.D. and Predecessor Agencies	6.0	55.6	61.0	53.2	87.5	527.5	748.1	3.4	744.7
Loans	—	—	10.1	7.4	18.6	47.3	48.2	3.4	44.8
Grants	6.0	55.6	51.0	45.8	68.9	480.2	699.8	—	699.8
(Security Supporting Assistance)	(5.0)	(55.0)	(50.0)	(45.0)	(87.5)	(456.7)	(452.1)		
b. Food for Peace (PL 480)	10.8	3.8	10.1	11.3	11.6	103.6	149.9	5.0	144.9
Loans	1.2	1.7	5.9	8.2	6.4	31.9	30.4	5.0	25.4
Grants	9.6	2.1	4.2	3.1	5.2	71.7	119.5	—	119.5
Title I Total	1.2	1.7	5.9	8.2	6.4	31.9	30.4	5.0	25.4
Repayable in U.S. Dollars—Loans	1.2	1.7	5.9	8.2	6.4	28.2	26.7	3.8	22.9
Payable Foreign Currency Planned for Country Use	—	—	—	—	—	3.7	3.7	1.2	2.5
Title II Total Grants	9.6	2.1	4.2	3.1	5.2	71.7	119.5	—	119.5
Emergency Relief Econ. Development & World Food Program	6.7	0.4	3.2	2.0	3.4	49.9	84.7	—	84.7
Voluntary Relief Agencies	2.9	1.7	1.0	1.1	1.8	21.8	34.8	—	34.8

c. Other Economic Assistance	—	—	—	—	0.2	0.2	1.5	—	1.5
Loans	—	—	—	—	—	—	—	—	—
Grants	—	—	—	—	0.2	0.2	1.5	—	1.5
Peace Corps	—	—	—	—	—	—	—	—	—
Other	—	—	—	—	0.2	0.2	1.5	—	1.5
II. Military Assistance—Total	59.8	56.2	54.8	45.7	104.6	399.9	415.5	36.2	379.3
Credits or Loans	30.0	10.0	—	—	30.0	99.0	99.0	36.2	62.8
Grants	29.8	46.2	54.8	45.7	74.6	300.9	316.5	—	316.5
a. MAP Grants	28.8	40.3	36.0	40.5	69.9	253.3	268.3	—	268.3
b. Credit Sales Under FMS	30.0	10.0	—	—	30.0	99.0	99.0	36.2	62.8
c. Military Assistance Service-funded (MASF) Grants	—	—	—	—	—	—	—	—	—
d. Transfers from Excess Stocks	1.0	5.9	18.8	5.2	4.7	47.6	48.2	—	48.2
e. Other Grants	—	—	—	—	—	—	—	—	—
III. Total Economic and Military Assistance	76.6	115.6	125.9	110.2	203.9	1,031.0	1,315.0	44.6	1,270.4
Loans	31.2	11.7	15.9	15.6	55.0	178.2	177.6	44.6	133.0
Grants	45.4	103.9	110.0	94.6	148.9	853.0	1,157.3	—	1,137.3
Other U.S. Government Loans and Grants	—	—	6.6	7.9	—	24.6	24.2	7.8	16.4
a. Export-import Bank Loans	—	—	5.9	3.9	—	19.9	19.5	5.4	14.1
b. All Other									
Loans	—	—	0.7	4.0	—	4.7	4.7	2.4	2.3

promised on 16. Saudi Arabia is paying for the purchase. As *The Economist* described it:

> The cost of the Hawk-based system is being reduced in four ways: the Americans are shaving the selling price; the number of Vulcan machine guns is being cut; training in the United States (some of which has already been done) is being reduced in favor of more training in Jordan; and fewer spare parts are now to be stocked in the Jordanian depot. All this should bring the new price below $500m.[4]

Jordan's Hawk missiles have the unsettling effect of creating a Hawk radar detection system that covers much of Israel. Together with Syria's Soviet SAMs, Arab radar systems now cover the whole of Israel.

Military Assistance to Jordan: July 1975-September 1977
(in millions of dollars)

	FY 76 (July 1, 75- June 30, 76)	Transition Quarter (June 30, 76- Sept. 30, 76)	FY 77 (Oct. 76- Sept. 30, 77)
Foreign Military Sales	82.500	——	75.000
Military Assistance Program (Grant)	55.000	——	55.000
International Military Education Training	.787	——	.800

FOOTNOTES

1. These figures are drawn from Colonel Trevor N. Depuy, Lieutenant Grace P. Hayes and Colonel John A.C. Andrews, *The Almanac of World Military Power* (1974).
2. *Supplement to the Air Force Policy Letter for Commanders*, No. 1-1976, p. 18.
3. *The Economist*, (London), August 7, 1976, p. 41.
4. *Ibid.*

Soviet-Jordanian Relations

By OLES M. SMOLANSKY

In examining the brief but turbulent history of this Hashemite Kingdom, an observer is struck by the marginal impact the U.S.S.R. has had on its domestic and foreign policies. Even under Nikita Khrushchev, when the Soviet Union made a determined effort to enter the Middle East, the Kremlin's activities were centered on such Arab states as Egypt, Syria, and Iraq, and involved Jordan only to a much lesser degree. It is true that on a number of occasions, such as the domestic crises of 1957 and 1970 as well as the Arab-Israeli wars of 1967 and 1973 (and their aftermath), the Kingdom came to attract considerable Soviet attention. These facts do not, however, alter the basic proposition that in terms of Moscow's *total* involvement in the Arab world, Amman has occupied a position of secondary (and often tertiary) importance. More often than not, it was treated with "benign neglect," emerging from its relative obscurity only as a result of the Russian preoccupation with larger regional issues.

The above observation does not imply that this basic Soviet stand has resulted from the Kremlin's own preferences. Rather, it has been conditioned by two important factors, neither of which the U.S.S.R. has been able to affect in any significant fashion. First, the country's kings, especially 'Abdallah and Hussein, have traditionally held staunchly conservative and anti-Communist views, making a meaningful rapprochement between Jordan and the Soviet Union difficult to achieve even after the establishment of diplomatic relations on August 20, 1963. Second, both because of their *Weltanschauung* and a number of practical considerations, the Jordanian rulers, in international and regional politics, have preferred cooperation with and reliance on the Western powers and conservative Arab states, above all Saudi Arabia. A glance at the Soviet literature dealing with Jordan leaves little doubt

Dr. Smolansky is Professor of International Relations and Chairman of the Department of International Relations at Lehigh University. He has contributed articles on Soviet policy in the Middle East to numerous books and journals. His book, *The Soviet Union and the Arab East Under Khrushchev,* was published by the Bucknell University Press, 1974.

The discussion of the Jordanian Communist party, including its interaction with both Amman and Moscow, has been omitted from this chapter. In making this decision, the author has been moved by the following considerations: (1) the JCP has never been able to reach the degree of relative prominence in the affairs of its country enjoyed by its counterparts in such states as Syria or Iraq and has not, therefore, been regarded by the Kremlin as a particularly useful instrument in efforts to influence Jordan's policies; (2) a discussion of the JCP's activities would do little more than shed additional light on the proposition, accepted by this author, that the various pro-Soviet Arab Communist parties are used by the U.S.S.R. to advance its own state interests.

about Moscow's awareness of the uniqueness of the problems which the U.S.S.R. has encountered in the Hashemite Kingdom.

The creation of the Emirate of Transjordan in March 1921 is generally attributed to London's determination to bolster the military-strategic position of the British Empire in the post-1918 Middle East. Specifically, the United Kingdom is said to have endeavored to establish a link between its mandates of Iraq and Palestine (while, at the same time, excluding the territory east of the river Jordan from the "National Home" promised to the Jews under the terms of the Balfour Declaration) in order to prevent France from penetrating Iraq and the Arabian peninsula.[1] Throughout the interwar period, Great Britain dominated the Emirate by means of strengthening its "feudal and tribal oligarchy" and by assisting them in the suppression of "popular resentment" against "foreign domination" and "domestic oppression."[2]

In the post-World War II period, the United Kingdom was forced to review the premises upon which its relations with Transjordan had previously rested. Among the factors which influenced London's decision were: the growth of anti-colonial sentiment in Egypt, Syria, and Lebanon, which made it imperative for Great Britain to strengthen its presence elsewhere in the region, above all Iraq and Transjordan; the fear of U.N. "meddling" in the affairs of Palestine and Transjordan; and the support of the "Greater Syria" project in which London, through Amman, was hoping to play a dominant part. The first step in securing the British position was the signing of the 1946 treaty which transformed the Emirate into a Kingdom but had no effect on London's control over its affairs. Encountering strong popular resistance, King 'Abdallah, in 1947, requested that the treaty be revised and, in light of its difficulties in Palestine, Great Britain complied with his wishes. A new treaty, limiting the British military presence to a few designated areas, was signed in March 1948.[3]

The creation of the State of Israel and the war of 1948 transformed the country in a number of important ways. Territorially, a large part of the West Bank was joined with the Kingdom's Transjordanian area. The addition of nearly one million, whom the Soviets characterized as "workers, artisans, peasants, intelligentsia, and the national bourgeoisie, rich in experience in anti-imperialist struggle," to some 400,000 relatively backward fellahs and nomads drastically changed the political and economic make-up of the state. Opposition to the King's pro-Western orientation and domestic repression continued to grow, resulting, among other things, in 'Abdallah's assassination at the hands of a Palestinian refugee in 1951. His successors Talal (1951-1952, removed because of his anti-British attitude) and Hussein persevered in 'Abdallah's determination to suppress domestic reforms. Nevertheless, the "progressive elements" asserted themselves. In 1954, the "National Front," led by the National Socialist party under Sulayman al-Nabulsi, called for the annulment of the 1948 treaty, the withdrawal of British forces from

Jordan, the recall of British officers from the Arab Legion, and the termination of reliance on Western economic aid.[4]

A new stage in the "anti-imperialist struggle" was reached in 1954, when Great Britain was forced to withdraw its forces from the Suez Canal Zone and attempted to replace this loss by drawing Jordan into the Baghdad Pact. In the ensuing domestic turmoil, the Jordanian parliament was dissolved, and several cabinets were forced to resign. In early 1956, Hussein no longer found it possible to resist the will of the "popular masses." On March 2, the King dismissed Glubb Pasha, the commander of the Arab Legion, replacing him with Abu Nuwar, a Jordanian officer, well-known for his anti-Western attitudes.[5]

The elections of October 21, 1956, resulted in a victory of the "patriotic forces," led by the National Socialist party. Sulayman Nabulsi became Jordan's new prime minister and, under his leadership, the country's domestic and foreign policies were significantly "liberalized." However, apprehension over what he perceived as an alarming growth of "progressive influence" in Jordan led the King, in April 1957, to execute an anti-government coup, restoring the "reactionaries" to power and resuming close cooperation with Iraq and the Western powers. Domestically, a "reign of terror" against the "progressive elements" was reinstituted, reaching its climax under the premiership of Haza' al-Majali (1959-1960).[6]

"Positive changes" in Jordan's foreign and domestic policies were effected by the government of Wasfi al-Tal, who assumed the premiership in January 1962. Of particular significance, according to Soviet sources, was the new prime minister's "White Book" on foreign policy, published in July 1962. In it, the refusal to join non-Arab military pacts was combined with a declaration of support for the national liberation movements and of intention to establish diplomatic relations with the U.S.S.R. Domestically, Tal expressed himself in favor of general amnesty for political prisoners, including members of the Jordan Communist Party, and of the legalization of political parties.[7]

Following the establishment of diplomatic relations on August 20, 1963, Jordan and the U.S.S.R., in March 1965, signed their first cultural and technical cooperation agreement which provided, among other things, for the opening in Amman of a Soviet cultural center. Subsequently, Jordan also established diplomatic and economic relations with a number of East European states, including Czechoslovakia, Hungary, Bulgaria, and Yugoslavia.[8]

Relations between Amman and Moscow began deteriorating sharply in 1966, when Hussein repeatedly expressed his concern about a possible "Communization" of Syria and Soviet publications responded by accusing Jordan, in cooperation with the CIA and British intelligence, of planning to invade its neighbor.

The June 1967 war, which led to a drastic transformation of the Middle Eastern scene, resulted also in a reappraisal of Soviet and Jordanian policies.

This time, the initiative for rapprochement emanated from the Kremlin and, as a result of a Soviet invitation, King Hussein visited Moscow in October 1967. In a joint communiqué, both sides expressed their determination to seek the withdrawal of Israeli forces from all territories occupied in June and the compensation by Israel for all the material losses suffered by the Arabs during the war. The extent to which Jordan was willing to go in an effort to secure Moscow's cooperation in the "liquidation of the consequences of the 1967 war" was evidenced by Hussein's subscription to the Soviet thesis that "in the face of aggression in the Near East, particular significance is assumed by the unity and solidarity of all Arab countries based on anti-imperialism and anti-colonialism." The latter principles were declared a "necessary prerequisite for the successful joint struggle for the strengthening of independence and sovereignty" of the Arab states. Both sides also noted that their relations were based on "complete equality, friendship, and mutual understanding" and reiterated their determination "to strengthen and develop . . . mutually beneficial ties in the economic, cultural, political, and other spheres."[9]

As events continued to evolve, another low in Moscow-Amman relations was reached in September 1970. Alarmed by what he regarded as Palestinian attempts to seize power in Jordan, the King moved to liquidate the autonomy which the *Palestine Liberation Movement* had enjoyed until then. Unable to intervene effectively on behalf of the PLM, the Kremlin engaged in unsuccessful diplomatic maneuvers while the Jordanian army crushed the commando units and repelled a Syrian tank column sent to their assistance. It is noteworthy, however, that *Black September* failed to affect, significantly, Moscow's attitude toward Hussein; in late 1972, Jordan was listed as one of the Arab states with which the U.S.S.R. was said to be maintaining "friendly relations."[10] These relations were further improved in the aftermath of the 1973 war.

As noted, the tenuousness of Soviet-Jordanian relations became particularly visible during the crises of 1957 and 1970.

As indicated, the national elections of October 21, 1956 led to the victory of the National Socialist party. Its program contained, *inter alia,* the following planks: annulment of the 1948 Anglo-Jordanian treaty; liquidation of British military bases; withdrawal of British forces; opposition to the Baghdad Pact, and the establishment of diplomatic relations with the Soviet Union.[11]

On October 25, four days before Nabulsi was installed as Jordan's new premier, Amman signed a defense agreement with Egypt, Syria, and Saudi Arabia. It came too late to be of practical significance in the Suez war: Jordan did not participate in the hostilities and limited itself to the severing of diplomatic relations with France but not Great Britain. Only in March 1957 did Amman move to abrogate the 1948 treaty and come out openly in opposition to the Eisenhower Doctrine. These steps were preceded, in December 1956, by Jordan's acceptance of a joint Egyptian-Syrian-Saudi offer to replace the annual British subsidy of £12.5 million.[12] These "progressive" steps were applauded by the U.S.S.R. At the same time, however, the King's attitude was a source of concern to the Kremlin.

In early 1957, Hussein was growing openly apprehensive about what he perceived to be an alarming growth of the "progressive" influence in Jordan. An early indication of his attitude was contained in the February 2, 1957 message to Premier Nabulsi in which the King attacked "the Eastern camp [for] render[ing] the greatest support to our enemy . . . [by] help[ing] it usurp a part of the Arab homeland." He then called for government repression of the Communists and their sympathizers on the ground that "if we allow Communist doctrine which calls for fraternity between the Arab Communist and the Zionist Communist to gain a foothold among us, we shall lose all our tradition as a nation with ideals, aims, and a history."[13]

The crisis reached a climax in April 1957. According to Soviet sources, it was brought to a head by Nabulsi's decision, announced on April 3, to establish diplomatic relations with the U.S.S.R. and the Chinese People's Republic and by his insistence on the removal from the governmental apparatus of persons "guilty of cooperation with the imperialists."[14] One day later, the premier expressed his government's willingness to accept Soviet aid, accompanied by a refusal to receive U.S. economic assistance, on the ground that it was designed to undermine the growing friendship between Jordan and Egypt.[15]

On April 10, Hussein, having secured the support of the Arab Legion's Bedouin units, forced the resignation of Nabulsi's cabinet and dismissed the parliament. However, the new government under Husayn Fakhri al-Khalidi, in which Nabulsi was retained as foreign minister, did not significantly deviate from the foreign and domestic policies of its predecessor: the new premier also favored the establishment of diplomatic relations with the U.S.S.R.[16] The King intervened again, this time decisively. A new cabinet, headed by Ibrahim Hashim, was installed on April 24, and, within a few days, initiated a wave of repression against the "patriotic force." According to Soviet sources, Hussein's "reactionary activities" enjoyed the "secret support" of Iraq, Saudi Arabia, Great Britain, and the United States. The latter, in particular, intervened on several levels: the Secretary of Defense announced his willingness to dispatch U.S. ground forces to Jordan; the Sixth Fleet sailed into the eastern Mediterranean and its commander threatened the use of atomic weapons in Hussein's defense; and the American embassy in Amman served as a "center" directing the coup against the "popular forces."[17]

Moscow's official reaction to the Jordanian events was contained in the April 30 statement by the Ministry of Foreign Affairs. Noting that "Jordan . . . has become the object of imperialist intrigues," the Kremlin held that "the situation . . . cannot fail to arouse the serious concern of the . . . Soviet

Union, the interests of whose security call for peace and order in the Middle East." The U.S.S.R. could not ignore these occurrences because they were "the result of flagrant foreign interference, . . . of a new imperialist plot which constitutes a grave threat to peace" and warned that the continuation of such activities "is fraught with grave danger. It may lead to dire consequences."[18] Amman responded on May 11, accusing the Soviet Union of plotting the overthrow of the Saudi, Libyan, Iraqi, and Jordanian monarchies. Moscow, thereupon, reiterated its insistence that the Jordanian developments were the result of "imperialist intrigues" and there the matter was allowed to rest.[19]

The 1957 crisis and Moscow's reaction to it provides significant additional evidence for the contention that, in the latter 1950s, Soviet policy in the Middle East was conducted from a position of weakness which references to "dire consequences" were unable to conceal. Confronted with Washington's determination to keep Hussein in power, the Kremlin, in spite of its sympathy for the Jordanian "progressives," had no choice but to limit itself to mere moral support. At the same time, however, the crisis also illustrates Moscow's determination to "hang in" in the Middle East and to attempt to undermine Western positions in the region until such time as the U.S.S.R. might be able to meet its rivals on more or less even terms. In the pursuit of these objectives, the Soviets suffered some political setbacks — as in the 1957 Jordan crisis — but it appears in retrospect that such reverses simply spurred the Kremlin to new efforts. In brief, the Russians not only clung to the positions which they were able to establish in such countries as Egypt and Syria, but they were also actively looking for new opportunities to expand their presence — in this instance, in Jordan. In spite of their best efforts, however, Moscow's ability to influence Jordanian events has remained marginal, as was demonstrated in the crisis of 1970.

As a result of their credible performance during the 1967 war, the Palestinian resistance organizations in Jordan gained considerable strength and, in the next three years, emerged as a serious threat to Hussein. His initial efforts to curb their political activity in the country and their raids into Israel (which invariably resulted in retaliation against Jordanian targets) proved futile, as did also his attempts at political accommodation. The tension eased somewhat in March 1968, when the major Palestinian groups in the country, including *al-fatah,* pledged "not to endanger [the King's] position."[20] Uneasy calm prevailed until February 1970, when the promulgation of a government decree which prohibited civilians from carrying arms resulted in bloody clashes between the army and the *fedayeen.* Serious outbreaks of violence occurred in the summer. In September, the radical *Popular Front for the Liberation of Palestine* (PFLP) hijacked three civilian airliners. They were flown to a Jordanian desert airport at Zarqa and destroyed on the ground. Although the hijackings were condemned by the main body of the *Palestine Liberation*

Movement which embraced most resistance organizations, the action impressed upon Hussein the inevitability of a final showdown with the Palestinians over control of the country.

On September 16, the King formed a military government and called on the PLM to disarm and disband its forces. The order was refused and, in the ensuing hostilities, the Palestinian units were forced to withdraw from Jordan. For a few days, the confrontation threatened to develop into a regional and even international conflict, as Syrian armor crossed the border to assist the PLM. In the ensuing battles, the Palestinians and the Syrians were driven back and, by November, all of northern Jordan had been brought under Amman's control.[21]

Of particular interest in the context of this discussion are the respective positions taken by the superpowers. From the very outset of the crisis the U.S.S.R. favored the PLM and attacked the "few isolated extremist groups" for hijacking civilian aircraft and for "efforts to prevent the attainment of a political solution of the . . . [Arab-Israeli] question." At the same time, Moscow was equally critical of the "reactionary circles of Jordan" which were said to have used the extremists' excesses "to deal a blow at the armed units and the refugee camps of the Palestinians."[22]

In contrast, Washington came out squarely in support of Hussein. On September 17, one day after the King's decision to confront the PLM, units of the Sixth Fleet appeared in the eastern Mediterranean. In addition, American forces in West Germany and the United States were placed on alert in a clear indication that Washington was prepared to intervene militarily (in cooperation with Israel) should the Jordanian army prove incapable of repelling the Syrian incursion. The magnitude of the U.S. reaction, which may have been prompted "by chagrin at Russian violations [in early September] of the Suez cease-fire agreement,"[23] leaves little doubt that it was directed mainly at the U.S.S.R. Specifically, the American show of strength was designed to demonstrate resolution and, in so doing, to warn the Kremlin not to take any precipitous steps on Damascus' behalf which might result in a superpower confrontation. The Soviet response was conciliatory in the extreme. On September 18, Moscow, in an urgent note, assured the United States that it was endeavoring to stop foreign intervention in Jordanian affairs. A few days later, Soviet diplomats in London and Washington were spreading the word that the U.S.S.R. "was doing all it could to stop" the Syrian incursion into Jordan.[24]

On September 23, the very day of the Syrian withdrawal, the Soviet Foreign Ministry announced that Russian ambassadors in Damascus, Baghdad, and Amman had conveyed to these governments Moscow's "firm conviction . . . that everything should be done to end the fratricidal fighting in Jordan as soon as possible, as this fighting can only play into the hand of forces which do not want lasting peace to be established in the Middle East."

The statement went on to note that "in view of the increasing concentration of the . . . Sixth Fleet in the area, the Soviet Government has called [Washington's] attention . . . to the need for all States to display caution . . ., and also to the fact that any interference from the outside in the events in Jordan would further complicate . . . the international situation."[25]

As might have been expected, Moscow's admonition to end the war in Jordan fell on deaf ears. Hostilities ceased only after the main bulk of the invading Syrian armor and the Palestinian forces had left Jordanian territory. Similarly, the Kremlin's posture had no apparent effect on Washington and Jerusalem, which were prepared to intervene on Hussein's behalf had their assistance been required. Typically however, these considerations did not prevent the Soviet government from subsequently claiming that its "diplomatic intervention against foreign interference in Jordanian affairs" had successfully foiled "the U.S.-Israeli plot to invade Jordan and Syria."[26]

Did the Kremlin know in advance of the Syrian decision to move tanks into Jordan and, if so, did it, in fact, sanction or even encourage this step? Ro'i argues convincingly that, in view of the large presence of Soviet advisers in the Syrian armed forces, the Russians must have been aware of Damascus' intention. Moreover, Soviet Ambassador Nuretdin Mukhitdinov's two meetings with Syrian President Atasi on September 18 (the day of the Syrian entry into Jordan) leave little doubt that the subject had been discussed.[27] The second question is more difficult to answer. Some commentators have argued that because the invading tanks were Soviet-made and their crews were Russian-trained, "obviously they would not have moved without . . . [Moscow's] approval."[28] Others are inclined to believe that the Kremlin played an even more active role, "probably encouraging an ineffectual Syrian intervention" and backed off only "after the Syrians were mauled and the Palestinians largely annihilated."[29] These arguments tend to minimize the fact that, at the time of the crisis, Moscow displayed considerable caution, as evidenced (in addition to material presented above), by the TASS statement of September 19.[30] In addition, in his admittedly *ex post facto* speech of September 30, Brezhnev insisted that "we believed and believe that any *foreign* military intervention in the events in Jordan is absolutely unacceptable."[31]

It could be argued that the public caution exhibited by the Soviet government was but a camouflage used to disguise an aggressive stance whose real motive was, at the maximum, to overthrow the pro-Western regime in Jordan or, at the minimum, to continue probing Washington's resolution in the wake of Soviet-Egyptian violation of the Suez Canal disengagement agreement. This and similar arguments are vulnerable on the following counts: (1) they presuppose Moscow's willingness to test American resolve on a Middle Eastern battlefield (in contrast to the violation of the Canal agreement which occurred in a non-warlike setting) at a time when the U.S.S.R. was determined to avoid fighting a war with the United States; and (2) they assume that

Russia's Arab clients are in the habit of seeking the Kremlin's approval before engaging in operations (including military) which are, for whatever reason, deemed desirable or necessary.

This writer is inclined to believe that the initiative for the military incursion into Jordan came from a powerful group within the Syrian government which routinely appraised Moscow of its intentions. Since the Soviets appear to have judged (correctly) that neither they nor Damascus had much to gain from such an adventure (in view of the expected U.S. and Israeli opposition), they may in fact have attempted to dissuade their clients from embarking on it. When the Syrians went ahead anyway, the U.S.S.R. exerted pressure to limit and, eventually, to end their intervention in the Jordanian civil war.

The *Black September* crisis demonstrated that, in spite of achieving relative strategic parity with the United States, the Soviet Union, because of its continuing tactical weakness in the eastern Mediterranean, was not prepared to challenge Washington seriously in a situation where the latter's interests were being threatened by a third party. Another intriguing and illuminating consequence of the crisis has been the lack of any significant effect on Moscow's attitude toward Jordan. As noted above, in 1972, the latter was officially classified as an Arab state with which the U.S.S.R. has maintained friendly relations.[32] One obvious inference to be drawn from this interesting fact is the relative lack of importance which the Kremlin, at that time, attached to the Palestinian problem. Relations with an established Arab government — albeit a pro-Western one — were considered more important than the fate of the *Palestine Liberation Organization* (PLO).

The fluctuations in the more recent relations between the two states are best illustrated by an examination of Moscow's reaction to some of the outstanding problems facing the Hashemite Kingdom.

a) *The Palestinian Issue.* One of the main purposes of the Arab summit meeting, held in Rabat (Morocco) in October 1974, was to reach a consensus on the future status of the PLO. Since most Arab leaders favored its recognition as the "sole legitimate representative" of the Palestinian people — a stand heartily endorsed by the organization itself — their attitude brought them into a conflict with King Hussein who resented having to relinquish his claim to the West Bank. In the end, unable to withstand the pressure, the King bowed to the collective will of his fellow-rulers, a move sweetened by the Saudi offer of $300 million in economic aid.

As manifested by the reaction of the Soviet press, the Kremlin closely followed the developments at Rabat. Its interest was understandable: in addition to the conflict between Hussein and the PLO, the conference addressed itself to two other problems which were of major concern to the U.S.S.R. They were, in Soviet phraseology, "coordination of actions by the Arab states in the struggle for the liquidation of the consequences of Israeli aggression" and the subsequent "efforts to establish lasting peace in the Near East." In the context of the competition between Hussein and Yasser Arafat,[33] Moscow's sympathy was unmistakably on the side of the Palestinians. Commenting on the King's resistance to the PLO's demand to represent the West Bank Palestinians, *Pravda* criticized his attitude because it called into question the principle of "full-fledged Palestinian representation" at the Geneva peace conference and was, therefore, "not conducive to the early resumption of its activity." *Pravda* went on to say that the Arab states rejected Hussein's approach on the ground that "it would offer the Israeli aggressors additional opportunities . . . to sabotage peaceful regulation of the Near Eastern problem."[34]

It is equally noteworthy, however, that the King's subsequent attempts to circumvent the spirit and the letter of the Rabat decision by means of a continuing *de facto* involvement in the affairs of the West Bank have by and large gone unnoticed in the Soviet press.[35] Moscow's relative caution has been caused by a number of factors: its growing difficulties in the Arab East (particularly in relations with Egypt); rapprochement with Syria which, for reasons of its own, has established close cooperation with Jordan; the events in Lebanon; and, more recently, the possibility of concluding a major arms agreement with Amman.

Put differently, in the 1970s, while the Kremlin sympathized with the PLO, the exigencies of Russia's involvement in regional politics have dictated the adoption of policies which often clashed with its expressed preferences. The conflict between Hussein and the PLO is a case in point. At Rabat, the U.S.S.R. lent its moral support to the PLO, partly because of its preferences but mainly because this stance reinforced Moscow's call for the reconvening of the Geneva conference in which the Palestinians were to participate as a full-fledged member. Moreover, the PLO deserved Soviet support as one of the main opponents of Kissinger's "step-by-step" diplomacy, an effort which, among other things, has been aimed at excluding the Russians from the decision-making process.

Political problems of a major magnitude have arisen as a result of the Lebanese civil war. While Moscow's sympathies throughout the conflict have remained with the PLO and its "progressive" Lebanese allies, the Kremlin's break with Sadat forced the U.S.S.R. to strengthen its ties with Syria, of whose pro-Christian and anti-PLO stand in Lebanon it strongly disapproved. Since Damascus had by then also established close cooperation with Amman, any exacerbation of Soviet-Jordanian relations made no political sense either. In short, confronted with an extremely complex and delicate situation in the Arab East, the Soviets have adopted a pragmatic and opportunistic approach. In the specific context of relations between Jordan and the PLO, as noted, this has meant continued political and material support of the PLO, combined with official silence on its continuing problems and competition with Hussein. Another reason for Moscow's circumspect treatment of the King was, as indicated, the anticipated opportunity of providing Jordan with large quantities of Soviet weapons.

b) *The "Missile Deal."* Hussein's determination to procure a viable air defense system and other modern weapons stemmed from several interrelated considerations. For one thing, it was stimulated by awareness on the part of the King and his military that Jordan had been left hopelessly behind in the regional arms race which accelerated significantly after October 1973. The acquisition of surface-to-air (SAM) missiles in particular, was regarded by Amman as an absolute minimum requirement for the maintenance of an effective air defense. Moreover, both Assad and Hussein agreed that, in case of another Middle Eastern war, an Israeli attack on Syria would be carried out not through the heavily fortified Golan area but through the sparsely defended northwestern Jordan. The establishment in that region of an effective air defense system was therefore regarded as absolutely essential by both Amman and Damascus.

In his search for SAM missiles, Hussein, with the active encouragement of Saudi Arabia (which agreed to finance their acquisition provided they were purchased from the United States), first turned to Washington. After an initial accord, it became obvious that the amount of money allocated for the purchase by Riyadh fell far short of what Amman wanted to spend. In the ensuing squabble, Hussein publicly threatened to turn to the U.S.S.R. Negotiations with the United States were broken off in the spring of 1976, providing the Soviet leaders with what may have appeared to them as an opportunity to detach Jordan from its pro-Western orientation and reliance on Washington and Riyadh. The contention that the Kremlin was eagerly trying to exploit the situation for its own purposes is supported by the following facts. In May 1976, Marshal Pavel Kutakhov, Commander of the Soviet Air Force, arrived in Amman for what the Jordanians described as a "successful" visit. It was quickly followed by a dispatch of a Jordanian military mission to Moscow and by Hussein's second state visit to the U.S.S.R. (June 17-28, 1976). It now appears that, in the course of high-level negotiations, the Soviet government offered the King substantial quantities of advanced military equipment, including SAM missiles, at terms superior to those advanced by the United States. In the end, however, Hussein proceeded to renegotiate a SAM deal with Washington. (Otherwise, the visit resulted in a promise to increase economic, technical, and cultural cooperation between Jordan and the U.S.S.R.)[36]

Some Western commentators believe that Hussein's decision was made against the advice of Assad who supposedly encouraged the King to conclude a major arms deal with the Soviet Union on the ground that such a move would greatly facilitate a coordination of the Syrian and Jordanian defense systems. There is a ring of truth in this argument, which explains some of the reasons which probably prompted Hussein not to go through with the Soviet deal. For one thing, he must have been reluctant to tie himself too closely to Syria for fear that, in the process, Jordan would be reduced to a pawn in Assad's military and political plans. Moreover, heavy military reliance on the U.S.S.R. was likely to result in a serious alienation of the United States and Saudi Arabia which have consistently supported Amman as a bulwark against the aspirations of the "radical" Arab states. Their financial assistance, without which Jordan could not survive (unless it were prepared to accept other sponsors), might be severely curtailed or even discontinued. In short, it appears that Hussein had used his negotiations with Moscow as a leverage against Washington and Riyadh. His intention was to extract concessions from them more favorable than those they had been prepared to make in the spring of 1976. The King succeeded. In early September, it was announced in Amman that Jordan would receive 14 *Hawk* SAM missile batteries at an estimated cost of $540 million from the U.S. The Soviet missile deal was off and relations between Amman on the one hand and Washington and Riyadh on the other had once again returned to "normal."

Nevertheless, Moscow's failure to establish close working relations with the Hashemite Kingdom does not mean that major agreements involving sophisticated military hardware may not be negotiated in the future. Much will depend on the evolution of the general situation in the Middle East and, more specifically, on the political fortunes of Hussein himself. It is obvious that he prefers to steer clear of a close relationship with the U.S.S.R. It is equally clear, however, that, if placed in an (from his viewpoint) untenable position, he will deal with the Kremlin or anybody else. Staying in power remains his primary concern. As for the Soviet Union, it has tenaciously explored all the possibilities to expand its presence in the Middle East. Moscow may be expected to broaden its cooperation with Jordan significantly, should the opportunity present itself.

FOOTNOTES

1. "Iordaniia" in Akademiia nauk SSSR. Institut narodov Azii, *Noveishaia istoriia arabskikh stran (1917-1966)* (Moscow: Izdatel'stvo "Nauka," 1968), p. 136. (Henceforth referred to as "Iordaniia.") For more details, see L. N. Kotlov, *Iordaniia v noveishee vremia* (Moscow: Izdatel'stvo vostochnoi literatury, 1962), pp. 19-30.

2. Control of Tranjordan was secured officially by means of the 1928 Treaty which transformed the country into a British protectorate. "Iordaniia," p. 139. Details in *ibid.*, pp. 140-141. See also Kotlov, *op. cit.*, pp. 30-45.

3. "Iordaniia," pp. 142-143. For details, see Kotlov, *op. cit.*, pp. 56-81.

4. "Iordaniia," pp. 144-146. See also Kotlov, *op. cit.*, pp. 81-170.

5. "Iordaniia," p. 148. For details, see D. E. Mel'nikov and D. G. Tomashevskii, eds., *Mezhdunarodnye otnosheniia posle vtoroi mirovoi voiny* (Moscow: Politizdat, 1965), Vol. 3, p. 619, and Kotlov, *op. cit.*, pp. 170-185.

6. "Iordaniia," pp. 149-153. See also Kotlov, *op. cit.*, pp. 185-193.

7. "Iordaniia," p. 154.

8. "Iordaniia," p. 155.

9. *Izvestiia,* October 5, 1967. An agreement on cultural and scientific cooperation between the two states was signed on October 4. It provided for cooperation in the fields of science, higher education, health, tourism, artistic and sports exchanges. I. A. Kirilin *et al.,* eds., *Vneshniaia politika Sovetskogo Soiuza i mezhdunarodnye otnosheniia. Sbornik dokumentov. 1967 god* (Moscow: Izdatel'stvo "Mezhdunarodnye otnosheniia," 1968), p. 344, n. 70.

10. R. Petrov, "The Soviet Union and Arab Countries," *International Affairs* (Moscow), No. 11 (1972), p. 24.

11. "Iordaniia," p. 149.

12. *Ibid.,* p. 150 and Yaacov Ro'i, *From Encroachment to Involvement: A Documentary Study of Soviet Policy in the Middle East, 1945-1973* (New York: John Wiley and Sons, 1974), pp. 219-220.

13. *Documents on International Affairs, 1957,* pp. 262-263, as quoted in Ro'i, *op. cit.,* p. 220.

14. "Iordaniia," p. 150. See also Mel'nikov and Tomashevskii, *op. cit.,* Vol. 3, p. 619.

15. Ro'i, *op. cit.,* p. 220.

16. Raphael Patai, *The Kingdom of Jordan* (Princeton: Princeton University Press, 1958), p. 67.

17. Mel'nikov and Tomashevskii, *op. cit.,* Vol. 3, p. 619 and "Iordaniia," pp. 151-152.

18. Ro'i, *op. cit.,* pp. 221 and 223, respectively.

19. Patai, *op. cit.,* pp. 69-70. For a detailed Soviet account of the 1957 crisis, see Kotlov, *op. cit.,* pp. 194-224.

20. Ivison Macadam, ed., *The Annual Register: World Events in 1968* (New York: St. Martin's Press, 1969), p. 288.

21. Ivison Macadam, ed., *The Annual Register: World Events in 1970* (New York: St. Martin's Press, 1971), pp. 195-197 and Ro'i, *op. cit.,* p. 536.

22. I. A. Kirilin *et al.,* eds. *Vneshniaia politika Sovetskogo Soiuza i mezhdunarodnye otnosheniia. Sbornik dokumentov. 1970 god* (Moscow: Izdatel'stvo "Mezhdunarodnye otnosheniia," 1971), p. 239, n. 70.

23. For details, see Jon D. Glassman, *Arms for the Arabs: The Soviet Union and War in the Middle East* (Baltimore: The Johns Hopkins University Press, 1975), p. 82.

24. Ro'i, *op. cit.,* p. 539.

25. *Pravda,* September 24, 1970. English translation in Ro'i, *op. cit.,* pp. 539-540.

26. Kirilin, *Vneshniaia politika . . . 1970 god,* p. 240, n. 70. See also A. A. Gromyko and B. N. Ponomarev, eds., *Istoriia vneshnei politiki SSSR, 1917-1975* (Moscow: Izdatel'stvo "Nauka," 1976), Vol. 2, pp. 444-445.

27. Ro'i, *op. cit.,* p. 538.

28. Henry Brandon, "Jordan: The Forgotten Crisis," *Foreign Policy,* No. 10 (Spring 1973), p. 166. It is noteworthy, however, that no Russian advisers crossed into Jordan with the invading Syrian force. Glassman, *op. cit.,* pp. 82-83.

29. *Ibid.,* p. 86.

30. Text in Ro'i, *op. cit.,* p. 538.

31. As quoted in *ibid.,* p. 540. Italics added.

32. See above, p. 7.

33. Head of *al-fatah* and the leader of the PLO.

34. *Pravda,* October 29, 1974.

35. For example, the February 1976 dissolution of the Jordanian parliament and the resignation of the cabinet — moves designed to reiterate Hussein's claim to the West Bank — were bitterly criticized by the PLO but evoked no official Soviet comment. *Ibid.,* February 10, 1976.

36. *Ibid.,* July 4, 1976. The visit also served to air the tactical differences separating the two parties, particularly with respect to the growing Syrian involvement in Lebanon. In his speech honoring Hussein at a Kremlin dinner, President Podgornyi argued that the Lebanese should be enabled to settle their differences "without outside interference," while the King praised Syria's "humane national endeavors" in Lebanon. *Ibid.,* June 19, 1976.

VI

The West Bank

THE WEST BANK

THE WEST BANK

Geography of the West Bank

By NORMAN DLIN

When the Israeli-Jordanian Armistice Agreement took effect in 1949, King Abdallah's Legion had control of the Old City of Jerusalem and a portion of the city outside of the Old City walls that was known as East Jerusalem.[1] In addition, the Jordanians won control of two large areas extending from the Jordan River westward into the hill country of Samaria in the north and of Judea south of Jerusalem. This whole territory was referred to as the West Bank.

The areas of Judea and Samaria, which comprise the West Bank, form the mountainous spine of Palestine's Central Region. This line of mountainous terrain which forms the largest continuous range in Palestine has a length of 81 miles and an average width of 25 miles and is bounded in the south by the Be'er Sheba and Arad Basins, and in the north by the Bet She'an and Yizre'el Valleys.[2]

The total Arab population of Judea and Samaria (as of April 1976) was 688,600. This population is distributed amongst 457 settlements, 25 of which are towns with an urban population of 157,000.[3] Such statistics would strongly indicate that at least 77 per cent of the West Bank population is rural in character. The population of the West Bank is concentrated in and around a series of main towns which form an almost straight line, north-south, in the middle of the uplands: Jenin, Nablus, Ramallah, (Jerusalem), Bethlehem, and Hebron. The Judean Desert lies to the east of the line of towns. The area is barren, dry and practically uninhabited. It is a region in which only a few thousand Bedouin exist. Where there is sufficient water, as in Jericho, irrigation allows for production on small, intensely cultivated patches of land.

The climate of the West Bank can be described as one of short, cool, rainy winters with occasional snowfall in the higher elevations and long, hot, dry summers. In the hill country there is an average of 20 inches of precipitation, relatively high humidity, and relatively low evaporation. Temperatures are mild and even, and the growing season lasts six to seven months, with natural rainfall, and can be year-round with the utilization of irrigation. In the Jordan Valley, precipitation is between two to five inches annually, and the very high rate of evaporation is a result of low humidity. Temperatures are high in the summer. There is virtually no rainfall farming season, but in the vicinity of an oasis (such as Jericho) the growing season can be year-round with the application of irrigation.[4]

Dr. Dlin is a member of the Department of Social Sciences at Louisiana State University-Shreveport. His publications include maps and geographical studies.

Samaria

Samaria is the smaller of the two regions, but contained (in 1967) about half of the West Bank population (excluding East Jerusalem). Settlement in Eastern Samaria is less dense than in the center and west, owing to the predominance of rock and the diminishing amount of rainfall.[5] In the northern portion settlements are still fewer but larger, probably owing to their proximity to the Bet She'an Valley, which until the beginning of the twentieth century was the dominion of the Bedouin. The largest village is Tubas, (the biblical Tevez) which is situated on a wide plateau and had a population of 5,300, in 1967.

The basins of Samaria, especially in its northern sections, facilitated the development of routes from the earliest times of human activity in this region of the world. These routes developed more in an east-west movement than north-south. Considering the fact that only few roads cross Samaria, it would be wrong to define Samaria as more open than Judea. It would be more reasonable to state that the towns of Samaria were harder to defend because they were located on the lower slopes of hills or in the margins of valleys, while in Judea they were located on the upper slopes or on top of high hills.[6]

The combination of rounded topography, wide valleys, soils easily worked, numerous springs, and reliable rainfall, has made Samaria a most favorable region for human settlement for thousands of years. Archaeological evidence points to the existence of many settlements since the early Bronze Age and usually at locations presently occupied by villages. Whereas other parts of the country experienced periods of retreat (or partial retreat) of settlements Samaria can boast of continuity of settlement. There was one break in settlement which occurred during the Assyrian exile in 722 B.C. (of the ten tribes of Israel) but the interval was short as new Jewish settlers from all over the Assyrian Empire occupied the mostly vacated territory and became known, eventually, as Samaritans. Today, the Samaritans have dwindled down to a few hundred, living in two communities;[7] a Quarter in Nablus and in Holon, near Tel Aviv.

The continuity of settlement in Samaria also can be determined by present day village names, which still adhere to their biblical names, although phonetic changes have taken place. It is only along the eastern and western margins of Samaria that a number of settlements ceased to exist during insecure times but most of these places were resettled at the beginning of the Turkish rule, or during Egyptian occupation under Ibrahim Pasha.

As the best cultivable lands lie in the basins and since the upper slopes of the chalk hills are most often covered by a thin, hard crust, locally termed *nari,*[8] most of the villages are located on the lower hill slopes. There was population variation, as expected, during fluctuations in the political and economic situation but even during such times the population was the highest in the country. And it is due to this dense population and maximum utilization of all cultivable soils, that modern Jewish colonization found no foothold in Samaria.[9]

Almost equidistant from all four corners of the Samarian quadrangle and at the intersection an east-west, north-south axis of communication lies the town of Nablus[10] with a population of 44,000 (as of 1967). The town is located at the focus of converging valleys which provide adequate cropland. Nablus is an important urban center to the West Bank and during Jordanian rule it stood only second to East Jerusalem in importance. It has grown and spread so that its urban area now includes the adjoining villages of Rafidiya (to its west), El Balata and Askar (to its east), as well as two large refugee camps. It is the only town on the former West Bank of Jordan which developed a number of industries.[11] Nablus is also considered the main market for Samaria's agricultural products and is a collecting center for agricultural exports to Jordan and to the Persian Gulf countries.

The other Samaritan towns have developed from rural backgrounds since the beginning of the 20th century and owe their importance mainly to the construction and presence of a now defunct narrow gauge railway. The most important of these smaller towns is Tulkarm (population 9,000 as of 1967) built on an isolated hill which slopes west to the Sharon Plain and to the east towards a southern tributary of Nahal ("river") Shehem. Tulkarm gained importance as the terminus of this narrow gauge railway line from Afula (in Israel) and since 1918 served as the trans-shipment point to the standard gauge line which runs just west of the town in a north-south direction. Even when the narrow gauge line no longer operated, in 1942, Tulkarm was a break of bulk point (from railroad box car to truck) to carry products from Samaria to the coast and to the port of Jaffa. Its hinterland included not only villages in Samaria, but also Arab villages on the coastal plain. When Israel became a state in 1948, Tulkarm lost the western portion of its hinterland and all connections to the coast and it became a dead-end city. It partially recovered by developing secondary education institutions and the only teachers' seminary in the West Bank, but it lost a large number of people to emigration who, in turn, sent money back to their families, and this encouraged capital investment for commercial development.[12]

At the northern end of Samaria lies the town of Jenin (with a 1967 population of 13,400). It is located at the northern end of the gorge through which the Kishon River meanders from the Valley of Dotan to the Valley of Yizre'el. This gorge is the main transportation route from the center of Palestine to the north and the now dismantled narrow gauge railway that snaked its tortuous way from Tulkarm and Nablus through to Jenin and on to Afula further north. Despite its strategic location, Jenin never achieved any important position in history.

In modern times its hinterland extends only to Mount Gilboa and to the

Dotan Valley; it has almost no connections northward where the Yizre'el Valley was initially malaria-infested and uncultivated and later on was developed and built up by Jewish settlers. Only along the southern fringe of the Yizre'el Valley are some large Arab villages which oriented themselves towards Jenin. Since these villages were a part of the West Bank after 1948, Jenin remained essentially intact with respect to its economic hinterland and needed no change in its economic structure.[13]

Judea

Judea exhibits the most compact mountain mass which extends, without interruption, over fifty miles in length and its crest, whose width varies between nine and sixteen miles, stays above 2,460 feet above sea level, and in places reaches 3,280 feet above sea level. Its flanks descend steeply to the Shefela to the west and to the Jordan Valley and Dead Sea to the east. Judea can also be described as a barren, unbroken upland plateau with very few diversifying elements. Limestone and chalky marl are the predominant rock types, often with little or no soil cover. Characteristic of the Judean desert wilderness are wide areas of exposed rock, numerous boulders and scree, and small valleys carved in the slopes of hills that present a barren and dry landscape and having numerous caves and sub-surface drainage.

The only important settlement in the Judean Desert is the oasis of Jericho. Excavations, initially carried out at the end of the nineteenth century, and more recently since 1952, have brought to light the remains of houses and walls that date as far back as 7,000 B.C., which makes Jericho the oldest known town in the world. Jericho has had a long history but for our purposes we need concern ourselves with the town since the early twentieth century, when it had the status of a village. It began to grow again and during the British Mandate it reached the status of a small town and began to attract tourists, mainly during the mild and warm winter months. At the same time a large number of churches were built in the town although the population is mainly Muslim.

After 1948 the area of Jericho, due to the warm winter temperatures and the absence of precipitation, was the place that received the largest number of Palestinian refugees—some 70,000 of them being housed in mud buildings in a number of camps in the vicinity of Jericho. In 1967 most of these refugees fled to the east side of the Jordan, in contrast to the inhabitants of refugee camps in the mountains of the West Bank, who chose to stay in their camps. Jericho itself grew in size and in importance by providing services to the refugees and the available cheap refugee labor force was utilized in large banana, citrus, and other subtropical fruit plantations. Water for irrigating these plantations emanated from nearby Wadi Qilt and from all of the many springs in the area. A large number of irrigation canals (up to a distance of six miles from the town) turned Jericho into a lush garden of green fruit and vegetables in the midst of the harsh dryness and bareness of the desert.

The town (10,000 inhabitants in 1967) also developed tourist services, hotels, and especially restaurants for the population of Jordanian Jerusalem and Amman, and for European tourists. With Israel's occupation in 1967, the economic base of the town was largely erased. There was an exodus of refugees and a discontinuance of tourism. Apart from the sale of its agricultural products to Jerusalem and to the Arab countries, via the Allenby Bridge across the Jordan River, Jericho really has very little of an economic base.[14]

Marginal to the Judean Desert and just north of Jerusalem the only urban settlements are the Christian town of Ramallah (population of 12,100 in 1967), and the Muslim town of Bireh (population of 9,700 in 1967). The development of Ramallah was not due to its supposed functions as a regional center, but rather to its proximity to Jerusalem. Because of its higher altitude and cooler summer temperatures, Ramallah became a recreational town and a dormitory suburb of East Jerusalem; a town favored by tourists from Arab countries and by Christian pilgrims. It also developed a number of small industrial enterprises besides its main income from tourism. Since the Israeli occupation in 1967 Ramallah, like Jericho, has been hard hit economically.

The Jerusalem Saddle is a region of easier topography and communications owing to lower elevations. The eastern rim of the saddle is the only area in the Judean Mountains where Senonian chalks appear on the crest of the mountain. Since these soils have always been preferred, a number of villages east of Jerusalem and also Bethlehem and its suburb, Beit Sahur, are based on them. Generally, the saddle's environment is more favorable to settlement and communications, and this has found its expression historically in higher population density and in the centrality of Jerusalem. The agriculture is similar to that found in the Ramallah area, subsisive on poorer soils with olives and vines on better soils. In the vicinity of Bethlehem the vine predominates, possibly because of the Christian population, which was not affected by the Muslim prohibition on the consumption of wine.

In 1948 a wedge in the western part of the area remained within Israel's boundaries and became known as the "Jerusalem Corridor." With the exception of the Arab population of Abu Gosh, the Arab population in the "Corridor" fled during the fighting to other areas of the West Bank. On the north and south flanks of the "Corridor" the Arab villages within Jordanian jurisdiction continued with their traditional agriculture of olives and vines but also increased their production of a variety of fruits.

The urban center for this region is the city of Jerusalem which became a divided city, as a result of the 1948 fighting. The Jordanian part included the Walled City and the northern and southeastern quarters outside the wall. The Jewish Quarter, inside the Old City, was demolished for the most part; Arabs took over the Quarter and all the Jews who were captured after a negotiated surrender were expelled and handed over to the Israelis who were in control of the western and southern (or new) portions of Jerusalem. Arabs who had lived in Israeli-held areas fled to the Jordanian areas. In addition, Israel held onto Mount Scopus (which contained the Hebrew University and Hadassah Hospital) as an enclave within Jordanian territory.

Jordanian-held East Jerusalem was affected by partition of the city as much as the western (Israeli) side. However, it did not become isolated like the Israeli side and it retained its connections with parts of the country to the north and to the east. Only the connection with Bethlehem, to the south, required the creation of a long and tortuous detour across the Qidron Valley. The severance of all connections with the coast deprived the city of its role as a transit station for goods and of most of its wholesale trade. The severance of the functions as a capital after the British departure from Palestine, hit East Jerusalem harder than the western portion, as the number of Arabs involved in government services were much more numerous than Jews. These functions were never restored for East Jerusalem because of the policy of the Jordanian government to foster Amman in all aspects of the economy and to shift and centralize all industrial development over to the East Bank. Despite these major set-backs, East Jerusalem retained some of its former functions. Its importance as a Muslim religious center increased; the Christian Holy Places still attracted international pilgrimages, although not in any great numbers for the first ten years of Jordanian rule because of a lack of suitable hotel accommodations. Only the Jewish Holy Places ceased to attract tourists, since no Jew was allowed to visit Jordan, and the Jewish Quarter, with its many synagogues and the cemetery on the Mount of Olives, were destroyed.

East Jerusalem also retained its functions as a regional center for Judea and its sukhs (markets) continued to serve the large rural population of its surroundings. It also had to cope with the problem of refugees from "Israeli" Jerusalem. Since most of these refugees were of a higher income group, it was easier for them to find employment or opportunities elsewhere and many of them moved to Bethlehem, Ramallah, and Amman. The population of East Jerusalem thus declined in the first years after partition and remained constant at around 60,000.[15]

A change in the economic situation of East Jerusalem occurred when the Jordanian government decided to encourage tourism as the main source of the city's income. In a short time a large number of hotels (of all categories) were built and the resultant increase of tourism also provided income for a large number of souvenir shops, restaurants, taxi drivers, and guides. Rural residents also flourished from income derived from money sent by members of their families living in Europe or in other Arab countries, and from an increase in agricultural produce shipped out to other Arab countries and consumed locally because of a stimulated economy. The 1960s brought an era of prosperity to East Jerusalem but it also created strong social differentiation, as wages remained low owing to the plentiful labor force existent in nearby refugee camps.

Both portions of the city (east and west) grew, and both had, to an extent, overcome the overwhelming trauma of partition. In both cases tourism served to bring badly needed money to each side of the border. Both parts increased their area considerably in a direction away from the border; West Jerusalem to the west, and East Jerusalem to the north and east. Whereas the border zone in both parts declined sharply in economic and social significance, both sides developed new economic activities and commercial centers. Both were subjected to strong competition from rival cities (Tel Aviv and Amman) although East Jerusalem suffered more, because Amman competed with it as a capital city, and on an economic level, while West Jerusalem was the center of government for the State of Israel and competed with Tel Aviv only on an economic basis. Because of the importance of Amman and the direction of all economic and governmental matters to that city, East Jerusalem had trouble keeping its population while Israel had become a land of immigration and, thus, West Jerusalem had grown by almost double its population of 1948 (from 100,000 to 196,000 in 1966).

Reunification after the Six Day War in 1967 has affected life in East Jerusalem more than in the western part of the city, as connections with Jordan and other Arab countries were severed, in part, after having been developed for twenty years. Muslim tourism has almost completely disappeared, and Christian tourism has only partly revived. In their place, Israelis and Jews from abroad have come in much greater numbers but their tastes and preferences are much different from those of Muslims and Christians and the Arab souvenir shopkeepers have suffered the most; their adjustment to the "new" tourist being a slow one. Building activity came to a sudden halt because Amman froze all the assets deposited in its banks. However, many construction workers from the east side have found employment on the west side and the hotels have changed their character in order to cater to Jewish tourists.

East Jerusalem is also regaining its former connections with coastal outlets, rather than Amman, and the fortuitous trade and travel between the West and East Banks, via the Damiyah and Allenby Bridges, has again stimulated trade and economy for Arabs on both sides of the Jordan River.

Closely tied to East Jerusalem's tourism (whether united or partitioned) Bethlehem is located but ten minutes drive due south of Jerusalem. In spite of its religious significance, Bethlehem was always only a small town based mainly on agriculture on the easily worked rendzina soils. It becomes very active only at Christmas time, when its Manger Square is crowded with Christian pilgrims wishing to visit the Church of the Nativity (the traditional birthplace of Christ). Bethlehem also developed a small souvenir industry based on mother-of-pearl and olive wood. The town began to develop tourism, and prospered, during Jordan's rule. When the Israelis took over in 1967, Bethlehem and the two nearby Christian villages of Beit Jala (located to the west) and Beit Sahur (situated to the east) together with some refugee camps, comprised an urban area with a population of 28,000. The population of Bethlehem alone was 14,000; 6,200 (or 44 per cent) of which was Christian.[16]

Unlike Ramallah and Jericho the economy of Bethlehem, although temporarily interrupted by the 1967 war, has continued to recuperate and has made progress from two main sources: tourism at Christmas time and employment opportunities in a united Jerusalem.

The Hebron Mountains

The Hebron Mountains occupy about half of the Judean Mountains and form the highest continuous area of Palestine, as most of the crest area lies 2,952´ above sea level. The transitional character of the southern part of the Hebron Mountains is also expressed by its climate; with diminishing elevation, precipitation decreases rapidly from 27 inches at the northern end of the mountains to 18 inches at Hebron and less than 12 inches on the southern slopes. Thus, the Mountains of Hebron have always had a close tie with the desert and through history, served as a defense against the Bedouin. The rocks of this region are mainly dolomite and limestone strongly influenced by karstic solutions which, through time, have weathered into stony wastes that are mostly unsuitable for cultivation. Almost all of the crest region north of Hebron consists of an alternation of narrow basins with rocky outcrops that rise as narrow ridges 160-490 feet above the basin floors. These basins have coverings of deep, stony, fertile soils. Since the basins are at altitudes of over 2,600 feet above sea level (which is the upper limit for olive growing) they have been utilized primarily for vineyards, for which Hebron is famous. The southern part of the mountains have rendzina soils but they are shallow and very stony and this combined with reduced precipitation in the south restricts agriculture in the region to marginal dry cereal crops.[17]

During the period of Jordanian rule agriculture in the area underwent a dramatic change owing to the influx of capital sent in by West Bank emigrants living in oil rich Arab countries. Almost all the high ground of the crest was converted into vineyards, not only in the basins and valleys, but also on the rocky outcrops, by the blasting out of terraces. Thus, the crest of the Hebron Mountains, except for the area south of Hebron, has been turned into an almost uninterrupted region of plantations.

The town of Hebron is the natural and historical urban center of the region. It never developed an important position outside of its region (such as in the case of Jerusalem) and it was destroyed many times by war and earthquakes. By the nineteenth century its population was approximately 10,000, living in three Quarters, each on a different hill, with the outer housing utilized as portions of walls to ensure security and privacy. By the end of the nineteenth century, people began to settle outside the "walls," mainly north along the road to Jerusalem, but later settlement spread over all the surrounding hills without plan, or pattern, or access roads, or a water supply.

There was always a small Jewish community in Hebron that kept alive Jewish tradition and learning—with only a few of these Jews engaged in economic pursuits. It was in the fourteenth century that Jews from Venice introduced the art of glass blowing into Hebron and it has, through the centuries, been taken over by the Muslims and is, today, one of the main economic activities in the town. In 1929 a large portion of the Jewish community was massacred during anti-Jewish rioting, and by 1936 Arab hostility had risen to the point where the continuance of Jewish settlement became impossible and they were forced to leave.

The town grew to a population of 38,000 (in 1967) and its special feature is the prevalence of agriculture (especially vineyards) in which 44 per cent of the town's people are still engaged. Hebron has some industry: glass manufacturing, which has revived since 1967; the processing of grapes (but not into wine because of the orthodox attitude of the Muslim population) and the processing of hides into leather goods. It still presents a picture of a traditional Muslim town, which it is, based mainly on trade and agriculture, with its regional population and Bedouin.[18]

FOOTNOTES

1. Bull, Vivian A. *The West Bank—Is it Viable?*, (Lexington, Mass.: Lexington Books, D.C. Heath & Co., 1975).

2. Karmon, Yehuda. *Israel: A Regional Geography*, (New York: John Wiley & Sons Ltd), 1971.

3. Israel Consulate General, New York City, 1976.

4. Bull, *op. cit.*, p. 28.

5. Karmon, *op. cit.*, p. 321.

6. *Ibid.*, p. 323.

7. Many Samaritans converted to Christianity during the Byzantine period and many converted to Islam when the Arabs conquered the region during the Islamic period. Those who identify as Samaritans meet every year to celebrate Passover on Mount Gerizim.

8. Orni, Efraim, Efrat, Elisha. *Geography of Israel*, (Jerusalem: Israel Program for Scientific Translations, 1966).

9. There were some 20 Jewish settlements, either of a para-military or civilian nature in Samaria as of 1976.

10. Nablus is located on the site of the ancient biblical town of Shehem.

11. The industries would be soap making, a match factory, a large number of carpentry shops, and car repairsm

12. Karmon, *op. cit.*, p. 325.

13. *Ibid.*, p. 325.

14. *Ibid.*, p. 335.

15. The census undertaken by the Israel Census Bureau in 1967 tabulated 65,857 Arabs in East Jerusalem.

16. Karmon, *op. cit.*, p. 328.

17. *Ibid.*, p. 329.

18. *Ibid.*, p. 331.

Continuity and Change in Palestinian Society

By JOEL S. MIGDAL

The long decay of Ottoman rule through the eighteenth and nineteenth centuries had a profound effect upon the peoples living in Palestine. By the nineteenth century, minimal control was exercised over the Arab provinces directly by the Empire. Instead, in the several administrative districts that made up the entity long thought of as Palestine, real power was left in the hands of local urban notables and rural sheiks. Through intimidation, use of the small numbers of Ottoman soldiers, and recruitment of their own private armies, urban notables took advantage of the institution of tax-farming to forge alliances with the sheiks in order to skim off produce from the poor and vulnerable peasants. A fairly rigid hierarchy, then, linked the rural and urban areas and resulted in exactions that at times resembled outright plunder.

The plight of the poor Arab was compounded by the minimal protection afforded by his rulers. Bedouin tribes roamed the coastal plain of Palestine victimizing the sedentary farmers. One major result of this lack of protection was the clustering of peasants in the towns (from which they often trekked long distances daily to their fields) and in villages situated on the hilltops and mountains in the eastern section of the country. Although the mountainous terrain was far from the most fertile in Palestine, it did afford greater protection against marauders. By the beginning of the nineteenth century, then, Palestine was greatly depopulated (about 200,000 Arabs), and the Arab population was concentrated in the coastal towns and principally in the hilly areas on the west bank of the Jordan River.

Following a brief period sandwiched between conquest by the Egyptian

Dr. Migdal is Associate Professor of Political Science in the Department of Government at Harvard University. He is editing a book on *Palestinian Society and Community: Continuities and Changes Under the Impact of Four Regimes.*

leader Muhammad Ali and reconquest by the Ottomans, Palestine became subject in the middle decades of the nineteenth century to the last gasp efforts at reform on the part of the Empire. New laws were enacted and enforced that were designed to bring greater central control to the provinces and a greater flow of resources (through taxes and other means) from the provinces to the center. These laws included prohibitions against common holdings and requirements for proper registration of lands. The reforms also significantly increased the security in many parts of the country.

In terms of movements of people, a pattern began to emerge in the 1860s that would characterize Palestinian Arabs for the next 80 years. That pattern was a steady movement westward into the coastal plain and fertile valleys in the more western portion of the country and into the towns and their surrounding villages on the Mediterranean shore. At first, this movement was tentative as peasants farmed areas that had long lain fallow but returned nightly to their "home" villages. In a relatively short time, new permanent communities dotted the western, lower lying parts of Palestine.

Stratification patterns began to change rapidly as well. The new laws of the reform period were utilized best by the notable families of the Arab provinces who were able to widen the gap between themselves and the peasants. The peasants lost title to their lands in many cases and went deeply into debt as they borrowed for short-term consumption loans. Notable families changed from tax-farmers into large landlords and moneylenders. Local village strongmen, such as the sheiks and the new muhtars, slowly began to lose their position of preeminence in Palestinian communities.

In a number of ways, British indirect rule that began after World War I merely led to a continuation of patterns already begun under the Ottomans. The Palestinian population more than doubled in the last hundred years of Ottoman rule to more than a half million and then more than doubled again in the thirty years of British rule. The Jewish investment in an economic and social infrastructure was augmented by British investments and these served as magnets that drew increasing numbers of Arabs to the Mediterranean coastal areas. In the decade of the 1920s, for example, greater Haifa and greater Jaffa were just about doubling their Arab populations while more eastern towns, such as Bethlehem and Nablus, were growing even more slowly than the overall rate of Arab natural increase. The center of gravity of Palestinian Arab society was shifting perceptibly westward. After a slowdown in the westward movement of people during the Arab Revolt of 1936-1939, the pace picked up considerably in the 1940s, spurred by British war investments on the coast and by the construction of military camps. In fact, despite the deep communal and political animosities among the Arabs, Jews, and British, a growing structural interdependence, centered along the coastal strip, characterized one aspect of their interrelations.

Some stratification patterns during the Mandate also continued to reflect those in the late Ottoman period. The position of village leaders and power-brokers, for example, continued to erode. Other stratification patterns, however, took new turns as the British had a dual effect on Palestinian leadership. On one level, British policy served to strengthen the position of the already dominant notables, led by the Husayni and Nashashibi clans of Jerusalem. In the early years of their rule, especially, when Palestine was a separate entity from its Arab neighbors (for the first time in centuries) the British choices as to whom among the Palestinians to deal with were critically important. The result was that British actions greatly helped the notables establish themselves as an all-Palestinian political and religious leadership based in Jerusalem. Although highly antagonistic to the British Mandate because of its legitimization of a Jewish National Home, the notables were able to achieve the highest political cohesion the Palestinian Arabs ever had—due, in part, to British policies. Even when the British struck out against the Arab leadership in the 1930s, they never seriously considered moving outside the circle of notable families in their political dealings.

On a second level, British investments and economic policies facilitated the development of a new elite situated in the growing cities along the coast. Consisting of labor union leaders, industrialists, and white collar workers, the new elite benefited from the shift of Arab population to the western portion of the country by beginning to establish a new Arab economic infrastructure. This infrastructure, and the temporary and permanent migrants who were absorbed into it, weakened the notable families' basis of control. The leverage that doling out tenancies and credit had brought to the old elite was declining significantly. On this level, then, the British (together with Jewish economic activity) posed a serious threat to the very elite that they were legitimizing on the political level. Although the conflict never became as overt and intense as that between the Husayni and Nashashibi factions, the existence of a new socio-economic elite did provide the basis for a possible struggle over the new pattern of stratification among Palestinian Arabs. Some signs of such a conflict became evident, as in the growing role of the *Istiqlal* Party, the party of many intellectuals, and in the emergence of a labor union movement. In short, a struggle began as to the geographic locus of power in Palestinian Arab society; between the old center of gravity in Jerusalem and the new in Jaffa and Haifa.

Events surrounding the British withdrawal from Palestine in 1948 precipitated a reversal of the long, steady pattern of westward movement of Palestinian Arabs and their concentration in coastal towns and cities. The 1948 war resulted in a de-urbanization of Palestinian Arab society. There was a stream away from the coast to the refuge of Arab controlled territory. The horror of those years in the late 1940s led to a renewed importance of the villages and the sleepy towns of Nablus and Hebron, among others on the West Bank, and to the creation of a new locus for the Palestinian population: the refugee camp. Also, for the first time in more than a century, a significant out-migration of Arabs from Palestine began. At times temporary and at times permanent, the emigration from the villages, towns, and refugee camps of the West Bank was encouraged by the Jordanian regime in the face of the sudden explosive growth of the West Bank population and the beginning of a severe economic depression.

Stratification patterns were also greatly upset in the 1947-1949 period. The old elite composed of the notable families was tremendously weakened. The debacle of the 1948 war discredited the old political leaders and also cut greatly into their primary resource, landholdings, especially in the fertile coastal plain. Parts of the Nashashibi clan were absorbed into the Jordanian government, while the Mufti of Jerusalem, Hajj Amin al-Husseini, tried unsuccessfully to establish his faction as a government-in-exile in Gaza. But for all intents and purposes, the era of the notables came to an end (although, somewhat later, a new generation of Palestinian leaders seemed to be drawn disproportionately from the same notable families).

The new infrastructure that had been constructed on the coast by white collar, labor, and industrial elites was completely destroyed. The two streams that had made up the upper elements of Palestinian society under the Mandate found themselves, after 1948, without the resources or credibility to continue to exert significant influence in Palestinian society as in the past. There was a dramatic reversal away from an all-Palestinian political leadership (based in Jerusalem) and from an all-Palestinian socio-economic leadership (based in Jaffa-Haifa). Instead, Palestinians witnessed the emergence of a new pattern of stratification, one that was characterized by the renewed strength of local kinship ties and by the reemergence of local-level powerbrokers. These powerbrokers, who were often large landowners *on a local scale,* were the connecting links between the East Bank Jordanian political leadership and the Palestinian population in the West Bank. The Jordanian regime rewarded these leaders for their roles but also acted so as to prevent those roles from expanding and developing an all-West Bank base.

The 1967 war and the subsequent Israeli rule on the West Bank served to maintain some of the established social patterns among the Palestinian Arabs. Out-migration from the West Bank was huge during the 1967 war and continued high, as in Jordanian times, after 1967. This out-migration continued the process of dispersal of Palestinians, feeding a growing Palestinian diaspora. In addition, the Palestinian population kept up its high rate of growth, doubling overall in the years between the wars of 1948 and 1967. Other trends were more reminiscent of the Mandate period. The 1967 war, for example, seemed to reestablish the westward flow of Palestinians to the coastal areas after an almost twenty year hiatus.

There was, however, a major difference from the migratory pattern established during the late Ottoman rule and the Mandate: all movement was now temporary. The old roads that had precipitated Arab urbanization and the creation of a new elite and economic infrastructure among the Palestinians during the Mandate period now served only as a daily commuting route. The constraints imposed by Israeli military rule and the twenty years of development of Israeli society precluded the new movement of people from creating a new all-Palestinian socio-economic leadership or a new economic infrastructure. Like the Jordanians before them, the Israelis adopted policies to block the creation of an all-West Bank elite. Stratification patterns, as a result, tended to continue to be local hierarchies, centering around the major West Bank towns.

British policy during the Mandate had fostered a traditional political leadership and, simultaneously, a new elite in a position to challenge the notables. Israeli policy created a similar anomaly but at a different level of Palestinian society. Israeli military administrators sought to deal through the traditional, *local* leadership including mayors and muhtars who had served under Jordanian rule. Simultaneously, Israeli economic policy, geared toward West Bank economic growth and utilization of West Bank Arabs in the labor force in Israel proper, has undermined the basis of authority of these traditional local leaders. Laborers have been earning more than landowning muhtars in many cases. New intellectual and professional elements have emerged. Unlike the pre-1948 period, however, these upwardly mobile elements do not have the social bases or infrastructure to exert an all-Palestinian leadership (i.e., there are no indigenous labor unions, no industries, no political machines).

Open hostility between the old powerbrokers and the new upwardly mobile, usually the young people, is not uncommon. In one village, several young men openly ridiculed the older powerbrokers. In other villages, the old leadership has quietly surrendered to the changes and sees itself as surrogates for the will of the new, young leaders. Israeli rule, in short, has led to new sources of income, a new distribution of income and new status bases among Palestinians and has thus undermined, even further, the old bases of social control in Palestinian society.

The changes in migration and stratification patterns over the last century and more, thus, have had significant effects on Palestinian social and political cohesion. By 1948, Ottoman reforms and British policy, along with Jewish immigration, had precipitated great changes in the structure and locational center of Palestinian society. Demographic changes and the growth of a new infrastructure were already undermining the social bases of the political elite—land ownership, money-lending, control over religious funds. The Palestinians' brief political cohesion was fraught with severe cracks after a generation of British rule.

It was the wars of the last generation, however, that led to the great discontinuities in changes in social patterns. The 1948 war destroyed the bases for an all-Palestinian hierarchy—both the all-Palestinian political leadership and all-Palestinian socio-economic leadership. These hierarchies had been the conduits for the political authority and social control that could serve as prerequisites for the development of a cohesive society. After the war, the Jordanian regime frowned on such cohesiveness and instead fostered local hierarchies through its support of local powerbrokers. But the shocks of the 1967 war and subsequent Israeli policy undermined even these leadership bases. By the 1970s, Palestinians found that they could lend expressive support to various political leaders (principally in the PLO), but that the real bases of social cohesion and social control in the society were now restricted to their simple families and clans that had weathered all the upheavals of the century.

The Jewish Presence on the West Bank

By MORDECAI S. CHERTOFF

"The West Bank" is a singularly imprecise designation, since it refers neither to a duly constituted political nor a naturally recognizable geographical entity. Historically, it was never a discrete political unit but rather an undistinguishable part of British Mandatory Palestine, as was Jordan itself before the first partition of 1922.

Ironically enough, there are almost as many different approaches to the disposition to be made of the West Bank among Arabs themselves as there are among the Israelis.[1] Whatever their differences concerning the disposition of the West Bank, however, Israelis are in accord over the past. Their awareness of the West Bank's place in Jewish history precludes any easy consensus about the area's future.

Between 1967 and 1974, the Israelis established some twenty-six settlements in the West Bank area — the ancient Judea and Samaria: seventeen in the Jordan Valley, a sparsely populated region along the 1967 ceasefire line,[2] five in the Hebron area and four in the vicinity of Jerusalem. The several thousand Israeli civilians now living in Judea and Samaria are few indeed when seen in the perspective of historical Jewish associations with the area.

Judea

The oldest such Jewish association is with Hebron, south of Jerusalem. It was in Hebron that the Patriarch Abraham bought the Cave of Machpelah as a

Dr. Chertoff has translated books and articles from Hebrew into English. He is the editor of *The New Left and the Jews,* Pittman Publishing Co., 1971 and the co-editor of *Israel: Social Structure and Change,* Transaction Press, 1973.

burial site for Sarah[3] and where he and the other Patriarchs and their wives —
with the exception of Rachel — were subsequently buried. It was in Hebron,
also, two millenia later, that David was annointed King over Judah[4] and
where he reigned for nine years before he established Jerusalem as the capital
of the united kingdom of Judah and Israel. Hebron was one of the levitical
cities[5] and a city of refuge[6] and one of the four holy cities with Jerusalem,
Safed and Tiberias.

The Jewish community of Hebron survived the destruction of both Temples
and maintained the continuity of Jewish settlement through successive con-
quests down to the Crusader period, when they were expelled in the year
1,100. However, one hundred years later Jews were already returning to
Hebron. By the beginning of the sixteenth century the Jewish community
there had already grown to such proportions and had achieved sufficient
economic status to make it worthwhile for the Sultan's deputy to put his
troops to the trouble of looting Hebron in the hope of gaining wealth. The fact
that a contemporary document[7] states that "they killed many people" attests
to the growth of the Jewish population. Over the centuries that population
fluctuated with the changing regimes, reaching a new low with World War I
and the conscription of its young men into the Turkish army. Following the
British conquest in 1918 the community recovered, only to be subjected to
Arab riots in 1929, when in the face of British passivity Arabs killed sixty-
seven and wounded another sixty people, among them women, children and
the aged. The community was destroyed, but two years later thirty-five
families returned and began to rebuild it. In the riots of 1936 it was all
destroyed again, and in April of that year the British evacuated the Jewish
inhabitants of Hebron. One Jewish family remained until 1947. The following
year Hebron was incorporated into the Kingdom of Jordan.

The Israel army captured Hebron in the Six Day War of 1967. On the eve of
Passover, 1968, a group of religious settlers went to reestablish Jewish settlement there. After initial opposition from local Arab as well as government
sources, Jewish settlement in the area (not within Hebron proper) was approved and the new suburb of *Kiryat Arba*[8] was created, renewing the four
millenia Jewish association with Hebron. By 1976, Kiryat Arba's population
had grown to over 1,500.

Neither Bethlehem nor Jericho, both rich in biblical history, have played
much of a role in modern Jewish history. Bethlehem was the center for the
tribe of Judah,[9] and the setting for the story in the Book of Ruth. It was also
the birthplace of David, and it was there that he was annointed king by
Samuel.[10] Jews lived in Bethlehem until the end of the Bar Kokhba rebellion
and Roman occupation of the city in 135 B.C. Jericho is the oldest known
town in Palestine and was a fortified city — already destroyed and rebuilt a
number of times — when Joshua sent his spies to investigate the defenses of
the Promised Land.[11] The Prophets Elijah and Elisha lived in Jericho.[12] The

city grew in the seventh and sixth centuries, and was destroyed by the Babylonians in 587 B.C. Resettled by Babylonian exiles[13] it contained a small community during the post-Exilic period, was abandoned during the Hellenistic period and destroyed again during the Jewish War (66-70). That Jericho subsequently did have Jewish inhabitants is indicated by the remains of a basilical-shaped synagogue dating to the seventh century. It was oriented toward Jerusalem, and had a mosaic pavement decorated with a *menorah,* the inscription "peace on Israel," and a memorial inscription in Aramaic[14] A third biblical town, Anatot, famous as the birthplace of the Prophet Jeremiah,[15] was in the vicinity of modern Anabta, an Arab village with some 1,260 inhabitants.[16]

East Jerusalem, annexed by Jordan in 1950 (an act recognized only by Britain and Pakistan and opposed by the Arab League), was retaken by the Israel army in the Six Day War and incorporated in the State of Israel. Since the gamut of Israel opinion on the future of the West Bank excludes Jerusalem, it is beyond the scope of this essay.[17]

An additional "West Bank" Jewish enclave, one without any known biblical antecedents, is the Etzion Bloc. Located in the Hebron Hills about fourteen miles south of Jerusalem, the first attempt at settlement there was made in 1926-27, and abandoned in the Arab riots of 1929. Further attempts in 1935 were frustrated by the Arab rebellion of 1936-39. However, in 1943 Kfar Etzion and three other settlements: Massu'ot Yitzhak, Ein Zurim and Revadim were founded by members of *HaKibbutz HaDati.* * The Etzion Bloc was subject to frequent Arab attacks during the war of 1948 and on May 12, 1948, was surrounded by the Arab Legion and vast numbers of Arab irregulars. After two days of desperate fighting, the bloc was overwhelmed and most of the defenders — men and women, the children had been evacuated earlier — were massacred by an Arab mob after surrendering to the Legion. The Etzion Bloc, together with the surrounding Hebron Hills, was retaken by the Israel Army in the Six Day War, on June 7, 1967. Three months later Kfar Etzion was resettled by members of *HaKibbutz HaDati,* including children of the original settlers massacred in 1948.[18]

Samaria

Despite the sentimental-historical Jewish affinities to Samaria, the northern portion of the "West Bank," modern Jewish settlement in the area was frustrated by two forces: Muslim fanaticism and the opposition of the British Mandatory Government,[19] which restricted Jewish land purchase and settlement in heavily Muslim areas.

Samaria (modern Sebaste) was the capital of the kingdom of Israel in the ninth-eighth centuries B.C. It was founded by Omri, King of Israel,[20] — the ruins of his palace and that of King Ahab have been excavated. It was

---

* The religious communal settlement movement.

conquered by Sargon II of Assyria in 722-21 B.C., and its inhabitants were deported.[21] Colonists from Bablyon and other places were brought in and together with the Israelite remnant formed the nucleus of the Samaritan population. During the Hasmonean reign Jews lived in Samaria once again, and Herod rebuilt it in 25 B.C.,[22] naming it Sebaste in honor of Augustus. It subsequently declined, was revived by Septimius Severus[23] and was finally destroyed by the Persians in 614. The Arab village on the site today has a population of some 1,300 people.

Shechem was another ancient Canaanite and then Israelite city, first mentioned in the Bible in connection with Abraham's arrival in Canaan.[24] It was the scene of the rape of Dinah[25] and the burial place of Joseph.[26] Joshua assembled the tribes there for the great covenant.[27] In the period of the Judges it was the center of the kingdom of Abimelech, the son of Gideon.[28] It was at Shechem, too, that Solomon's son Rehoboam was repudiated by the ten tribes of Israel, who crowned Jeroboam king in his place,[29] and Shechem served as Jeroboam's capital. It underwent a series of destructions and rebuildings, finally by the Samaritans, who had been expelled from Samaria by Alexander the Great.[30] The Hellenistic city was destroyed by John Hyrcanus in 107 B.C.[31]

Three additional Arab towns of any consequence — the "triangle" of Nablus, Jenin and Tulkarm — must be mentioned, even though none of these has any Jewish residents. Tulkarm, when taken by the Israel army in 1967, had a total of 10,157 inhabitants of whom 103 were Christians and the rest Muslims. Of the total population, 5,020 lived in a refugee camp.[32] Jenin, from which the Arab Liberation Army under Fawzi al-Qawuqji set out to attack the Israeli settlement of Mishmar HaEmek during the 1948 war, was also almost totally Muslim: there were 90 Christians out of 8,346 residents, while 4,480 were living in a refugee camp.[33] There is no record of Jewish settlement efforts in either of these cities.

Nablus, however, under early Muslim rule, contained a mixed population of Muslims, Persians, Samaritans and Jews.[34] A synagogue was built there in 362, while a Jewish community is known to have existed there in 1522.[35] This community remained until shortly after 1900, when it was abandoned. Following World War I, Jews again tried to live in Nablus but it was a center of Muslim fanaticism and the 1929 riots ended these attempts.[36] Nablus had a population of 44,000 in 1967, all Muslim except for 370 Christians and some 250 Samaritans. There were, in addition, about 26,000 people in the neighboring villages and the refugee camps next to the town.[37]

An attempt was made by a group of some thirty Jewish settlers to establish a permanent settlement near Nablus in early 1976. Camp Kaddoum, as it is called, has been a focus of controversy ever since the Rabin government insisted that these settlers would have to move to an alternate site to be offered to them by the government, while the settlers themselves have been insisting on the historical Jewish right to live in the area. The issue has not yet been resolved.[38]

One of the most recent Israeli ventures in the Judea area of the West Bank is Ma'ale Adumim, a barren site nine miles east of Jerusalem on the road to Jericho. A major new industrial park, expected to cover about 1,500 acres when completed, is being created.[39] While some housing is available there for people working in the area, it is not a settlement in the accepted sense of the term.

By the end of 1976, a total of sixty-eight settlements had been established in all of the Israeli occupied areas — the West Bank, the Golan Heights, Sinai, and the Gaza Strip. The Israeli Jewish population of the area, somewhat over 3,000, comprises 0.3 percent of the total. By contrast, Arabs constitute 14.7 percent of Israel's population.[40]

FOOTNOTES

1. Yigal Allon, "Israel: The Case for Defensible Borders," in *Foreign Affairs Quarterly*, Vol. 55, No. 1, October, 1976. pp. 38-53, especially pp. 50-51.

2. *Judea and Samaria*, by H. Zeev, M. Gihon and Z. Levkowich, Carta, Jerusalem, 1974, p. 2.

3. Genesis 23:17-20.

4. 2 Samuel 2:1-4.

5. Joshua 21:13.

6. 1 Chronicles 6:14.

7. Japheth b. Menasseh of Corfu, quoted in Encyclopedia Judaica, Vol. 8, p. 231.

8. Based on the biblical reference (Joshua 14:15) ". . . the name of Hebron formerly was Kiryat Arba . . ."

9. 1 Chron. 2:51, 54.

10. 1 Sam. 16:1-13.

11. Josh. 2:1.

12. 2 Kings 2:4, 18-11.

13. Nehemia 7:36.

14. Encyc. Jud., Vol. 9, pp. 1369-1370.

15. Jer. 1:1.

16. Encyc. Jud., Vol. 2, p. 927.

17. However, see "Jerusalem," ed. Msgr. John M. Oesterreicher and Anne Sinai, The John Day Company, New York, 1974, for full treatment of its history, demography, political, sociological and religious importance and development, etc.

18. Encyc. Jud., Vol. 10, pp. 800-1.

19. "British Rule in Palestine," by Bernard Joseph, Public Affairs Press, Washington, D.C., 1948. See Chapter 12, pp. 122-189; especially pp. 141-146.

20. 1 Kings 16:24.

21. 2 Kings 17:6, 18:11.

22. Encyc. Jud., Vol. 14, pp. 724-5.

23. *Ibid.*

24. Gen. 12:16.

25. Gen. 33:18ff.

26. Joshua 24:32.

27. Joshua 24.

28. Judges 9.

29. 1 Kings 12.

30. Encyc. Jud., Vol. 14, p. 1333.

31. *Ibid.*

32. Encyc. Jud. Vol. 15, p. 1429.

33. Encyc. Jud., Vol. 9, pp. 1340-1.

34. Encyc. Jud., Vol. 12, p. 745.

35. *Ibid.*

36. *Ibid.*

37. *Ibid.*

38. Terence Smith, "Israeli Settlements a Clue," *New York Times,* May 11, 1976.

39. Terence Smith, "Covert Israeli Land Deals on West Bank Stir Furor," *New York Times,* April 12, 1976, p. 1.

40. "Israeli Settlements in the Administered Areas," Ministry for Foreign Affairs, Division of Information, Jerusalem, June 1973.

Jordanian and Israeli Policy on the West Bank

By SHAUL MISHAL

Demographic and geographical factors have made Jordan and Israel the major political elements directly involved in the Palestinian issue.

Geographically, the West Bank of the Jordan River, with its more than 650,000 Palestinian Arab inhabitants, is a sort of island surrounded on all sides by Israel and Jordan. Demographically, more than 1.5 million of a total of 2.3 million Palestinians lived on the West Bank, the East Bank and the Gaza Strip (600,000 on the East Bank; 400,000 in the Gaza Strip) as of 1974.[1] PLO estimates provide an even higher figure. According to these, 994,000 Palestinians lived on the East Bank, 654,000 on the West Bank and 500,000 in the Gaza Strip in the same year, as part of a total Palestinian population of 3.3 million.[2] The PLO statistics include the 460,000 Israeli Arabs among the

Dr. Mishal is a Visiting Fellow and Lecturer in the Department of Political Science at Yale University. He is the author of *Palestinian Reality and Jordanian Policy, 1949-1967,* Yale University Press, 1977.

The second part of this article is based on a study by the author and Dr. Dan Horowitz, Hebrew University, Jerusalem, entitled "The Tacit Modus Vivendi: The West Bank Political Elite Under the Israeli Rule."

total Palestinian Arab population, which would mean that some 2,000,000 Palestinians live under Jordanian and Israeli rule. These figures serve to dramatize the involvement of the two states in the Palestinian issue.

Neither government can ignore the fact that the PLO has steadily become the dominant ideological and political force among the Palestinian population since the war of 1967. Yet even at the height of its power and prestige, the PLO may have been strong enough to gain the Palestinians' political allegiance but not to achieve its objectives; it has always had to take the Jordanian and the Israeli positions seriously into account.

For Israel, the Palestinian issue became a concrete problem in 1967. For Jordan, however, the problem began in 1948.

Transjordan, in 1948, had a population of about 450,000. Its annexation of the West Bank added 900,000 Palestinians. Many of them remained on the West Bank or moved to the East Bank, becoming the majority in the Kingdom of Jordan. The Palestinians perceived the 1948 war as having ended in utter failure. The Hashemite regime saw it as having served to increase its power, both militarily and politically. These opposing evaluations of the war affected the way each party defined its own objectives in the continuing conflict with Israel. The Jordanians tended toward acceptance of a stabilization of the status quo; they embarked on a process of political arrangements with Israel.[3] The Palestinians on the other hand, sought a change in the status quo by military means. Nevertheless, although they constituted the majority of the population of Jordan, enjoyed socio-economic superiority and a high degree of political consciousness, they did not succeed in posing a serious threat to the Jordanian regime.

Mainly, this was due to the regime's skillful handling of the situation and its use of certain ideological mechanisms and political tactics. The Jordanian declarations always maintained that Jordans political objectives were identical with those of the Palestinians, and especially on issues such as the restoration of Palestine by the extermination of Israel, the struggle against colonialism and the goal of Arab unity. In this sense, Jordan's expressed ultimate objectives vis-à-vis Israel coincided with those of the Palestinians and with those of other Arab states. But at the same time, the Jordanians also generally succeeded in furthering their own real political interests, and these were not compatible with the Palestinians' demands. The regime managed to slur over these differences by presenting the fulfillment of the ultimate objectives as long-term policy goals while presenting their day-to-day policy as a series of temporary arrangements to deal with short-term needs. The liberation from colonialism, the restoration of Palestine, Arab unity — these, the regime argued — were objectives requiring long-term preparation. Until that time, the demands of survival and daily existence had to be met.

The Jordanians emphasized this distinction between the short and long-term objectives, which became the cornerstone of their Palestinian policy. This

212 JORDAN AND THE WEST BANK

was not without precedent. Transjordan itself had been created in this way. The idea of establishing a political entity on the east bank of the Jordan River was first discussed in 1921 on the terrace of the King David Hotel in Jerusalem, when Winston Churchill, then the British Colonial Secretary, agreed to support 'Abdallah, King Hussein's grandfather, for a period of six months — and these six months stretched into fifty-six years. Much has changed since then, but the basic Jordanian political outlook has remained the same. Politics is, above all, a matter of making temporary arrangements which, when skillfully manoeuvered, can become political patterns of rela- tively long duration. Temporary and enduring — these are the key words of Jordanian politics. "War and peace," 'Abdallah declared in his colorful style, "are things that mankind will continue to experience until the Resurrec- tion, just as season follows season, summer, autumn, winter and spring, and as day follows night. It is the way of God with his creations."[4]

It was this distinction between the temporary and the ultimate goals — the short-term and the long-term — that enabled the Jordanians to carry out and justify a policy that was in fact incompatible with the Palestinians' political goals.

This Jordanian policy was made possible by the Hashemites' monopoly of both military power and foreign economic aid, elements that largely deter- mined the dependence of the West Bank on Amman. Moreover, the Amman authorities were helped by the fact that the political leadership on the West Bank also, to a large extent, constituted a socio-economic elite. Most of this political leadership belonged to a social structure in which political power, political awareness and political participation were the preserve of a very narrow social stratum. The membership of most of the West Bank's political leaders in families with commercial and economic interests created a close inter-dependence with Amman and made it difficult for them to adopt views which could harm their economic interests. On the other hand, indulgence on the part of the authorities brought economic benefits to those who cooperated with them through appointments or elections to senior positions which carried control over resources. In fact, half the Senate and half the Jordanian Parlia- ment were Palestinians. They were appointed provincial governors, to posi- tions as representatives of refugee affairs, and in the economic, education and judicial sectors.[5] Palestinians also held senior administrative positions in the ministries of agriculture, economics, education, development and foreign affairs.

King 'Abdallah tended to apply this policy to placate not only his allies among the Palestinians who came mostly from the Nashashibi camp but also his rivals. Anwar Nusaybah, for example, who belonged to a Husayni family, and served as secretary of the All-Palestine Government in Gaza, found a place for himself in the Jordanian administration. So too did Husayn Fakhri al-Khalidi, who had formerly been a sharp critic of 'Abdallah's Palestine policy.[6]

At the same time, the regime kept fundamental Palestinian values outside the realm of discussion. It tried to appease the Palestinians with political platforms and official declarations coated with political slogans that were acceptable to them even though the actual policy the regime pursued was not compatible with their fundamental values. In late 1949, for example, 'Abdallah attacked the 1947 Palestine Partition Plan, firmly declaring that he would do everything in his power to prevent partition as long as he lived while behind the scenes actually negotiating a political settlement with Israel. In this respect, until 1967 the Jordanian regime made a careful distinction between Palestine as a fundamental issue and the Palestinians as a group with actual interests. The "Liberation of Palestine" was considered a matter of faith — and of long-term policy. The "Liberation of the Palestinians" was not a goal that the Jordanians could easily accept. It would only have served to emphasize their differences with the Palestinians.*

Ahmed al-Shuqaiyri, one of the key figures in Palestinian politics until 1968 claimed, in his memoirs, that it was dangerous for anyone to so much as mention the term "Palestinian entity" in Jordan.[7] In 1964, following the first Arab Summit Conference's Resolution,[8] when the Jordanians decided to change their political tactics by recognizing the PLO, they became more aware of the distinction between Palestine as a symbolic term and the Palestinians as a separate entity within the state. King Hussein expressed this clearly in 1965 when he said that he regarded Palestine as the goal but that "the organizations which seek to separate Palestinians from Jordanians are traitors helping Zionism in its aim of undermining the Arab camp . . . We have only one army, one political organization and one people's mobilization system in this country, into which the blood of the Palestinians and the Jordanians was mixed at Bab-al-wad and Kfar Etzion.[9]

Al-Shuqaiyri also writes of this Jordanian sensitivity toward the Palestinians' fundamental values. He cites the dramatic debate between the Jordanians and the PLO in 1964 about the site of the first Palestinian Congress. The Palestinians proposed holding it in the Jordanian-held Old City of Jerusalem. The Jordanians, seeking a less emotion-laden site, proposed Amman — which the Palestinians rejected. Thereupon, as a more or less veiled hint that the projected PLO Congress might die before it began, the Jordanians suggested Qalia, on the shores of the Dead Sea. This proposal was fiercely rejected. A compromise was finally reached; the Congress was held at the Inter-Continental Hotel, near Mount Scopus and in Jerusalem, but *not* in the Old City.

Thus both the instruments used by the Jordanian regime to satisfy the Palestinians on the material level and the delicate manipulation of symbols and values became mediating mechanisms between Jordanian policy and Palestinian political desires.

* When the West Bank came under Israeli occupation in 1967 it became much easier for the Jordanians to fuse the terms "Palestine" and "Palestinians."

What served most to keep Jordanian rule alive, enduring and undefeated in all these years, however, was the powerful idea of Arab unity. This idea which was recognized and accepted by both the Palestinians and the Jordanians reflected their flexible definition toward the national boundaries. This flexible definition is mainly derived from the distinction between two concepts. One is that of *qawmiyyah*, meaning people, group or tribe and is used to express the idea of ethnic nationalism — i.e. a political allegiance and commitment of individuals and groups in the Arab world to the realization of Arab nationalism through a grand unity. The second is that of *wataniyyah* — which can be defined as a political allegiance and commitment stressing patriotic attachment to a single country.

This distinction between *qawmiyyah* and *wataniyyah*, between a broad nationalism and a narrow patriotism, and the tension between them, had pro-Jordanian as well as anti-Jordanian implications.

In its pro-Jordanian sense it provided a broad mechanism for manipulating the Palestinians. The Palestinians of the West Bank had at least three options for defining their political allegiance: the pan-Arab (or pan-Islam), the Jordanian and the Palestinian options. There had always been people, especially during the first years of Jordanian rule on the West Bank, willing to give practical effect to the Palestinian option, as is indicated by the *All-Palestine Government* which was established in the Gaza Strip in September 1948 and which articulated oppositional attitudes toward Amman. From 1954 on, the West Bank Arabs tended to associate the pan-Arab option with the Nasser regime in Egypt, though some saw it embodied in the Damascus Ba'thist regime. Above all, their pan-Arab allegiance was coupled with pan-Islamic symbols. The name of the largest guerrilla organization — *Fatah* — means "a conquest for Islam gained in the Holy War." The three PLO Army brigades, *Qadisiyya, Hattin* and *Ayn Jalut*,[10] were named for a great victories won by Muslim arms. Alongside these two identities there was also an affiliation with the political entity of the Kingdom of Jordan. This "Jordanian identity" however, materialized mostly in Palestinian participation in Jordan's political life and in the dependence on resources allocated in Amman.

However, the absence among the Palestinians of clear criteria for the definition of their national boundaries was similar to Amman's political approach, which was crystallized by 'Abdallah. In this respect, he saw the realization of his political dream in a "Greater Syria" which would include Syria, Lebanon, Palestine and Transjordan. This political resemblance between the two parties in defining the collective boundaries even made it possible for the Jordanian regime to share, in some measure, in a common ideology with the Palestinians and on occasion even to cooperate with the most extremist of their Palestinian rivals.

This "antagonistic collaboration" also enabled the Jordanian regime to find Palestinian allies on almost any political issue and at any time, merely by redefining policy in the broad terms of Arab nationalism. The Jordanians thus preferred to talk about routing out "the enemies of Arab nationalism" while suppressing enemies of the regime and of arresting "Communists" and "traitors" while seizing PLO leaders.

Furthermore, the association of the West Bank elite with more than one Arab political center was used by the Jordanian regime to keep this elite from functioning as an effective and solid East-West Bank leadership. National leaders with pan-Arab pretensions like Nasser of Egypt or Abd al Karim Qassem of Iraq formed the political center during periods of unrest on the West Bank. A solid leadership comprised of intellectuals, many of whom had been educated in other Arab countries did emerge, but in the main, however, it remained a medium for transmitting popular identification with the pan-Arab leadership. In sum, the West Bank leaders' fragmentation and their splitting of political allegiance helped Amman to treat the Palestinians as objects to be manipulated rather than as an independent element in control of their own resources.

But the anti-Jordanian implications of the flexible boundaries definition were also exploited by the Palestinians, and on more than one occasion, in order to maneuver the Jordanians into political and military decisions which were incompatible with Jordanian interests. By creating an appropriate political and ideological climate and by using the same pan-Arab slogans, the regime's opponents succeeded in obtaining the dismissal of Colonel Glubb and other British officers from the Jordanian army in March 1956; in facilitating the rise to power of the pro-Egyptian and anti-Western government of al-Nabulsi in 1957 and in bringing about the political and military maneuvering which brought Jordan into the war of 1967. It also led to the great prestige and the military and political power that the Palestinian guerrilla organizations attained in the East Bank from 1968 to September, 1970 and to the official Jordanian position at the Arab Summit Conference at Rabat in October 1974, when Jordan accepted the resolution declaring the PLO the sole representative of the Palestinian people. It led to the Jordan-Syria rapprochement, which is based on Jordan's assumption that this new alliance will make it easier to challenge the PLO. Thus, Jordan's status-quo policy toward the Palestinians was propelled by the same dialectic toward Jordan's involvement in the Palestinian cause.

It is possible to conclude, in the light of events, that the Arabs' ideological distinction between "broad" nationalism and "narrow" patriotism is not only a myth or a cultural decoration but is also a sharp weapon which can be used as a political boomerang in political conflicts. Membership in the Arab political club, with its flexible definition of the collective boundaries, demands that one must be prepared not only to manipulate one's rivals but also to be manipulated by them; that one must be ready not only to ride them, to paraphrase 'Abdallah's statement about the Palestinians, but also to be ridden by them.[11] This ideological orientation led the Jordanians to see their political salvation not only in the eradication of the Palestinian problem on the West Bank by decisive measures but in the careful application of their basic belief that politics is above all a matter of maintaining temporary arrangements which can become political patterns of long duration.

This perception, which gave room for cooperation between the West Bank leadership and Amman, also continued to play a significant role under the Israeli administration. It was reflected in the traditional leaders' behavior. They concentrated on day-to-day activity in their relationship with the Israeli military government while the solidary leadership functions were fulfilled, as under Jordanian rule, by Palestinian or Arab bodies outside the West Bank. In this respect, the differentiation between the daily-instrumental functions and those of solidarity helped the local leaders to regard the political future of the West Bank as an issue for negotiation between Israel and external political elements outside the West Bank rather than between themselves and the Israeli authorities. This political approach helped the West Bank leaders evade the need to make a clear-cut commitment to Israel, Jordan or the PLO.

There have been Palestinian groups inside and outside the West Bank which constituted a challenge to the traditional West Bank leadership and which were willing to adopt these behavior patterns because it opened the way for cooperation with the Israeli authorities. However, radical political activity did not become the main feature of the West Bank's Palestinian leadership. The daily relations between the Israeli authorities and this leadership continued, even during periods of riots and demonstrations.

This pattern of day-to-day cooperation was made possible mostly by Israeli policy. Nevertheless, some aspects of this policy may have worked simply because these coincided not only with the Palestinian leaders' self interests but also with those of Jordan and, paradoxically, even with those of the PLO. Israeli policy gave priority to the maintenance of tranquility and the assurance of cooperation in everyday matters by the local leaders and the population. It did not attempt to involve them in efforts to search for political solutions to the West Bank's future. This political issue, according to the Israeli government, had to be negotiated with Amman.

The guideline of Israeli policy, thus, was concern for the normalization of life, by a minimal demonstration of the Israeli presence and non-intervention in the management of their day-to-day affairs.[12] In the economic sphere, this policy took the form of "open bridges" across the Jordan River, which enabled the movement of people and merchandise between the two Banks.[13]

The employment of workers in Israel and the development of agriculture guided by the Israel Ministry of Agriculture has brought about changes in the population's income level and has created prosperity among certain groups, such as manual workers, whose prestige and political influence under the Jordanian rule were extremely low.[14] The merchants, who had always constituted a moderate element in comparison to the well-educated groups, were also among the beneficiaries of this economic prosperity. Israel's activities in the provision of such services as health, welfare and technical advice, especially in the agricultural sphere, also contributed to the emergence of a social process that may be termed "creeping modernization."

The tranquilization of everyday life, through cooperation on the instrumental level was aided by the absence of a political leadership which might have developed a consistent and independent initiative for the West Bank's political future. It is true that during the first few months after the Six Day War some attempts were made by West Bank Palestinian leaders to carry on a dialogue with the Israeli government; for example, it was reported that thirty notables were ready to sign a formal declaration of political cooperation with Israel provided the Israel government accepted the idea of establishing a Palestinian state on the West Bank. Apart from a few attempts, however, this type of political initiative declined and became very sporadic.[15] It is possible that any real political effort by the West Bank leaders to deal with Israel on the future of the West Bank would only have served to underline the internal conflict among themselves regarding the desired settlement. Moreover, their approach, of concentrating on day-to-day activity, coincided with the Jordanians' interest in maintaining some influence on the West Bank.

The principal instrument for this maintenance of Jordanian influence was the money distributed on the West Bank via those loyal to the Jordanian authorities. Jordan has continued to pay salaries to Jordanian civil servants, who also receive salaries from the Israeli authorities (although Jordanian salaries to certain employees, such as policemen, are no longer paid.)[16]

This cooperation did not exist in the first period of Israeli rule on the West Bank, during which the Jordanian authorities attempted, by means of this money, to prevent cooperation between the local leadership and the Israeli authorities. Since 1970, however, the Jordanian government has reconciled itself to the situation of current daily contact between the Israeli authorities and the West Bank's mayors and notables. They have sought only to prevent local political initiatives which could limit their influence on the West Bank's political future.

This Jordanian policy can be seen as the emergence of a "tacit understanding" pattern between the Israeli authorities and the Jordanian government, based on a "division of labor" between areas for which Israel felt it should be directly responsible and areas which the Jordanians were particularly sensitive about. It may be argued that this kind of understanding made possible the sustenance of a complex relationship between the local leadership and the Israeli and Jordanian authorities.

Mayors in the West Bank who did not adjust to this network of relationships encountered difficulties in their activities and lost their positions. This was the case with Hamdi Kana'an, Mayor of Nablus, who sought to turn his position into a regional and even national leadership, and Nadim Zarou, Mayor of Ramallah, who was known for his radical nationalist views.

Hamdi Kana'an hoped to play a significant role as representative not only of inhabitants of the West Bank but of all the Palestinians in any future political developments. He had tried to turn the Nablus municipality into a political body of some importance by replacing members of the City Council with individuals with broader political experience as ministers in the Jordanian government and members of parliament. When some of these individuals refused to join him, and as his relationship with Amman, which feared any local political initiative, was undermined, he resigned and became an advocate of a West Bank political initiative under Israeli rule. As the first step he called for municipal elections.[17]

Nadim Zarou, on the other hand, found it difficult to satisfy the daily needs of his town's inhabitants because of the introduction of nationalist political considerations into the sphere of the Ramallah town council's relationship with the Israeli authorities. This situation was expressed in the town council's pondering about getting a loan from Israel for the town's development and in activity aimed at preventing laborers from Ramallah and its surroundings from working in Israel. The Mayor's approach became an obstacle in the path of the normalization of daily life in Ramallah during his tenure of office. Despite the differences in their approach, however, Hamdi Kana'an in Nablus and Nadim Zarou in Ramallah shared a tendency to take political initiative beyond the instrumental level of cooperation. This initiative was not consistent with the local leadership nature of activity or with the Israeli and Jordanian "division of labor" approach.

The West Bank leaders' tendency to concentrate on day-to-day activity as against taking a political initiative, also coincided, to some extent, with the PLO's political interest in the West Bank. The PLO claims that it is the authoritative representative of the Palestinians on the West Bank, and not Amman or leaders living under Israeli rule. The acceptance of this argument by the West Bank leaders, whether for ideological or tactical reasons, emphasized the West Bank leaders' lack of direct involvement in efforts for the West Bank's future.

The Israeli authorities' ability to gain tranquility on the West Bank through the cooperation of the local leadership was dependent, therefore, on the political behavior of elements outside the West Bank. The traditional elite's ability to maintain a balance between the influence and the interests of Israel, Jordan and the PLO began to wane as, after 1973, the PLO began to achieve a high level of recognition (at the Arab Summit Conference in Algiers in November 1973; the Islamic Summit Conference in Lahore in February 1974; the Arab Summit Conference in Rabat in October 1974 and in the United Nations General Assembly in November 1974).

Other PLO political successes in the international arena in late 1975 and in the beginning of 1976 — its participation in the U.N. General Assembly with Observer Status and the rumors about contacts between American officials and PLO representatives — strengthened the belief among broad sectors of the West Bank population that the PLO, and not Amman, would be successor to the Israelis.[18]

Under these circumstances, the attempts by Israeli extremists to establish a new settlement in the Nablus area and the decision by a magistrate in Jerusalem allowing Jews to pray on the Temple Mount accelerated riots and demonstrations in many West Bank cities in late 1975 and early 1976. Yet, as one writer put it, ". . . None of these ostensible provocations was a new Israeli policy and none in the past had elicited such violent response on the part of the Arab population. What was different in 1975-1976 was the particular matrix of outside forces that destabilized the emotional climate of the West Bank."[19]

The PLO's elevated position in West Bank eyes was also reflected in the 1976 municipal election results. As in the 1972 elections, educated individuals who did not belong to the traditional leadership attempted to fill the vacuum created by the political passivity of the leadership. While most of the candidates in the 1972 election failed to obtain any significant gains, they showed impressive success in the 1976 election. The mayors of the two largest cities, Nablus and Hebron, and landlords and businessmen who served as members in many municipalities were replaced by blue collar workers, some of whom were connected with radical parties like the *Ba'th* and the Communists or by PLO supporters.[20]

The election results spurred many observers to predict that this was a turning point in the West Bank's relations with Israel and Amman. However, the newly elected leaders, especially the new Mayors of Nablus and Hebron, continued to behave like their predecessors: they concentrated on day-to-day activity rather than on taking a political initiative beyond these contacts. The events in Lebanon, which hurt the PLO, probably encouraged this conservative style of behavior and prevented the PLO from trying to take advantage of the new political development and the linkage between external events and domestic behavior will continue to play a central role in West Bank political life. From this viewpoint, the continuous patterns from the Jordanian to the Israeli period since 1967 are showing a stronger vitality than are the tendencies toward change.

FOOTNOTES

1. *Israel Ministry for Foreign Affairs,* "Information Briefing," November 21, 1974, No. 470, (Jerusalem) p. 2.

2. "Al-Tali'a" as cited in *Ibid,* p. 1.

3. For the Israeli-Jordanian discussions over the possibility of political settlement see, for instance, Abdallah al-Tall, *Zikhronot Abdallah al-Tall,* ("The Memoirs of Abdallah al-Tall") (Tel-Aviv, 1964) pp. 308-309; also David Ben Gurion, "The negotiations reached an advanced stage. Israel agreed to grant Jordan a free port — at Haifa or Jaffa — and a corridor to it. The parties were discussing the width of the corridor when King 'Abdallah was shot and killed . . . If 'Abdallah had not been murdered *a full peace agreement would have been signed between Israel and the Kingdom of Jordan."* In Jon and David Kimche, *Mishnei Evrei Hagiv'ah,* ("Both Sides of the Hill") (2nd. ed.; Tel-Aviv, 1973) p. 263.

4. See King 'Abdallah, *My Memoirs Completed.* Translated by H.W. Glidden, American Council of Learned Studies, (Washington, D.C. 1954), p. 11.

5. For more details see *Hamizrah Hehadash,* (The New East), Vol. I, No. 1 (October, 1949), p. 60, Jerusalem, Israel (in Hebrew).

6. See Clinton Bailey, *The Participation of the Palestinians in the Politics of Jordan,* (Unpublished doctoral dissertation, Columbia University, 1966), pp. 97-99.

7. Ahmed al-Shuqairy, *Min al-Qimma ila al-Hazima ma-al-Maluk Wa-al-Rua'sa,* ("From the Summit to Defeat with Kings and Rulers"), (Beirut, 1971) p. 69.

8. *Ibid,* p. 50, on this conference, see also L. S. Kadi, *Arab Summit Conference and the Palestine Problem,* PLO Research Center, (Beirut 1966).

9. See *Al-Wathaiq al-Filastiniyya li-Am 1966,* ("Palestinian Documents — 1966"), Institute of Palestinian Studies, (Beirut, 1967), Document No. 125. p. 303.

10. All three battles, as Bernard Lewis points out, "were won in holy wars for Islam against non-Muslims, Qadisiyya against the Zoroastrian Persians, Hattin against the Crusaders, Ayn Jalut against the Mongols. In the second and third of these, the victorious armies were not even Arab; but they were Muslim, and that is obviously what counts . . ." Bernard Lewis, "The Return of Islam," *Commentary,* Vol. 61, No. 1, January 1976.

11. As quoted by Yoseph Nevo, *Mediniuto Hapalestinait shel Abdallah, 1945-1948.* ("Abdallah's Palestinian Policy"). M. A. thesis, The Hebrew University, Jerusalem 1971. p. 38.

12. This policy was expressed in a statement by the Israeli military governor who maintained that the aim of the military government was that "an Arab may be born in Bethlehem, obtain his birth certificate, grow and be educated, get married, bring up his children and grandchildren to a ripe old age without the need of any Israeli civil servant or clerk and without even seeing one at all." *Bamachane,* Israel, 12.3.68 (Hebrew). For a general survey of Israeli policy in the administered territories, see Brigadier-General Shlomo Gazit, "The Administered Territories — Policy and Action" *Ma'arachot,* Israel, (January, 1970), (Hebrew), and his "Israel's Occupation Policies," *New Outlook,* Israel, Vol. 11, No. 6, July-August, 1968. For a description of the Administrative aspects of Israel government in the Administered Territories see: Nimrod Raphaeli, "Military Government in Occupied Territories: An Israeli View," *Middle East Journal,* Washington, D.C. (Spring, 1969), pp. 177-190, and Ann Mosely Lesch, *Israel's Occupation of the West Bank: The First Two Years,* Rand, RM-6296-ARPA, August, 1970.

13. The estimated imports from Jordan to the West Bank was I.L.13 million in 1970, I.L.14 million in 1971 and I.L.19 million in 1972. The exports from the West Bank to Jordan amounted to I.L.60 million in 1970, I.L.80 million in 1971 and I.L.121 million in 1972. See *Statistics of the Administered Territories,* Vol. 4, No. 1, April, 1974 (Israel Central Bureau of Statistics, Jerusalem).

14. The income of inhabitants of the West Bank who worked in Israel almost trebled in 1969 and doubled the 1971 figure in 1972. The gross disposable income on the West Bank increased from I.L.481 million in 1969 to I.L.754 million (at current prices) in 1971. See *Statistical Abstract 1973,* Israel Government, pp. 700-716. Unemployment among male workers has dropped to a minimum of 1.3% from 7.6% in 1967. See Bruno Michael, "Israeli Policy in the Administered Territories," in Howe, Irving, and Gershman, Carl, Eds., *Israel, the Arabs and the Middle East,* (New York, Bantam Books, 1972), p. 256.

15. For more details on those attempts, see Mark Allan Heller, *Foreign Occupation and Political Elites: A Study of the Palestinians,* (Unpublished doctoral dissertation, Harvard University, September 1976), pp. 228-230.

16. On the salaries paid by the Jordanian government see Raphaeli, *op. cit.,* p. 186, *Al-Anba,* January 4, 1974 (Arabic). In 1974 Jordan granted I.L.34 million to the West Bank municipalities. See *Jerusalem Post,* Israel, February 13, 1975. According to Heller, who cites private sources, the ex-mayor of Nablus, Hamdi Kana'an received I.L.200,000-300,000 in the first 2-3 years of the Israeli rule on the West Bank as Jordanian funds. See Heller, *op. cit.,* p. 237.

17. For more details see my article, "Anatomy of a Municipal Election in Judea and Samaria," *Hamizrah Hehadash,* (Hebrew). Vol. XXIV, No. 1-2, 1974, pp. 63-67.

18. See for instance Heller, *op. cit.,* p. 278.

19. *Ibid,* p. 276.

20. See *Ha'aretz,* Israel, April 30, 1976. For a discussion of the election results see Heller, *op. cit.,* pp. 274-289; also Michael Walzer, "Israeli Policy and the West Bank," *Dissent,* Summer 1976, pp. 234-236.

The West Bank
Under the Israeli Administration

The West Bank is the most populous of the areas under Israeli administration although not the largest. It was part of Mandatory Palestine until 1948. Then it was annexed by Transjordan, which became the Hashemite Kingdom of Jordan with the merger of the East and West Banks of the Jordan River. The area's main towns are Hebron, Bethlehem, Ramallah, Nablus and Jenin, which lie along its hills. In 1967, its economy was found to be based on farming, small-scale industry and services, especially tourism. There were twenty refugee camps in the area, consisting of shanty-towns built on the outskirts of the towns. Most of the refugees were employed outside the camps.

The war of 1967 and the subsequent occupation of the area by Israel created economic dislocations caused by a flow of refugees to the East Bank and by the fact that the area suddenly found itself cut off from the East Bank, which had been the center of all Jordanian economic activity. The West Bank was governed by Jordanian law, which continues to be in force. Its inhabitants are Jordanian citizens.

In Israel, the West Bank is known as Judea and Samaria, the site of Jewish history and settlement, but no change in the status of the area has been made since its occupation. No area has been annexed except for that part of Jerusalem known as East Jerusalem — the Old City — which had been occupied by Jordanian forces during the war of 1948 and had been ruled by Jordan as part of the West Bank. The reunification of East Jerusalem with West Jerusalem (that part of Jerusalem that was in the State of Israel prior to June 6, 1967) took place immediately following the passing of the Israel *Knesset* (parliament) Law and Administration Ordinance (Amendment), Law

5727-1967 on June 27, 1967, Section 1 of which provides that "the law, jurisdiction and administration of the State shall extend to any area of *Eretz Yisrael* (the Land of Israel) designated by the Government by order."

Two governmental committees deal with the major policy issues of the occupied areas. These are the Committee of Cabinet Ministers, which coordinates all political and security matters, and the Committee of Directors-General, which is concerned with civil and economic affairs. Decisions affecting the areas are coordinated by the Israel Ministry of Defense and the General Staff, in order to assure a consistent policy and direct control by the supreme civil authority. The Israel Defense Forces appointed a military governor for each occupied area. He acts as the senior authority in the area and is responsible for both the military and the civilian branches of the administration. Each branch is headed by an army officer: the military arm deals with problems of security while the civilian arm coordinates all civilian activities, including economic and social services. The officers responsible for civilian activities are seconded from and work in coordination with the respective Israel ministries, but are directly under the command of the military governor.

In the main, the area's agricultural activity was not radically disrupted by the war, and war damages were minor — most of the battles were fought along the major highways and did not involve towns or villages.

The declared aim of Israeli policy is the maintenance of a "low profile" Israeli presence, non-intervention in local affairs and "Open Bridges" across the Jordan River, (with the consent of Jordan). The offices of the administration were placed on the outskirts of the towns and the individual West Banker is less frequently, over the years, required to see the military authorities when he seeks permits and licenses. Non-political crimes are the responsibility of a local Arab police force, most of whose personnel (who carry arms) served in the local police forces prior to the war. The Israeli military units are stationed in abandoned Jordanian army camps located outside the towns.

In 1975, some 545 Israeli officials worked in Judea and Samaria and the Gaza Strip, with 14,000 Arab officials. Nineteen Israelis worked in the school system and 8,700 local Arab inhabitants, who were school principals, teachers and maintenance workers. Israel intervened in the school system to check textbooks and exclude inflammatory anti-Israel and anti-Jewish passages. This was done with the approval of a committee of the United Nations Educational, Scientific and Cultural Organization (UNESCO) which had previously checked the Jordanian and Egyptian publications in use. Syllabi and curricula remain unchanged. In Judea and Samaria, an examinations committee whose members are elected by local representatives prepares the final examination papers, which are recognized by Jordan as equivalent to the Jordanian matriculation examinations. The town of Ramallah was granted permission, in 1975, to establish a locally-run, independent university.

The Open Bridges policy was initiated when West Bank farmers found themselves with large stocks of foodstuffs and vegetables that could not be transported across the Jordan River. Exports to the East Bank were at first quasi-legal: the Israeli authorities permitted them to cross the river without hindrance. Temporary crossing points were then established and thereafter the main bridges across the Jordan River, the Allenby Bridge and the Damyah Bridge were opened to traffic. Beginning as a one-way movement, imports were next permitted from the East Bank. The sole restriction at present is confined to security matters and crime: preventing the smuggling of arms or prohibited goods into Israel.

Visits to and from the East Bank were first permitted in October 1967. A permit from the military commander was at first required for those West Bankers wishing to visit the East Bank. These permits are no longer needed.[1] In the category of summer visits, West Bank residents who applied were granted permission to invite kin from the East Bank to visit them for a period of from one to three months. The requirement that the visitor's passport be endorsed with an Israeli stamp has not deterred these visits, which reached 153,000 in the summer of 1973. Since mid-1973, incoming visitors can receive permits to stay for thirty or ninety days, depending on the circumstances, all year round.[2] Special arrangements exist for visits from the East Bank to the Christian and Muslim Holy Places in Israel. Repatriation permits, under the Family Reunion Scheme, now permit displaced members of West Bank families living in any of the Arab countries since the war of 1967 to return to their homes. 44,000 were granted permission to return between 1968-1975.

There is no death penalty in Israel or in the occupied territories. Although provided for by law in the gravest breaches of security, no military prosecutor has demanded it, and it has administratively been laid down that the courts shall not pass a death sentence that cannot be appealed.

The law does provide that houses may be blown up if they are found to have been used by terrorists as a base of operations against the Israeli security forces or against civilians. Demolition is one procedure; the second is evacuation of the house and its sealing off, a procedure followed, as a rule, when the terrorist hide-out is in an apartment in a house tenanted by a number of families which have no connection with the terrorist act or a house which would render its neighbors unsafe if dynamited. This practice is exercised under Regulation 119 of the British Mandatory's Emergency Regulations of 1945, which are an integral part of the judicial system of the West Bank (and the Gaza Strip) and also of Israel. A number of houses were blown up in abandoned villages, mainly in the Jordan Valley, the reasons given being to prevent their use by infiltrating terrorists. In cases where a house is demolished in a populated area, each is reviewed by the Minister of Defense (in person), following three reviews at lower levels.

The sanction of banishment is applied to persons who have organized acts of civil disobedience or aided terrorist activity and to terrorists who have served lengthy prison terms and whose release is claimed to entail a serious security risk. Seventy of those banished to the East Bank from 1967-1975 have petitioned the Israel authorities to permit their return and some half of all those banished have been permitted to return (others may return for brief visits for special family events).

Regarding detention, provisions exist against any person's imprisonment for his political opinions: only those accused of participating in terrorist actions or giving aid to terrorists may be so detained (under Regulation III of the Mandatory's Emergency Regulations of 1945). Political criticism may be made verbally or in writing. Under the Regulations cited above a military commander may detain a person for several years, but the Israeli authorities have ruled that the military commander may not do so for a period exceeding one month. He cannot, in addition, act to detain any person unless and until a special committee, including lawyers, has reviewed all the facts of the case and recommended administrative detention. The military commander must then submit the file with his recommendation to the Minister of Defense, whose personal approval must be given before the detention is confirmed — and even in this case, for a period not exceeding twelve months. Each file is then reviewed every six months by a committee headed by a lawyer. Those detained must clearly be proven guilty of terrorist activity. The Red Cross is supplied with itemized information on each prisoner and detainee, including changes in the place of detention. Red Cross representatives visit every prison or detention camp at least once each month. They see all prisoners except those undergoing first interrogation and are allowed to talk with each prisoner or detainee without witnesses. The Red Cross assists in arranging visits of relatives, in many cases from Jordan and the other Arab states.[3]

Municipal elections were held on the West Bank in 1972 and 1976, in the 25 West Bank municipalities. The first elections took place in the municipalities of Samaria on March 28, 1972 and the second in those of Judea, on May 2, 1972. Elections to village councils were introduced in 1975. The subsequent municipal elections were held in Judea and Samaria on April 12, 1976. The elections were held in accordance with the Jordanian Municipality Law No. 29 of 1955, which determines that the period of office of a Municipal Council shall be four years and that the number of council members (7-12) are to be determined by the Jordanian Ministry of Interior, i.e., on the criterion that linked the number of council members to the size of the local population. According to Jordanian law, eligible voters are males, aged twenty-one and over, who own property and have been residents of the municipality for at least one full year prior to the elections. The administration has extended the vote to those who have paid at least one dinar in local taxes (whether property, an education tax or a license fee for industry and commerce, etc.) and to women. The rise in the standard of living in the area, increased municipal incomes from taxes, and the imposition of new taxes, such as the Annual Tax for Sanitation Services, also led to an increase in the number of eligible voters (there were 32,000 voters in 1972 and 85,000 in 1976, some 36% of these being women). The mayor is not chosen by the municipal council but is appointed by the Council of Ministers at the recommendation of the Minister of the Interior (in effect, however, the Government accepted the recommendations of the councils regarding the designation of the mayors — thus a number of the new mayors are openly and vociferously antagonistic to the Israel administration and may express themselves as against the existence of the State of Israel).

Jordanian law empowers the authorities to appoint two additional members to a municipal council and also to appoint one of them as mayor. This has not been followed by the Israel administration, but although the 1972 elections were held in strict conformance to Jordanian Law, the 1976 elections were not: Edict No. 627 of December 28, 1975 dropped the words "of male gender" from the Jordanian law (the trend to broaden the voting base and to extend suffrage to women is also present in Jordan today) and residents who paid only service taxes (non property owners) were also eligible to vote. No legal or other restraints were placed — former detainees and persons who had been tried for security offenses were also permitted to vote — and in several cases an administrative detainee put forward his candidature for office.

Towns and village councils or institutions or clubs are permitted independent activity and may mobilize capital in the Arab countries. Free and voluntary associations and trade unions exist. Central and municipal services are run by local personnel. Access to all Holy Places is free and protected by law, and religious and cultural life is undisturbed.[4] The Arabic language press is independent, subject only to the laws of the State of Israel. The Arabic language daily, *Al Quds,* now published in East Jerusalem has, from the outset, advocated an end to the Israeli occupation and recognition of the "national rights of the Palestinians." Other dailies and journals are regularly published on the West Bank and circulate freely, although expressing opinions extremely hostile to Israel.

Local courts may examine the legal validity of orders by the military governor and exercise the right of examination. Persons may petition the Israel High Court of Justice against the Government of Israel, its Ministers and civil servants, and against the area commander and other officer-holders of the military government. They may also submit appeals in the nature of *habeas corpus* to the High Court in every case of arrest which they find is illegal. They are also entitled to engage in litigation with the Israel Defense Forces or other authorities of the State of Israel in respect of losses caused to them by the Israel Defense Forces or the said authorities. They may appeal to a quasi-judicial committee of appeal against decisions of such administrative authorities as the Custodian of Government and Abandoned Property, the

Customs Staff Officer or the Internal Affairs Staff Officer, and against decisions of the pensions and personnel committees. Bodily harm inflicted on an
inhabitant at the hands of Israeli soliders must be immediately investigated
and those found guilty must be brought to justice.[5] Damage to property is
similarly handled.

In accordance with the Conventions of the International Labor Organization, West Bank residents employed in Israel through the labor exchanges
opened in the area by the Israel Employment Service and who receive their
earnings via these exchanges, are protected by statute and within the compass
of collective labor agreements by *Histadrut* (Israel's General Federation of
Labor), which must ensure their rights through the trade unions and by means
of its overall apparatus. Unorganized employment also exists from these areas
in Israel. These workers are not immune to undercutting of wages by Israeli
employers or by Arab agents.

Unemployment on the West Bank fell from 13% in 1968 to 0.9% in 1974.
Women have penetrated the labor market to an increasing extent and the
expansion of the educational network has made child labor increasingly rare.

There has been no expropriation of privately owned land, but this land can
be sold by the owner to another West Bank resident or to an Israeli citizen, if
he so chooses. In certain cases, where privately owned land which lies along
front-line sectors or elsewhere is required for use by the Israel Defense Force,
the owner must be paid compensation or a proper rental. Land for public
purposes, such as roads, is acquired according to law, with compensation to
the owner. These legal procedures also apply to citizens of the State of Israel
whose property is needed for the purposes of public development.

The Jordanian Dinar and the Israeli Pound are legal tender.

Jordan's Civil Service Regulations are in force in the area. Since 1967,
however, several changes have been introduced, providing for clearer defini-
tions and job descriptions, improvement in welfare benefits and social services, etc. The Jordanian Government resumed paying salaries to West Bank
civil servants who had been in its employ in May 1967, although with a
disruption from 1972-1974.

The population of the West Bank is taxed according to the former Jordanian
system and tariff of direct taxation. Since no customs barriers exist between
the West Bank and Israel, there is symmetry in the rates of indirect taxes and
service fees. No contributions have been levied in the area to date.

FOOTNOTES

1. Security restrictions and the state of war existing between Jordan and Israel nevertheless impose many hardships on those crossing from the West Bank to the East Bank and vice versa. On the Jordan side of the river, they are thoroughly checked and made to wait for long hours in the sun, without any facilities. On the Israel occupied side of the river they are minutely searched, as are all goods coming or going, although water and benches and other facilities are available on this side for those waiting for inspection. Even on normal days, the nerve-wracking process may take many hours for those crossing either way. To add to the difficulties, the Israeli authorities have sometimes instituted curfews, changes in the form of identity cards, additional checkpoints and limits on travel in order to make the movement of terrorists more difficult. Both the Jordanian and the Israeli authorities have at times suddenly halted the movement of trade, for these and other reasons.

2. Citizens of the Arab states may also enter the occupied areas and continue, if they so wish, to Israel, for purposes of tourism, pilgrimage, trade, medical care and employment. Since 1967, the military administration has invested several million Israel pounds in buildings, installations and manpower to facilitate arrangments of crossing the bridges. A (*circa* $3) fee is charged for crossing, which subsidizes maintenance and servicing. Some 5,000,000 persons had crossed the bridges in both directions by the end of 1976.

3. As of the end of 1976, some 2,000 persons were tried and sentenced. 500 were in custody pending trial and 37 were administrative detainees. Parents of minors have been detained, in certain cases, under the Juvenile Offenders Ordinance of 1937. Trials of demonstrating minors have sometimes been held at night on the ground that this spares them the hardship of having to spend a night in prison. Israel Defense Forces units entered the Karri Tukan secondary school in Nablus in 1976. The explanation given was that the school is situated on a highway and the students, who threw stones and other missiles at the forces, had blocked a main link between two towns in the district.

4. In cases, such as the Machpela Cave in the Tomb of the Patriarchs in Hebron, holy to both Muslims and Jews, Jews and Muslims pray side by side. In some cases, e.g., where a Mosque is also the site of an ancient synagogue, different hours are set aside for each religion. When a verdict, pronounced by an Israeli Magistrate's Court on January 28, 1976 acquitted Israelis charged and prosecuted for the offense of doing public mischief by worshipping on the Temple Mount in Jerusalem, the Israeli Government stood by its decision to prohibit Jews from worshipping on the Mount (the site most holy to Jews and third ranking in holiness to Muslims).

5. Any member of the Israel Defense Forces found guilty of infringing the proscriptions of the 1949 Geneva Conventions or of any other Convention is an offender under Section 133 of the Military Judgment Law (Israel) 1955 and is liable to imprisonment.

Regulations in Force on the West Bank

Regulations promulgated by the British Mandatory Government in Palestine in 1945 which were in force in the area which is now the State of Israel, the West Bank and the Gaza Strip, are followed by the Israel Military Government. The Regulations came into effect following World War II. They were promulgated by the High Commissioner for Palestine, acting under the authority of Article VI of the Palestine (Defense) Order in Council 1937, to assure public safety, defense of Palestine, the maintenance of public order, the suppression of mutiny, rebellion or riot. The Order in Council expressly authorized the promulgation of Regulations concerning administrative detention, confiscation of property, work on land—including demolition, entry into premises and the conduct of searches therein, as well as the establishment of military tribunals empowered to try civilians for violation of the Regulations and similar orders.

The following provisions mark the character of the Regulations and the broad judicial and administrative powers vested by them in military authorities:

The establishment of a system of military tribunals empowered to try civilians.

Under Regulation 58, the *death penalty* is imposed for the use of arms or explosives, for the unlicensed bearing of arms or the carrying of explosives, or for belonging to an organization one or more of whose members have committed such an offense. (This death penalty was not abolished in Israel, even when the *Knesset*—Parliament—abolished capital punishment for murder in 1954). The death penalty has, in fact, been passed by a military tribunal in three instances only since the establishment of the State of Israel in May 1948, and in all three instances the sentence was remitted by the Military Court of Appeal.

Under Regulations 72, 75 and 76, the power of search and arrest is granted to military personnel as well as to police.

Regulations 86-100 are the legal grounds for the maintenance of censorship.

Regulations 109-111 authorize a military commander to restrict, by Order, the movements of an individual and his employment, to impose police control on his residence, and to require his administrative detention for an unlimited period of time.

Regulation 112 authorizes the High Commissioner to order the deportation of a person from the country and the prevention of a person's entry into the country.

Regulation 119 authorizes a military commander to order the forfeiture of property where there is reasonable ground to believe that such property has been fired from; and also to order its demolition.

Regulation 124 authorizes a military commander to impose a curfew.

A military commander is authorized to order the closing of any area so that ingress thereto and egress therefrom shall be by permit only.

Regulation 129 authorizes a military commander to open businesses closed as a result of an organized strike, and to order the closing of business premises.

The Regulations were in effect on June 6, 1967 on the West Bank, never having been rescinded by the Government of Jordan.

Jordanian Enactments

On May 13, 1948, a Supplement to the Defense of Transjordan Law, 1935 was enacted in Amman, whereunder the provisions of the Defense of Transjordan Law, and any Regulations issued or to be issued under it, would apply to any country or territory in which the Arab Jordanian Army was stationed or wherever that Army was entrusted with the duty of protecting security and order. The Supplement also empowered the Prime Minister to authorize others to exercise the powers vested in him. Any privilege or immunity given in the Defense of Transjordan Law, or in Regulations made under it, to the British forces or to Mandatory officials was annulled.

On May 24, 1948, General Hashem issued Proclamation No. 1, in which his appointment as Military Commander of the West Bank was made public. On the same day, Proclamation No. 2 was issued, which provided that all Laws and Regulations in force in Palestine at the end of the Mandate, on May 15, 1948, shall remain in force throughout the regions occupied by the Arab Jordanian Army, or wherever the Army is entrusted with the duty of protecting security and order, except where that is inconsistent with any provisions of the Defense of Transjordan Law, 1935, or with any Regulations or Orders issued thereunder.

On December 1, 1949, the Law of Modification of Administrative Procedures in Palestine became effective, stipulating that "all Laws, Regulations and Orders in force at the end of the Mandate over Palestine shall remain in effect until abolished or modified." The Law added that "all Laws, Regulations, Orders and other legislation issued by the King, the military governor or the general administrative governor shall be regarded as having been and still being in effect."

Jordan's Law Concerning the Laws and Regulations Prevailing on Both Banks of the Hashemite Kingdom of Jordan, of September 16, 1950 prescribed that the Laws and Regulations prevailing in each of the two Banks should remain in force until such time as the National Council and His Royal Highness issued unified, general codes of law for both Banks.

No such unified general codes had been enacted by June 6, 1967.

Israeli Enactments

On June 7, 1967, General Herzog, commander of the Israel Defense Forces in the area of Judea and Samaria (the West Bank) issued a proclamation providing that "The law which existed in the Region on June 7, 1967 shall remain in force, insofar as it is not inconsistent with the provisions of the Proclamation or any Proclamation or Order issued by me and compatible with the changes resulting from the establishment of an Israel Defense Forces military government in the Region.'' Arguments by local attorneys on the West Bank that the Defense (Emergency) Regulations of 1945 were not valid were not accepted by the Israeli Military Courts, which found that the military government is authorized to act within the terms of local law by Article 64 of the Fourth Geneva Convention of 1949, which declares that the penal laws of the occupied territory shall remain in force.

West Bank: Population

Population[1] Judea and Samaria

Average	At end of Period	Month	Year
632.0	639.3		1972
650.6	657.4		1973
669.5	674.5		1974
680.4	681.4		1975
675.6	676.7	I	1975
676.8	677.0	II	
677.6	678.2	III	
679.4	680.5	IV	
681.6	682.7	V	
684.0	685.2	VI	
685.2	685.2	VII	
684.1	683.0	VIII	
683.2	683.3	IX	
681.3	679.2	X	
677.4	675.6	XI	
678.5	681.4	XII	
682.5	683.5	I	1976[2]
684.3	685.1	II	
686.1	687.1	III	
687.9	688.6	IV	
690.3	692.0	V	
692.9	693.9	VI	
696.0	698.1	VII	
697.6	697.1	VIII	

1. De Facto population.
2. By registration.

Source: *Administered Territories Statistics Quarterly,* Israel Bureau of Statistics, Jerusalem, Vol. VI, 3, 1976.

SOURCES OF POPULATION GROWTH: 1972-75

	Judea and Samaria			
	1972	1973	1974[1]	1975
Natural increase (thousands)	18.8	17.8	19.9	19.9
Birth rate (per thousand)	45.0	45.0	44.7	44.7
Mortality rate (per thousand)[1]	15.8	17.7	14.9	15.5
Rate of natural increase (per thousand)	29.7	27.4	29.7	29.2
Net migration balance (thousands)	−5.1	0.3	−2.8	−13.8
Total population growth (percent)	2.2	2.8	2.6	0.9

1. The mortality rate was estimated by extrapolating from 1967 census data.

WEST BANK: GROSS INVESTMENT, 1968-75
(IL million, at 1974 prices)

	Judea and Samaria			
	Average 1968-69	1973	1974	1975
Public sector investments	43	47	59	82
Private sector investments	56	262	350	382
Thereof: Construction	37	193	270	311
Machinery, equipment, and transport vehicles	19	69	80	71
Total gross fixed investment	99	309	409	464
Change in inventories	8	−46	126	−81
Total gross investment	107	263	535	383

Source: *The Economy of the Administered Areas, 1974–1975,* by Arie Bregman, Bank of Israel Research Department, Jerusalem, December 1976. From Table 11-5, p. 20.

WEST BANK: BALANCE OF PAYMENTS, 1968-75
(IL million, at current prices)

Judea and Samaria

	1968 C	1968 D	1972 C	1972 D	1973 C	1973 D	1974 C	1974 D	1975 C	1975 D
Total	265	265	703	703	827	827	1,280	1,280	2,056	2,056
Total goods and services	148	225	543	561	648	762	985	1,188	1,566	1,891
Goods	97	176	216	414	243	556	426	885	699	1,466
Services	51	49	327	147	405	206	559	303	867	425
Transportation	—	4	—	17	8	21	24	33	33	50
Insurance	0	1	5	9	9	17	10	19	16	31
Travel abroad	33	32	26	34	23	61	35	80	50	119
Income from investments	4	—	3	1	4	1	5	1	6	1
Government	—	5	—	5	—	6	—	9	—	13
Labor	14	6	293	12	361	12	485	16	762	20
Other	—	1	—	69	—	88	—	136	—	191
Unilateral transfers	117	1	160	42	93	65	146	92	178	165
Private institutions	73	—	94	—	86	10	111	17	128	27
Israel government[1]	—	—	—	—	—	—	35	75	50	138
Total net capital movements[2]	—	39	—	100	86	—	149	—	312	—

C = credit; D = debit.

1. Includes incentives and national insurance benefit payments.
2. Includes errors and omissions and savings through social insurance funds.
Sources: Central Bureau of Statistics.

Source: *The Economy of the Administered Areas, 1974–1975*, by Arie Bregman, Bank of Israel Research Department, Jerusalem, December 1976. From Table V-1, pp. 47-8.

WEST BANK: FOREIGN TRADE
IL million (Israel pounds)

Judea and Samaria
1 9 7 6

	1973	1974	§1975	I-III	IV-VI	VII-IX	X-XII
A. IMPORTS—TOTAL	555.7	881.8	1,462.3	425.9	517.4		
FROM ISRAEL—TOTAL	496.7	790.0	1,296.2	370.6	476.0		
Agricultural produce	84.5	125.9	205.0	62.7	..		
Industrial products	412.2	664.1	1,091.2	307.9	..		
FROM JORDAN—TOTAL	16.5	21.3	35.9	9.2	8.8		
Agricultural produce	3.9	3.4	5.4	2.1	1.7		
Industrial products	12.6	17.9	30.5	7.1	7.1		
FROM OTHER COUNTRIES—TOTAL	42.5	70.5	130.2	46.1	32.6		
Agricultural products	8.2	13.2	44.6	19.5	9.7		
Industrial products	34.3	57.3	85.6	26.6	22.9		
B. EXPORTS—TOTAL	242.6	409.6	690.4	190.9	224.1		
TO ISRAEL—TOTAL	174.7	287.3	442.1	113.4	154.0		
Agricultural produce	35.6	54.9	66.3	96.9	..		
Industrial products	139.1	232.4	375.8	16.5	..		
TO JORDAN—TOTAL	66.2	119.5	220.6	64.8	63.4		
Agricultural produce	25.4	34.5	70.7	25.2	33.8		
Industrial products	40.8	85.0	149.9	39.6	29.6		
TO OTHER COUNTRIES—TOTAL	1.7	2.8	27.7	12.7	6.7		
Agricultural produce	—	—	18.6	11.0	4.7		
Industrial products	1.7	2.8	9.1	1.7	2.0		
C. SURPLUS OF IMPORTS OVER EXPORTS—TOTAL	313.1	472.2	771.9	235.0	293.3		
In trade with Israel	322.0	502.7	854.1	257.2	322.0		
In trade with Jordan	−49.7	−98.2	−184.7	−55.6	−54.6		
In trade with other countries	40.8	67.7	102.5	33.4	25.9		

Source: *Administered Territories Statistics Quarterly*, Israel Central Bureau of Statistics, Jerusalem, Vol. VI, 3, 1976.

The West Bank Refugee Population

In a report entitled *Some Sociological and Economic Aspects of Refugee Camps on the West Bank* (The Rand Corporation, August 1971), Yoram Ben-Porath and Emanuel Marx furnish a picture of the Jalazon camp in 1967-68. This camp is situated in a valley west of the Jerusalem-Nablus trunk road, near the twin towns of Ramallah-Bireh.

The camp looked much like a small village. It had a primary school, the UNRWA's official's office and house and other camp institutions, such as a food distribution center, stores, a youth club, a basketball court, a cook house where daily meals for the camp's children were prepared, a dispensary and a mother and child clinic and a police post (empty following the Israeli occupation). A water tank served the whole camp. There were three coffee-houses, a small mosque and a barbershop. The twenty-seven small stores were all run by their refugee owners. The bus company which serviced the camp was owned by refugees formerly from the Israeli town of Jaffa, who did not live in the camp.

The standard dwellings were of thin concrete, with tin or asbestos roofs. The municipalities of Nablus, Ramallah and Bethlehem had installed electric street lighting in the camps near these towns and many of the houses were connected to the network. UNRWA does not consider these services essential for a temporary population although Jalazon, which had neither electricity nor piped in water, had "graduated" from tents to tin and concrete in 1949. UNRWA took over the administration of the camps in 1950. In 1953, each refugee household was assigned a plot of 100 square meters, on which a concrete cubicle of 3 by 3 meters was constructed. Larger households received somewhat larger dwellings and the refugees themselves added rooms, surrounded their plots with walls and used the extra space for planting vegetables and fruit trees. The dwelling units were officially called *malja* (shelters), because the refugees resisted any idea of permanence; there was resistance even to the concrete dwellings in the permanent camps set up between 1955-1957, though these could not shut out the cold and the damp and though the asbestos roofs broke frequently.

The Jalazon camp population included persons who had arrived in 1948, but half the households had arrived from 1950 onward and the movement into the camp had continued at a steady annual rate of about 15%. Most of this influx was, however, offset by a movement out of the camp, so that the actual number of inhabitants remained more or less stationary.

Those who left moved to other camps, seeking to improve their chances of steady employment. Most had never lived in a camp before and had moved into it for the sake of the advantages it offered. Thus, young men going abroad placed their parents in the camp so that they would be looked after. Men who had failed in business or become chronically ill or had decided to retire moved in with their families. Some came because they had relatives in the camp; others so as not to have to pay rent — with the payment of "key money" to the former occupant, a man could live in a camp dwelling free of rent and taxes, or some of the inhabitants rented out rooms to individuals, not necessarily refugees, or if they left the camp, charged a monthly rental to tenants. (If the new occupant can show refugee status, UNRWA does not evict the tenant or take him to court.)

By 1967, the refugees had grown to believe that the camp had come to stay for a long time and this feeling was translated into a growing interest in making improvements. Some had built concrete houses in the camp or its periphery. Others had acquired the land on which they built their home.

Most of the camps' inhabitants had come from rural areas and each camp on the West Bank had drawn people from the same district, and the attraction of kinship and common origin has tended to continue. In Jalazon, Ben-Porath and Marx found, the population had come mainly from villages in the area of Ramallah-Lydda. The rate of intermarriage had been high, and most of the inhabitants of each village were related, but neither in Jalazon nor in other West Bank camps were there associations of former co-villagers. The old structure had, apparently, broken down.

In Jalazon, some one fifth of the households were headed by women, mostly widows with several young children, who derived most of their small incomes from UNRWA and in fact, preferred this to assistance from relatives which, the majority of camp residents complained, was difficult to come by.

UNRWA employs only refugees, but since its staff security depends on the continued existence of the refugees, its definition of "who is a refugee" is as wide as possible. To the ordinary camp dweller, his ration card constitutes proof of his refugee status. Many refugees, however, though they claim the right to return to their fomer homes and to be compensated for their lost property, try to free themselves of the need to live in camps and to draw food rations.

The UNRWA estimate of the camp population in 1967 was 73,000, with under 75,000 living outside the camps. (The Israeli authorities' census of September 1967 placed the camp population at around 58,000.) Clearly, thus, the total refugee population of the West Bank constituted less than one tenth of the area's total population.

Like the settled residents of the West Bank, the refugees are also Jordanian citizens. In 1967-68, 57% of the adult men were gainfully employed (the ratio for both refugees and non-refugees was 59%). Most of the refugee labor force was engaged outside the camp. Almost three quarters of the refugees employed in the camps described themselves as wage earners as compared with only half the non refugees and 62% of the refugees living outside the camps.

Some of the refugee families had relatives working in the oil states and elsewhere, but the percentage of families receiving private transfers from abroad was smaller in the refugee camps than outside them (6.9% in the camps and 14% outside). Although UNRWA provided assistance in the form of loans and grants and the Jordan Development Bank had set up, with 80% UNRWA financing, loans for projects for refugee employment and for small businesses, the refugees themselves were suspicious of all forms of rehabilitation. When it was realized, for example, that the refugee problem would remain for a long time, UNRWA Director General J. Blandford recommended the establishment of a $200,000,000 rehabilitation fund to be spent over a three year period.[1] The chief projects planned were the large-scale Yarmuk River-Jordan Valley and the Sinai irrigation projects. These went on at a very slow pace. UNRWA reports reflected this disappointing effort quite early in the projects, and blamed the refugees, the Arab governments and Israel.[2] A plan to create six refugee agricultural settlements for 300 families at a cost of some $600,000 was equally disappointing. Some of the projects failed completely and those that survived cost far more than had been planned. As UNRWA reported:

> Years of camp life and dependence on the agency for care and maintenance,
> plus the political aversion to group resettlement, have made it difficult for
> the refugees to adjust themselves to living in agricultural settlements.[3]

UNRWA's education programs, however, proved both popular and highly acceptable since they did not overtly imply resettlement outside the State of Israel (although training in fact equipped a refugee to work in the Arab oil states and elsewhere — thus facilitating emigration).

As early as 1954, UNRWA reported that "many refugee camps are . . . increasingly taking on the appearance of villages and towns with school buildings, small workshops and communal facilities." This is much the case today. Like the rest of the area's population, the men are gainfully employed, working either in Israel or in the area. The women are moving increasingly into the labor market. Housing has vastly improved in many areas and TV antennaes blot the skylines everywhere. The Israeli authorities have constructed apartment buildings in the towns and any refugee family who wishes to do so may move into them, but the process is slowed by the fact that a refugee, although he legally retains his refugee status if he moves out of the camp, must pay taxes and rates to the municipality — an obligation he is free from if he lives in a refugee camp, with all its hardships and handicaps.

The West Bank refugee population was estimated to consist of 125,000 persons in 1975 (this number was estimated by the Bank of Israel on the assumption that the ratio between the number of refugees and the total population remained as it was in the 1967 census). They make up 18% of the total population of the West Bank. The refugees' rate of participation in the work force, employment in Israel and on the West Bank, and income from work, increased continually from 1968 to 1974 but declined in 1975. The refugees have been rapidly integrated into economic activity in the area but are still the marginal workers among the employed, and when the demand begins to drop off in Israel, the refugees are apparently the first to be laid off and the last to be absorbed in the economic activity of the area — in enterprises owned by non-refugee residents. The number of those employed in seasonal work in agriculture has, however, remained stable, at about 20,000. The percentage of refugees employed in the service sector of the area is, however, strikingly high; most fill positions appropriate to persons with a higher education.

FOOTNOTES

1. U.N., *Assistance to Palestine Refugees – Special Report of the Director and Advisory Commission of the U.N. Relief and Works Agency for Palestine Refugees in the Near East*, Supplement No. 16A (A/1905/Add. 1), Paris, 1951.

2. UNRWA Report, 1954.

3. UNRWA Report, 1957.

The Christian Communities in Jerusalem and the West Bank, 1948-1967

By DAPHNA TSIMHONI

When Jordanian rule began in the West Bank in 1948 Christians constituted about eight percent of the population. Ninety percent of the Christians were indigenous and Arabic speaking and formed a religious minority identifying itself with the Muslim majority in culture and national identity. The majority of Christians lived in the towns surrounding the Holy Places: Jerusalem, Ramallah, Bethlehem, Beit Jala and Beit Sahur. These towns were traditionally considered as Christian though the proportion of Christians had been steadily decreasing since the end of the First World War. This process was the outcome of constant Christian emigration abroad and a higher Muslim birthrate. Another factor in the proportional increase of the Muslim population in these towns after 1948 was the surrounding refugee camps whose inhabitants were devout Muslims. As a result, Jerusalem and Ramallah no longer came to have a Christian majority, although a considerable proportion of the population was still Christian. Only Bethlehem and the neighboring

Dr. Tsimhoni is a member of the Middle East Department at Haifa University, and specializes in the problems of minorities in the Middle East.

Reprinted from *Middle East Review*, Vol. IX, No. 1, Fall, 1976.

villages of Beit Jala and Beit Sahur retained a Christian majority. Still, Christians formed a substantial minority in these districts.

For hundreds of years Christians had been living under Ottoman-Muslim rule as *dhimmis* (protected believers of an inferior religion). While acknowledging their inferior position the Christian communities enjoyed a substantial amount of autonomy in conducting their own communal and religious life as prescribed by the *millet* system, which included maintenance of religious courts of law, educational and charitable institutions, and the right to own property. The British mandatory government in Palestine, although introducing some changes, had accepted the *millet* system as the basis for its relations with the various religious communities. When, after thirty years of rule by a Christian power under the British mandate, authority reverted to the Muslim Jordanian government, the Christian communities were understandably anxious regarding their status.

The Jordanian constitution, which was promulgated on 8 January 1952, recognized Islam as the official religion of the Hashemite Kingdom and of its King (*arts*, 2, 28). In so doing Jordan did not differ from most of the Arab states with a majority of Muslim citizens. Freedom and equality before the law was guaranteed to all citizens regardless of their religion or race (*arts*. 6, 14). The constitution also recognized the right of Christian and foreign communities to maintain their own educational institutions provided these were supervised by the Government (*art*. 19). It granted the ecclesiastical law courts equal jurisdiction to that of the Muslim *Shari'a* law courts (*art*. 109).

The Christians in Jordan, realizing that they were a small community living in a Muslim country, accepted recognition of Islam as the official religion of the state. Because the new constitution granted Christians internal autonomy and equal status before the law it was welcomed by Christian circles as "the most liberal of all constitutions in the Arab countries, at least concerning the status of the Christians."[1] A major question remained: What would be the implications for Christians as citizens, and for their institutions, of the declaration of Islam as the official religion.

One immediate effect was the exclusion of Christian festivals from the list of national holidays. Only Muslim festivals were now officially recognized. For several years, however, a three-day official holiday during Christmas was declared in the cities of Jerusalem and Bethlehem. The declarations were announced one at a time, "according to the King's will and by recommendation of the prime minister."[2] They were issued as a gesture and not by law. Christmas was not recognized as an official holiday in the other Jordanian towns and villages, even including Ramallah which was traditionally regarded as a Christian town. Except for the years in which these declarations were issued, Christmas was regarded as a normal weekday in Jerusalem and on the West Bank. But, as a concession Christians in government and municipal services were permitted to absent themselves from work, in accordance with their respective religious calendars.[3] In spite of the demands of Christian dignitaries, no other Christian festival was recognized as an official holiday in any of the Christian towns.

Even though the Christian religion was not granted an official status, a few other gestures were made towards the Christian citizens. Friday was the official weekly holiday but Christians were allowed to come to work at 10 a.m. on Sundays. On Christian holidays and Sundays the Jordanian Broadcasting Corporation transmitted prayer services for the Christian communities but, typical of the status of the Christian religion, these programs were temporarily discontinued during the month of *Ramadan*.[4]

The most important implication of the communal autonomy granted by the Jordanian constitution was recognition of ecclesiastical law courts. The Jordanian constitution (*art.* 9) granted the Christian courts equal judicial rights with those of the Muslim *Shari'a* courts. By this act their status was improved as compared with the British mandatory period, during which the Muslim courts had enjoyed a higher status than that of the Christian and Jewish communal courts.[5] Other expressions of autonomy, such as the maintenance of communal educational and charitable institutions, were also allowed to continue. However, in 1953 the *Charity Associations Law* (No. 36, 16 February 1953) and the *Law of Maintaining Properties by Religious Personalities* (No. 61, 16 April 1953) were enacted. The Jordanian government published these laws in order to limit Christian influence and activity in Jerusalem and the West Bank.

The *Law of Maintaining Properties by Religious Personalities* included severe restrictions on the purchase of properties by Christian institutions, especially foreign ones. Above all, it prohibited all Christian charitable and religious institutions, both local and foreign, from buying properties in the neighborhood of the Holy Sites without special permission from the Cabinet (*art.* 7). The publication of this law caused great anxiety among the Christian communities. Protests were sent and communal delegations met with the authorities in order to dissuade them from promulgating the new law. Most active were the Catholic clerics. The Pope himself brought up this issue during the discussions concerning the Christians' position in Jordan, when King Hussein visited the Vatican in 1953.[6] As a result, a new amended law was published on 17 January 1954. However, the article prohibiting Christian institutions (Jordanian as well as foreign) from buying new properties in the neighborhood of the Holy Places was not changed. The enactment of this law was the result of pressure by Muslim circles on the government. They warned that Christians might gain possession of properties surrounding the Holy Places by taking advantage of the poverty of the Arab citizens living there.[7] These circles were not satisfied with the new law of 1954 and demanded a total prohibition on the purchase of properties in Jerusalem and its outskirts by Christian institutions.[8]

With the growth of nationalist Muslim pressure on the government a new amendment was published in 1965. The new law prohibited Christians from acquiring properties in the entire district of Jerusalem by any means, whether by buying, hiring, accepting gifts, creating *waqfs,* etc., and repeated all the restrictions imposed by previous laws. Christian institutions had apparently managed to evade the 1954 law by assigning local Muslim citizens to buy properties in their name. It seems that the new detailed law of 1965 was aimed at eliminating such a possibility. The new restrictions were carried out very rigorously regarding foreigners, church personalities and institutions both European and Arab.

This enactment was an expression of the traditional nationalist Muslim identification of Christianity with the Western powers which had often attempted to seize control of the Holy Land. This feeling was not absolutely groundless. Since the Eastern communities were usually very poor, most properties were in fact purchased by Western Christian institutions. But, although the restrictions in the new law were aimed at foreign Western institutions, the law was formulated to include all Christian institutions in general and thus acquired an anti-Christian tinge.

The *Charity Associations Law* (No. 36, 16 February 1956) restricted the activity of Christian and Western institutions in Jordan even further. It demanded the reestablishment and registration of all associations and included articles that assured a strict supervision of their activities. Furthermore, it asserted that all the institutions engaged in charity work would be put under the control of the law. This, naturally, caused apprehension among the Christian institutions, and especially the Catholic ones (they being the most active). They were afraid that it might lead to the limiting of their activities and even to the diminishing of their unique religious character. As a result of protests and discussions between the representatives of the communities and the authorities a new amendment to the law was published on 17 March 1956. It clearly asserted that the law would not affect the Christian institutions and monasteries but only their social and charitable activities, and reaffirmed all the articles of the previous law supervising and limiting this work. These articles were rigidly carried out, particularly regarding foreign Christian charity institutions.

Christian schools also suffered legal interference. A very large number of the educational institutions in the West Bank towns, particularly in Jerusalem, was Christian. They were mostly owned or supported by Western Christian bodies, and represented the continuation of missionary activities started during the nineteenth century. The teaching in these schools was conducted according to European methods and standards and the languages of instruction were also European. The raison d'être of these schools was the propagation of the Christian faith, specifically that of the denomination of the owners of the institution. Very few of their graduates had however become converted to

Christianity since the establishment of the British Mandate in Palestine. These institutions, particularly the secondary schools, attracted growing numbers of Muslim students — children of families who wished to give their offspring a Western education and in particular a knowledge of European languages.

Following the promulgation of the laws limiting the purchase of properties by Christian institutions in 1953, nationalist circles demanded that the government should closely supervise the activity of Christian educational institutions, especially the foreign ones, in order to restrict their influence.[9] Despite numerous protests and contacts with the Government made by communal representatives, the *Public Education Law* was published on 16 April 1955. It included far-reaching restrictions and aroused anxieties among the Christians that the Christian character of the communal educational system might be destroyed. The main provisions of the law were: (a) the adoption of the study-program, teaching methods and text-books of the Ministry of Education (*arts* 2, 4, 6, 41) (these were of a far lower standard than those in Christian schools); (b) the use of Arabic as the only language of instruction and the teaching of foreign languages according to the Ministry of Education's program (*art*. 33), (this meant that only one foreign language would be taught whereas the Christian schools taught several European languages and prepared their students for European matriculation examinations); (c) the closing of schools on Fridays and national holidays (*art*. 39), (even though this meant Muslim but not Christian festivals); (d) the teaching of religion according to the community to which the student belonged (*art*. 35). Provisions (a) and (b) were aimed at providing national education to all Jordanian students. Provisions (c) and (d) were intended to eliminate possible Christian missionary influence on Muslims.

The law aroused protests by all the Christian communities, which tried to join forces in order to postpone its implementation. The law was mainly opposed by Roman Catholics since most of the Christian educational institutions were organized and run by them. Due to this opposition, the law was not implemented. In 1966, however, as a result of the growing pressure of nationalist Muslims on the government, the law finally came into force.[10] It remained in force for no more than one year, until the 1967 war, and in that short time did not manage to change the character of Christian educational institutions in Jerusalem and the West Bank.

The activity and influence of Christians in political and public life exceeded their proportionate numbers in the West Bank population. Just as in the mandatory period, this influence was a result of their higher educational level, their higher concentration in the towns and their higher concentration in white collar professions.

Christians were employed in government administration; some of them even attaining high positions. Also, traditionally, in every Cabinet one to three portfolios were given to Christians, although no Christian held the post of prime-minister. Christians were rarely appointed to key public posts such as that of district governor.[11] They did not attain high rank in the police force and the army. Discussing the problem with Christian dignitaries, this author was told that there was discrimination in employing Christians in the civil service, though nobody admitted this publicly. Moreover, the increasing percentage of educated Muslims aroused fears among Christians of being pushed out of the civil service.

Except for the years 1954-1957, proportional representation was achieved for Christians in Parliament. Elections were based on district-communal distribution which preserved seats for the Christians according to their proportional numbers in the population of the district. Several Christian personalities expressed the idea that this system limited the Christians' activities. They maintained that according to their education and abilities Christians could have occupied more seats in Parliament if this sectarian key had not existed.

The Jordanian government did not encourage the preservation of the Christian character of the towns of Ramallah, Bethlehem, Beit Jala and Beit Sahur. For statistical and administrative purposes the neighboring refugee camps, inhabited almost entirely by Muslims, were integrated into these towns. Accordingly, a Muslim majority was created in their municipal institutions. The government had, also, intended to set up a single municipal council for Ramallah and el-Bireh, the poor neighboring Muslim town, but this was not carried out owing to the decisive opposition of the Christian citizens of Ramallah.

The Christian communal establishment maintained correct and even friendly relations with the Jordanian authorities. Leaders of the communities and Jordanian high officials met frequently in order to discuss problems concerning the communities and paid each other courtesy visits on religious and other holidays. Christian dignitaries manifested their loyalty to the King especially during the crucial period 1956-1957.[12] In contrast to the good relations of the Christian establishment with the government, the participation of Christians in the political opposition to the Hashemite regime was outstanding. Christians were among the prominent leaders of the illegal parties and organizations. Jawdah Shahwan, Yusuf and Abdallah Bandak from Bethlehem, 'Adil Qasis from Ramallah, and Emil Harb from Jerusalem were eminent figures in the communist party. Abdallah Hanna from Taibeh was one of the founders of the *Ba'th* party and one of its active leaders, as was also Fu'ad Nasr.

One might suggest a few reasons to explain this phenomenon:

1. Christians formed an important component of the intellectual elite in the Jordanian towns — as has been the case everywhere in the Arab world. They had played an outstanding role in the intellectual leadership of the Arab national movement in its formative years.

2. Many Christians felt that they were discriminated against when trying to

obtain posts in the Jordanian administration. This resulted in frustration and pushed them toward extreme opposition to the government.

3. Because of latent Muslim suspicion of Christians, the latter wished to demonstrate that they were no less nationalistic than the Muslims.

4. A major part of the opposition to King Hussein's rule came from Palestinian circles, particularly the Palestinian town-dwellers who regarded themselves as superior to the East Jordanians and resented the latter's political dominance over them. Many Christian intellectuals on the West Bank believed that they were discriminated against not because of their religion but because they were Palestinians. In this sense they regarded themselves as belonging to the same category as did the Muslim Palestinians as compared with the East Jordanians.

Christian participation in nationalist and opposition organizations was limited to the leadership stratum. Among the masses the barrier between Muslims and Christians still existed. Among the lower classes latent Muslim suspicions that the Christians were in league with the West continued to exist. These latent feelings occasionally burst into violent clashes and attacks on Christian churches and properties. This was particularly the case during periods of crisis in Jordan, such as 1956 and 1966-1967.[13] In the light of these outbursts, educated and middle-class Christians from the towns were made very much aware of their insecure position as a religious minority living in a Muslim-dominated country. This was true even though the barriers between them and the Muslims were not so significant, since their education, occupations and everyday lives were to a large extent similar.

Summing up, although the status of Christianity in Jordan was inferior to that of Islam, the constitution provided all citizens with freedom and equality before the law. Christians did not usually protest against the recognition of Islam as the official religion of the Kingdom, but against the restrictions imposed upon them as a result of this declaration. The links between Arab nationalism and Islam worsened relations between Muslims and Christians, especially in the period of rising nationalism. The Christians' activities and influence in public and political life far exceeded their proportionate numbers in the total population. Yet, in spite of their success, as a religious minority many felt the presence of an underlying discrimination and suspicion.

FOOTNOTES

1. *Proche-Orient Chrétien (P.O.C.)* Vol. 2 (1952) p. 84.

2. Declaration for 1956 *P.O.C.* Vol. 6 (1956) p. 364, 1961; *Filastin,* 26 December 1961, 1962; Israel State Archives (I.S.A.) 23-193, 1964; I.S.A. 23-193.

3. See for instance, *Filastin* 26 December 1961.

4. *Filastin,* 30 March 1960.

5. For a detailed discussion of this issue see D. Tsimhoni, *The British Mandate and the Arab Christians in Palestine 1920-1925* (A London University Ph.D. Thesis, 1976) pp. 129-140.

6. *P.O.C.* Vol. 3 (1953) pp. 371-372.

7. *P.O.C.* Vol. 5 (1955) p. 62.

8. *Filastin,* 19 January 1955.

9. See for instance the call of the General Assembly of Jordanian students, *P.O.C.* Vol. 3 (1953) p. 268.

10. *Filastin,* 23 February 1966.

11. An exception was the appointment of a Christian as the district governor of 'Aqaba for a short time.

12. *Filastin,* 28 April 1957.

13. Reports in *Filastin,* 24 April 1956, 3 May 1956; *al-Hayat* 28 April 1956; *al-Difa'* 4 May 1956. Complaints by communal leaders regarding Muslim acts of violence against Christians, *I.S.A.* 192-3; 1302-29; 245-6.

VII

Views on the Future
Of the West Bank

West Bank Attitudes:

THE HONORABLE BASAM SHAK'A, Mayor of Nablus

MAYOR SHAK'A: The Palestine problem is very complicated. It began in 1947, when the Zionist movement, abetted by America, Britain and Russia, managed to extract a resolution from the U.N. supporting the creation of the state of Israel. This state was established against the will and the wishes of the Arab people to whom the land belonged. A conflict inevitably ensued, and the state of Israel was imposed on the inhabitants of the area. As a result, the rights of the Palestine Arabs—in the occupied land and elsewhere—have not yet been recognized. Israel still refuses to implement any of the U.N. resolutions. More than a million Palestinians were driven out of Palestinian town and lands, but throughout the years they have never forgotten their rights; they have persisted in demanding them. Israel ignores these legitimate and just rights and wars against the Palestinian people with arms, murder and violence. In 1967 Israel was able to occupy all the Palestinian lands and still rules in Palestine by force of arms. Israel has consistently refused to implement any of the resolutions passed by international bodies; it has persistently denied the rights of the Palestinian people everywhere. Israel does not even acknowledge their existence. Nevertheless, the Palestinian people have clung tenaciously to demanding their rights, in the face of oppression. They are reacting as would any other people in the same situation.

QUESTION: Why were there no demands for recognition of Palestinian rights under Jordanian rule?

MAYOR SHAK'A: The struggle for the rights of the Palestinian people has been going on since 1948. There was no enmity between King 'Abdallah or King Hussein and the Palestinians. They are Arabs and we are Arabs. But there may have been certain differences regarding the future of the Arabs as a whole, or regarding methods of approach to the problem. King 'Abdallah did not surrender the Palestine cause to Israel and neither has King Hussein ever announced that he was ready to relinquish the struggle for Palestinian rights to Israel. The Palestinians of the West Bank made the decision to annex this area to Jordan, on condition that we would, together, struggle for the liberation of Palestine; it would have been impossible for the West Bank to survive on its

Mr. Shak'a is a member of the PLO. He was elected mayor of Nablus on April 12, 1976.

Excerpted from a briefing by Mr. Shak'a to a Study Mission of *American Professors for Peace in the Middle East,* June 1976. The briefing was taped and the transcript has been edited. It is presented in as true and faithful a fashion, in keeping with the ideas expressed, as is possible. In no way have these ideas been altered. [*Eds.*]

Mr. Shak'a's remarks were translated from the Arabic by Mr. Victor Sasson, hwo is a Ph.D. candidate at New York University.

248   JORDAN AND THE WEST BANK

own. But then a political conflict arose between the Palestinian people and the
Jordanian people — against King 'Abdallah and against King Hussein —
regarding Jordan's political structure and the ways of achieving the liberation
of Palestine.

QUESTION: Why was there no demand for a Palestinian state?

MAYOR SHAK'A: Our conflict is with Israel. We were not initially interested
in a Palestinian state, but changing political circumstances in the Arab-Israel
conflict and in the Arab world in general made us realize that we should think
in terms of a Palestinian entity. This idea began to crystallize while we were
still united with the Hashemite Kingdom of Jordan. We gave expression to it
through the PLO, the organization recognized by all the Arab states. The idea
of a Palestinian entity has been recognized by King Hussein, by the Arab
states and by the world at large as a result of our planning, our work and our
struggle.

QUESTION: What would you see as the borders of a Palestinian state?

MAYOR SHAK'A: That is a difficult question to answer. So far, our relations
with Israel have been those of a life-and-death struggle; a "we-or-they" issue.
Israelis want a state from the (Mediterranean) Sea to the River (Jordan),
and maintain that we have no rights whatsoever. We want to establish that we
have all our legitimate rights. Our objectives will perhaps be achieved in
stages, and these stages will be shaped by the nature of the conflict and by the
way it develops.

QUESTION: Are you willing to accept Israel as a state existing side by side
with a Palestinian state?

MAYOR SHAK'A: Suppose we were to agree to a state of Israel existing
within the 1967 borders, would that mean that we must surrender the pre-1967
rights of the Palestinian people? And how does Israel view this issue? Israel
wants to take over all of Palestine, while we aspire to achieving our rights
regarding Palestine. Our conflict with Israel is over our rights in Palestine; in
all of Palestine. However, we want peace. The borders of a peace settlement
will shape themselves as the conflict evolves. It depends on Israel's response.
It has to do with negotiations. The nature of our future relationship (with
Israel) will be the result of negotiations, of mutual understanding; it will be
the result of the conflict that today exists in every part of the Palestinian land.
Israel is the obstacle to peace. It has not recognized that the Palestinians have
any rights. It has not even defined its own borders as a state. If Israel were to
say, "We are ready to withdraw to the 1967 borders," then we would accept
a Palestinian state (beside) these borders. We would be prepared to negotiate.
Once the problem of borders is solved, we could lead a life of cooperation and
brotherhood; a life with a common destiny. The political trends in the Zionist
movement and among the Great Powers and the consequences of fascism all
combined to create a solution to the Jewish problem—in a land that was not

deserted and at the expense of another nation. They solved one problem and created a more serious one; an international problem. There are Jews here from America building a state in a land that is not theirs — a racist state — against the wishes and the interests of the people of the land. The issue is not that of Jewish persecution but of Zionist ambitions in the area. If this problem is solved—if the Jewish people can become independent of American interests and can bring their aspirations into harmony with the area where they live then, I believe, we will be able to live together in peace and friendship and on equal terms, in a country in which we can have common goals and common aspirations.

QUESTION: If Israel were to recognize the right of the Palestinian people to a state, would you recognize the right of Israel to exist as a state?

MAYOR SHAK'A: I would like you to put that question to Israel. We have consistently urged that we be recognized. The PLO urges Israel to recognize the organization and to sit down and talk with it. Israel has consistently rejected this demand. If it becomes responsive, if it becomes a harmonious part of this region, we will then have no objection—although I think this is a very remote possibility.

QUESTION: We have found that many Israelis feel that the prevailing sentiment among Palestinians is that while Jews would be welcome in the area, Israel as an independent state, is not considered legitimate. Do you recognize Israel as a legitimate state in the area?

MAYOR SHAK'A: I know that there is this feeling in Israel and that this sentiment does exist among Palestinians. It is the natural result of the conflict. The reason is that they have a state and this state is only concerned with its own self-interest. If they were to approach the other party—if they gave a thought to the rights of the other nation—they would find a willing response. But this problem will find its own solution.

QUESTION: Do you demand an Israeli withdrawal in addition to the creation of a Palestinian state? Would this state consist of the West Bank and the East Bank?

MAYOR SHAK'A: I would say that would be a possibility. But it depends on Israel. For example, I told the Military Governor here that the people must be permitted to express their feelings. He replied: "Do you expect us to pack up and leave *peacefully*?" I said: Why do you insist on being *forced* to leave? Does that mean you have no intention of leaving except by force?"

QUESTION: What led to the demonstrations and unrest in Nablus?

MAYOR SHAK'A: There is a constant struggle here, whether it is overt or covert. The fact of occupation makes people suffer. Our suffering began in 1967, and we have since that time expressed this in various ways. Now we feel it can no longer be endured. Israel keeps establishing settlements, confiscating lands, creating colonies on land belonging to Arabs who still live here.

The military government takes harsh and repugnant measures. We see the Jews striking roots in our country, on our land, and we are not about to ignore this. In the absence of democracy, we demonstrate, as the only way to express ourselves, and then the army comes in. In this atmosphere, calm political effort and calm discussion are useless. There are demonstrations, there is tension, military curfews are imposed and people are killed. It is all the result of the occupation.

QUESTION: What role does the Jordanian Federation of Labor play on the West Bank?

MAYOR SHAK'A: The workers and the people marched on May Day—Labor Day—but the authorities came to stop them. We repeatedly demand the right to free and complete expression. If we had it, there would be no confrontations. Eventually, a suitable atmosphere would be created for mutual understanding. There would be mutual recognition of our shared rights, developed in an atmosphere of democracy. Instead, the army beats us, shoots us down, interns us, enters our houses by force, insults our women and children and our aged. This leads to more violence and tension and more curfews and the situation keeps getting worse.

QUESTION: You insist that the PLO is your voice, but the PLO calls for a secular state in the entire area that was Palestine, and hence the elimination of the state of Israel. How do you reconcile your position with that of the PLO?

MAYOR SHAK'A: The only political trend on the West Bank is support for the political unity of the Palestinian nation everywhere. All the people support the PLO. We did not vote for a single candidate who was not PLO. The list of candidates for the office of mayor included a union representative and also physicians and merchants. I myself am a merchant and property owner— although not, of course, a tycoon!

QUESTION: The Israelis have told us they are reluctant to negotiate with terrorists. In view of the difficulty of achieving negotiations between Israel and the PLO, could West Bank representatives negotiate with Israel on behalf of the Palestinian people?

MAYOR SHAK'A: Human experience in general and the history of political agreements would be sufficient to answer your question. There are undoubtedly many ways of creating legal and binding agreements leading to political unification, and these could lead to solutions to various situations. What is important is that Israel must see itself as an integral part of this area and not as alien to it. As things stand at present, Israel exists only to preserve a particular situation in the area and it wants to preserve this situation for its own special reasons. Therefore the secular state could very possibly provide a solution. I can envision a secular state in the distant future. It would be a kind of paradise of the end of days if it became a reality. But prior to that, certain commitments have to exist; a belief in peace, in human brotherhood and in human life.

As far as terrorism is concerned, the PLO does not like what it has done or might still have to do. Acts of murder have been condemned by various bodies in the organization on various occasions. This has also been the case regarding acts planned and undertaken by the PLO itself. The people committing these acts have explained what impelled them to commit them—because the Palestinian people are oppressed and the world is unmindful of them—out of revenge and retaliation against certain acts committed by the Israeli government. We have very painful memories. Rightly or wrongly, as long as mankind closes its ears to certain human outcries, people will find a way of making their voices heard. We must eliminate the basic root of the problem in order to make a real move toward peace.

Concerning West Bank negotiations with Israel, we did not receive a mandate from the people to negotiate the creation of a Palestinian state; the elections were held for the municipal councils only. We are not here as a substitute for the PLO and we do not represent the whole of the Palestinian people.

QUESTION: The Palestinians are the most educated people in the Arab world, yet they allow themselves to be exploited and victimized by everyone — and mainly by their own Arab brothers. If they recognized the realities of the twentieth century instead of hearkening back to the past, they would see that Israel exists, as a legitimate state, and that violence only triggers violence. There are two rights in this area, the rights of the Israelis and the rights of the Palestinians. Recognizing this fact, could you not declare, openly and frankly, that you are prepared to live side by side with the state of Israel?

MAYOR SHAK'A: That is a very broad question. Americans and Europeans have gone through all the stages of development in the past in order to achieve independence and freedom. You are economically advanced and have few problems, so you feel there are easy answers to everything. I cannot remain calm when the rights you enjoy are denied to me. Facts cannot be imposed; they have to be willingly accepted. What we demand for ourselves and for others—for the Jews as well—is that human relationships be created in order that we can achieve (mutual) understanding. Realities must not be created by force. They must not be imposed by the governments of the Arab states or by others with certain political commitments who try to force upon the Palestinians what is in these governments' interests, or who take certain measures and then claim that they are existing realities. We reject any attempt to force us to act as the leadership of the Palestinian people because we feel this would be a source of weakness which could eventually affect the unity of the whole nation. Therefore we consider this as an interference that is neither right nor beneficial to us.

DR. HATEM ABU-GHAZALEH (Nablus)

DR. ABU-GHAZALEH: The Palestinians-Israel dilemma on the West Bank and elsewhere involves the problem of justice and peace. A pragmatic approach is needed. The first step must be taken by the stronger party to this conflict — and the two parties are the Palestinians and the Israelis; not the Israelis and the Arab states. Because the Israelis are the stronger party, they must issue, frankly and openly, what I call a "Declaration of Intentions," spelling out Israel's readiness to withdraw to its 1967 borders, its recognition of the PLO as the sole legitimate representative of the Palestinian people and its readiness to accept and recognize the rights of the Palestinians. This declaration must be specifically endorsed by [all the political parties; by] the Israel Knesset and it must be the recognized and official policy of Israel, which cannot be revoked by any future Israeli government. I believe that this Declaration will be followed — and it must be followed — by the readiness of the Palestinians and the PLO to negotiate with Israel as a state; by their readiness to recognize Israel's right to exist and to have recognized borders; by their readiness to create a new life side by side with the State of Israel as a twin state in the area. When a Palestinian state is created, with its own territorial borders, which is ready to sit down and to negotiate directly with Israel, a completely new pattern of life and relations between the Palestinians and the Israelis will be established. I can see no other solution. I have said so since 1967 but I have found it unacceptable to Israel. Therefore I have designed a pragmatic program for the establishment of a just peace in the area; a program for peace. I propose that the U.N. Security Council pass a resolution placing the territories occupied in the June 1967 war, under U.N. sponsorship (mandate). These would then be administered by a High Commissioner nominated by the Security Council. He would have to be a man of experience, who understands the Middle East and the Arab-Israel conflict. He would be assisted by a Board of Councilors, consisting of eight persons, who would serve as his executive branch. Of these eight persons, three would be nominated by the PLO and three would be elected by the population of the occupied territories (one from Samaria, one from Judea, the third one from the Gaza Strip), by direct ballot. The remaining two persons would be elected by the Arab League, but they too must be Palestinians. The High Commissioner, as the representative of the

Dr. Ghazaleh, a former member of the Jordanian parliament, twice imprisoned by Jordan and once by Israel for his political activities, is a practicing physician in Nablus. He is a member of the PLO National Congress.

The above is excerpted from a Briefing to a Study Mission of the *American Professors for Peace in the Middle East* in June 1976. The Briefing was taped and the transcript has been edited. It is presented in a true and faithful fashion in keeping with the ideas expressed. In no way have these ideas been altered. Where lack of facility in the English language on the speaker's part called for it, the necessary changes were made for the sake of greater comprehensibility and clarity. [*Eds.*]

U.N., and the Board of Councilors would constitute an Executive Committee. The Israelis would not oppose this program because it would be under U.N. supervision. A local U.N. police force would be responsible for security. The Arab states and the PLO would not oppose the program because three members of the Executive Committee would be nominated by the PLO. The Arab League would be satisfied because two of the Executive Committee members would be its own nominees. Thus the main parties to the conflict — Israel, the Arab states and the Palestinians — would be neutralized, since they would all be under U.N. supervision. Following the transition of power from Israel to a U.N. administration, this U.N. administration would resettle the 400,000-500,000 Palestinian refugees who were displaced from the territories occupied by Israel after the June 1967 war. Their rehabilitation and resettlement will not cost the U.N. anything because they already have their own homes, farms and villages in the territories. The area would then have a population of over 1.5 million, all of them Palestinians. This population would elect, after a period of, say, two to three years, some 100 or 150 Deputies, on the basis of one Deputy per 10,000 of population. These elected Deputies would form fifty percent of the Palestinian National Congress. This Congress, as at present constituted, is the PLO's legislative branch, which convenes annually in Cairo. Half the Deputies to the Congress would represent parties outside the territories; from Jordan, the PLO, Syria, Lebanon, Saudi Arabia — wherever there are Palestinians in the world, including the United States and Canada. All these Palestinians would have the right to elect their own Deputies, in the framework of one per 10,000 people. This new legislature would make changes in the PLO Covenant, since the Israelis are so sensitive about this Covenant and especially about Article 4, which stipulates that the whole area is Palestine and that Israel does not have the right to exist as a state. As a first step therefore, this particular Article in the Covenant would be changed, in order to give the Israelis more confidence in the Palestinians' good intentions. Then, this new PLO National Congress would elect a Provisional Government. This Provisional Government would enter into direct negotiations with Israel in order to work out the final, permanent peace settlement between both parties. If they fail to attain a final peace agreement, then the U.N. Security Council would have the right to prolong the existence of the High Commissioner and of its mandate over the territories, until such time as both parties attain a final peace settlement.

QUESTION: How receptive have the PLO and the other factions in the Arab world been to your program?

DR. ABU-GHAZALEH: I have not discussed it with the PLO, but I believe the PLO will not oppose it because there would be a Palestinian National Authority similar to the one adopted at the Palestinian National Congress in 1972, which voted for the creation of a Palestinian National Authority. My program however, is to create a Palestinian National Authority with a U.N. hat on its head. If I find that there is a readiness on the part of Israel to accept such a program, I will contact the PLO and offer it to them as well. If both parties reject it, then, in the interest of international security and peace, the U.N. Security Council must adopt this plan and must impose it on both parties. Peace is more important than local conflicts.

QUESTION: The PLO may be under a different leadership at the time. How would that affect your program?

DR. ABU-GHAZALEH: If my program is endorsed, a new Executive Committee will be elected after the creation of the new Palestinian National Congress. Whoever the new PLO Chairman may be — whether he is George Habbash or Yasser Arafat or anyone else — my program would be carried out under U.N. auspices.

QUESTION: I suggest that there are internal political problems in the PLO which would determine PLO acceptance of your program.

DR. ABU-GHAZALEH: That is precisely why I propose the creation of a new PLO, through the democratic process. The PLO might have certain sensitivities about me if I approach them with my program; they might not accept me as a sponsoring authority. I am a member of the PLO National Congress, although I have not been able to attend its meetings since 1967. Nevertheless, my experience of life under Israeli rule and my contacts with many international forums have convinced me that a move must be made. Unless Israel is prepared to accept and to recognize the Palestinians as a nation, with the PLO as its representative, we are not ready to accept Israel as a nation and as a state. We are in a position of stalemate. I offer a workable solution.

QUESTION: If the Israelis accept a return to the 1967 borders, and recognize an independent Palestinian state — with national sovereignty or in an East and West Bank combination — would that be acceptable?

DR. ABU-GHAZALEH: Yes, definitely. If international legitimacy is given to Israel's border as the 1967 line, I would accept that. But it must also be accepted by the Israelis and the Palestinians, not only by the U.S. The Palestinian-Israeli conflict is based on two issues — on recognized and acceptable borders, following an Israeli withdrawal, and on Palestinian rights in the state of Israel. We want the implementation of all the U.N. resolutions — these are our *international* rights. Our *national* rights will be satisfied if we have our own Palestinian state.

QUESTION: Would acceptance of Israel, under those circumstances, be an acceptance of Israel as an inherently *Jewish* state, or do you demand that Israel become a ''secular democratic'' state, as in the PLO parlance?

DR. ABU-GHAZALEH: If we do not want the Israelis to impose their concepts on us, we must not impose our concepts on Israeli nationalism.

QUESTION: Does your definition of the "international rights of the Palestinians" include the right to return to land that is now a part of the state of Israel?

DR. ABU-GHAZALEH: I would not make my own interpretation of "international legitimacy" a hindrance to peace. The 1947 Partition Resolution says explicitly that any disputed problems between the Arabs and the Jews will be referred to an international court of justice. I believe that we are ready to accept the resolution adopted by the International Court of Justice concerning any issue over which there are differences or a conflict of interests.

When this area comes under the U.N. flag the borders will still be open. The new relations will be between the Israelis as a people and the Palestinians as a people. Today, the Israelis do not regard themselves as an occupying force; they do not see themselves as oppressors but we see them as the occupying force and we regard them as oppressors. Sensitivities will have to change radically on both sides.

QUESTION: Do you propose that the West Bank be demilitarized?

DR. ABU-GHAZALEH: Yes, to be supervised by an international U.N. force, or a U.N. force composed of local personnel.

QUESTION: Would this U.N.-controlled West Bank Palestinian state be economically viable?

DR. ABU-GHAZALEH: We would not be the first state in the world to start with nothing. The budget of the Hashemite Kingdom of Transjordan in 1923 was £5,000, given annually by the British High Commissioner. If we have the opportunity to build our economy we will do very well. We have never been given the right to grow independently. We have always been in the middle of the conflict, first under the British, then under King Hussein and now under Israel. But we are the lifeblood of the Arab world. The state of Kuwait would never have come into existence without us, or Jordan, or Saudi Arabia or the Gulf States. The Palestinians, in terms of population percentage, have more academicians, intellectuals and professional people than any other Arab country. This would not be a weak state, and the good will of the international community would help to give it life and prosperity. The Palestinians have had to pay the price for the dispersion and the humiliation of world Jewry. Jewish participation and help will enable us to live peacefully in our own land.

SHEIK MUHAMMAD ALI AL-JAABARI (Hebron)

As long as there is a body called the PLO which behaves in the way it does, there will be no solution to the Palestine question. I think that the Arab people of the West Bank should be brave enough to admit this and courageous enough to know what is in its true interest. This people should authorize Jordan to negotiate on its behalf, so that afterwards it will have the opportunity of self-determination.

The PLO, too, must be courageous and realistic enough to admit that it has failed. This organization should turn to Jordan—or perhaps to another Arab country—and ask it to negotiate on behalf of the Palestinians. The PLO is incapable of negotiating. The PLO wrought havoc in Jordan and now it is destroying Lebanon. It would do the same thing here, given the chance.

Sheik Muhammad Ali al-Jaabari, former Mayor of Hebron, in a statement to Tawfiq Khoury (an Israeli Arab journalist). *Yediot Aharonot*, (Israel Daily), October 14, 1976.

Israeli Attitudes:

YITZHAK RABIN (Labor Party-Mapai)

I believe that we cannot ignore the fact that the Palestinians exist and that a Palestinian problem exists. But we are still far from recognizing what is called, without any further specification, a Palestinian entity. We must solve the problem in such a way that the Palestinians may be allowed, if they so wish, to make their voices heard, but only within the framework of a Jordanian-Palestinian State.

We are firmly convinced that there is no room for a third nation between Israel and Jordan, for the very simple reason that those who call for its establishment maintain that it would only represent the first step towards their final goal, which is the destruction of Israel. On the other hand, this mini-State would not be in a position to solve the Palestinian problem. On the other, it would introduce into the region a real time-bomb, which our enemies might explode at their convenience. Finally, a place must be found for the transfer of the 250,000 refugees now crowded in the Gaza Strip. This place can be found only in Jordan, within which the Palestinians have already been integrated to the point that half of the ministers of the present government are Palestinians.

However, I want to emphasize the following very strongly: Israel will never negotiate with the terrorists. First, they are not the legitimate representatives of the Palestinians, since nobody has elected them. Second, we do not see why we should negotiate with people who want to eliminate us from the face of the earth and who seek to murder civilians, including women and children. Finally, on principle, we will deal only with sovereign States — otherwise we risk having to face a myriad of organizations, each one claiming that it is a representative body.

From an interview with Livio Caputo in *Epoca* (Italy), July 27, 1974, with Prime Minister Rabin.

▼

Until 1967, Israel did not hold an inch of the Sinai Peninsula, the West Bank, the Gaza Strip or the Golan Heights. Israel held not an acre of what is now considered disputed territory. And yet we enjoyed no peace. Year after year Israel called for — pleaded for — a negotiated peace with the Arab Governments. Their answer was a blank refusal — and more war.

The reason was not a conflict over territorial claims. The reason was, and remains, the fact that a free Jewish State sits on territory at all.

It is in this context that the Palestinian issue must be appraised. That issue is not the obstacle to peace, as some would suggest. Certainly, it has to be solved in the context of a final peace. But to assert that this is the key to peace, the formula for peace, or the breakthrough to peace, is to misread the realities. It is to put the proverbial cart before the horse.

The Palestinian issue began with, and is a product of, the overall Arab posture on the legitimacy of a Jewish State of Israel. Only when that posture changes will the Palestinian issue be constructively and finally tackled.

The clock of history cannot be put back. It was not Israel that prevented the establishment of a Palestinian State in 1947, as the Partition Plan had proposed. What did prevent it was the Arab declaration of war on the Plan itself, because it called for a Jewish State.

For nineteen years no Arab Government saw fit to establish a Palestinian State, even though the West Bank and the Gaza Strip were under Arab control. Neither was there a Palestinian demand to do so. In January 1964, the organization that calls itself the PLO was established by Arab Heads of State. Yet, even then, statehood in those territories, when held by Jordan and Egypt, was never the objective. We know what the objective is. It is written large into the Palestinian Covenant which is their binding constitution. Every paragraph of it spits out the venom calling for Israel's destruction.

These are the truths that lie at the heart and the core of the Arab-Israel conflict. And since, to date, the Arab version of peace does not depart from these truths, no honest being can blame us for refusing to cooperate in our own national suicide.

From an address before the Joint Session of Congress, Washington, January 28, 1976, by Prime Minister Rabin.

▼

Q. *Isn't it clear that the Palestinians and the Arab countries both look upon the PLO as the voice of the Palestinians, not the Government of Jordan?*

A. If this is true, why, of the 670,000 people who live on the West Bank and hold Jordanian citizenship, have none decided to give it up? All of them adhere to their Jordanian citizenship, according to the Geneva Convention. We are there on a temporary basis, and we have to tolerate Jordanian law and respect it. The fact is that the people there are Jordanian citizens and want to remain so.

From an interview on "Meet The Press," NCB-T.V., February 1, 1976, with Prime Minister Rabin.

YIGAL ALLON (Labor Party-Mapai)

II

The polarized asymmetry between the size and intentions of the Arab states and those of Israel, and the extreme contrast in the anticipated fate of each side in the event of military defeat, obliges Israel to maintain constantly that measure of strength enabling it to defend itself in every regional conflict and against any regional combination of strength confronting it, without the help of any foreign army. To our deep regret, this is the first imperative facing us, the imperative to survive. And I would venture to say every other state in our place would behave exactly as we do.

There are, of course, many elements constituting the essential strength that Israel must maintain, ranging from its social, scientific and economic standards, as well as its idealistic motivation, to the quality and quantity of its armaments. A discussion of all of these elements is not within the compass of this article; my concern here is with one of them — but one essential to them all and without which Israel might well lack the strength to defend itself. I am referring to the territorial element; to what can be defined as defensible borders that Israel must establish in any settlement, as an essential part of any effective mutual security arrangements and without any desire for territorial expansion per se.

The most cursory glance at the map is sufficient to ascertain how little the armistice lines of 1949 — lines which were never in the first place recognized as final — could be considered defensible borders. And even the most superficial fingering of the pages of history should be enough to demonstrate how attractive these lines have been to the Arab states as an encouragement to try their strength again against us. The truth of the matter is that Resolution 242 of the United Nations Security Council has already recognized, in its original English text, the need to provide Israel with secure and recognized boundaries, in other words, that changes must be introduced in the old lines of the armistice agreements.

It is no coincidence that this resolution does not speak about Israel's withdrawal from *all* the territories that came under its control in the war that was forced upon Israel in June 1967, nor even from *the* territories. In the original text (which was the outcome of long and exhaustive negotiation), Resolution

242 speaks only of withdrawal from territories. That the meaning was clear was demonstrated by the statement of the United States at the time, made by its U.N. Ambassador Arthur Goldberg on November 15, 1967, in the Security Council discussions that preceded the passage of Resolution 242. He stated: "Historically, there never have been secure or recognized boundaries in the area. Neither the Armistice Lines of 1949, nor the Cease-Fire Lines of 1967, have answered that description."

As is known, Israel expressed more than once its willingness to withdraw from the cease-fire lines of 1967, within the framework of a peace agreement. On the other hand, it is clear — even according to the Security Council decision — that Israel is not obliged to withdraw to the armistice lines of 1949 that preceded the 1967 war, but to revised lines. The question is what borders will provide Israel with that essential minimum of security? And without such security it is difficult to expect to pacify the area and provide a lasting solution to the conflict within it.

If the sole consideration were the purely strategic-military one, then possibly the most convenient security borders would have been those Israel maintained following the Six-Day War, or perhaps those which it maintains today. There is even a basis for the claim that the 1973 Yom Kippur War — begun as a surprise attack in concert by the armies of Egypt and Syria — proves that these lines were ideally the best. Had the Yom Kippur War commenced on the 1949 armistice lines, for example, there can be little doubt that the price Israel would have had to pay in repelling the aggressors would have been unimaginably higher than that paid so painfully in October 1973. But we are not merely talking about purely military-strategic matters, to the extent that they ever exist in isolation. Nor are we discussing the maximum security that borderlines can provide Israel. As stated, our preoccupation is only with the essential minimum.

One does not have to be a military expert to easily identify the critical defects of the armistice lines that existed until June 4, 1967. A considerable part of these lines is without any topographical security value; and, of no less importance, the lines fail to provide Israel with the essential minimum of strategic depth. The gravest problem is on the eastern boundary, where the entire width of the coastal plain varies between 10 and 15 miles, where the main centers of Israel's population, including Tel Aviv and its suburbs, are situated, and where the situation of Jerusalem is especially perilous. Within these lines a single successful first strike by the Arab armies would be sufficient to dissect Israel at more than one point, to sever its essential living arteries, and to confront it with dangers that no other state would be prepared to face. The purpose of defensible borders is thus to correct this weakness, to provide Israel with the requisite minimal strategic depth, as well as lines which have topographical strategic significance . . .

III

Fortunately, the geostrategic conditions that have existed in the Middle East over the past nine years permit a solution based upon a fair political compromise. This could provide Israel with the minimal defensible borders that are indispensable without impairing, to any meaningful extent, the basic interests of the other side, including those of the Palestinian community. As with every other compromise, so, too, is this one likely to be painful in the short term to both sides. But this compromise will, in the long run, grant advantages that both sides do not currently possess nor, without it, ever would in the future.

According to the compromise formula I personally advocate, Israel — within the context of a peace settlement — would give up the large majority of the areas which fell into its hands in the 1967 war. Israel would do so not because of any lack of historical affinity between the Jewish people and many of these areas. With regard to Judea and Samaria, for example, historical Jewish affinity is as great as that for the coastal plain or Galilee. Nonetheless, in order to attain a no less historically exalted goal, namely that of peace, such a deliberate territorial compromise can be made.

For its part, the Arab side would have to concede its claim to those strategic security zones, which, together with a number of effective arrangements to be discussed below, will provide Israel with that vital element so lacking in the pre-1967 war lines: a defense posture which would enable the small standing army units of Israel's defense force to hold back the invading Arab armies until most of the country's reserve citizens army could be mobilized. These security zones would thus guarantee enough time to organize and launch the counteroffensive needed to defeat any such aggression . . .

A reasonable compromise solution can be found for all these weaknesses in the current geostrategic and demographic situation existing in the Middle East. Without going into details or drawing precise maps, an activity that must await direct negotiations between the parties themselves, in my opinion the solution in principle ought to be along the following general lines.

Both to preserve its Jewish character and to contribute toward a solution of the Palestinian issue, Israel should not annex an additional and significant Arab population. Therefore the strategic depth and topographical barriers in the central sector, so totally absent in the lines preceding the 1967 war, cannot be based on moving these lines eastward in a schematic manner, even though this would be logical from a purely strategic point of view. Rather, apart from some minor tactical border alterations along the western section of "the green line," this same goal can be achieved through absolute Israeli control over the strategic zone to the *east* of the dense Arab population, concentrated as it is on the crest of the hills and westward. I am referring to the arid zone that lies between the Jordan River to the east, and the eastern chain of the Samarian and Judean mountains to the west — from Mt. Gilboa in the north through the Judean desert, until it joins the Negev desert. The area of this desert zone is only about 700 square miles and it is almost devoid of population. Thus this type of solution would leave almost all of the Palestinian Arab population of the West Bank under Arab rule.

Cutting through this zone, which continues from north to south, it would be possible to delineate a corridor from west to east under Arab sovereignty. This would permit uninterrupted communication along the Jericho-Ramallah axis, between the Arab populated areas of the West and East banks of the river. In this manner the only realistic solution becomes possible — one that also helps resolve the problem of Palestinian identity that could then find its expression in a single Jordanian-Palestinian state. (After all, the population of both banks, East and West, are Palestinian Arabs. The fact is that the great majority of Palestinians carry Jordanian passports while almost all of Jordan's inhabitants are Palestinians.)

Jerusalem, Israel's capital, which was never the capital of any Arab or Muslim state, but was always the capital and center of the Jewish people, cannot return to the absurd situation of being partitioned. The Holy City and adjacent areas essential for its protection and communications must remain a single, undivided unit under Israel's sovereignty. Because of its universal status, however, in that it is holy to three great religions, as well as the mixed nature of its inhabitants,[1] a solution for the religious interests connected with it can be found, a *religious* and not a political solution. For example, special status could be granted to the representatives of the various faiths in the places holy to them, just as it might be possible to base the municipal structure of the city upon subdistricts that take ethnic and religious ciriteria into account . . .

In my view the city of Gaza and its environs, which is heavily populated by Palestinian Arabs, could comprise a part of the Jordanian-Palestinian unit which would arise to the east of Israel, and serve as that state's Mediterranean port. In this case, it would be necessary to place at the disposal of traffic between Gaza and the Jordanian-Palestinian state the use of a land route (as distinct from a land corridor) similar to that, for example, connecting the United States with Alaska. But Israel must continue to control fully the strategic desert zone from the southern part of the Gaza Strip to the dunes on the eastern approaches of the town of El Arish, which itself would be returned to Egypt. This strategic zone, almost empty of population, would block the historic invasion route along the sea coast which many conquerors have taken over the generations to invade the land of Israel, and further north . . .

Let me stress again that defensible borders are vital to Israel not out of any desire to annex territories per se, not out of a desire for territorial expansion, and not out of any historical and ideological motivation. Israel can compromise on territory but it cannot afford to do so on security. The entire rationale of defensible borders is strategic. This is also the only rationale for the selective

1. From the middle of the nineteenth century Jerusalem has had a Jewish majority. Today, the population consists of 260,000 Jews, 84,000 Muslims and 12,000 Christians.

settlement policy that Israel is pursuing, as an integral part of its unique defense system, in those strategic zones so vital to its security.

Of course, when the peace for which we strive is achieved, the borders will not divide the two peoples but be freely open to them. In short, good fences make good neighbors . . .

IV

. . . According to the principles I have already outlined, if Israel were to forfeit the densely populated heartland of Judea and Samaria, it would not be able to forego — under any circumstances — the effective demilitarization of these areas. Apart from civilian police to guarantee internal order, these areas would have to be devoid of offensive forces and heavy arms. In the same way as any other country, Israel would be unable to abandon areas so close to its heartland if they were liable once again to become staging areas for full-scale, limited or guerrilla attacks upon its most vital areas.

In short, Israel cannot permit itself to withdraw from a large part of the West Bank unless the area from which it withdraws is shorn of all aggressive potential. For this purpose, absolute Israeli control, as proposed above, of a strategic security zone along the Jordan Basin will not be adequate. Effective demilitarization of the areas from which the Israel Defense Forces withdraw will also be essential. Here as elsewhere, the two elements are interwoven: without a security zone, Israel cannot be satisfied with demilitarization alone; without effective demilitarization, Israel cannot be satisfied with just the security zone.

It should be clear from what I have said, that Israel does not hold most of the territories that fell into its hands in the war, which was imposed on it in 1967, as an end in itself. Despite the paucity of its territory compared with the vast areas of the Arab countries, and despite the historical, strategic and economic importance of these areas, Israel would be prepared to concede all that is not absolutely essential to its security within the context of an overall peace settlement. It is holding most of these territories now only as a means to achieve its foremost goal — peace with all its neighbors . . .

Excerpted from "Israel, the Case for Defensible Borders" by Yigal Allon, as Minister of Foreign Affairs, in *Foreign Affairs,* October, 1976. Reprinted by permission.

SHIMON PERES (Labor Party-Mapai)

[My concept constitutes] a program for an Israeli Federation which will give autonomy to the inhabitants of Judea, Samaria and the Gaza Strip, who can define themselves as Palestinians if they so wish. Such a federation could constitute the first step toward the establishment of a future confederation with Jordan, but that should be viewed as an additional option and not as a condition

Excerpted from an interview with Mr. Peres as Minister of Defense in *Davar* (Israel Daily), June 27, 1975. By permission.

for the establishment of the [proposed] Israel Federation or for the creation of relations between it and Jordan.

[This] federal solution [would be] based on [creating] three levels of government . . . The municipal level [would be] concerned with local matters, with the right to vote . . . granted to all residents and not only to citizens of the state. On the top level . . . the right to vote . . . [would be] granted to citizens only, and the right to acquire citizenship if they freely will it would be granted to all the inhabitants. This level would be confined to a number of the most important areas, such as foreign affairs, security and currency. The intermediate level, which is the regional level, would deal with a variety of matters which are beyond the scope of the local level but are also not on the national level—education, health, tourism, transportation, trade, agriculture, police and justice.

The right to vote for the regional legislature would be granted to all inhabitants and not to citizens only. This would make things easier for many Arab inhabitants who wish to retain their foreign passports but who also want to make their own decisions about the education of their children and their own way of life. The Israel Federation would comprise the three regions of Judea, Samaria and the Gaza Strip, plus a suitable number of regions of the former territory of the State of Israel which are at present under a centralized government and which still do not meet the needs of orderly government functioning . . . In the future Israel Federation, every citizen will be able to decide what his nationality will be, which school his children will attend and which elections he will not wish to participate in. This state will not determine the destiny of the citizens; rather, the citizens will determine their own destiny, where they live, where they educate their children, and which borders they will defend.

Demographically, in order to eliminate [some Israelis'] fears that the present Jewish majority would be lost in a Federation, the present balance of representation of two-thirds Jews and one-third Arabs could be frozen by agreement on the national level in the Federation for several dozen years . . .

. . . I believe that many Israelis would agree to a "European solution," to a "triangle" of the three regions: Israel, Jordan and Judea, Samaria and the Gaza Strip. Within such a solution it would be possible to set up a common market between the three regions, with a council of ministers and a parliament similar to the European Parliament, with a common army in addition to the national armies, Jordanian and Israeli, with the national armies meeting the needs of national security and the common army dealing with common dangers both internal and external . . . it is still a vision of things to come; nevertheless it is worthwhile considering and developing [this] concept and perhaps making progress toward it in stages, step by step, as is also the case with the federal solution, which is a prior stage toward the confederation, toward which we can only advance gradually, step by step, on the basis of the deep, stable foundation already laid down for it in the realities of Israel-Arab coexistence in Judea, Samaria and the Gaza Strip . . .

Judea and Samaria are not only a source of conflict between Israel and the Arab States but also among the Arabs themselves. The best proof of this can be found in the Rabat Conference. There the legal claimant to Judea and Samaria was eliminated and a vacuum was left. In [this vacuum] Israel is entitled to cancel Jordanian law since Jordan itself gave up its claims and rights . . . When the Jordanian government wanted to deprive the inhabitants of the West Bank of their Jordanian passports and give them Palestinian passports they raised a great outcry of protest . . . At present this is an area under Israeli control, inhabited by Jordanian citizens and intended by them to become part of a state which does not yet exist and which does not desire to exist solely in this territory alongside of Israel.

. . . In 1967 Arab society in Judea and Samaria was feudal. In it a small minority of landowners and industrialists enjoyed a monopoly supported by the monarchy while the vast majority were tenant farmers who were poor, depressed and exploited, deprived of all rights and receiving a subsistence wage . . . The influence of the landowners and industrialists has declined and that of the workers and farmers has increased . . . Most important, for the first time in this entire region we have had here truly free municipal elections in which representatives of the younger generation were chosen—a generation of Arab intelligentsia who defeated the representatives of the large, rich, powerful families . . .

There have also been physical changes . . . new channels of transportation and employment . . . of agricultural methods and of marketing produce have also been established. In [this] situation . . . I cannot see any possibility of wielding a political axe at the head of this new living reality. Territorial partition is impossible not only because it will destroy a structure of living ties and relationships but also because it cannot bring with it any agreement or produce peace or create security . . .

Partition did not bring a solution of the Palestinian problem . . . The original concept, which Israel accepted, was to establish a Palestinian state on the West Bank, in the Triangle and in part of Galilee and of the Negev. All the Arab countries decided that they were Palestinian and they have since created doubt as to the Palestinian identity, since the Palestinians look upon themselves as part of the Arab world, and the Arab world as a whole sees itself as the custodian of the Palestinian problem . . .

. . . If a [West Bank] Palestinian state is established . . . the West Bank bulge will immediately be filled with new weapons of Soviet manufacture or from the arsenals of Libya. It is also not difficult to foresee a situation in which George Habbash will attempt to do to Arafat what Arafat tried to do to Hussein and what the two of them have been trying to do to Lebanon. In addition to a Palestinian state which will be armed from top to toe, there will also be bases in it of the most extremist forces of *fatah*, and they will be equipped with anti-aircraft and anti-tank shoulder rockets which will constitute a threat not only to every passerby but to every plane and helicopter . . . to every vehicle moving along . . . the coastal plain . . . It is doubtful whether territorial space can grant any state complete deterrent ability, but the lack of minimal territorial space places it in a position of total lack of such ability, which represents a perpetual temptation to attack Israel from all sides . . . The idea of demilitarizing the West Bank seems highly dubious . . . The main problem is not that of reaching agreement on demilitarization but of the observance of the agreement in practice . . .

LABOR PARTY (Mapai) Election Platform, 1977

Excerpts:

Consistent striving for peace: The central objective of Israel is the attainment of peace with the neighboring states and the weaving of the fabric of cooperation between the peoples of the region. Israel has been striving for this target ever since it came into being, and the fact that it has not been reached is due to the policy of hostility, war and boycott pursued by the Arab States all these years. Nonetheless, the political efforts to reach permanent peace in defensible borders with Egypt, Jordan and Syria are to be continued with readiness for territorial compromise with each of them, and with Lebanon — with the present boundaries.

Israel will support the convention of the Geneva Conference without delay, composed of the participants as agreed in December 1973. This agreement constitutes the base for the Peace Conference and should not be deviated from. Israel rejects the invitation of representatives of PLO and terrorist organizations.

At the Peace Conference and through all channels of international relations, Israel will strive for peace agreements to be arrived at by negotiation without precondition, without pressures, and without attempts by any party to impose anything.

The peace agreements should ensure:

a) Cessation of all elements of hostility, blockade, and boycott.

b) Defensible borders enabling Israel to defend itself efficiently against military attack or attempts at blockade, and based upon territorial compromise. Peace borders should replace the cease-fire lines. Demilitarization provisions and political arrangements are to be included in the peace agreements, additional to agreed and recognized defensible borders, and not instead of them. Israel will not return to the borders of June 4, 1967, which constituted an incitement to aggression.

c) United Jerusalem is the Capital of Israel. In the peace arrangements, the special religious status of the places holy to Islam and Christianity should be safeguarded, under autonomous administration.

d) The Jewish character of the State of Israel so as to realize its Zionist destination and its tasks in immigration and ingathering of the exiles.

e) The beginning of an era of regular relationships between Israel and the neighboring states in the political, economic, social and cultural fields.

The peace agreement with Jordan is to be based upon the existence of two independent states: Israel with its capital in United Jerusalem, and an Arab state to the east of Israel. Israel rejects the establishment of an additional separate Palestinian Arab State to the west of the Jordan River. In the neighboring Jordanian-Palestinian state, the independent identity of the Palestinian and Jordanian Arabs will be able to find its expression, in peace and good neighborliness with Israel.

Any peace agreement is to be signed subject to approval by the Government and the Knesset.

MENACHEM BEGIN (Herut and Likhud)

The Likhud government will take a peace initiative. We shall do so not through the U.N. General Assembly, where the majority is hostile to us . . . We shall ask a friendly Government which has regular diplomatic relations with Israel and with our neighbors, to transmit our proposal for starting negotiations for peace treaties. The negotiations will have to be direct, without prior conditions, and free from any externally devised formula for a settlement . . .

A special focus of interest will be the relationship between Israel and the United States, which should be founded on an awareness of mutuality on both sides . . .

Such a partnership of interests exists with relation to the demand for the establishment of a so-called Palestinian State in Judea and Samaria. Such a state would be an existential danger to the Jewish state, but also a serious danger to the whole free world; for it would inevitably become a central Soviet base in the Middle East . . .

· · ·

Judea and Samaria are an inseparable part of Israel's sovereignty. It must be clear that whoever is prepared to surrender Judea and Samaria to foreign rule, inevitably prepares the ground for a Palestinian State. If the Labor Party is sincere in its opposition to a "Third State" between the sea and the Jordan, we appeal to its leaders to desist entirely from their statement about surrendering Judea and Samaria to any foreign rule. We shall call on all citizens of Israel, to whatever party they belong, to help save Judea and Samaria to ensure the country's security of existence and the prospects of peace . . .

· · ·

Members of the Arab nationality, which we recognize, will be given a free choice between adopting Israeli citizenship and retaining their previous citizenship. If they opt for naturalization, they will have full rights, including the right of voting for the Knesset, like Jewish citizens; if they do not apply for our citizenship, they will have full rights, except that of voting for the Knesset, like Jewish residents. The Arab nationality in Eretz Israel will enjoy cultural autonomy. The refugee problem will be solved humanely and understandingly by providing the refugees with housing and employment.

· · ·

Menachem Begin is chairman of the *Herut* Movement and the leading candidate of the *Likhud* Bloc. Excerpted from a Keynote Address by Mr. Begin at the opening session of the thirteenth *Herut* Convention, January 2, 1977.

LIKHUD Election Platform, 1977

Excerpts:

a) The right of the Jewish People to the Land of Israel is eternal, and is an integral part of its right to security and peace. Judea and Samaria shall therefore not be relinquished to foreign rule; between the sea and the Jordan, there will be Jewish sovereignty alone.

b) Any plan that involves surrendering parts of Western Eretz Israel militates against our right to the Land, will inevitably lead to the establishment of a "Palestinian State," threatens the security of the civilian population, endangers the existence of the State of Israel, and defeats all prospects of peace.

c) In spite of the preparations of Israel's enemies for another war, war is not inevitable. The Likhud Government will resort to a combination of political and military means and maintain a staunch and credible stance in order to deter aggression and prevent another war.

d) The peace initiative of the Likhud Government will be *positive*. Israel will invite her neighbors to hold direct negotiations with a view to signing peace treaties between them without preliminary conditions from any party whatsoever and without any formula for a solution *provided by third parties*.

e) Upon the peace treaties being signed, the state of war shall be terminated, the borders shall be determined, and normal political, diplomatic and economic relations shall be established on a mutual basis between all Middle East countries.

f) The Likhud Government will call on the younger generation in Israel and the Diaspora to settle in all parts of Eretz Israel and will assist any group and individual in the task of settling the Land, while having due care that no one shall be deprived of his land.

g) The so-styled Palestine Liberation Organization is not a national liberation movement, but a murder organization which serves as a political tool and military arm of the Arab States and as an instrument of Soviet imperialism. The Likhud Government will take action to exterminate this organization.

h) Those Arabs of Eretz Israel who will apply for citizenship of the country and declare their allegiance to it shall be granted citizenship. Equality of rights and duties shall be maintained for all citizens and residents without distinction of race, nationality, religion, sex or ethnic origin. Full autonomy of culture, religion and heritage, and complete economic integration, shall be assured to all parts of the population.

The Views of the National Religious Party

By LOUIS BERNSTEIN

To many Americans, the most adamant and inflexible Israeli political party on the question of Israel's future borders appears to be the National Religious Party. However, like other Israeli political parties, the NRP is splintered into factions and subfactions. On the issue of peace negotiations and possible future borders, the movement is split and divided. There are three distinct positions. There are extreme "doves" like Moshe Unna, the member of a religious kibbutz who has represented the party in the *Knesset,* and "hawks" like S.Z. Shragai, the NRP's veteran ideologist.

Even the *Kibbutz Hadati,* the NRP's collective settlements movement and the party's moral conscience, is divided on this vital issue. Yitzchak Fuchs, a member of kibbutz Tiral Zvi and of the *Kibbutz Hadati'*s secretariat, asserts that the religious kibbutz members seem to be evenly divided on the issue. The younger kibbutz members tend toward *Gush Emunim* (literally, "faith Bloc") and a more militant approach while the older ones tend to flexibility and broader bargaining positions.

There is, however, one basic difference between considerations that determine NRP attitudes and those of the secular parties. Whereas security and political considerations are predominant in most Israeli thinking on Israel's future borders, within the NRP theological considerations have a direct bearing. The opinions of leading rabbinical authorities carry considerable weight in molding both official doctrine and individual opinion.

The activist approach is championed by Rabbi Zvi Yehuda Kuk, the eighty-five-year-old son of the saintly late Chief Rabbi Avraham Yitzchak Kuk. He is the head of *Yeshivot Merkaz Harav,* which differs even from some other yeshivot.* The *Gush Emunim* leaders were or are his disciples. Rabbi Kuk views the restoration of Jews in Israel as part of the Divine process leading to ultimate redemption of the Jewish people and of humanity. In his *yeshivot, Yom Ha'atzmaut* (Independence Day) and *Yom Yerushalaim* (Jerusalem Day)—the former commemorates the establishment of the State in 1948 and the latter the liberation and unification of Jerusalem in 1967—are observed as religious holidays and even the observance of limited mourning during the period between Passover and the Pentecost are lifted on these days. Rabbi Kuk's disciples have established pioneering settlements beyond the

Dr. Bernstein teaches Jewish History at Yeshiva University and is the President of the Religious Zionists of America and the spiritual leader of Young Israel at Windsor Park, Bayside, N.Y. He has contributed numerous articles to the Hebrew press.

*A *yeshiva* is an Orthodox religious school. The *yeshivot* referred to here are all on the graduate level. [*Eds.*]

"Green Line," in Kiryat Arba (Hebron), Ofra, Kaddoum, Ma'ale Adumim, and Eilon Moreh. For them, there is only the divine imperative of Jewish settlement in all of Israel's historic boundaries. His supporters buttress their theological arguments with strategy and security considerations.

The other side of the theological coin is best summarized by the position of Rabbi Joseph Soloveitchik (of Yeshiva University, New York), the towering sage of the twentieth century whose religious and moral leadership extends to the entire religious Jewish world unbounded by oceans and other geographical considerations. For him, the main consideration is security, i.e., the preservation of lives. The sanctity of human life supersedes the sanctity of religious shrines, preservation of the Cave of Machpela and possibly even the Western Wall (of Solomon's Temple in Jerusalem), for the Jewish State cannot justify the unnecessary loss of life. Security is a military and political consideration. Safe and defensible borders can be determined only by military experts and by diplomats. Whereas religion gives primary consideration to security, it leaves the determination of the best security posture to generals rather than to rabbis.

National Religious Party intellectuals have organized the *Oz Veshalom* movement ("Strength and Peace") which has also been characterized as the "Movement to Save Religious Zionism." This organization stands squarely opposed to *Gush Emunim,* which enjoys the strong support of many NRP members. Paradoxically, the *Oz Veshalom* also leans ideologically on the late Rabbi Kuk's teachings. Zvi Yaron, one of the moving spirits of this small group, is the author of "Mishnat shel Harav Kuk," a systematic analysis of the religious philosophy of the late Chief Rabbi of Israel. He emphasizes the humanistic and universalistic aspects in Rabbi Kuk's thinking. These contrasting ideologies are reflected in the differing political approaches within the NRP to Israel's projected stance at a hoped-for peace conference. The NRP's party platform assumed a maximalist stance and refers to the historic boundaries of Israel. The NRP entered Golda Meir's government on condition that any territorial concessions for peace be preceded by a plebiscite on the issue. The party is united on the issue of a united Jerusalem, incorporated into the State of Israel, although the NRP probably would not oppose concessions granting extra-territorial rights to Holy Places of other faiths. A chain of several settlements and a *yeshivat hesder* (a Torah academy whose students also serve as soldiers) in Ramat Hamagshimim (on the Golan Heights) makes the party's position on the Golan Heights abundantly clear. The same may be said for Kiryat Arba, which overlooks Hebron. The Etzion Bloc, a series of settlements which defended Jerusalem before falling to the Arab Legion in 1948, was recaptured in 1967 and immediately resettled by families of the original settlers. A new *Hapoel Hamizrachi* (Religious Labor organization) moshav (cooperative farm settlement), Elazar, is a clear demonstration that the NRP and the State of Israel do not intend to permit Jerusalem's southern flank to become vulnerable again.

The differences within the NRP are, however, substantial on the other issues. The youth faction (a relative term) led by Zevulun Hammer, a former cabinet member, and American-born and educated Dr. Yehuda Ben Meier is the most "hawkish." It almost swung the party into the orbit of Menachem Begin in the post-1973 War *Knesset* and may yet do so in the future. Hammer favors incorporating into the Jewish state all of pre-1948 Palestine. Even as a minister, he attended functions of *Gush Emunim* beyond the Green Line, brushing aside criticisms of such an action by a minister.

An intermediate position is taken by Dr. Yitzchak Raphael and his center faction. Raphael speaks about the "historic land of Israel" which, he maintains, is historically Jewish. Within this definition, he would incorporate Judea and Samaria into the State. Raphael's position, therefore, does not preclude concessions in the Gaza Strip, or possibly Jericho and other areas that do not fall within the scope of his definition.

The most reserved and cautious NRP leader is Dr. Joseph Burg, the head of the *Lamifne* faction. Since it is the largest faction, Dr. Burg is titular head of the movement and has served as its senior cabinet minister for many years. As Minister of Interior in several governments, he is particularly sensitive to the demographic problem of the large and increasing Arab population. Of all the conflicting factions within the National Religious Party, *Lamifne,* led by Dr. Burg, is most likely to support significant territorial concessions, but only in return for a genuine peace. It must, however, be emphasized that although *Lamifne* is the largest faction, it represents less than 30% of the party. Ideological and political unity, a luxury enjoyed only rarely in the NRP, simply does not exist on the questions of borders and negotiating stance.

UNITED WORKERS PARTY (Mapam)

1. The 7th Convention of Mapam calls upon the government of Israel to formulate a program for an inclusive Israeli-Arab peace agreement.

2. The program will be based upon the following assumptions:

a. Peaceful relations will be founded on recognition of the independence and sovereignty of the State of Israel, the cessation of hostile propaganda and the economic boycott . . . with the aim of attaining normal relations between the countries.

b. Israel will be prepared to conduct negotiations without any preliminary conditions with all the Arab countries together or with each one of them separately.

c. Israel will also be prepared to negotiate the termination of the state of war as well as interim or partial agreements as a state towards peace.

d. The State of Israel is not looking for annexations but for guarantees for its security. Israel will declare its readiness to evacuate the territories occupied by it in Sinai, the West Bank and the Golan Heights and to make far-reaching withdrawals with necessary border modifications obligated by security needs.

Resolution on the Occupied Territories passed at the Seventh Convention of Mapam, June 9-12, 1976.

e. Israel will be guided by its concern to maintain its character as a Jewish state, ingathering its exiles and fulfilling its Zionist mission.

3. Peace and Secure borders.

a. Golan Heights: In order to assure the safety and welfare of the settlements in Upper Galilee and the Jordan Valley, the border between Israel and Syria will be on the Golan Heights.

b. Egypt: Peace agreement with Egypt will be based upon wide demilitarization in the Sinai Desert and border modifications vital for Israel's security. The Gaza Strip will not return to Egyptian rule; the political status of the Strip will be determined according to Israel's security needs and the will of the inhabitants.

c. Jordan: In its negotiations with Jordan, Israel will favor a political solution based on the existence of two independent and sovereign states, Israel and an Arab-Jordanian-Palestinian-state. At the same time, Israel will respect the democratic decisions of the Palestinians and the Jordanians concerning self-determination, sovereignty and independence beyond Israel's borders. Israel will be prepared to negotiate with any Palestinian element recognizing the State of Israel's right to exist and sovereignty and rejecting and avoiding any acts of violence or sabotage (on the basis of Security Council Resolution 242).

Face To Face With Our Neighbors

By ARIE LOVA ELIAV

After the Six Day War Israel found herself not only within new borders but also in a totally new situation with respect to the Palestinian Arabs. Israel has not yet given herself, the Arabs, or the world a clear statement of her position concerning these Palestinian Arabs. Israel has dealt with the Palestinian Arabs pragmatically. [It] has developed the system of open bridges across the Jordan, which makes possible business, transport and tourism, and the passage of relatives and students between the West Bank and the Hashemite Kingdom of Jordan. After the Six Day War many tens of thousands of Palestinian Arab workers on the West Bank started crossing daily into Israel to work in construction, agriculture, industry, and services. In a certain respect it may be said that all of Israel is now serving almost all the Palestinian Arabs as a kind of huge school for high-grade vocational training — by guidance and training given in the administered areas, by jobs provided in new trades, or by the training and experience that make it possible for workers to improve their skills.

This policy has borne considerable fruit. The standard of living of the

As a member of the Israel *Knesset* (parliament), Mr. Eliav has twice served as a Deputy Minister and was the Secretary-General of the Labor Party *(Mapai)* from 1969-1971. He is Israel's leading "dove." Mr. Eliav's latest publication is *Sulam Yisrael, Halom u'Shivro* (Israel's Ladder, the Dream and its Meaning), published by *Zmora Bitan Modan*, Tel Aviv, 1976.

The above is excerpted from *Land of the Hart*, by Arie Lova Eliav, The Jewish Publication Society, Philadelphia, 1974, by permission of the author and the publisher.

Palestinian Arabs on the West Bank has risen steadily. There is no doubt at all that laying the groundwork for a higher standard of living and providing vocational training are most important steps forward in the developing relations between Israel and the Palestinian Arabs.

But the Palestinian Arabs have not yet received any answers to the question that they ask — and must inevitably ask — that are beyond bread and butter. What will their future be? What national options are open to them? What does Israel want from them? The reason that they have not yet received answers is that Israel has not yet given herself any clear-cut answers to these questions.

In dealing with this question from an Israeli standpoint, we touch an extremely sensitive spot. There is no question that in the Six Day War, Israel conquered — some say liberated — the historical cradle of the Jewish people. In antiquity the Jews lived mainly in the mountains of Judea and Samaria — which today constitute the southern and northern parts of the West Bank.

Who will ignore the feelings of the Jews upon reaching these precious areas after a bloody and valiantly fought war? It would seem that all that remains for us to do now is to settle these areas as quickly as possible, build Jewish villages and towns in them, annex them unequivocally to the sovereign State of Israel, make them a part of the body of Israel, and thus complete the historical act of restoring all of western *Eretz Yisrael** to the Jewish people. To those who think this way, the problem of the Palestinian Arabs living in these areas in such density is a problem, to be sure, but one that takes second place to the annexation and settlement of the areas.

Some among us seriously think that this problem will be solved more easily if we annex the administered areas. For them, they think, the Arabs living in them will know that they are destined to become a national minority in the State of Israel. The Arabs will then reconcile themselves to their fate, in due time acquire Israeli citizenship and full civil rights, and become fully integrated into Israel's economic and political life. There is an extremist nationalist-religious school among us whose members have managed to find scriptural evidence attesting to the sanctity of every last inch of western *Eretz Yisrael*.

Another sensitive aspect of the problem has to do with security. For nineteen years we lived in a state with accidental, tortuous, and intolerable borders. And now the Israeli army is encamped along the Jordan River. Anyone wishing to invade us must first come up to the mountains which we control. We have sealed the invasion and infiltration routes. How — it is argued — can anyone think of withdrawing from these strategic positions? If we withdraw our life will turn into a hell again, and sooner or later we will once again have to capture — and who knows at what price? — these vital strategic areas.

Anyone who doesn't understand the magnitude of these emotions and arguments concerning western *Eretz Yisrael* cannot begin to understand present-day Israel.

* The Land of Israel.

What Israel must do is declare her readiness in principle to return — "return" not "withdraw from"; there is a tremendous difference between these two terms — to the Palestinian Arabs most of the West Bank and a large part of the Gaza Strip, so that in these areas plus Jordan they may set up an independent and sovereign state of their own whose future form of government or name (Jordanian Palestine, Palestinian Jordan, or any other combination) will be up to them.

The historical, undivided Land of Israel is the Land of the Twelve Tribes: the area, more or less, which the British acquired as a mandate from the League of Nations — in other words, western *Eretz Yisrael* (Mandatory Palestine) and the part of Palestine that is east of the Jordan River (Mandatory Transjordan). In this land our people was born and lived; here, in these 20,000-odd square miles, we have full historical and national rights.

To that very same number of square miles the Palestinian Arabs also have national-historical rights. [They] have been living here for thirteen hundred years.

In the 1930s our leaders said to the Arab leaders: "Let us divide up the land. In one part we will set up a Jewish state, and in the other part you will set up a Palestinian Arab state." But the Palestinian Arab leaders responded: "Never! The rights to this land are exclusively ours . . ."

After the establishment of the State of Israel we again said to the Arabs: ". . . We will undertake to content ourselves with our present borders forever . . . These borders are not of the undivided, historical Land of Israel. We also have rights to other parts of the Land of the Twelve Tribes. We do not waive these rights. We will insist on the right to visit and pray at those of our historical sites that are in your control. But we will waive the implementation of these rights, if only you will make peace with us. We know that you, too, have rights in our part of *Eretz Yisrael*, but by the same token we ask you to waive the implementation of your rights."

This was Israel's position from 1948 to 1967. But the Arabs totally rejected it. Now it behooves us to return to our principles.

There is room in the Land of the Twelve Tribes for the State of Israel and a Palestinian-Jordanian Arab state. In exchange for a full and permanent peace we will waive implementing part of our historical rights in this Arab state.

It is precisely we Jews who must begin discussing this subject in principle, because we, and not the Palestinian Arabs, are the victors: it is we, not they, who have the upper hand — and that is precisely why we can allow ourselves to rise to the occasion and discuss principles.

To the standard argument that there is no one to talk to it can be said that this may be due precisely to the fact that we are not clearly stating any principles concerning the problem of the Palestinian Arabs and their and our national-historical rights, and are obscuring the subject of the future of the areas of western *Eretz Yisrael*. If we were to start discussing principles, first of all

among ourselves, we might stir the Arabs into discussing them among themselves and then with us.

If we are proud of what Israel has done in the territories, this pride can have
only one justification: that whatever we are doing there is being done on the
premise of open options in the future for the inhabitants of the areas.

If we leave the Palestinian Arabs open national options, and if we speak of
the principles of two nations and two states, then our positive activity in the
areas has better prospects for the future. If we do not discuss principles then no
act of ours in the territories can be understood; every act is interpreted as part of
a Jewish plan for "creeping annexation" by creating reality — and every road
is a created reality, every electrical link-up is a created reality.

[The solution to the security problem] must be unconventional and flexible.
It will depend on when the negotiations with the Palestinian-Jordanian Arabs
take place and who represents them, on whether the settlement with those
Palestinian-Jordanian Arabs takes place before, during, or after a settlement
has been reached with any or several of the other Arab states. It will also depend
on the general situation in our region and on the relations between the superpowers.

We should not sign a peace treaty with the Kingdom of Jordan unless that
country represents and offers a solution to the Palestinian Arab problem.

In the short run, the establishment of a little Palestinian Arab state on the
West Bank, perhaps together with parts of the Gaza Strip, might appear easier
— and perhaps safer for Israel. But such a state will not solve the Palestinian
Arab problem, because about half of the Palestinian Arabs will be mainly in
Jordan, and this nation — split in two — will not consider this a solution to its
problems. On the other hand, a Palestinian-Jordanian Arab state comprising
Jordan as well as most of the West Bank and parts of the Gaza Strip will, like
Israel, have access to two seas: the Red Sea and the Mediterranean — with
Israel permitting the transfer of goods and free passage through her territory.

Categorical demilitarization of the West Bank and the Gaza Strip will be
guaranteed not only by written agreements, but also by concrete guarantees;
[by] Israeli supervision or joint supervision by the two states.

Jewish settlement on the West Bank and in the Gaza Strip is open to several
possibilities in the future: some settlements will be officially and finally
annexed to Israel at the conclusion of negotiations between Israel and the
Palestinian-Jordanian Arab state (the Etzion region, for example); some may be
turned into temporary bases for military forces and patrols, under the security
arrangements agreed upon by the two states; and some will remain within the
borders of the new Arab state.

We must speak candidly to our Jewish settlers [on the West Bank] and tell
them, now, that when peace comes they may have to make new decisions
regarding where and how they are to live [so that they] will accept the idea that
[their settlements are on land that may] when peace comes, be in sovereign
Arab territory.

There is need for a clear and public declaration — for ourselves, for the Arabs, and for the world at large. Such a declaration in the name of the Israeli government will itself serve as an impetus toward changing the situation in our region. I believe that such a declaration by Israel will find support among some Palestinian Arabs living in the West Bank and the Gaza Strip; and maybe in time even among those in Israeli prisons (it would not be the first time in history that leaders emerged from among men in prisons); among leaders in Jordan; and among some young Arabs studying in the universities of the Middle East, Europe and other parts of the world.

I believe that such a declaration by us will have a tremendous impact not only among the Palestinian Arabs but also in the Arab states. The Arabs will, in the course of time, become aware that the Jews are ready to give the Palestinian Arabs their due. They will also realize that the establishment of a Palestinian-Jordanian Arab state alongside Israel is the maximum that Israel can concede, and that demands for any further concessions — such as the relinquishment of territory inside the 1948-67 borders or the return of Arab refugees to Israel — will be seen by Israel as part of an effort to destroy her.

Besides issuing a declaration and educating the public to moderation, there are a few other steps that Israel must take in order to advance peace. The most important of these is to begin to tackle in a serious way the Palestinian Arab refugees under Israeli rule in the Gaza Strip and on the West Bank.

[After the Six Day War] Israel left the camps and the conduct of day-to-day affairs in them to UNRWA. This agency, set up after the Arab-Israel War of 1948, turned into a bureaucracy employing thousands of Palestinian Arabs whose main concern was to preserve the camps as they were — "till the 'return' and the liberation of Palestine." Many of these UNRWA officials were hostile to any new initiatives in the matter of the refugees. They flourished by virtue of the preservation of the status quo. Even the attempts of some of the non-Arab UNRWA heads to do something unconventional ran up against this conservatism and vested interest.

If Israel had set about dealing with the Arab refugee question with some fresh, vigorous thought and implementation after the Six Day War, we would now be at the beginning of the road toward a solution to this problem. Most of the camps could have been broken up and, as an interim step toward the solution of the problem, the refugees could have been settled in an orderly fashion on the outskirts of the West Bank and in Gaza Strip towns.

It may well be that the failure to act stems from our general inability to think clearly regarding the administered territories and the Palestinian Arabs. This makes it all the more urgent for Israel to come up with a declaration of intent.

In [the] complex issue of Jerusalem, so charged with irrational emotions, we must make a few things clear: united Jerusalem is the capital of the State of Israel and so she shall remain. We will never allow this city to be split in two. We will not allow it to be restored to Arab rule, nor will we again expose its streets to snipers and machine gunners. This price — and it is a heavy one — the Arabs will have to pay for peace with us.

But fate has decreed that Jerusalem is not only the city of David and Solomon. Fate has decreed that Jerusalem is also the city of Jesus and Peter. Jerusalem is also the city of the Arabs who fought under Khalid ibn al-Walid; of Abdel Malek who built the Dome of the Rock.

The solution of the religious questions lies in some sort of Vaticanization — the establishment of a clearly defined holy area within the secular city. This area should receive all municipal services from the city but should enjoy a symbolic sovereignty and its affairs should be conducted independently by clergymen.

The Muslim-Arab question, comprising at once religious and national aspects, and therefore being all the more delicate and complex, might be solved by the creation of a territorial corridor from the Palestinian-Jordanian Arab state to be established when peace comes; the borders of this state would be very close to Jerusalem.

At the same time, we must make it clear to the Muslims and Arabs, as well as to the whole world, that we will be ready to deal with the Jerusalem issue only at the end of the process of reconciliation and peace, not at the beginning.

The Third-State Pitfall

By AMNON RUBINSTEIN

What, in effect, are the arguments in favor of the establishment of another Arab state in the Middle East, with boundary lines so close to, indeed almost touching, Israel's main urban centers?

Three major arguments are presented:

* Such a state would be the embodiment of the right of the Palestinian nation to self-determination, a right which could also take into account its desire to separate into a number of national units.

* A third state would be friendly toward Israel, since it would be sandwiched between Jordan and Israel, would depend on Israel economically — outlet to the sea, etc., — and would even be able to call upon Israel's assistance in the struggle with other elements in the Arab world.

Translated and reprinted by permission of Ha'aretz (Israel Daily), August 6, 1976. Dr. Rubinstein is Professor of Constitutional Law at Tel Aviv University, a member of the Editorial Board of Ha'aretz (Israel Daily) and a member of the Secretariat of the Democratic Movement For Change. His publications include Jurisdiction and Illegality, Oxford University Press, 1956. His monograph, The Constitutional Law of Israel, was published by Schocken Books, Tel Aviv, 1974. He has contributed articles on legal issues and international relations to numerous international journals.

* The question whether such a state should be established, separate from Jordan, should not concern Israel. She should only set the conditions affecting her security, and should not interfere in determining the manner in which this eastern neighbor is organized, whether as one national unit astride the Jordan, or as two separate entities. If Israel responds with a flat negative to the idea of a separate state, her international isolation will increase even more.

The first two arguments are easily dealt with . . . even from the abstract standpoint of the right of self-determination, there is no reason to split the two population groups into separate units. However, Israel is not concerned with the issue of Palestinian-Jordan self-determination in the abstract. We must respond to the Palestinian problem because, in the long run, there is no alternative to coexistence with the Arab nation in Palestine and, in the short run, we must fend off the diplomatic-propaganda offensive directed against us.

However, the primary moral issue is that of our right to self-determination. The Jewish problem is the true problem of the Middle East, since we are the only ones threatened by a powerful military and economic alliance. Nobody poses a threat to the existence of the Palestinians. The supreme moral dictate is, therefore, that of our own existence, accompanied by the commitment that this very existence shall encompass, inherently, the obligation to consider others.

Moreover, the principle of self-determination plainly does not entitle every group to itself determine its own political framework. Even when the concept of self-determination was most popular — following World War I — it was not translated into action in a simplistic and mechanical way. In fact, after Europe was repartitioned, many national minorities remained within other nations. As a result, an international convention was signed especially to ensure protection of these minorities. Thus, for example, an entire German population was annexed to the new Czechoslovak state which was created at the time.

For these two reasons alone, I consider inadmissible the fundamental argument that the Arabs of Palestine are entitled to decide for themselves how they will organize their political life. The issue is an international one and Israel, as the party most liable to be hurt, has the right and the duty to express her opinion and take action for the adoption of her stand.

The second argument, which maintains that such a third state would necessarily be friendly to Israel, is based on pure speculation. Who will guarantee that the Arabs of the West Bank will, in fact, feel themselves isolated and in need of Israel's help in their struggle with whoever may emerge as the enemy of the Palestinians at any given time? . . .

Above all, where is the assurance that this process will indeed come about? A third state on the West Bank might just as easily become a spearhead aimed at Israel's heart and backed by the entire might of the Arab world, rather than an isolated enclave. And, if this third state is granted sovereignty and independence, surely it cannot be deprived of the right to maintain an independent military force, to sign international treaties, to invite foreign advisers, etc. Who will guarantee that all these rights would not be exploited, in the most extreme fashion, to harm us; to threaten our urban centers?

. . . a distinguished group of persons all of whom I admire, [say] that if we are threatened by artillery from Qalqiliya, we shall threaten Qalqiliya in turn with our own artillery. But the answer is pathetically simple: the Arab world can manage, can live, prosper and grow stronger, even if our guns threaten Qalqiliya and even if we hit it. Small, exposed Israel will not be able to exist and to prosper if her urban centers, her vulnerable airport and her narrow, winding roads are shelled and sabotaged. This is the basic difference between ourselves and the Arab world. This is the terrible danger inherent in the existence of a third independent, sovereign state between Israel and Jordan.

What, then, are Israel's demands concerning the future of Judea and Samaria? We now come to the third argument, which maintains that Israel should be content with defining her own conditions, and should not dictate the form of organization of Palestine's Arabs to them. In my view, Israel's terms must deal with her own security, and Israel's security necessitates the imposing of substantial military restrictions over any area west of the Jordan which would revert to Arab sovereignty.

First and foremost, these restrictions must include the demilitarization of Judea and Samaria, prohibiting the presence of any substantial military forces; of armored and of air forces. Such demilitarization would also necessitate a degree of joint supervision, and entitle Israel to use the air space over all of the area west of the Jordan. Only such security arrangements would effectively prevent the return of Arab armies to the boundaries from which they have attempted in the past — and might attempt in future — to strike against Israel.

It should be noted that such arrangements constitute, in effect, a very grave restriction of sovereignty. This is the major difficulty. Any third state established west of the Jordan would have to be either fully sovereign — and would therefore pose a constant threat to Israel's heartland — or a state subjected to the above security arrangements which are so vital to us. Of all the states in the U.N. this would be the only one whose sovereignty is restricted; the only one without an army or an air force; the only second class state in the world.

Such inferiority — which would never be acceptable to enemies or, for that matter, to friends — would intensify Palestinian "humiliation," and lead to increased hostility toward Israel and the perpetuation of the Arab-Israeli conflict. This is the real danger of the proposals to establish a separate Palestinian state between ourselves and the desert.

The situation would be entirely different if Jordan — or even a Syrian-Jordanian federation — served as a large Arab unit in which the right of the West Bank and Gaza Strip Arabs to be free of Israeli rule would be fulfilled. We would then be dealing with an independent, sovereign state, in which one region — a small fraction of its total area — would be demilitarized, with restricted sovereignty. Such an arrangement — which, naturally, is not free of difficulties, either — has both precedent and parallel, and avoids the pitfall of becoming a "first or second class third state."

It may, of course, be claimed that, from the tactical-propaganda standpoint, Israel should be content with stating her security demands and handing the burden of the pitfall over to the Arabs. This would have its tactical advantages. But it is important to know what lies beyond tactics: a vital issue, the solution of which must rule out the establishment of a separate Palestinian state west of the Jordan.

The Attitude of Jordan: Hussein and the West Bank

By ASHER SUSSER

Historical ties between the east and west banks of the River Jordan existed long before Jordan's annexation of the West Bank after the Arab-Israel war of 1948. These ties, further enhanced by the annexation, form the basis of the concept—equally accepted, ironically enough, by Palestinian, Jordanian and Israeli spokesmen—that the Jordanians and the Palestinians are essentially one entity; that there is a Jordanian-Palestinian—or Palestinian-Jordanian— people. The basic problem in this assumption is whether the Palestinians or the Jordanians are to rule this Jordanian-Palestinian entity. Jordan's special interest in the Palestinian question is therefore understandable, particularly since almost half the population of the East Bank itself is of Palestinian extraction. One of Jordan's main considerations is the fear that historical ties and demographic reality might lead, eventually, to a solution of the Palestinian problem at Jordan's expense; that it could lead to the "Palestinization" of Jordan. It is therefore imperative, in Jordan's view, to ensure its influence by "Jordanizing" the political fate of the Palestinians.

The resolutions of the Arab summit conference at Rabat of October 1974 marked the zenith of the PLO's success in its competition with Jordan over the right to determine the fate of the Palestinian people. The PLO's role as the "sole legitimate representative" of the Palestinian people was recognized by all the Arab states, as was its right to establish a "national authority" in any area of Palestine from which Israel withdrew. Jordan formally accepted the resolutions of Rabat but continued to regard the preservation of its influence and control on the West Bank as a vital interest. The political goals of the PLO, as defined in June 1974, called not only for the establishment of an "indepen-

Dr. Susser is head of the Jordan Desk at the Shiloah Center for Middle Eastern and African Studies at Tel Aviv University.

dent fighting national authority'' in any Palestinian territories from which Israel withdraws; the plan also called for a struggle to establish a ''national democratic regime in Jordan that would join together with the Palestinian entity.'' The PLO's strategy thus regards the overthrow of the Hashemite regime and the ''Palestinization'' of Jordan as a primary objective that would guarantee the existence of the political entity it seeks to establish. But the establishment of such a PLO entity on the West Bank would be a serious threat to the regime in Jordan—particularly since, in terms of the Rabat resolutions, the PLO represents about half (and according to it, the majority) of the East Bank's population. It would lay the groundwork for the undermining of the legitimate existence of the Hashemite regime.

The conflict between Jordan and the PLO is not, therefore, only over the West Bank but over control of the East Bank as well, and over political control of the majority of the Palestinians concentrated on the East and West Banks. Both the PLO and the inhabitants of the West Bank are fully aware of the importance of the East Bank for the survival of any future Palestinian state or entity on the West Bank and the historical, economic and family ties between the two banks also serve to strengthen the desire for political connections between them. The PLO strategy, as mentioned, sees the overthrow of the regime as a prerequisite for such connections—as, most probably, do their supporters on the West Bank. However, there are also West Bankers who hold less radical views. An article in the West Bank daily, *al-Quds,* of March 1976 reflected this situation. It maintained that any Palestinian ''national authority or state'' on the West Bank would have no choice but to find some form of understanding with the East Bank, ''without reference to who rules it.''[1] It is this kind of thinking on the West Bank that provides the Hashemite regime with an extremely important advantage over the PLO: Hussein is the ruler of the East Bank.

Jordan was not required by the Rabat resolutions to sever its ties with the West Bank. Its economic, political and legal ties with the territory have been maintained, and it took no steps, following the Rabat resolutions, that might signify its detachment from the area. Jordan continued to pay salaries to West Bank government officials and to provide aid to West Bank municipalities. It continued to control freedom of movement and of the import and export of goods going to and from the West Bank across the Jordan River bridges and thus preserved a measure of West Bank dependence on Jordan.

In its competition with the PLO for influence on the West Bank, Jordan's major drawback has been its lack of legitimacy—in the eyes of the Palestinians and the Arab world in general—as the custodian of the Palestine cause, as was signified by the Rabat resolutions. Since Rabat, Jordan has spared no effort to re-establish itself as a legitimate party to the determination of the West Bank's political fate, acting on the assumption that the pragmatic political considerations of the Arab states and the West Bank population would eventually lead to its reinstatement in their eyes.

Since Rabat, a number of factors have worked in Jordan's favor in this respect. These were:

• Israel's refusal to recognize or negotiate with the PLO;

• The fact that the political process in the Middle East crisis has remained tied to U.N. Security Council Resolutions 242 and 338, accepted by Jordan and rejected by the PLO;

• Sadat's interest in incessant political momentum—and therefore in Jordan's involvement in negotiations to overcome the PLO obstacle—as expressed in Sadat's interview of December 30, 1976 with the *Washington Post,* in which he called for formal ties between Jordan and a future Palestinian state;

• Jordan's close relationship with Syria, which has given rise to Syrian readiness to agree to make concessions to Jordan at the PLO's expense.

Since Rabat, Hussein has been implementing a policy designed to demonstrate, to the West Bank population, that their most realistic political solution is one in which the Hashemite regime must play a decisive role, since Jordan has a better chance than has the PLO of achieving an Israeli withdrawal. When the Jordanian Parliament was reconvened in February 1976,[2] it was attended by delegates from both the East and the West Banks. The Jordanians explained the reconvening of Parliament as a constitutional necessity, but it also served as an opportunity to demonstrate Jordan's continued political attachment to the West Bank and its readiness to act on the West Bank's behalf in the diplomatic sphere. Premier Rifa'i, in his address to Parliament on February 5, stressed that the "political horizons" of the Middle East crisis "continued to be closed."[3] and the Jordanian media explained that the West Bank population had the right to try to extricate itself from the dead end their problem had reached. This was clearly designed to drive home the point, to the West Bankers, that since the PLO had proved unable to achieve any change in the West Bank's situation, it would be in their interest to reconsider the Jordanian option.

Parliament had been reconvened to amend the Constitution so that parliamentary elections could be indefinitely postponed. This postponing of elections was necessary in order to prevent the formal detachment of the West Bank from Jordan—which the holding of elections on the East Bank alone would have signified. Such a detachment, the official explanation maintained, would have paved the way for the application of Israeli law on the West Bank and would have changed the area's status. It was Jordan's way of seeking to convince the West Bank population that preservation of its legal and constitutional ties with Jordan formed an obstacle to an Israeli annexation.[4]

Nevertheless, the reconvening of parliament, coming shortly before the municipal elections on the West Bank, had little impact on the outcome of these elections. Held on April 12, when the PLO was still riding high in the Arab world and on the West Bank, the election results strengthened the PLO supporters in the newly elected town councils at the expense of the traditional leadership, which was known for its generally favorable relationship with the

Hashemite regime. In the important towns of Nablus and Hebron, pro-Jordanian leaders like Hajj Ma'zuz al Masri and Sheik Muhammad Ali al-Jaabari were replaced by leaders of a new generation who had repeatedly expressed their allegiance to the PLO. Hussein was not particularly perturbed by this development. He maintained that only time and the behavior of the PLO would tell whether the newly elected leaders really supported the organization.

A basic characteristic of West Bank politics, of which Hussein is no doubt well aware, is the influence of external factors on the political behavior and attitudes of the local population. Lacking an independent power base of their own, West Bankers have repeatedly been compelled to contend with developments in the inter-Arab and international arenas, over which they have very little influence. In the period of Israeli rule, the ups and downs of the relative stature of Jordan and the PLO in West Bank eyes have been clearly discernible and have reflected the changes in the relative strength and stature of the PLO and Jordan in the inter-Arab and international arenas. The PLO's ascendancy since the war of October 1973, the Rabat resolutions and the steadily increasing international recognition of the organizations inevitably led to an upsurge in the PLO's popularity and influence on the West Bank. Its position was weakened in the latter half of 1976, as its stature in the Arab world sank to an all-time low following its resounding defeat by the Syrians in Lebanon and this led to the steady enhancement of Jordan's position in the Arab world.

The new situation provided Jordan with the opportunity for which it had been waiting and preparing. At the end of July, Jordan officially recognized the results of the West Bank municipal elections and invited the newly elected mayors to Amman to discuss the resumption of financial support for the municipalities, which Jordan had cut off shortly before the elections.

The first of the West Bank mayors to accept this invitation was the new mayor of Hebron, Fahd Qawasame, who visited Jordan in mid-August. He was followed by delegations of mayors from Bethlehem, el-Bireh and Araba in mid-November and from Bir Zayt, Anabta and Salfit in December.

The mayors' visits, which included audiences with King Hussein and Premier Badran, were widely publicized by the Jordanian media, which enveloped the visits in an atmosphere of importance and officialdom. In this way Jordan clearly sought to exploit the municipalities' dire need for funds for its own political ends in its struggle with the PLO. It was a demonstration of Jordan's *rapport* with the newly elected West Bank mayors and of the mayors' readiness to give their sanction to Hussein's involvement in West Bank affairs. Mayors Qawasame and Elias Frej of Bethlehem explained that there were no political strings attached to the promises made by the Jordanian government to renew aid to the municipalities. However, this aid was not specifically promised to those municipalities whose mayors had declined to visit Jordan. Thus the question of aid was clearly made to serve as a means of pressuring West Bank mayors to show a readiness to cooperate with Jordan, and although the visiting mayors did not produce statements of loyalty to Jordan, the very fact of their visits demonstrated that they were consciously helping Jordan to use their visits to further its own political aims. These visits, firmly opposed by the PLO and its supporters on the West Bank, reflected a weakening of the PLO's influence—at least some of the mayors showed they were obviously prepared to make moves that the PLO did not approve. In this atmosphere of growing Jordanian involvement, a number of the more moderate mayors, like the mayors of Hebron, Qalqiliya and Jericho, made statements favoring future ties between the West Bank and Jordan on the basis of "equality"—i.e.—not under direct Jordanian rule but also not ruling out a federative concept, which Hussein supports. Mayor Fahd Qawasame, responding to criticism of his visit to Jordan, stressed that a distinction had to be made between ties to the Hashemite dynasty and ties to Jordan. Qawasame did not spell it out, but those favoring ties with Jordan, in the present political set-up, cannot avoid favoring ties with the Hashemite regime.

To date, Jordan's pressure on the mayors has met with only partial success. Some have refused to travel to Amman at all, notably Mayors Karim Khalaf of Ramallah, Hilmi Hanun of Tulkarm[5] and Basam Shak'a of Nablus, the three most prominent PLO supporters. Khalaf maintained, in November, that if the Jordanians were ready "to give us money without conditions . . . we will take it. But we cannot give our loyalty to the Jordanian regime because our loyalty is to the PLO, to our people . . . to our country, Palestine."[7] Khalaf was also, reportedly, the leading figure in an effort, in mid-December, to organize opposition to Jordan and to its attempts to manipulate the West Bank leadership. This effort resulted in the signing of a petition by many West Bank mayors criticizing Jordan's methods and expressing support for the PLO.

Jordan's only partial success with the West Bank municipal authorities led it to extend its efforts to other elements, such as members of the Supreme Muslim Council (its seat is in East Jerusalem and it has maintained a favorable relationship with the regime in Jordan since 1967) and to prominent pro-Jordanian personalities like Anwar al-Khatib, the former Governor of Jerusalem and Sheik Jaabari, the former mayor of Hebron. Jaabari visited Jordan for the first time since 1967 at the end of December 1976. While in Amman, having had an audience, no doubt, with his host, the King, Jaabari called for the formation of a new Palestinian party—the "Party of the Land"—to represent the Palestinians and to be created, not necessarily in place of the PLO but certainly not as part of the PLO. He was, thus, undermining the PLO's claim to sole representation of the Palestinians and implying a Jordanian-West Bank leadership alternative.

On the same day, President Sadat made his statement proposing formal ties between the future Palestinian state and Jordan. It was fully endorsed only by the mayor of Bethlehem, Elias Frej, known for his pro-Jordanian leanings. It was also reportedly well received in political circles in East Jerusalem and Judea. But staunch PLO supporters like Karim Khalaf, Basam Shak'a and

Hilmi Hanun were more reserved. They reaffirmed their support for the PLO as the sole authorized spokesman of the Palestinians and maintained that the Palestinian state must first be established—only then would this state decide what ties to have with Jordan—or Syria—or any other Arab state. Frej, on the other hand, answered that once the Palestinian state was established, its *elected government* (i.e., not necessarily the PLO) would enter into a confederation with Jordan, on the basis of "equality." *Al-Quds* maintained that formal ties with Jordan would provide the solution to the Israeli opposition to a third state between Israel and Jordan.

The West Bank leadership has, thus, not been able to establish a consensus on the political future of the area and Jordan's policy since Rabat has been to provide an alternative to the PLO and to encourage support for itself by advocating a solution which would allow for some form of Palestinian self-determination—but in close relationship with Jordan. Jordanian policy statements have consistently differentiated between the PLO and the right of the Palestinians to self-determination. Hussein has sought to convince West Bankers that following an Israeli withdrawal (brought about by Jordan) the right of the Palestinians to self-determination would be respected.

However, Hussein has also repeatedly stressed that it is the inhabitants of the West Bank themselves (i.e., not the PLO) who must decide their own fate, "free from all pressure or coercion" (thus implying that the PLO may impose itself on the West Bank against the will of the population). In June 1976, asked in an interview in Vienna whether he still supported his federation plan, Hussein said that he believed that the ties between the Palestinians and the Jordanians "originally one and the same people" were strong and durable. The Palestinians "in the occupied territories themselves" must decide what ties to have with Jordan, but he was sure that, in the end, they would make "the right choice."[8]

The Jordanians' accelerated effort to strengthen their influence on the West Bank in the latter half of 1976 was accompanied by a stepped-up propaganda campaign against the PLO in the context of the Lebanese crisis. Hussein frequently asserted that the Palestinian leadership "must rise to the level of events and face its responsibilities in order to extricate the cause of the Palestinian people from the bloody conflict in Lebanon and save its people from aimlessness. It must be a leadership capable of shouldering the responsibility and [of] leading the Palestinian people"[9]—something it had obviously not been, in Hussein's view. The Palestinians, he maintained, had to choose a "courageous and constructive leadership,"[10] or, alternatively, the Palestinian leadership must "rise to the level" expected of it "so that we can cooperate with it."[11] The point Hussein was clearly seeking to drive home to West Bankers was that the PLO, in its present form, was not capable of leading the Palestinians or of solving the problem of the Israeli occupation, while Jordan was.[12]

Clearly, Hussein believes that by neutralizing the PLO or forcing it to cooperate with Jordan (with the help of Syria and Egypt) he can pave the way toward establishing Jordan's legitimacy and creating a situation in which, given the opportunity, West Bankers would choose to preserve their ties with Jordan, along the lines of Hussein's federation plan, for lack of any better choice.

The Rabat resolutions may never be formally revoked, but present developments do not exclude the possibility that Jordan might eventually succeed in doing away with them.

FOOTNOTES

1. *Al-Quds,* March 7, 1976.

2. It was dissolved in November 1974, ostensibly in compliance with the Rabat resolutions, to prevent dual representation of the West Bank by the PLO and the Jordanian Parliament.

3. *Radio Amman,* February 5, 1976; *Daily Report* (Amman), February 10, 1976.

4. West Bankers of all political persuasions support the continued application of Jordanian law, obviously preferring this to Israeli law, the only feasible alternative. Jordan has often sought to exploit this support as a sign of loyalty. Though not reflecting loyalty to Jordan, it is yet an example of how West Bank ties with Jordan are supported for lack of any other alternative, a situation from which Jordan profits.

5. In December 1976, a member of the Tulkarm town council visited Jordan, thus not closing the door altogether.

6. Opposition within the Nablus town council to Shak'a and his refusal to visit Amman is led by the pro-Jordanian Deputy Mayor, Safir al-Masri. There have been reports of Jordanian attempts to undermine Shak'a's position with the help of the Masri family. In mid-December, Jordan imposed a ban on the export of agricultural produce from the West Bank to the Persian Gulf and Saudi Arabia. The explanation was that a shortage existed in the Jordanian markets. However, a few days later, Hajj Ma'zuz al-Masri succeeded, during a visit to Jordan, in lifting the ban on 50% of the West Bank exports. It is quite possible that the Jordanian authorities were signalling to Nablus that the Masris were in a better position to further the town's interests than was Shak'a, who refused to cooperate or to receive funds for the municipality on Jordan's terms.

7. *Guardian,* November 16, 1976.

8. *Radio Vienna,* June 16, 1976; *Daily Report,* June 17, 1976.

9. *Radio Amman,* October 11, 1976; *Daily Report,* October 12, 1976.

10. *Radio Amman,* November 13, 1976; *Daily Report,* November 15, 1976.

11. *Destour,* November 6, 1976.

12. Jordan has also made a concerted effort to bolster its nationalist posture in the eyes of the local population by frequently denouncing Israeli policy on the West Bank. It has stepped up its incitement to unrest, praised the "steadfastness" of the population in face of the "occupation and the tyrant enemy" and demonstrated its concern for the "Arabness" of the area, by repeated pronouncements of death sentences on West Bankers for the "crime of selling property to the enemy."

Q: If a West Bank-Gaza state were established, what links would you accept?

A: In view of the closeness of the people of both sides, we are willing to look at any possibility, but the people of both Jordan and the West Bank would have to express their views in absolute freedom. Some years ago, we had the vision to suggest a federation of Palestine and Jordan [which was rejected by other Arab states]. Now maybe this plan will be looked at again.

King Hussein, February 14, 1977. Reprinted by permission of *Time* The Weekly Newsmagazine; © Time Inc. 1977.

PLO Attitudes: 1970-1977

If the slogan of a Democratic State is designed only to reply to the contention that we aim to throw the Jews into the sea, then it is a successful slogan and and efficient political and propaganda act. But if we wish to see it as the final strategic aim of the Palestinian and Arab national liberation movements—then I am convinced that it requires continued consideration . . .

Shafiq al-Hout, PLO Executive Representative, at a symposium organized by Al-Anwar, Beirut Daily, on the creation of a Democratic Palestinian State, March 20, 1970.

There is agreement between the various components of the resistance movement that the practical translation of the idea of a Palestinian State means the elimination of the Zionist entity . . .

When the slogan of the Democratic Palestinian State was brought up, it was implied that it was intended to pacify progressive public opinion and the world Leftist movement. However, the idea cannot be realized by flinging about slogans that are not implementable . . . We are convinced that no State created in Palestine will be able to stay democratic for long—irrespective of who heads it—in circumstances of Arab disunity and the imperialistic influence and schemes prevailing in the area today.

Representative of the Arab Liberation Front at the symposium organized by Al-Anwar, March 20, 1970.

As to the question: What if Israel agrees? . . . Our answer is: Israel will not agree to this idea (of the Democratic State), and it is not possible for it to agree, because it means the dissolution of the State of Israel . . . and there has never in history been a class force or a social-political system that has agreed to self-destruction . . .

The (Democratic Palestinian) State can be established only on the ruins of the Zionist entity and the destruction of the State of Israel.

Representative of the Popular Democratic Front at the symposium organized by Al-Anwar, March 20, 1970.

. . . Despite all that the Palestinian resistance movement said, from the day it fired its first shot up to Black September 1970, to the effect that it only came into existence to liberate Palestine and the occupied territories, and despite the consistent attitude it has always adopted and what it has endured as a result of adopting this attitude—to the effect that the central contradiction which it came into existence to combat is the Zionist presence and the Israeli occupation—despite all this the Jordanian regime has insisted on offering itself as an accomplice for the Zionist enemy . . .

. . . King Hussein concentrated in his proposal on the relations of the one people in the Jordanian-Palestinian field without making any serious reference to the central problem, which is the problem of liberation . . .

> Statement by the PLO's Executive Committee
> on King Hussein's proposal to establish the
> United Arab Kingdom, March 16, 1972.

The October War has put before us a difficult choice: On the one hand, our nationalist upbringing, the heritage of 50 years, means rejecting everything that is proposed with regard to our cause. This rejection is bound up with our historical right to the whole of Palestine.

On the other hand, we find ourselves in a new situation, facing a new reality that will grow out of the settlement. We must confront this situation with realistic solutions, that will not abrogate our historical right. At the same time one cannot ignore present gains—I prefer to call them gains and not rights—which our people may achieve, while struggling to keep these gains out of the framework of concessions over the right of our people to reject recognition of Israel and peace (Sulh) with it.

Out of faith in our masses and sympathy with them in their present test, when they have to choose between the Israel occupation and the Hashemite oppression, we shall continue to uphold the right of these masses to self-determination and to the establishment of a national authority on any land that the settlement may apply to. . . .

The nationalist forces are called upon to struggle so that this land will constitute a revolutionary base for our people. . . .

It is the fighters who establish the facts on any land they tread on. It is they who are able to stiffen the attitude of their people so that it continues the struggle. They constitute the true framework for this Palestinian land, being taken from Zionist occupation. . .

If the question is—how is it possible to achieve the present gains without damaging the historical right of the Palestine people to establish the democratic State of Palestine and liquidate the Zionist entity?—then our reply is clear: The present gains can certainly not be at the expense of the historical right. The price cannot be recognition of Israel and peace (Sulh) with it.

> Abu Ayad (al-fatah), in an interview
> with the Lebanese paper Al-Balagh, Beirut,
> December 24, 1973.

We believe that the ultimate solution of the conflict in the Middle East is the establishment of a national State in partnership with the Israeli Jews . . .

> Said Hammami, PLO representative in London
> in an interview with the Jewish Chronicle,
> London, April 5, 1974.

We have no knowledge of these things. They do not express the view of the organization. The strategic aim of PLO is the establishment of a democratic State on the whole land of Palestine . . .

> From an official statement issued by the PLO
> repudiating the Hammami statement, published in
> An-Nahar, Beirut, April 5, 1974.

Q: What is your view on the future of the Palestinian territories that will be included in any settlement in the area?

A: . . . The existing trend (in the PLO National Council) says that the Palestinian people have the right to establish their national-popular-independent-fighting authority over every inch of land from which Zionist occupation withdraws and which is liberated. There are no differences over this point and we firmly insist that this land is Palestinian and shall remain so, whether the Zionists agree or not.

> Voice of Palestine, Cairo, May 31, 1974, broadcast of
> an interview by French Television with Yasser Arafat.

Jordan is ours, Palestine is ours, and we shall build our national entity on the whole of this land after having freed it of both the Zionist presence and the reactionary-traitor [i.e., Hussein] presence.

> Yasser Arafat in a letter to the Jordanian Student
> Congress in Baghdad, as reported by the
> Washington Post, November 12, 1974.

The solution for our revolution is unequivocal; that is why al-fatah emphasizes that it does not differentiate between Jew and Jew, either now or after victory and liberation, in accordance with our definition. The most democratic and just criteria shall be ''everyone by his ability and everyone by his actions.''

What is meant by this concept is every person will be judged and be accorded treatment in relation to his active role and position against Zionism and its institutions. Al-Fatah also rejects the notion that the democratic state would include Israelis and Palestinian Arabs. It is neither a matter of compromise between two historical and right concepts nor an agreement between Israelis and Palestinian Arabs. The question is one of a fundamental, historic conflict in which the only solution is the disappearance of one of the parties in this conflict. Since it is impossible, historically, for the Palestinian people or the Palestinian land to disappear, Palestine shall regain its historically right place in society and Palestinians will govern it regardless whether they are Muslim, Christian or Jew.

The creation of a new Palestinian society requires a long-range revolution which is the consequence of a national struggle for emergence. The new Palestinian will be Arab, either by origin or by imitation. A democratic Palestine, in addition to being our primary goal, is also our plan of battle and liberation. This long-range battle plan is the only way to overcome the imperialistic Zionist enemy and to build a new Palestine.

Assimilation is the only solution to the Jewish problem in Palestine, as well as in the rest of the world. This assimilation can be achieved only through the development of true democracy within an integrated society. Undoubtedly, the absence of social democratic governments has prevented Jews from assimilating in the countries in which they reside.

After the collapse of this Zionist system [the State of Israel] and its political, military, and cultural institutions, only vestigial conditions will remain. Of course, these vestiges are also reactionary and are the result of the reactionary nature of the Zionist existence.

Therefore, Jews must be assimilated. No doubt, this will be a difficult, long-range task which can be accomplished by democratic means. However, it must be by assimilation and not be granting of special rights to develop special and individual cultures. Acceptance of demands for individual rights would thwart our historic plans and would permit the formation of ghetto societies in liberated Palestine to replace that vast ghetto society called Israel.

The liberation of Palestine and the return of its people cannot be accomplished, nor can Palestine develop and prosper, until all Arab nations and Palestine become one Arab united and progressive state in the Near East. . . .

> From ''The Democratic Palestine-Goal Program and
> Historic Realization,'' by Dr. Machjub Amar,
> prominent PLO spokesman, in Sha'un Falastin,
> the official PLO organ, January-February 1975.

Kaddoumi . . . said the Palestinians are firm in their resolve to establish a democratic Palestinian State in Israel and Israeli-occupied territories, and they consider another war inevitable to achieve that end. ''This can be said to those people who are looking for political settlements. This is an armed struggle,'' Kaddoumi said . . .

Decrying Israel for ''aggressiveness, racism, expansionism,'' Kaddoumi predicted a ''democratic State of Palestine where Israel is not existing and only we have one Palestine. This is within 15 years.'' A Palestinian independent State in Gaza and the West Bank ''can be regained in less time,'' he said, pointing to a map in his office.

> From an interview with Farouk Kaddoumi,
> PLO Political Department Head,
> the Chicago Daily News, December 30, 1975.

The PLO is going to amend the National Covenant with a view to setting up a Palestinian State in a part of Palestine as a transitional stage leading to a secular State that will be established on the entire Palestinian territory.

> Naim Khader (PLO Liaison and Information Center
> Director in Belgium), quoted by Al-Quds,
> Jerusalem, November 23, 1976.

The establishment of a Palestinian State in every part of Palestine that will be liberated is of political rather than geographical significance: it will be considered the beginning of the realization of the final goal—which is the establishment of the Democratic Palestinian State.

> Khaled el-Hassan (al-fatah Central Committee
> member) in an interview in Kuwait quoted
> by Al-Quds, Jerusalem, December 5, 1976.

The question of a West Bank—Gaza solution for us, as the PFLP, is impossible—100 percent impossible, 1000 percent impossible. We simply believe as we always have that we are fighting for the cause of one democratic Palestinian nation and the partition or recognition of the occupying force (Israel) is unthinkable.

> George Habbash (PFLP), as reported by
> the Los Angeles Times, December 5, 1976.

The establishment of a Palestinian State in every part of Palestine that will be liberated is of political rather than geographical significance: it will be considered the beginning of the realization of the final goal—which is the establishment of the Democratic Palestinian State.

> Khaled el-Hassan (al-fatah Central Committee
> member) in an interview in Kuwait, quoted
> by Al Quds, Jerusalem, December 5, 1976.

I follow the resolutions (passed in 1974) of our Palestine National Council, which states that we will establish a national authority on any part of Palestine liberated from Israel or which Israel will evacuate. This is clear.

> Yasser Arafat, in an interview with
> Time Magazine, December 13, 1976.

My people are readying a new campaign of terror, unprecedented in scope, against every Israeli and against every target in Israel and throughout the world.

> George Habbash (Head of PFLP) in an interview
> with the BBC, quoted by Yediot Aharonot,
> Tel Aviv, December 16, 1976.

These topics [the establishment of a Palestinian state on the West Bank and in the Gaza Strip, and agreement to participate in the Geneva Conference] were placed on the agenda of the Palestinian National Council, which will convene this coming February at the latest. They will be discussed within the framework of the guidelines outlined in previous resolutions of the Council, and in the 'Ten Points,' as a stage-by-stage schedule for the Palestinian revolution, without any changes or amendments, no matter how minor.

> Farouk Kaddoumi, speaking of the resolutions
> of the PLO Central Committee, as reported
> in Sha'un Falastin, Beirut, December 18, 1976.

. . . the meeting between the two Presidents referred not merely to the 10 years after 1976 and the 30 years since the rights of the Palestinian people were usurped, but that the Arabs will render Israel an account which includes not only Jerusalem, Nablus, Gaza, Sinai, and the Golan, but primarily Tel Aviv, Haifa, Jaffa and Nazareth. The Arabs will not only demand the West Bank and the Gaza Strip, but all of the land conquered since

1948 . . . The slogan that the rights of the Palestinians be restored and Palestine liberated can have but one meaning—the elimination of Israel.

> Radio Damascus, "Palestine Corner,"
> program, December 22, 1976, in reference
> to the joint communique issued by
> Presidents Sadat of Egypt and Assad of Syria
> at their meeting of December 21, 1976.

Our consent to the establishment of a Palestinian State on any piece of land that will be liberated from the occupation does not constitute a renunciation of PLO principles. On the contrary, it is part and parcel of the Ten-Point Program approved by the 12th National Council in 1974 . . .

The resolutions of the General Assembly concerning the establishment of an independent Palestinian State do not obligate us to concede so much as an inch of Palestinian soil. The fact that the Assembly confirmed the right of self-determination of the Palestinian people on its soil serves to consolidate our right to fight, by every means at our disposal for the attainment of our rights . . .

Any political gain registered by the Palestinian Revolution will not loosen our people's grip on the gun. For it is only by means of the gun that we have achieved what we have achieved—and thus it will be in the future.

In the course of a campaign of liberation, it becomes necessary, on occasion, to exercise political flexibility at certain stages, in order to ensure freedom of action at all levels. However, this certainly does not mean that we will compromise the national goals for the sake of which we have taken up arms.

> Voice of Palestine, Lebanon,
> December 25, 1976

There will be no settlement and there will be no peace. We must all prepare for the battle against Israel.

> Abu Salah (al-fatah Central Committee
> member), Voice of Palestine, Lebanon, January 7,
> 1977.

We will accept a state on any land in Palestine, but we are not prepared to pay a price for that state in terms of conciliation with or recognition of Israel, or in terms of being a fake state affiliated with Jordan, or with any side not in harmony with the Palestine Revolution or people . . . We oppose those who believe that through giving in and offering major concessions we can obtain something.

> Abu Iyad (Salah Khalaf, original commander
> of Black September) in a speech to a seminar
> of the Palestinian Student Federation in Cairo,
> broadcast over the Voice of Palestine, Cairo,
> January 18, 1977, quoted in Afro-Asian Affairs,
> London, No. 43, January 31, 1977.

Speaking at a graduation ceremony of Fatah officers Arafat said:

"We must be prepared for our task, which is the struggle against the Zionist foe and against all the enemies of our Arab nation—without and within . . . The Popular War of Liberation is the only way to liberate the land."

> Yasser Arafat, quoted by Voice of Palestine,
> Lebanon, February 1, 1977.

From time to time we read reports, in the Arab and foreign press, alleging that the Palestinian Revolution is prepared to make concessions in exchange for the attainment of the rights of the Palestinian people. Some of these reports go so far as to raise doubts as to the firmness of the Palestinian Revolution's strategic positions and aims.

We wish to emphasize that the Palestinian Revolution continues to adhere to the hopes and aspirations of the Palestinian masses—and, in particular, the aspiration to the *total liberation* of the Palestinian soil.

> Voice of Palestine, Lebanon,
> February 11, 1977.

We say that after the establishment of a Palestinian state there should be peace . . . there should be other ways to regain our rights: the repatriation of Palestinians to their homeland, the rest of our land. We should follow all means. But we have to be flexible, in order to establish peace in this part of the world. So we have to accept at this stage that we have this state on only part of our territory. But this doesn't mean that we are giving up the rest of our rights . . . There are two [initial] phases to our return. The first phase to the 1967 lines, and the second to the 1948 lines . . . The third stage is the democratic state of Palestine. So we are fighting for these three stages. I hope Mr. Yitzhak Rabin knows this also.

> Farouk Kaddoumi, in an interview in
> Newsweek, March 14, 1977.

▼

Arafat, the PLO and the West Bank People

By THOMAS A. IDINOPULOS

The failure of Jordan and Israel, from 1967 to 1974, to achieve an agreement about the Palestinian Arabs on the West Bank of the Jordan River created a vacuum that began to be filled by Yasser Arafat, leader of the Palestine Liberation Organization. As late as May 1974, when Israel and Syria began their military disengagement, any proposal coming jointly from Jordan and Israel would probably have been favored by Egypt's Sadat, and hence have been acceptable to the Arab nations as a whole. If Arafat had succeeded in gaining control of the West Bank, Jordan and Israel would have been no less to blame for putting the wolf at their doors than the United Nations, which, in inviting Arafat to address the General Assembly, granting the PLO Observer Status, and allowing it to participate in Security Council debates on the Middle East, garbed the wolf in sheep's clothing.

At the Arab summit meeting in Rabat in October 1974, Arafat achieved his most important political breakthrough when he was declared the "sole legitimate representative of the Palestinian people." Even King Hussein of Jordan acquiesced, under massive Arab pressure. But whether Arafat is in fact the "legitimate representative" of all the Palestinian people is open to question. It is a question I have asked of Israelis and Palestinians in East Jerusalem and the West Bank since 1974.

It is true that Arafat, who seeks to regain what the Arabs lost during and after the war of 1948, speaks for the thousands and their descendants languishing in refugee camps in Lebanon, Syria and Jordan. But it is doubtful that he represents the aims of the Palestinians who are integrated into and prospering in these countries, who are not about to give up their places to follow a revolutionary leader "back to Palestine." As for the West Bank, there were of course demonstrations of support by young Arab students in Jerusalem and other West Bank towns after Arafat's U.N. speech— demonstrations organized and led by their teachers. But except for the *circa* 700,000 refugees out of the *circa* 3 million Palestinians in the Middle East and elsewhere, it is hard to make a case for Arafat as the "sole legitimate representative of the Palestinian people." What is closer to the truth is that

Dr. Idinopulos is Professor of Religion at Miami University, Oxford, Ohio. He has written extensively on religion and politics in the Middle East today and is the author of *The Erosion of Faith: An Inquiry into the Origins of the Contemporary Crisis in Religious Thought*, Quadrangle, 1971.

The first part of the above article is reprinted, with editorial changes by the author, from "Yasir Arafat and the West Bank People" in *Christian Century*, February 19, 1975, by permission.

Arafat was elevated at Rabat because his revolutionary aim to regain Palestine fits in nicely with the consistent Arab strategy—led by Egypt, Syria and Saudi Arabia—to neutralize Jordan, harass Israel and exert pressure on the United States, all the while expressing the wish to negotiate every issue affecting the peace and security of the Middle East.

But one cannot govern a Palestinian state from Cairo or Damascus or Riyadh; it must be done from the Jerichos and Nabluses of the West Bank. So the question of support for Arafat is crucial in determining whether he could in time become the West Bank Palestinians' "sole legitimate representative."

In early 1974, one experienced news analyst told me that in the minds of virtually all West Bankers, the choice was between ballots and bullets. If the West Bankers could have a fair plebiscite, they would in overwhelming numbers choose Hussein over Arafat. If Arafat should come with bullets, they would not want him; but they were not about to say so openly. The pressure on West Bankers to either keep quiet or publicly avow Arafat was great, as witnessed by the turnabout of *al Quds*, Jerusalem's influential daily newspaper, which had long opposed Arafat but then announced support for him.

The West Bankers, in 1974 and 1975, played a game they are good at—the waiting game, in which all bets are hedged. They were betting that Israel would never willingly permit Arafat to control the West Bank; but in case Israel should bend to external pressure, they were hedging their bet by not opposing him. They were betting, too, that the sudden prominence of Arafat would alert Jordan and Israel to the need for a realistic agreement vis-a-vis the West Bank. Here the hedge was that precisely because of the threat of Arafat, no agreement need be accepted by them that automatically returned King Hussein to his accustomed authoritarian rule on the West Bank. They have not forgotten Jordan's Arab Legion, which jailed thousands of Palestinians at the merest hint of unhappiness with life under the Hashemite Kingdom. The talk among West Bankers was of a confederation in which Hussein would be acknowledged as king but the West Bank would have its own democratically elected regional government, linked in some fashion to Jordan's parliament but not controlled by it.

No person with whom I have spoken within the past several years, Arab or Jew, expressed the belief that the West Bank could survive as a sovereign state. This state could not defend itself against external threat except with a military force, and an armed West Bank state would be viewed by both Jordan and Israel as a grave threat. Economically, a sovereign state could survive only by means of close ties to Jordan and Israel. Such a tie is now the case under Israel's "open bridges" policy linking the West Bank to the East Bank of the Jordan, and further by the employment of hundreds of Arab workers in Israel proper. But if in the future Jordan or Israel should refuse to do business with the Palestinian state, its economy would collapse within weeks. A sovereign Palestinian state is not viable, but an independent Palestinian state, self-governing and protected from external enemies by defense alliances with both Israel and Jordan, is. It is in the interests of both Jordan and Israel to work toward the creation of such a state.

What is often overlooked by political analysts is the social make-up of West Bank Arab life. About all the people can now agree on is that, since fully 90 per cent of the Palestinians are Muslims, the future leader must be a Muslim. Beyond that, people's loyalties are tied most closely to their villages and towns. The society of the West Bank is tribal; rule stems from the wealth, power and influence of family clans, many of which have lived for 400 years in the same place. Hussein extended national government over clan rulers partly because he understood and respected them, and partly because if they did not always love him, they respected him as king. One of the gravest mistakes not admitted by some Israelis is the failure, since 1967, to encourage clan leaders to organize with a view toward putting forth national representatives—an action of political self-expression that might have pre-empted Arafat and the PLO. In any case, the coming of Arafat threatens the West Bank "notables" because they view him as an all-out revolutionary with no respect for family, tradition or order.

The growing class of professional people, drawn largely from the Arab Christian communities in or near Jerusalem, does not differ markedly from the older traditionalists. They, too, see the coming of Arafat as a threat to the order under which they have flourished. One doctor told me, in 1974, that if Arafat came to power he would immediately emigrate to Latin America, as have many Palestinians in recent years. The one professional class that seems to favor Arafat is the teachers—this out of a mixture of liberalism and nationalism.

It is clear that military occupation of the West Bank by Israeli soldiers is resented by all classes. On occasion the civil rights of individual Arabs have been violated through arrests and deportations whose purpose was not so much the defeat of sabotage and terror as the suppression of political activity. But in the present climate of fear, Israelis find it difficult to be sure which Arab nationalist may or may not be a murderer.

The task of security places an immense burden not only on Israel's physical resources but on its psychological ones as well. The strains are beginning to show. The daily fear, the diplomatic setbacks, the constant pressure to make territorial concessions which undermine Israeli security but salvage Arab pride—all this has produced a deep depresssion among Israelis. They definitely will not capitulate to an arrangement that would result in the control of the West Bank by Arafat—nor should they. Arafat, they argue, has identified himself with terrorism, and even if he does not commit the murders himself, or even personally order them, he would nonetheless tolerate murderers to work in a Palestinian state against Israel. The Arabs of the West Bank do not want Arafat for roughly the same human reasons.

This of course leaves the resettlement of the Palestinian refugees as the most important argument for Arafat's return. But the refugee youth, if not their parents, are schooled in hatred and revenge, and are feared by both Israelis and West Bankers—not to mention Jordan.

The refugee problem may never be solved socially or psychologically. But it could have been solved years ago if Arab leaders had wanted it solved. In 1974 an Iranian diplomat in Teheran told me that, in his opinion, if the late King Faisal of Saudi Arabia had taken seriously his own talk about Arab solidarity, he alone could easily have solved the economic problem of the refugees. He did not want to, the Iranian added, "for political reasons."

Until the Lebanese civil war, Arafat had center stage and any agreements proposed by Jordan and Israel vis-a-vis the West Bank could not have carried weight with the Arab states, or with the United States and the Soviet Union, each of which has had its own balancing act to perform with all parties concerned. All that could be hoped for was that Arafat, out of failure to realize his stated goal of "liberating Palestine," would be overthrown, most likely from within the ranks of the PLO, and that in the interim Jordan and Israel might propose something workable, having already worked out secretly on paper an agreement in conjunction with principal figures among the West Bank people.

In the summer and fall of 1976, however, conversations with West Bank Arabs and others in the Jerusalem area convinced me that the Lebanese war has damaged (perhaps irreparably) the authority of the Arafat-led PLO as a stable, effective organization for representing West Bank Palestinians in any future negotiations with Israel and Jordan over the question of an independent Palestinian state. The bloody havoc wrought a few kilometers across the border in the conflict between Lebanese Christians on one side and Lebanese Muslims aided and abetted by Palestinians on the other, confirmed for the West Bankers what they already knew: the PLO is fractionalized, divisive, unpredictable, and explosive. It is feared that what happened in Lebanon could just as easily happen on the West Bank if the PLO succeeded in "liberating Palestine" only to use it as a base for action against either Israel or Jordan or both. However, West Bankers are still not about to criticize the PLO openly for the same shrewdly self-serving reasons that characterize politics in this region. In the nine years since they came under Israeli military control, they fully appreciate how deeply they are caught in the crossfire between the radical politics of the PLO, the conservative monarchy of Hussein, and the deeply resented Israeli soldiers who each day patrol their streets and alleyways. The style of West Bank politics has not changed since 1967: Don't close out any option so that advantage can be gained in whatever happens in the future. This basically pragmatic, non-ideological style was amply illustrated in the April 1976 elections in which virtually all the candidates expressed some degree of sympathy or support for the PLO, while simultaneously disavowing the PLO's stated objective of destroying Israel's "Zionist state," and while carefully doing and saying nothing which would alienate Hussein and cut-off the financial support which Hussein has given and will continue to give West Bank officials and notables.

Just as there are Israelis who view as an error the prohibition of independent political organization and activity among West Bankers early in the occupation, so there are now Israelis who view as an error the granting of a free, democratic election—which surprised Arabs and Israelis alike by resulting in the defeat of a large number of the older, traditionalist clan leaders who cooperated with the Israelis in administering the West Bank, and elected in their place younger, more militant-sounding figures who say they are not about to obey any and every dictate of the Israeli government. A total of 148 new municipal councilmen were elected out of 191, a remarkable turnover of 77%. In 10 of 24 towns new mayors were elected who represent the new "National Bloc" party, and the fledgling Communist and Syrian Ba'thist parties. However, as noted, it would be a mistake to suppose that West Bank politics have been radicalized *a la* PLO, or that the traditional conservatism of this predominantly rural, feudally-minded society has ended. The election results signified a fresh expression of Arab self-will; they also signified a protest against the overly-long Israeli occupation, especially in light of the 1976 demonstrations.

The election results signalled support more for the PLO's objective of an independent Palestinian state, than for the PLO's leaders and organization. These results suggest increased self-identity amongst West Bank Arabs and more confidence and pride in running things themselves. One doubts that West Bankers are eager to see the return of the exiled Palestinian "heroes" who will certainly seek to take things over. Thus, when West Bankers now speak of the "PLO" they seem to be referring not so much to their brothers in Beirut, as to themselves. The term "PLO" has become a political-emotional slogan which they are using to advance their own internal interests.

The election results signalled a political and social generation gap which was highlighted in the nine years of Israeli occupation. The old patriarchal clan leaders, like eighty-two year old Sheik Ali al-Jaabari of Hebron, lost to younger men because of the many new voters which the Israelis created by changing the Jordanian election laws which restricted registered voters to the male head of a property owning family. With women, young people and workers voting, and with the incumbents doing little if anything to "politik" with these new groups the younger candidates received many more votes than they could have otherwise expected. It is doubtful that the old clan leaders were defeated because they were viewed as "collaborators" with the Israelis; and it is equally doubtful that the West Bankers expect the newly elected leaders to effectively oppose the Israeli government. It is significant that most of the new leaders belong to the same powerful family clans as the older traditionalists which have ruled West Bank towns for generations. If anything hurt the incumbents it was the heavy-handed efforts of the Israelis themselves to insure their re-election by speaking against some of the more militant candidates, and deporting two of them, Ahmad Natshi of Hebron and Abdul Azzia Haj Ahmed of el Bireh.

The election results also signalled a protest against the ever-rising inflation and taxes spiral of the Israeli economy which hits the West Bank Arabs particularly hard. While it is true that Israel employs hundreds of West Bankers in their construction projects, it is no less true that Arabs are chafing against a cost of living which they find increasingly difficult to meet. The newer candidates speak about opposing Israeli taxation, but it remains to be seen what they can do about it. Since the elections, the Israelis have imposed on the West Bank the value-added tax which they earlier applied to themselves, and this led to protest demonstrations and business shutdowns, but the tax continues.

The election results signalled a strong protest against the personal treatment of West Bank Arabs by the Israeli military authority, which has increasingly in the last two years relied on strong-arm tactics to break up demonstrations, search homes, arrest, detain or deport those they regard as in any way making trouble for them. The West Bankers care little about ideology, but the expressed militancy of the younger candidates unquestionably appealed to voters fed up with nine years of military occupation which, given the resistance to rock-throwing and tire-burning that resulted in beatings and killings, can no longer be regarded as peaceful. The violent demonstration which took place in January 1976 in the Old City, an Arab protest against the Israeli magistrate who legalized Jewish worship on the Temple Mount in the vicinity of Al Aksa Mosque, brought to the surface the gradual deterioration of relations between West Bank Arabs and the Israeli occupying authority.

The emergence of *Gush Emunim* within the past two years has tremendous significance for present and future West Bank-Israeli relations. This right-wing religio-political movement in Israel claims that the occupied West Bank and Gaza are an integral part of Israel's patrimony, the fulfillment of the bibilical prophecy of Israel's inheritance of the land (Ezekiel 36:8-11), hence the actual, historical beginning of the era of messianic redemption of the Jewish people. Its members have established communal settlements at Kiryat Arba in Hebron, at Kaddoum (near Nablus) and at Ofra (near Ramallah). It is difficult to gauge *Gush Emunim's* true strength and following; but I was impressed in the summer of 1976 with the number of politically moderate Israelis who expressed sympathy with the *Gush's* ideals and activities. If the *Gush* has not yet persuaded the Israeli populace into annexing the West Bank, it has unquestionably worked to harden attitudes against territorial concessions in any future agreement—and for this reason it has drawn the fire of the government which seeks to retain some flexibility on the question of the return of Arab lands.

The question of land here is in a sense deeper than politics; it is in essence a spiritual question—an expression of a people's sense of self-identity in the region as related to its history. Israelis like *Knesset* member Lova Eliav recognize that both Jews and Arabs have an equal claim to Palestine—and that it should therefore be divided between them. But it is precisely this politically pragmatic solution that *Gush* is pledged to fight against. Thus *Gush Emunim* works not only to intensify the already tensely complicated political picture in Israel; it threatens to place Israeli Jews permanently at swordspoint with West Bank Arabs, whose most vital interest is the integrity of their lands.

Out of fear of being driven off the land, West Bank and Israeli Arabs demonstrate with increasing violence, whereupon the military comes down on their heads and right-wing Israeli politicians seize the occasion to argue that if the West Bank were given back to Jordan, it would quickly pass into the hands of the PLO, which argument serves to justify Israeli expansion into the West Bank . . . and the cycle begins again. It is obvious that the only way to break the cycle is a comprehensive peace-and-territory agreement between Israel and the major Arab nations in the region, an agreement that would entail assigning Jordan the major responsibility for the future political stability of the West Bank. If Sadat's suggestion *(The New York Times,* January 4, 1977) of a future Jordan-West Bank link is sincere, it reflects his own post-Lebanese war disenchantment with Arafat's PLO as an effective political instrument. Whatever Sadat's ultimate intentions are, however, it is clear that only such a West Bank-Jordanian link would prove acceptable to Israel, assuming adequate security arrangements can be worked out.

This territorial issue may prove extremely difficult to resolve. Reviewing Israel's 1968 security settlements on the West Bank and in the other occupied territories (established according to the Allon Plan) which appear to give a clue to Israel's future territorial policy, and in the light of King Hussein's rejection of the plan as totally insufficient, "the territorial question," Terence Smith *(The New York Times,* May 12, 1976) concludes, "would be subject to negotiation, of course, but a possibility exists that Israel's vigorous settlement policy has already eliminated the prospects of a negotiated agreement on the West Bank."

It remains to be seen whether Smith's prognosis is prophetic or overly pessimistic.

The West Bank Within a Plan for Regional Development

By VIVIAN A. BULL

In evaluating the potential viability of the West Bank, the following serves as a working definition: an area will be regarded as economically viable if its economic characteristics permit it to experience sustained economic growth and rising welfare per capita.

In an analysis of the sectoral development of the West Bank, stress must be placed on sociopolitical and religious determinants as they affect development in the Territory. It is sometimes claimed that such constraints, which are difficult to assess and almost impossible to quantify, are rather rigid. Perhaps their strength has been overestimated, for it appears that man and religion are more adaptable than many had believed, at least within the frame of reference of this study.

But there is one very important constraint that must be taken into consideration explicitly when discussing the potential of the West Bank Territory—that is, the political relationship of the Territory with its neighbors. Though we do not know the precise political settlement that will eventuate in the Middle East, let us examine three major possible solutions and evaluate the potential economic prospects of the Territory within each of these. As a means of testing the viability concept, these possibilities will be considered: (1) the West Bank Territory in some close relationship or federation with Israel; (2) the Territory in federation with Jordan; (3) the Territory as a "Palestinian region." There are other alternatives, but for the sake of testing the viability definition, let us concentrate on these proposals.

In my book, various developmental conditions are discussed, with regard to labor force characteristics, entrepreneurship, capital and social overhead requirements, and so forth. It is also concluded that another prerequisite for development is an extensive market. There are several potential markets for the West Bank Territory, but the full development of these markets will depend upon political considerations—that is, on the Territory's integration with and access to other markets in the region. Let us then examine the realization opportunities for developmental conditions as they would exist under each of the proposals for political settlement.

Dr. Bull is Professor of Economics at Drew University. She has made frequent visits to the Middle East since 1957 for the purpose of research and archaeological excavations and has written articles on Middle East problems.

The above has been excerpted, with editorial changes by Dr. Bull, from Chapter 8 of *The West Bank–Is It Viable?* By Vivian A. Bull, Lexington, Massachusetts, Lexington Books, D.C. Heath and Company, 1975, and is reprinted by permission.

Federation with Israel

The quality and position of West Bank labor have been greatly improved since 1967, and some credit for these changes must go to the Israeli Government. Investments in vocational education and training are being undertaken though the programs are geared to the current needs of the market. Israel has had extensive experience in retraining and integrating labor into its economy, and it has directed similar efforts at improving the quality of the Territory's work force. Israel has instituted social welfare programs, and workers now have available an increasing number of medical and health benefit schemes as well as various social benefits similar to those offered in more developed areas. The Labor Exchanges have facilitated mobility of labor and have also offered protection and counseling to the employees. Though these Exchanges are now geared primarily to the requirements of the Israeli labor market, with some modifications they could also serve the Territory's local market.

Knowledge, skills, capacities, and attitudes are all undergoing change. There is beginning to be a shift in emphasis in the formal education system as it adjusts to new demands for a problem-solving and work-oriented educated class. When full-employment is achieved, future sources of labor will depend upon fuller employment of members of the Palestinian refugee population, and increased entrance of women into the work force. A major source of job opportunities for the population of the Territory is employment in Israel, and this source would be maintained in the federation. This may become an efficient and quantitatively important method through which Israeli entrepreneurship and capital can be combined with excess labor in the Territory. In the long run, it would of course be undesirable if the population of the West Bank would depend on employment opportunities in Israel. As seen during the current recession, these workers are the first to be laid off. Employment opportunities within the Territory must open up in tandem with industrial development. To these possibilities we turn next.

The Rand Study on the *Economic Structure and Development Prospects of the West Bank and the Gaza Strip*,[1] estimated the expected rate of endogenous industrial growth in the West Bank Territory to be almost 5 percent per year.[2] This estimate conforms to the expected growth of domestic demand for industrial products. The study emphasized that Israel could assist by relaxing some existing constraints on output and by increasing the potential demand for West Bank industrial products.

One must be cautioned not to overestimate the likely effectiveness of Israel's assistance, however, since Israel's own industry is lagging because of a severe scarcity of some of the prerequisites for growth. Israel can become a source for additional stimulation to the West Bank's industrial growth by purchasing industrial products, and some of this is being done through subcontracting arrangements between Israeli firms and local firms within the Territory. With the effect of this Israeli aid and trade, the basic rate of growth of industrial production might increase from 5 percent to 10 percent per annum.[3]

Israel has already attempted to provide the West Bank Territory with some of the necessary technical infrastructure. Extensive road building has been undertaken, and the roads are well maintained. There has been some expansion of the electrical systems to tie in areas not previously electrified as well as to improve service in existing systems. Some areas have been allowed to import generating equipment while other areas have been tied into the Israeli electrical grids. Further improvement of the infrastructure will depend upon the amount of available capital.

Israel has provided the Territory with an extensive market and has also allowed the Territory's agricultural sector to participate in Israel's export trade.

As the agricultural sectors have become integrated, the interdependence of the Territory and Israel has increased. Some products in which the Territory was formerly self-sufficient are now imported from Israel.

Although the Territory would gain much from federation with Israel, there are important constraints to consider. The Palestinians would probably find themselves severed from the rest of the Arab world. This would not only interfere with traditional family ties, but would also limit the available market for both agricultural and industrial commodities. This federation would also create a bi-national state, and bi-national states have never functioned successfully, nor would any party accept such a state.

Israel would be financially burdened to take on such a responsibility as well, for the various benefits that now are available only to those Arabs working in Israel would have to be extended to the total West Bank population.

In federation with Israel, the West Bank Territory would benefit from an integrated, but limited, agricultural sector and an integrated labor market. It is unlikely that much additional investment would be directed to the Territory, for Israel has great investment needs of her own to fulfill. Arabs who might be potential investors would be cut off from the Territory or might be unwilling to invest in the Territory. The West Bank Territory would lose contact with the Arab world, and this would include a diminution of the size of her potential markets. Israel would again be in a position in which she is cut off from trade with her immediate neighbors. Under these circumstances, it is unlikely that the Territory could achieve a rate of growth much beyond 6 percent per annum, which would not allow her to participate fully in the growth and welfare prevailing in the region.[4] While such a rate might be compatible with the economic aspects of the viability definition, the political aspects are not likely to be met.

Federation with Jordan

Another possibility for the West Bank would be for the Territory to rejoin Jordan in a new affiliation, as proposed by King Hussein. The return to Hashemite rule, even under a federation arrangement, is not appealing to the

West Bank residents nor to the Palestinians abroad. Although the Palestinians are more culturally advanced and better educated than the Jordanians, the Jordanians have become more politically cohesive as a result of their interaction with a "center," in this case, a kingdom. The Palestinians always have lacked a center and thus are fragmented politically. It is reasonable to assume that even in a federation the difficult relationships between the Jordanians and the Palestinians in the pre-1967 period would reassert themselves.

What of the economic conditions of development under such circumstances? Prior to 1967, little effort was directed at vocational training, except by international agencies. If the labor market in Israel were closed to the residents of the Territory, as it well might be in a new Jordanian federation, there would be an immediate dislocation of some 40,000 laborers with varying degrees of skills. Some of these could be absorbed within the local economy. In the past, Palestinians emigrated to various Arab countries to find employment, but they were usually the better-educated, better-trained workers, and professional people. There has been little Arabic foreign demand for the unskilled and semi-skilled workers, since the surrounding countries have an abundance of these workers in their own economies. There would thus probably be wide-spread unemployment in the Territory.

Jordan would have little to offer the West Bank Territory in either entre-preneurial or managerial skills. Traditionally the Palestinians have been the suppliers of these skills to the Jordanians, but as we have seen the Territory itself is now in need of trained people to provide these functions.

In the pre-1967 period, Jordan expended little effort towards industrial development of the West Bank Territory. Whatever capital was available was used in the East Bank areas, particularly to expand the industrial area around Amman. As long as political control lies in the hands of the East Bankers, it is reasonable to assume that the same situation would exist within a new federa-tion. It is probable, however, that the Territory would benefit from investment by the various oil-rich countries who are directing some of their new financial efforts toward development of the Arab world.

Since 1967, there have been structural changes in various sectors, particu-larly in the agricultural sector. In case of federation with Jordan, it would be necessary for the Territory to establish new trading relations with countries outside the Arab world to obtain maximum benefit from her crop specialization programs. It is questionable how well Jordan would be able to assist her in these efforts.

In the pre-1967 period, Arab tourists traveled to the West Bank as reli-gious pilgrims or for recreational purposes. This tourism provided an impor-tant source of revenue for the Territory. Much of this tourism, with the exception of family visits, was stopped after the Six Day War, but federation with Jordan would once again allow for the free flow of Arab tourism to the West Bank. This would provide employment as well as foreign exchange.

In comparison with the first solution and with present conditions, federation between the West Bank Territory and Jordan would restrict, rather than encourage, development of the Territory. It is unlikely that the Territory would benefit from capital inflows because of the traditional preference given to the development of the East Bank. Although the Territory would benefit from an expanded Arab market, it is impossible to conceive of a rate of growth in excess of 3 to 4 percent per annum under these conditions of a federation with Jordan. The Territory could not achieve economic viability.

A Palestinian Region

The final alternative is the possibility of a "Palestinian region" that could arise in cooperation with Israel, in cooperation with Jordan, or more probably through a settlement with both of them.[5] The region might be restricted to the present Territory, or it might include the Gaza Strip and other areas. The disposition of the Jerusalem problem will have to be an integral part of the solution. The regional solution need not involve statehood of an area but could specify a semi-independent status. This type of political arrangement is not new, but it would have to be adapted to specific requirements of the Territory and its neighbors. The regional solution could arise from the practical relations with Israel, based on economic necessities and strategic requirements, as a result of a political settlement between Jordan and Israel.

There are definite economic advantages to be gained within the region. A Palestinian region may not be the realization of full justice, but at least it might be a step forward toward "practical justice."[6]

All of the benefits to be gained from federation with either Israel or Jordan individually might be had with the development of a Palestinian region supported by both: an extensive, well-developed labor market, with the continuing development of vocational and training programs, and a labor exchange; availability of entrepreneurial and managerial skills; interest in and development of a technological infrastructure; and extensive potential markets for a great variety of agricultural and industrial products. It is also reasonable to assume that with some political stability in the area, there would be more interest in investing by Arabs as well as by international institutions. Oil-rich Arab countries might also be prepared to participate in joint ventures requiring capital and technology inflows. An important advantage to be gained from good relations with the Arab world involves access to markets for both agricultural and industrial output of the Territory, and the benefits from specialization that this entails. It also would tend to increase the stability of the market (and thus, the economy) by diversifying across sources of demand and reducing the dependence upon any one source. Finally, this solution would imply a political stability that is not as likely to exist in previously discussed scenarios.

The Rand Study, in evaluating the potential of the Territory, estimated that agricultural production will increase on the average during 1973-78 at a rate of about 6 percent.[7] A growth rate of 6 percent would not be as impressive as the rate of growth in the period immediately following the Six Day War, but that rate was a short-term achievement, as idle resources were re-employed and agricultural methods were upgraded in a once-and-for-all way. But a rate of 6 percent would be achieved only if free trade with all neighbors—that is, *all* regional markets—were maintained. If there were relative political stability and if efforts toward regional development were fostered, it is reasonable to assume that there would then be greater inflows of capital available for the development of water supplies. The growth rate would of course be higher with an increase in the water supply.

Likewise, within the context of regional development, it would be possible for the endogenous expected rate of industrial growth in the West Bank Territory to be greater than the originally estimated rate of 5 percent,[8] which conforms only to the expected growth of domestic demand for industrial products. A greater rate of growth (8 percent) was estimated when free trade with the neighboring Arab countries was considered possible.[9]

The labor force in the Territory has continued to grow and develop as a result of an integrated labor market between the Territory and Israel. If there were free mobility of labor within the region, the Arab states would also benefit, for they too would have access to a trained and skilled labor source. Perhaps, of greater importance, if capital inflow occurs and if broadly based development could proceed relatively securely and without interruption, there might be a return of the Palestinian diaspora—those Arabs of the entrepreneurial and professional classes who originally left the Territory for lack of job opportunities. This, of course, raises the problem of the absorption capacity of the Territory—that is, how many returnees can be integrated into the economy—but this must await further analysis.

There is yet another sector in which the West Bank Territory would benefit as a result of regional development: tourism. In the pre-1967 period, tourists were mainly European and American pilgrims and those from Arab countries coming for religious and recreational purposes. The lack of peaceful relations with Israel, difficulties in transportation between the West Bank and Israel, restriction on travel, and prohibition of the travel of Jews in Arab countries prevented the full development of tourism in the Territory for foreign tourists. The free flow of tourists between the West Bank, Israel, and neighboring Arab states would increase the attractiveness of all areas.

Since 1967, Israeli facilities for tourists, which are mostly superior to those of the West Bank, have attracted the majority of tourists. The West Bank has had some benefits from tourist purchases of souvenirs and food during excursions in the Territory; however, the main source of tourism for the West Bank could be tourists from Arab countries which could provide an important source of revenue for the Territory. Revenues from tourism would provide the Territory with foreign currencies that could be used for development purposes. These revenues would also help to improve the balance of payments.

The regional solution opens the possibility for more rapid agricultural development, enhancement of industrial growth, and the revival of tourism. This would permit a less extreme form of "unbalanced growth" and would improve the conditions for the economic viability of the region. The West Bank Territory should continue along a path of unbalanced growth. Any investment funds available should be directed towards improvement in the agricultural sector, particularly towards the development of water supplies. Improved methods of production and marketing will make possible a greater export trade with Europe and other non-Arab countries, as well as with regional trading partners. The industrial sector is so poorly developed and would need such massive inflows of capital and technology to accomplish development that rapid development is literally impossible.

Additional funds available should be directed toward the continuing improvement of the labor force. More vocational and skill training centers should be established and greater efforts exerted toward training and retraining all potential members of the work force. This will also involve the development of an improved attitude towards the work ethic.

Few countries have been able to become viable when dependent upon agriculture alone. The West Bank would have a comparative advantage, for with a regional development plan she could specialize in agriculture. Continued development of the labor force through training and skill development would provide another source of growth for the Territory, particularly if there were free mobility of labor within the region.

The development of a Palestinian region might also help to alleviate some sociopolitical problems. There are certain actions by the Israel government that have not aided the economic condition of the Territory, and these have to do with decisions regarding territorial claims. The annexation of East Jerusalem has removed from the Territory the natural capital and market center. But of even greater importance, the religious center and one of the three most important sites of Islam has been lost to the Arabs. If agreement cannot be reached on internationalization of that part of Jerusalem known as the Old City, then the control of the city by Israel will have long-term adverse political implications for cooperation between Arabs and Jews. Furthermore, the settlement of the land in the Jordan Valley and the establishment of paramilitary kibbutzim have deprived the Territory of the last potentially productive, but undeveloped agricultural areas available. These territorial claims, in addition to reducing the size of the Territory, are serious sources of tension and unrest.

Also, some settlement of the refugee problem will be necessary in order to achieve a degree of peace. The refugees must be incorporated into society for they not only can serve as a source of labor, but the existence of the camps constitutes a destabilizing center of discontent.

All of these problems might be somewhat alleviated under the terms of a

Palestinian region. If there were freedom of tourism, the religious center of Jerusalem would be available to all. Regional development must allow the area in the Jordan Valley to be developed for the benefit of the Arabs, particularly with reference to water sources. Any regional development plan would have to incorporate the refugees into the general population and labor force, and the resources available for improved housing, education, and training would be greater than under any plan of federation.

Only under regional development might adequate monetary arrangements be established. The regional integration outlined above, with the West Bank serving as a politically acceptable economic intermediary between Israel, Jordan, and other Arab states, might, in economic terms, indicate an optimum currency area. Yet the history of the different monetary systems of the various countries (with the Jordanian dinar being a convertible currency and the Israeli lire being inconvertible), together with the political constraints on a Palestinian region, will inevitably mean the continuance of two currencies in the region. The lire—as the currency received from exports to Israel, as wage payments and as the currency in use at higher levels of integration of government budgetary expenditures—will account for a growing share of total receipts by West Bank residents. The convertibility of the two currencies will be dependent upon the foreign exchange policies of Israel. On the other hand, a federation of the West Bank with either Jordan or Israel would, almost by definition, dictate a financial system dominated by and integrated with the system of the partner in the federation.

In summary, federation with Israel may work economically, but it will not work politically. Federation with Jordan may work politically, but it will not work economically. Neither solution meets our viability criterion. Of the three possible settlements, there is, in my opinion, only one that can be considered both economically and politically feasible: a Palestinian region. Assuming the Territory has economic and political relations with both Israel and the Arab world, one can estimate an overall growth of 8 percent per annum for the West Bank Territory, which rate is significantly greater than that estimated under either of the two federation proposals. It may still be several years before the West Bank Territory can experience sustained economic growth, but economic viability will be approached in a shorter period under conditions of regional development than under any other possible plan. Social and political stability will surely be enhanced if regional partners can cooperate in economic endeavors. A Palestinian region could serve as an intermediary between Israel and the Arab world.

The hope for the future of the Middle East lies in the establishment of peaceful regional development. A Palestinian region might be the first building block in such a scheme. Economic necessities might create political realities.

FOOTNOTES

1. Haim Ben Shahar, Eitan Berglas, Yair Mundlak and Ezra Sadan, *Economic Structure and Development Prospects of the West Bank and The Gaza Strip* (Santa Monica, California: The Rand Corporation, R839FF. September 1971).

2. *Ibid*, p. 102.

3. *Ibid*, p. 104.

4. The estimated growth rates are based on data for the period 1968-1972. More recent data and general economic conditions indicate that the estimates are probably too high. However, the relationships among the rates are probably consistent.

5. This idea has also been proposed by Y. Harkabi in *The Problems of the Palestinians* (Jerusalem: *Israel Academic Committee on the Middle East,* 1973).

6. *Ibid*, p. 9.

7. Ben Shahar, et. al., *op. cit.*, p. 95.

8. *Ibid.*, p. 102.

9. *Ibid.*

VIII

Jerusalem

Jerusalem: The Search for a Political Solution

By MERON BENVENISTI

Israel's policy on the political future of Jerusalem was determined in the middle of June 1967, when the Government decided upon the unification and the borders of the city. This policy was phrased in differing ways, but there was unanimous agreement that the unified city — at least within those borders fixed in June 1967 — would remain under the exclusive sovereignty of Israel, and that no compromise would be considered which would give political-sovereign status to any other state. This policy has remained unchanged over the years and has been accepted by all of Israel's leaders, including those who, in return for peace with the Arabs, were originally in favor of an almost total retreat from the 1967 cease-fire lines. When questioned as to how this uncompromising position conforms to Israel's willingness to conduct negotiations "without prior conditions," officials reply that Jerusalem's future will also be discussed in direct negotiations, and that there is no contradiction between the absence of prior conditions and "claims made by either side."

Despite this resolute position, Israel's leaders have had difficulties in deciding what to offer the Arabs, if and when negotiations do take place. One school of thought maintains that the Jerusalem problem is so difficult that it had best be left to the final stage of negotiations. A second school of thought maintains the opposite — in other words, precisely because the problem is so difficult, it is best to solve it at the beginning of negotiations, because otherwise no progress will be made on any issue. Contacts between King Hussein and Israeli ministers, as well as between high-ranking Israeli and Jordanian officials, have proved, as expected, that the Jerusalem problem is the main stumbling block to an agreement between the two countries. Contingency-planning groups of Israeli experts were asked, on a number of occasions, to suggest a plan whose objective, in the terms of reference established for one of the groups, was "to ensure the unity of the city under our sovereignty and, at the same time, to satisfy non-Israeli (especially Jordanian) interests." The room for maneuver, within this framework, was extremely limited. As a first

Dr. Benvenisti, from June 1967 to 1971, was the Jerusalem Municipality Administrator of the Old City and East Jerusalem. He has been a member of the Jerusalem City Council since 1969 and Deputy Mayor of Jerusalem since 1974. He is the author of several books, including *The Crusaders in the Holy Land*. Macmillan, 1970.

The above forms Chapter Twenty-Two (entitled "The Search for a Political Solution") of Dr. Benvenisti's book *Jerusalem: The Torn City*, University of Minnesota Press, 1976. Reprinted by permission.

step, an attempt was made to satisfy Muslim religious interests, in the hope
that this would also satisfy Arab political claims.

Israel was not prepared to recognize the national claims of the Arabs,
whether local or Jordanian, but was prepared to recognize the religious interests of the Muslims and Christians in the Holy City. In order to do so, Israel
proposed the autonomous administration of the Holy Places. During the extended dialogue with the Vatican, the Government suggested that extra-
territorial status be granted to the Christian Holy Places. A similar approach
was proposed for the Muslim Holy Places, and it was suggested that the
mosques on the Temple Mount be given extra-territorial status and be administered by Jordan, "which would represent the Muslim world." This
proposal was suggested in the summer of 1967 by the Minister of Defense,
Moshe Dayan. When the experts started to consider the details of the proposal, various ideas were raised, among them, allowing the Jordanians to hoist
their flag over the mosques on the Temple Mount, and to place a special guard
— like the Swiss Guard in the Vatican — on the Mount. In order to ensure
Muslims from Arab countries free access to the mosques, and in order that
King Faisal of Saudi Arabia "would not have to step on Israeli soil and
receive an Israeli visa on his way to the al-Aksa mosque," it was suggested
that a special road be paved which would be "under the sovereignty" or
"under the control" of the Jordanians. At a later date, it was suggested that,
instead of paving a road, a tunnel should be constructed. None of these
proposals was ever fully crystallized.

All the proposals referred to "the Temple Mount," but when experts
pointed out that the Muslims do not distinguish between the mosques on the
Temple Mount and the other sections of the Mount, opinions were divided as
to whether extra-territoriality should apply to the whole area or just to the two
mosques. There was no doubt that Israel could not give up her sovereignty on
the Temple Mount, but the exact meaning of "extra-territoriality" was not
clear. Nor was it clear whether Jordan would be given "symbolic" or "real"
authority over the road.

Proposals were also put forward in other spheres, such as allowing
Jerusalem's Arabs to keep Jordanian citizenship, and the establishment of
municipal autonomy for the Arabs of East Jerusalem. In the latter instance,
several possibilities were suggested. One was to divide the Old City into three
sub-units, according to ethnic groups, while another was to create "a single
municipal district with dual sovereignty."

This last proposal called for the creation of a new municipal district —
"Greater Jerusalem" — which would include united Jerusalem, under Israeli
sovereignty, as well as Bethlehem, Beit Jallah and a number of other villages
which are not under Israeli sovereignty since they were not annexed by Israel.
The administration of this district with dual sovereignty would be similar to
that of the Greater London Council, that is, there would be a division into

boroughs or sub-municipalities with an overall, federal or "roof"-municipality, each of which would have defined areas of responsibility and authority. The author of this proposal claimed that in this manner it would be possible to ensure a united Jerusalem under Israeli sovereignty while, at the same time, satisfying non-Israeli interests; through the non-annexed sub-municipalities or boroughs, the Arabs could influence the actions of the federal or roof-municipality. But nothing ever came of these proposals, either.

During the contacts with the Jordanians, these ideas concerning the Temple Mount, the road (or tunnel) and municipal autonomy were raised as general proposals, without going into details. They were never fully crystallized for two reasons: firstly, the contacts never developed into a meaningful dialogue; the distance between the two sides was too great for them to attain a common denominator, without which it made no sense to formulate practical sugges-tions. Secondly, the leaking of these ideas to the Israeli public led to a public outcry so strong that statesmen were forced to deny their existence, let alone the fact that they were seriously suggested. As early as July 1968, an official of the Ministry for Foreign Affairs complained that the suggestion to allow Jordan to hoist its flag over the mosques on the Temple Mount, which had been made earlier by the Minister of Defense without arousing any protest, now encountered strong opposition. He was convinced, "after checking the situation, that there is a hardening of the Israeli position," and in his opinion "a hard fight will have to be waged in order to persuade people on the flag issue."

In April 1971 the proposal to create a "single municipal district with dual sovereignty" was leaked. A campaign of villification, which included tele-phoned threats of murder, and slogans smeared on the walls of Jerusalem calling for his trial as a "traitor," was organized against the author, who formulated this suggestion in July 1968 as a member of one of the contingency-planning groups. In a *Knesset* debate, called as a result of the public controversy, the Foreign Minister, who was under attack not only from the opposition but also from members of his own party, was forced to deny that he had ever heard of the proposal before it was leaked, and to state that it had never been adopted by his Ministry.

King Hussein's position on Jerusalem has undergone several permutations. In the period immediately after the war, his enemies — mainly Palestinian radicals — blamed him for refusing to defend Jerusalem. "As soon as the first shots were fired, Jordanian troops retreated from Jerusalem," they insisted, and only after a great deal of effort did Hussein manage to free himself of these accusations. During this period, the King demanded that total control of East Jerusalem be returned to him, and he left no room for compromise. When it became apparent that this position would not advance his cause and did not elicit support even from the Western powers, he tried to retreat into the

past and proposed internationalization of the whole city, including West
Jerusalem. When he realized that this position, too, would not succeed, he
began to hint that he would be satisfied with sovereignty over only part of the
eastern sector. At the end of 1971 he suggested that "the Jewish Quarter of
the Old City be left under Israeli sovereignty" and that Israel be granted free
access to it. At the beginning of 1972 he made this change in his position
public and told an Israeli journalist that he claims "sovereignty over the city,
or part of it." Explaining this statement, Hussein made it clear that he was
"prepared to give up the Armenian Quarter, as well as the Jewish Quarter
with the Western Wall plaza." In other words, he was ready to accept a new
border which would pass through Jaffa Gate, along David Street and the
Street of the Chain, with the southern half of the Old City thus coming under
Israeli sovereignty. In his statements of 1972, he spoke in terms of "an open
city," of "a city of peace and cooperation" and of "a place where our two
peoples meet." These statements met with the fierce opposition of radical
Palestinians and several Arab leaders.

Despite the fact that Hussein's position on a territorial arrangement in
Jerusalem has changed and has become more flexible on the practical matter
of administering the city, no change has occurred with regard to his basic
claim, that sovereign status in the city be restored to him. In their political
thinking and actions, between 1948 and 1967, the Hashemites proved that for
them Jerusalem was not a focal point; but, at the same time, Hussein saw
himself as destined to protect the Arab character of Jerusalem, as the trustee
for all Muslims. In view of the refusal of all the Arabs and Muslims to
surrender the Arab character of Jerusalem, the Jordanian King cannot adopt a
position which will make him responsible for "the loss of the Holy City." At
the end of 1972, after he had declared that he was ready to relinquish parts of
the Old City, Hussein told an American reporter: "We cannot sign any
document in which we would give up sovereignty of the Holy City, simply
because future generations would cry out against such a signature." An Israeli
expert reached the conclusion that although Hussein

> can live with the military fact that Jerusalem has been conquered . . . he doesn't
> see himself being able, and perhaps not even entitled, to give legal approval to
> the existing situation, even though he is powerless to change it.

In his Jordanian-Palestinian Federation plan, which was published in
March 1972, Hussein designated Jerusalem as the capital of the Palestinian
region in the federal "United Arab Kingdom." To the Israeli proposals for
extra-territorial status for the Temple Mount, Hussein could not agree, both
because they did not return sovereignty in the city to him and because, in the
words of an Israeli expert,

> the Muslim religion . . . nurtured the idea of territorial expansion as a result of

religious expansion. From this stems the difficulty for Arabs to relate to the concept of 'extra-territorial rights,' as accepted in Christianity, or to the concept of 'free access.'

After the Yom Kippur War, King Hussein's statements hardened. In July 1974 he said:

There can, in fact, be no compromise. The return of Arab sovereignty over the Arab city of Jerusalem, over the Arab section of Jerusalem which was conquered in 1967, is a basic requirement. There can be no peace so long as the Israelis are in control of the whole of Jerusalem.

Yet, Israeli sources reported in 1975 that "Jordanian sources agreed to see Jerusalem as a united city, under two sovereignties and with minor border changes." And, in March 1976, Hussein stated:

In the framework of peace, if sovereignty over the Arab part of the city is returned, I see no reason why it should be a divided city; Jerusalem must be a city of all believers.

These fluctuating positions of King Hussein were, however, much less rigid than those of other Arabs. The position of the Saudi Arabians was particularly uncompromising and that of the leaders of the PLO, naturally, made no contribution towards a political settlement.

Reviewing the positions of the two sides since 1967, it becomes clear that the crucial question is one of sovereignty. Israel is not prepared to grant the Arabs sovereign status in Jerusalem and Jordan is not prepared to relinquish such sovereign status. Despite this, however, Israel and Jordan agree on the principle of safeguarding the physical unity of the city.

This blind alley, and the feeling that without a political solution to the problem of Jerusalem a solution to the Arab-Israel conflict is unattainable, has impelled governments, various bodies, and research institutions to formulate ideas for the future of the city.

The official position of the United States has not changed since it was stated by Secretary of State William P. Rogers on December 9, 1969:

. . . we believe Jerusalem should be a unified city within which there would no longer be restrictions on the movement of persons and goods. There should be open access to the unified city for persons of all faiths and nationalities. Arrangements for the administration of the unified city should take into account the interests of all its inhabitants and of the Jewish, Islamic and Christian communities. And there should be roles for both Israel and Jordan in the civic, economic and religious life of the city.

The United States has never officially clarified which practical arrangements are to be made, in its opinion, in order to fulfill these principles. At the end of 1974 it was reported that the Americans support "a unified city with two separate administrations and the transfer of the Jewish Quarter to Israeli rule.'' In the spring of 1976, the U.S. representative to the United Nations, William Scranton, stated the American position in the following manner:

> That part of Jerusalem that came under the control of Israel in the June War, like other areas occupied by Israel, is occupied territory and hence subject to the provisions of international law governing the rights and obligations of an occupying power. Ambassador Goldberg said, in 1968, to this Council: 'The United States does not accept or recognize unilateral actions by any states in the area as altering the status of Jerusalem.' I emphasize, as did Mr. Goldberg, that, as far as the United States is concerned, such unilateral measures, including expropriations of land or other administrative action taken by the Government of Israel, cannot be considered other than interim and provisional and cannot affect the present international status, nor prejudge the final and permanent status of Jerusalem. The United States' position could not be clearer. Since 1967 we have restated here, in other forums, and to the Government of Israel, that the future of Jerusalem will be determined only through the instruments and processes of negotiations, agreement and accommodation. Unilateral attempts to predetermine that future have no standing.

This formulation, more critical than any which preceded it as far as Israel's actions were concerned, was met with a storm of anger by Israeli Jerusalem.

The American State Department has encouraged a number of groups, including the Brookings Institution in Washington, and the Aspen Institute, to study the Jerusalem problem and suggest solutions. And, in fact, suggestions for a solution have streamed in from various sources. Not many of those making the suggestions were aware of the fact that between the years 1917-1967 no less than three dozen proposals for the solution of the Jerusalem problem had been advanced. A few of these earlier proposals are outlined below.

The "Jerusalem Problem," as a subject demanding a political solution, secured in international agreements, was created in 1917 when the city was conquered by the British, after hundreds of years of Turkish rule.

The European powers, including the Vatican, decided to settle the various contradictory Christian claims to control of the Holy Places, to ensure orderly administration of these sites, as well as of the city in which they existed, and to ensure free access to them. More than a century earlier these claims had become international problems, rather than purely religious ones. The European powers became involved in the trivial conflicts between the various Christian communities because they saw these conflicts as a means towards expanding their political influence, both within their own countries and on the international plane.

In the period before the British conquest, and immediately after it, the European powers decided to solve the problem by placing Jerusalem under international rule. The Sykes-Picot Agreement of 1916 stated that, following the partition of the Ottoman Empire, the area between the Sea of Galilee in the north and Beersheba in the south would come under "an international administration, the structure of which will be decided upon in the future." However, the agreement was never implemented. National interests persuaded the signatories to agree to British rule over Palestine and Jerusalem, subject to a treaty (Mandate) between Great Britain and the League of Nations.

In the wake of this solution to the problem of sovereignty, attempts were made to solve the problem of the Holy Places within the framework of British sovereignty, by an international treaty which would, to a certain extent, limit this sovereignty. None of the proposals, however, was acceptable, and, at the end of 1924, it was decided that the British Administration would also be responsible for the supervision of the Holy Places. In this manner, the Jerusalem Problem was removed from the sphere of international relations, for the time being, and the city became the capital of Mandatory Palestine and the seat of its government.

But, of course, the Jerusalem Problem was not so easily solved. It now became an inter-ethnic bone of contention. The Jewish and Arab residents of the city began a long and on-going struggle for control of the Municipality. The Arabs, relying on precedent, claimed the mayorship and a decisive voice in the Municipality. They argued that, ever since the establishment of a municipality in Jerusalem in 1877, the mayor had always been an Arab, and that the Jewish residents in Jerusalem had to accept this state of affairs, based on precedent and tradition, and agree to the appointment of an Arab mayor. The Jews, on the other hand, argued that they constituted a majority in the city and claimed the right of a majority to choose its own mayor, in democratic elections. The British attempted to reach a compromise, the practical significance of which was a continuation of the *status quo,* in other words, preferred status for the Arabs. During the 1930s and '40s, Jerusalem always had an Arab mayor, a Jewish deputy mayor with special status, and a Christian deputy mayor. The membership of the City Council was fixed at six Jews, four Muslims and two Christians. In order to reach this balance, prior to the municipal elections the British manipulated the geographical constituencies, as well as the ethnic voting register. They also excluded Jewish neighborhoods from the municipal borders, or included them only together with areas populated by Arabs. The Jewish majority was dissatisfied with the privileged position of the Arabs and as early as 1932, Haim Arlosoroff, Director of the Political Department of the Jewish Agency, suggested that Jerusalem be split into two boroughs. Under his proposal the two Borough Councils would be subordinate to the Council of the united Municipality. The British immediately rejected this suggestion.

The Jewish-Arab conflct over control of the Municipality of Jerusalem was, however, only one part of the overall conflict between the two ethnic groups for hegemony in Palestine. Thus, when the Arab revolt broke out, in 1936, the local problem was absorbed by the general one.

In 1937, the Jerusalem Problem again became an issue which could only be solved on the international plane. The Palestine Royal Commission, appointed by the British and headed by Lord Peel, proposed the partition of Palestine and a permanent British Mandate for Jerusalem with extensive borders and a corridor to the Mediterranean Sea. As for the municipal government, Peel suggested leaving the situation as it was, with elections organized by geographical districts and an ethnic register.

The following year, the Palestine Partition Commission, headed by Sir John Woodhead, was appointed to recommend details of partition. The Jews suggested to the Commission (at the end of 1938) that Jerusalem be divided in two. Part of Jerusalem (the New City and Mount Scopus) would be attached to the Jewish State, and the Old City and the Arab quarters would be within the area of the British Mandate of Jerusalem. The city was to be divided into two boroughs, with integrated services and a single customs zone. The British rejected this proposal outright. In their opinion, the city was an integral unit and it was impossible to divide it. Furthermore, they said that administrative partition demanded close cooperation and good will. It was precisely because of the lack of good will between the Jews and the Arabs that the problem had arisen in the first place; thus, there was no question of dividing the city, given the existing tension between the two groups.

As a result of the total disagreement between Jews and Arabs on every proposal — which was clearly expressed by the failure of the St. James' Conference (winter 1939) — the British published the MacDonald White Paper, in May 1939, which declared the partition proposals "impracticable" and announced their intention of establishing an independent Palestinian state, with an Arab majority, within ten years. The capital of this state was, of course, to be Jerusalem, with no special status, apart from an undertaking that free access be ensured to the Holy Places. The White Paper was not approved by the League of Nations and met with bitter opposition from the Jews, but meanwhile, the Second World War broke out and the solution of the Palestine problem, including that of Jerusalem, was postponed.

However, the inter-ethnic conflict for control of the municipality continued. This conflict reached a climax in August 1944 when the Arab mayor died and the British appointed his Jewish Deputy, Daniel Auster, as his successor. The Arabs protested and the British suggested a rotation every two years, the first mayor being Jewish and the third, British (appointed). The Arabs boycotted the meetings of the City Council and the British dissolved it, appointing in its stead a Municipal Commission, composed of six British officials.

The British also appointed the Chief Justice of Palestine, Sir William Fitzgerald, "to enquire into and report on the local administration of Jerusalem and to make recommendations thereto." Fitzgerald's report was published in August 1945. He did not concern himself at all with the question of sovereignty, which was, of course, to remain British. He viewed Jerusalem not as a municipality but as a county, similar to London. The upper body which would administer the whole area, according to his proposal, would be an Adminstrative Council. Within the area managed by the Administrative Council would be two boroughs, one Jewish and one Arab, and an area that would be administered directly by the Council. Each borough would have a council and a mayor. The boroughs would have the authority to impose taxes and to fulfill the duties imposed on a municipality by the Municipal Ordinance. City planning would be delegated to each borough, but only after an outline scheme had been approved by the Administrative Council. Each borough would send four representatives to the Council, whose chairman would be appointed by the British High Commissioner. In addition, two representatives would be appointed who were neither Jews nor Arabs. The main job of the Administrative Council would be to co-ordinate the activities of the two boroughs, with a minimum of interference in their internal affairs. The Administrative Council would also deal with the Holy Places, under the direct responsibility of the High Commissioner.

When the Fitzgerald Report was submitted, after the end of the Second World War, the problem of municipal rule in Jerusalem had again been absorbed by the general conflict.

At the beginning of 1946, the Morrison-Grady Committee suggested that Palestine be transformed into a cantonal state consisting of an autonomous Jewish province, an autonomous Arab province, and two areas under the direct control of the central government, with a High Commissioner. One of these areas was to be the Jerusalem enclave and Bethlehem. The municipal administration proposal for Jerusalem was a regular city council, to which would be added several members appointed by the High Commissioner. Both the Jews and the Arabs, as well as the United States, rejected the plan.

The rejection of this last attempt to solve the Jerusalem Problem was among the factors which prompted the British Government to refer the entire problem of Palestine to the General Assembly of the United Nations. The United Nations Special Committee on Palestine (UNSCOP), presented its majority and minority reports in May 1947 . . .

Sixty years after it was first raised as an international political problem, and after thirty-six plans for its solution, the Jerusalem Problem still awaits a settlement. It is not enough that the elusive solution be a brilliant intellectual exercise, full of good will and objectivity. Jerusalem has experienced many of these. The real test of a solution is its accord with the changing reality and its practicability, but most important is the readiness of the two parties to compromise and cooperate. Without a readiness to compromise, no plan, however balanced and inspired, will succeed.

INTERNATIONAL VIEWS ON JORDAN'S OCCUPATION OF THE OLD CITY

. . . Jordan's occupation of the Old City — and indeed of the whole of the area west of the Jordan river — entirely lacked legal justification; and being defective in this way would not form any basis for Jordan validly to fill the sovereignty vacuum in the Old City. Jordan's prolonged *de facto* occupation of the Old City was protected exclusively by the Armistice Agreement which prohibited Israel from initiating action to displace Jordan; and Jordan's occupation could last no longer than the protection thus afforded. This bulwark was abandoned when Jordan destroyed the Armistice Agreement by its attack on Israel Jerusalem on 5th June 1967.

Elihu Lauterpacht, *Jerusalem and the
Holy Places,* 1968, p. 47.

· · ·

[T]he position of the State of Jordan on the West Bank and in East Jerusalem itself, insofar as it had a legal basis in May 1967, rested on the fact that the State of Transjordan had overrun this territory during the 1948 hostilities against Israel. It was a belligerent occupant there.

Julius Stone, *The Middle East Under
Cease-Fire,* 1967, p. 12.

IX

Jordan: A Political Directory

King 'Abdallah ibn Hussein al-Hashemi

King 'Abdallah was born in Mecca, the second son of Sharif Hussein of Mecca, scion of the Prophet Muhammad's Hashemite clan of the Quraish tribe. In 1891 he accompanied his father to Istanbul (where Hussein lived under Ottoman supervision) and was educated there. He became active in Arab literary circles in Istanbul and associated with the semi-secret Arab nationalist organizations. Hussein returned to Mecca after the Young Turks revolution of 1908, becoming its Emir, and 'Abdallah accompanied him but returned to Istanbul in 1912 as a Deputy for Mecca in the Ottoman parliament. He was later appointed Deputy-President of the House. Returning to Mecca via Cairo in 1914, he contacted the British Resident in that city with a view to receiving aid for a rebellion against the Ottoman Empire, and later participated actively in the Arab Revolt of June 1916, stirred up by his father against the Ottoman rulers following renewed contact with the British. 'Abdallah became his father's Foreign Minister and political adviser when the Emir assumed the title of King of Hejaz.

'Abdallah's younger brother, Feisal, was proclaimed King of Syria. A group of Iraqi nationalists, meeting in Damascus, offered the crown of Iraq to 'Abdallah in March 1920. The British, however, did not favor this proposal. In July 1920 the French, who had obtained the mandate over Syria, expelled Feisal from Damascus. 'Abdallah assembled troops with a view to marching through Transjordan to Damascus to avenge his brother and restore Hashemite rule in Syria. He entered Amman in March 1921, but was deflected from his purpose by the British Colonial Secretary's offer of Transjordan.

'Abdallah's dream of a "Greater Syria" (of Transjordan, Palestine, Syria and Lebanon) under his crown and a "Fertile Crescent" federation of this Greater Syria and Iraq made him many enemies, although the British to some extent supported this aspiration, as did some elements in Syria, Iraq and Palestine. He was violently opposed by the French, the Syrian nationalists and Hajj Amin al-Husseini, the Grand Mufti of Jerusalem and the other Arab rulers.

'Abdallah remained loyal to Britain during World War II. In 1941 he sent the Jordanian Army—the Arab Legion—to assist in quelling a rebellion in Iraq, which branded him as a British puppet in the Arab world. He also tried to maintain good relations with the leaders of the Palestinian Jewish community and favored Jewish settlements in Transjordan—a plan that never materialized, mainly because of British opposition.

'Abdallah was ready to grant the Palestinian Jews autonomy, if a vaguely defined one, and even some degree of independence, but had little sympathy for the creation of an independent Jewish state. Named Commander-in-Chief of the Arab armies which invaded Palestine upon the declaration of the State of

Israel in May 1948, 'Abdallah knew this would be a purely nominal title—he had little respect for, and less confidence in, the Arab leaders.

Following his Arab Legion commander's plan in the fighting, his army took over most of the area allotted by the 1947 Partition Resolution to a projected Arab State, avoiding attacking Israel in the area allotted to her by the Resolution—and opening himself to charges of collusion with the Israelis. Most of the fighting took place in Jerusalem and its vicinity, an area not allotted by the U.N. either to the Jewish or to the Arab State.

Secret negotiations conducted directly with the King facilitated settlement of the Israel-Jordan armistice agreement in April 1949. 'Abdallah maintained contact with Israel and in early 1950 negotiated a non-aggression pact. A final draft was ready for initialling in February-March, but 'Abdallah broke off negotiations following virulent opposition by the Arab states, who had learnt of them. Transjordan was again threatened with expulsion from the Arab League upon 'Abdallah's annexation of "Arab Palestine"—i.e., the West Bank.

He was assassinated in the al-Aksa Mosque in Jerusalem on July 20, 1951 by a Palestinian follower of the Grand Mufti of Jerusalem.

King 'Abdallah-Israel Contacts

The United Nations voted for the partition of Palestine into an Arab and a Jewish state in November 1947. It was clear, in the early months of that year, that the Arab states would not accept this partition resolution when it came and that they would take up arms against any attempt to create the Jewish state. The British-led Arab Legion was entrenched at Latrun, effectively cutting off the road between Tel Aviv and Jerusalem. Arab irregulars were waging continuous battles with the *Haganah* (the Palestinian Jews' underground army) and Palestinian Arabs had begun to abandon their villages and homes by the thousands, under the persuasion, it appeared later, of the Arab Higher Committee. As the fighting escalated, the leaders of the Palestinian Jews decided to make an effort to approach King 'Abdallah of Jordan, who had had friendly dealings with them on previous occasions and who had publicly advocated a settlement by peaceful means. The Palestinian Jews and 'Abdallah shared a common aversion for the Grand Mufti of Jerusalem, chief instigator of the Palestinian Arabs.

The King agreed to meet with Mrs. Golda Meir, in her capacity as head of the Political Department of the Jewish Agency—the Palestinian Jews' unofficial government. The first meeting took place in early November 1947, shortly before the U.N. vote. The King told Mrs. Meir that he would not join in any attack on the Jewish community and that if the U.N. should vote on partition he would annex the proposed Arab state to his kingdom. He promised friendship and gave assurances that he would accept partition. He asked what the attitude of the Palestinian Jews would be to the inclusion of the projected Jewish state in his kingdom (the response was negative) and expressed the hope that the Arab state to be created would not be so small that it would embarrass him.

Palestinian Jewish liaison with King 'Abdallah continued. Discussion via third parties on the status of Jerusalem found both sides opposed to its projected internationalization under the U.N. partition resolution. The King asked whether the Palestinian Jews were prepared to cede to him a part of the territory assigned to the Jewish state by the partition resolution—a concession that was refused. The Jewish leadership informed him that the boundaries established by partition would be valid only if peace were established.

By May 1948 'Abdallah found himself forced to join the Arab League in their commitment to war. Mrs. Meir requested a second meeting, which took place in Amman. 'Abdallah informed Mrs. Meir that he was not in control of his own destiny. He said he believed that the coming war (the State of Israel was to be proclaimed on May 14 and the meeting took place on May 10) could be averted and asked why the Jews could not postpone creation of their state. If they dropped their demand for immigration and were patient he would take over the whole of Palestine and give the Palestinian Jews representation in his parliament. He said that the *Deir Yassin* incident (when the Jewish terrorist *Irgun Tzvai Leumi* and Stern gang had attacked the Arab village of that name and massacred its inhabitants, including women and children, April 9, 1949) had greatly inflamed Arab feelings. Mrs. Meir reiterated the Palestinian Jewish community's determination to establish a state.

Renewed meetings between Israeli representatives and the King followed the end of the war of 1948. A meeting was arranged with 'Abdallah at the King's winter palace at Shuneh. The King had consented to release the Israeli Prisoners-of-War a month before the Armistice Talks began at Rhodes.

A series of intensive and prolonged meetings were held between November 1949 and March 1950. The main discussion revolved about an exchange of territory, especially in the Jerusalem area. There was to be an Israeli undertaking not to express opposition to Jordan's annexation of the West Bank and Jordan was to be allowed access to Gaza and the Mediterranean through a corridor in Israeli territory. The Israeli representatives were assured that Britain knew of the negotiations, and the King made no secret of them, introducing the Israelis to members of his Cabinet and other leading Jordanian personalities.

By December 17, 1949, the negotiations had reached the stage of the drafting of a peace treaty—which it was agreed, at 'Abdallah's urging, would be called a "paper" on "Principles of a Territorial Arrangement (Final)." The treaty was actually initialled, but 'Abdallah could not give it final ratification. Sir Alec Kirkbride, Britain's Minister to Jordan, would not agree that Jordan enter into a final arrangement with Israel while the other Arab states, mainly Egypt, had not yet done so. The King therefore requested that the "paper" be considered cancelled.

Subsequent meetings in 1950 afforded no results. Jordan signed the Armistice Agreement in 1949, but never complied with Article VIII of this Agreement whereby Israeli Jews and Arabs were to have free access to the Holy Places under Jordanian control.

The Arab Revolt

Also called "The Revolt in the Desert," the name was given to the uprising of Hussein ibn 'Ali, Sharif of Mecca and his sons, 'Ali, 'Abdallah and Feisal of the Hashemite family against the Ottoman Empire during World War I. The revolt followed an exchange of letters between Hussein and Sir Henry McMahon, in which Britain promised support for Arab independence after the war. The revolt was financed by a British subsidy of £200,000 per month and also arms, provisions and direct artillery support. Britain also sent Hussein guerrilla experts, among them T.E. Lawrence.

Starting with an army of Bedouin of about 10,000 and an additional 40,000 desert fighters loosely attached to it on occasion, the army's final strength was an estimated 70,000 men. It was joined by a small number of Syrian and Iraqi officers defecting from the Ottoman Army.

The rebels conquered Mecca (with British artillery support) and Aqaba (with British naval support). Medina remained in Ottoman hands, but was cut off and surrounded. The rebels sabotaged the Hejaz Railway.

In 1917-18 the army formed the right wing of Allenby's armies advancing into Palestine and Syria. It was allowed to enter Damascus (led by Feisal) and to raise the Arab flag there. The Hashemite heads of the Revolt became the chief spokesmen for the Arab cause at the peace conference and the settlement following the dismemberment of the Ottoman Empire.

Nationalists have called the Arab Revolt the "golden age of Arab nationalism." Several of its spokesmen became leaders in the Arab states in the 1920s and 1930s. T.E. Lawrence, in his books, brought it to general Western attention.

Winston Churchill and the Creation of Transjordan

The various divisions of Palestine throughout the centuries had generally linked the coastal plain with the east bank of the Jordan River in one way or another. The Palestinian Jewish community and the Zionist Organization which represented it had, as early as 1917, consistently reminded the British Government of the "vital necessity" of including the country east of Jordan in Palestinian territory when Britain's mandate over Palestine came into effect. David Ben Gurion and Yitzchak Ben Zvi, in their book *Eretz Yisrael* published in 1917, had pointed out that the eastern border of Palestine included the two former Ottoman *sanjaks* of Hauran and Kerak and also part of the *sanjak* of Damascus. In their statements before the peace conference on February 3, 1919, the Zionist representatives had defined the eastern border of Palestine as a line "close to and west of the Hejaz Railway terminating in the Gulf of Aqaba," while the first Article of the draft of the Feisal-Weizmann agreement (of January 3, 1919) had recognized the need to fix the boundary of "Palestine East of the River Jordan." Chaim Weizmann, as head of the Jewish Agency for Palestine, stressed in his correspondence with Sir Henry Wilson that it was "absolutely essential" for Palestine's economic development to have the territories east of the Jordan included in its borders, and this view was supported by Lord Milner. Lord Balfour, author of the Balfour Declaration, urged that Palestine's eastern frontier be drawn so as to give the widest scope to the agricultural development of the area across the Jordan, although this had to be consistent with leaving the Hejaz Railway in Arab possession.

The British government, after World War I, was torn between its interests in the Middle East and a public at home clamoring for demobilization and a decrease in military expenditures abroad. In Palestine, Sir Herbert Samuel, the British High Commissioner, reported that forces were not needed in large numbers and could be supported by local revenues, although the situation across the river was chaotic and would require the deployment of some troops. The new Colonial Secretary, Winston Churchill, was much more concerned about events in Mesopotamia and Syria. The French had occupied Syria and evicted King Feisal ('Abdallah's brother) who had marched into Syria with the victorious British forces and become King of Syria. The Arab nationalists were resentful and the situation in Iraq difficult. In the Hejaz, the Sharif Hussein, whom the British had promised an Arab kingdom, had permitted his second son, 'Abdallah, to start a march toward Syria with a view to regaining the throne for the Hashemites. Churchill saw all these events as extremely dangerous to British interests and told the Cabinet that they might involve serious military embarrassments and heavy expenditures.

The status of Transjordan remained unsettled into 1920. Samuel reported that Syrian nationalists expelled by the French had gathered in Transjordan and were creating serious problems. He called for an effective administration in the area to quell the general lawlessness. The Emir 'Abdallah, furthermore, had moved to Ma'an, and this was, he felt, a threat to British prestige as well as British authority.

Churchill called a conference in Cairo of all the political officers in the area, to settle the problem of Palestine and to discuss the future of Mesopotamia. The conference was scheduled for March 1921. As preparations were under way, Samuel informed Churchill that Arab raiders had already penetrated into Syrian territory, and that 'Abdallah had marched to Amman with an estimated force of 8,000 men.

The reaction was sharp. Samuel advised sending troops to Transjordan immediately. Churchill decided to confront 'Abdallah personally at a meeting in Jerusalem.

The Churchill-'Abdallah talks resulted in the entrusting to 'Abdallah of control over Transjordan for a six-month period. In this way Churchill felt he might yet succeed in avoiding direct military intervention in Transjordan— which would be expensive—while 'Abdallah would not lose face by failing to challenge the French. The agreement provided for the permanent constitution of Transjordan as an Arab province within Palestine under the ultimate supervision of the British High Commissioner for Palestine. Churchill instructed Samuel to make an immediate advance of £5,000 to 'Abdallah for his personal expenses. A chief political officer was appointed to advise 'Abdallah during the interim administration.

The Cairo Conference thus served to seal a situation initiated by Churchill; it introduced the idea of a separate Transjordanian entity.

'Abdallah's administration of Transjordan was sharply criticized by Samuel and the local British officials. The French demanded clarification of the new situation. In a letter to General Gouraud on March 31, 1921, Churchill explained: "I have made an arrangement with 'Abdallah of an informal and temporary character whereby he is to use his whole influence to prevent any disturbances in the French zone arising out of Trans Jordania." To the Cabinet, however, he hinted that 'Abdallah might remain into 1922. He informed Samuel that he was dissatisfied with 'Abdallah's administration and that he would invite him to London, where he would tell him to go back to Mecca. In his speech before the House of Commons, however, he praised 'Abdallah and implied that the initiative resided with 'Abdallah as to whether he wanted to stay in Transjordan or leave for Mecca. If he left, Churchill declared, Britain would find a suitable replacement.

'Abdallah, who had made overtures to the French, still believed that he had a chance to become King of Syria. He disliked "the wilderness" that was Transjordan, but if he gave it up, he told the British, he would lose everything. Churchill himself remained unconvinced of 'Abdallah's unsuitability, and T.E. Lawrence recommended that his administration continue but without any official announcement. Lawrence advised cutting 'Abdallah's subsidy by one half or more and also the publication of a statement in London that the application of the Zionist provisions of the Palestine mandate was not contemplated for Transjordan. Churchill, busy elsewhere, agreed.

Legal officers in the Colonial and Foreign Offices, given the task of drawing up the provisions for the future British mandates in the Middle East, deemed it advisable to insert in advance general clauses giving the future mandatory "certain discretionary powers" in applying the Palestine and Mesopotamia mandates to Transjordan and Kurdistan. It was finally agreed to introduce Article 25 into the Palestine mandate, to entitle Britain "to postpone or withhold" application of certain unsuitable provisions and to provide for a local administration for Transjordan. In the Colonial Office, Article 25 was understood to mean that Britain could act provisionally on the assumption that Transjordan was to be a province of Palestine, though an Arab one. Others, like Colonel Meinertzhagen, saw the Article as severing Transjordan from Palestine—a view shared by Sir Alec Kirkbride. 'Abdallah also appears to have shared this view. He had created the government of Transjordan, he wrote later, "by having it separated from the Balfour Declaration."

Sir John Bagot Glubb (Glubb Pasha)

Born in 1897, Glubb served as a British army officer during World War I in France and Iraq and in the Iraqi civil service, 1926-30. Transferred to the Arab Legion in Transjordan, he became its Second-in-Command and then Commander-in-Chief, 1938-56, succeeding Lieutenant-Colonel F.G. Peake, with the rank of Lieutenant-General. He served under contract but the nationalists saw him as a symbol of British imperialist domination in Jordan and blamed him for the defeat of the Arab Legion in the 1948 war, and particularly for the loss of Lydda and Ramleh (both in Israel), although the Legion had won control of the Old City and the Arab Quarter of Jerusalem. Hussein, aged 20, dismissed him without warning. He blamed Glubb for reluctance to promote Arab officers quickly to top posts in the Legion and for his strategy, which Hussein said he opposed. He said also that he felt that Glubb's Defense Plan was inadequate and accused Glubb of interfering in Jordanian politics (which Glubb has strongly denied). Hussein also accused him of encouraging Jordanian leaders to turn to him or to the British embassy before making any decision. Glubb was also accused by the British magazine *Picture Post* of behaving like the "uncrowned king of Jordan."

Glubb persisted in his support of Hussein and persuaded Britain's prime minister Eden to remain calm. His abrupt dismissal did not cause a break in British-Jordanian relations; Britain continued the Jordanian subsidy.

Glubb has published several books on the Arab Legion, Arab history and the Arab-Israel conflict. He writes with great affection for the Arabs—and particularly for the Bedouin—although this sentiment is not always free of a touch of irony. King 'Abdallah drew his greatest admiration and the Jewish State his greatest hostility.

The Hashemite Dynasty

In Muslim tradition, the Banu Hashem are the family or clan of the Quraish tribe from whom the Prophet Muhammad is descended. "Hashemite" has come to refer to the family of the Sharifs of Mecca. The Hashemites trace their descent from the Prophet through his daughter Fatima and his son-in-law 'Ali and their son al-Hassan.

The Sharif Hussein (an honorary title in the Hashemite family, handed down from father to son) was appointed Emir of Mecca in 1908. In 1916, following an exchange of letters and messages with Sir Henry McMahon, the British High Commissioner in Egypt promising aid and support for Arab independence, he proclaimed the Arab Revolt against the Ottomans, and declared himself King of Hejaz. He attempted to proclaim himself Caliph in 1924, but was forced to abdicate in order to save the throne for his dynasty, and died in exile. His oldest son, 'Ali, was on the throne for less than a year. He was driven out by Ibn Saud of the ruling family of an area of the Nejd who adopted the extremist Muslim *Wahhabi* creed and extended his power to Mecca and Medina, making it part of the modern country of Saudi Arabia.

'Ali died in exile in Baghdad. His brother Feisal (Hussein's third son) became King of Syria, ruling in Damascus under British auspices from 1919-1920, when he was expelled by the French. Also under British auspices he became King of Iraq. His grandson, Feisal II, ruled Iraq until the coup of July 1958 when he was assassinated. The Baghdad branch of the Hashemite dynasty thus became extinct.

Hussein's second son, 'Abdallah, was made Emir of Transjordan by Britain in 1921 and took the title of King in 1946. He became King of the Hashemite Kingdom of Jordan in 1949, changing the name of the country upon his annexation of the West Bank. 'Abdallah was assassinated in 1951.

The present King of Jordan, Hussein, is 'Abdallah's grandson and the only reigning Hashemite. Many members of the Hashemite family hold high positions in Jordan.

King Hussein ibn Talal

King Hussein of Jordan was born in Amman in 1935 and educated at Victoria College in Alexandria, Egypt and later at Harrow and the Sandhurst Military Academy in Britain. He succeeded his father in 1953 and was crowned in May of that year. In 1955 he married Princess Dina, a member of a distantly related branch of the Hashemite family based in Egypt—a union strongly favored by President Nasser. Hussein divorced Dina in a period of strain between Jordan and Egypt. He married Antoinette Gardiner, the daughter of a British Army officer stationed at Amman in 1961. She converted to Islam and assumed the name Muna al-Hussein (Hussein's Wish). Policy considerations—and nationalist pressure—led Hussein to declare that the eldest son of this union would be ineligible to succeed him. He chose his youngest brother, Hassan, as Crown Prince in 1965 (an older brother, Muhammed, is unstable). Hussein divorced Muna in 1972 and married Alia, the daughter of a Palestinian notable of the West Bank Tuqan family—her father was a Jordanian delegate on the United Nations—the same year. Alia, the first of Hussein's wives to be crowned queen, was killed in a helicopter crash in February 1977. The alliance had been aimed at uniting the blood of the Hashemites with that of the Palestinians in Jordan and particularly on the West Bank. Queen Alia told reporters upon their marriage that Jordanians were Palestinians and Palestinians Jordanians. (The wife of the King's brother Muhammed is also a Palestinian; she is a member of a notable family in Jenin on the West Bank).

Hussein, an effective ruler, has been an ally of the West through many periods of instability in the Arab world, at first of Britain and then of the United States. Given to spells of depression, he has also shown the ability to maintain a cool head in a crisis. He has, at times, had to make important concessions to the nationalist and extremist elements in Jordan and the Arab world, but makes all important policy decisions himself. Surviving a bloody civil war and frequent attempts at assassination, he has led Jordan to economic development and a measure of tranquility.

X

Appendices

PALESTINE AND SYRIA IN 1915

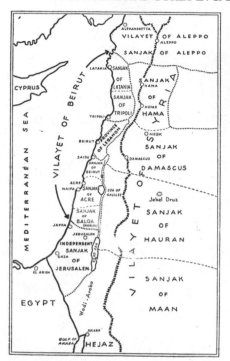

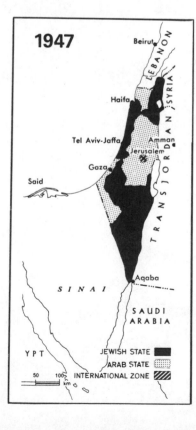

Permission to reprint this map which appears on
page 185 of Palestine: Jewish, Arab and British
Policies. (Yale University Press), was given by
ESCO Fund Committee, Inc.

JORDAN-ISRAEL ARMISTICE AGREEMENT, 1949

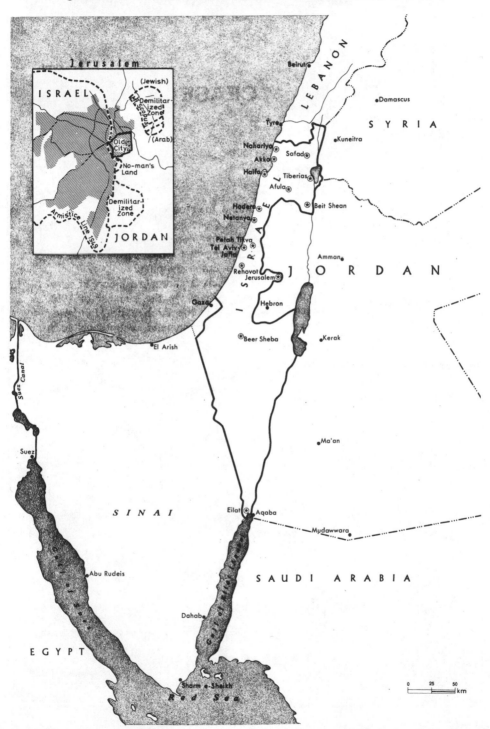

The West Bank (Judea and Samaria), 1974

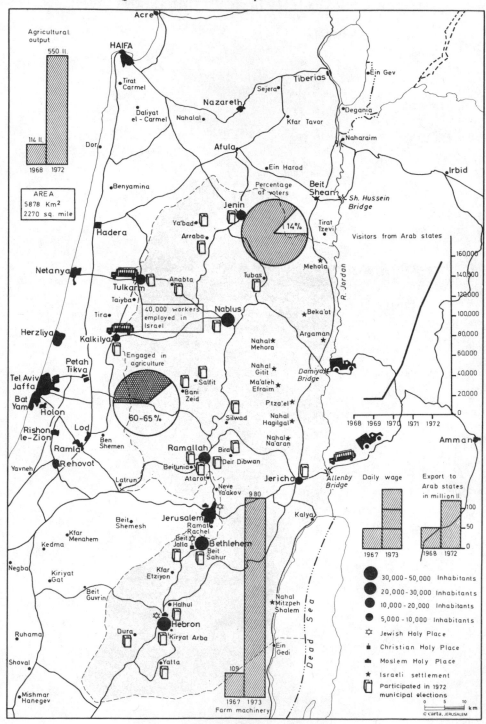

Agricultural output

550 Il.
114 Il.
1968 1972

AREA
5878 Km²
2270 sq. mile

Percentage of voters
14%

40,000 workers employed in Israel

Engaged in agriculture
60-65%

Visitors from Arab states

160,000
140,000
120,000
100,000
80,000
60,000
40,000
20,000
0
1968 1969 1970 1971 1972

Daily wage
1967 1973

Export to Arab states in million Il.
100
50
0
1968 1972

980

109
1967 1973
Farm machinery

- ● 30,000 - 50,000 Inhabitants
- ● 20,000 - 30,000 Inhabitants
- ● 10,000 - 20,000 Inhabitants
- ● 5,000 - 10,000 Inhabitants
- ✡ Jewish Holy Place
- ⌖ Christian Holy Place
- ⌂ Moslem Holy Place
- ★ Israeli settlement
- 🏠 Participated in 1972 municipal elections

0 5 10 km

© Carta, Jerusalem

Map labels: Acre, HAIFA, Tirat Carmel, Nazareth, Sejera, Tiberias, Ein Gev, Daliyat el-Carmel, Nahalal, Kfar Tavor, Degania, Dor, Afula, Naharaim, Benyamina, Ein Harod, Beit Shean, Sh. Hussein Bridge, Irbid, Hadera, Jenin, Ya'bad, Arraba, Tirat Tzevi, Mehola, Netanya, Tulkarm, Anabta, Tubas, Taiyba, Tira, Nablus, Beka'ot, Herzliya, Kalkilya, Salfit, Nahal Mehora, Argaman, Petah Tikva, Tel Aviv Jaffa, Bani Zeid, Nahal Gitit, Ma'aleh Efraim, Damiya Bridge, Bat Yam, Holon, Silwad, Ptza'el, Rishon le-Zion, Lod, Ben Shemen, Ramallah, Bira, Deir Dibwan, Nahal Hagilgal, Nahal Na'aran, Ramla, Rehovot, Beitunia, Atarot, Amman, Yavneh, Latrun, Jericho, Allenby Bridge, Neve Ya'akov, Kfar Menahem, Beit Shemesh, Jerusalem, Ramat Rachel, Kalya, Kedma, Beit Jalla, Bethlehem, Beit Sahur, Negba, Kiriyat Gat, Kfar Etzion, Beit Guvrin, Nahal Mitzpeh Shalem, Halhul, Ruhama, Dura, Hebron, Kiryat Arba, Ein Gedi, Dead Sea, Shoval, Yatta, Mishmar Hanegev, R. Jordan

U.N. General Assembly Resolution on the Partition of Palestine

29 November 1947
[Resolution 181 (II)]

Excerpts:

A

The General Assembly,

• • •

Recommends to the United Kingdom, as the mandatory Power for Palestine, and to all other Members of the United Nations the adoption and implementation, with regard to the future government of Palestine, of the Plan of Partition with Economic Union set out below;
Requests that

• • •

(c) The Security Council determine as a threat to the peace, breach of the peace or act of aggression, in accordance with Article 39 of the Charter, any attempt to alter by force the settlement envisaged by this resolution;

• • •

Calls upon the inhabitants of Palestine to take such steps as may be necessary on their part to put this plan into effect;
Appeals to all Governments and all peoples to refrain from taking any action which might hamper or delay the carrying out of these recommendations . . .

PLAN OF PARTITION WITH ECONOMIC UNION

• • •

3. Independent Arab and Jewish States and the Special International Regime for the City of Jerusalem, set forth in part III of this plan, shall come into existence in Palestine two months after the evacuation of the armed forces of the mandatory Power has been completed but in any case not later than 1 October 1948. The boundaries of the Arab State, the Jewish State, and the City of Jerusalem shall be as described in parts II and III below.

4. The period between the adoption by the General Assembly of its recommendation on the question of Palestine and the establishment of the independence of the Arab and Jewish States shall be a transitional period.

B. STEPS PREPARATORY TO INDEPENDENCE

1. A Commission shall be set up consisting of one representative of each of five Member States. The Members represented on the Commission shall be elected by the General Assembly on as broad a basis, geographically and otherwise, as possible.

2. The administration of Palestine shall, as the mandatory Power withdraws its armed forces, be progressively turned over to the Commission, which shall act in

conformity with the recommendations of the General Assembly, under the guidance of the Security Council. The mandatory Power shall to the fullest possible extent coordinate its plans for withdrawal with the plans of the Commission to take over and administer areas which have been evacuated.

. . .

3. On its arrival in Palestine the Commission shall proceed to carry out measures for the establishment of the frontiers of the Arab and Jewish States and the City of Jerusalem in accordance with the general lines of the recommendations of the General Assembly on the partition of Palestine . . .

4. The Commission, after consultation with the democratic parties and other public organizations of the Arab and Jewish States, shall select and establish in each State as rapidly as possible a Provisional Council of Government. The activities of both the Arab and Jewish Provisional Councils of Government shall be carried out under the general direction of the Commission.

6. The Provisional Council of Government of each State, acting under the Commission, shall progressively receive from the Commission full responsibility for the administration of that State in the period between the termination of the Mandate and the establishment of the State's independence.

10. The Constituent Assembly of each State shall draft a democratic constitution for its State and choose a provisional government to succeed the Provisional Council of Government appointed by the Commission. The constitutions of the States shall embody chapters 1 and 2 of the Declaration provided for in section C below and include *inter alia* provisions for:

(b) Settling all international disputes in which the State may be involved by peaceful means in such a manner that international peace and security, and justice, are not endangered;

(c) Accepting the obligation of the State to refrain in its international relations from the threat or use of force against the territorial integrity or political independence of any State, or in any other manner inconsistent with the purposes of the United Nations;

(e) Preserving freedom of transit and visit for all residents and citizens of the other State in Palestine and the City of Jerusalem, subject to considerations of national security, provided that each State shall control residence within its borders.

11. The Commission shall appoint a preparatory economic commission of three members to make whatever arrangements are possible for economic cooperation, with a view to establishing, as soon as practicable, the Economic Union and the Joint Economic Board, as provided in section D below.

. . .

C. DECLARATION

A declaration shall be made to the United Nations by the provisional government of each proposed State before independence. It shall contain *inter alia* the following clauses:

. . .

Chapter 1

Holy Places, religious buildings and sites

1. Existing rights in respect of Holy Places and religious buildings or sites shall not be denied or impaired.

2. In so far as Holy Places are concerned, the liberty of access, visit and transit shall be guaranteed, in conformity with existing rights, to all residents and citizens of the other State and of the City of Jerusalem, as well as to aliens, without distinction as to nationality, subject to requirements of national security, public order and decorum.

· · ·

Chapter 4
Miscellaneous provisions

· · ·

D. ECONOMIC UNION AND TRANSIT

1. The Provisional Council of Government of each State shall enter into an undertaking with respect to Economic Union and Transit. This undertaking shall be drafted by the Commission provided for in section B, paragraph 1, utilizing to the greatest possible extent the advice and cooperation of representative organizations and bodies from each of the proposed States. It shall contain provisions to establish the Economic Union of Palestine and provide for other matters of common interest. If by 1 April 1948 the Provisional Councils of Government have not entered into the undertaking, the undertaking shall be put into force by the Commission.

The Economic Union of Palestine

2. The objectives of the Economic Union of Palestine shall be:

(a) A customs union;

(b) A joint currency system providing for a single foreign exchange rate;

(c) Operation in the common interest on a non-discriminatory basis of railways; inter-State highways; postal, telephone and telegraphic services, and ports and airports involved in international trade and commerce;

(d) Joint economic development, especially in respect of irrigation, land reclamation and soil conservation;

(e) Access for both States and for the City of Jerusalem on a nondiscriminatory basis to water and power facilities.

· · ·

NOTE.

Geneva,
September 23rd, 1922.

ARTICLE 25 OF THE PALESTINE MANDATE

Territory known as Trans-Jordan
Note by the Secretary-General.

The Secretary-General has the honour to communicate for the information of the Members of the League, a memorandum relating to Article 25 of the Palestine Mandate presented by the British Government to the Council of the League on September 16th, 1922.

The memorandum was approved by the Council subject to the decision taken at its meeting in London on July 24th, 1922, with regard to the coming into force of the Palestine and Syrian mandates.

Memorandum by the British Representative.

1. Article 25 of the Mandate for Palestine provides as follows:—

"In the territories lying between the Jordan and the eastern boundary of Palestine as ultimately determined, the Mandatory shall be entitled, with the consent of the Council of the League of Nations, to postpone or withhold application of such provisions of this Mandate as he may consider inapplicable to the existing local conditions, and to make such provision for the administration of the territories as he may consider suitable to those conditions, provided no action shall be taken which is inconsistent with the provisions of Articles 15, 16 and 18."

2. In pursuance of the provisions of this Article, His Majesty's Government invite the Council to pass the following resolution:—

"The following provisions of the Mandate for Palestine are not applicable to the territory known as Trans-Jordan, which comprises all territory lying to the east of a line drawn from a point two miles west of the town of Akaba on the Gulf of that name up the centre of the Wady Araba, Dead Sea and River Jordan to its junction with the River Yarmuk; thence up the centre of that river to the Syrian Frontier."

Preamble.—Recitals 2 and 3.

Article 2. The words "placing the country under such political administration and economic conditions as will secure the establishment of the Jewish national home, as laid down in the preamble, and"

Article 4.

Article 6.

Source: LEAGUE OF NATIONS. MANDATE FOR PALESTINE, together with a Note by the Secretary-General relating to its application to the Territory known as Trans-Jordan, under the provisions of Article 25.

Article 7. The sentence "There shall be included in this law provisions framed so as to facilitate the acquisition of Palestinian citizenship by Jews who take up their permanent residence in Palestine."
Article 11. The second sentence of the first paragraph and the second paragraph.
Article 13.
Article 14.
Article 22.
Article 23.

In the application of the Mandate to Trans-Jordan, the action which, in Palestine, is taken by the Administration of the latter country, will be taken by the Administration of Trans-Jordan under the general supervision of the Mandatory.

3. His Majesty's Government accept full responsibility as Mandatory for Trans-Jordan, and undertake that such provision as may be made for the administration of that territory in accordance with Article 25 of the Mandate shall be in no way inconsistent with those provisions of the Mandate which are not by this resolution declared inapplicable.

Jordan-Israel Armistice Agreement, 1949

Excerpts:

Article I

With a view to promoting the return of permanent peace in Palestine and in recognition of the importance in this regard of mutual assurances concerning the future military operations of the Parties, the following principles, which shall be fully observed by both Parties during the armistice, are hereby affirmed:

1. The injunction of the Security Council against resort to military force in the settlement of the Palestine question shall henceforth be scrupulously respected by both Parties;

2. No aggressive action by the armed forces — land, sea, or air — of either Party shall be undertaken, planned, or threatened against the people or the armed forces of the other; it being understood that the use of the term *planned* in this context has no bearing on normal staff planning as generally practised in military organizations;

3. The right of each Party to its security and freedom from fear of attack by the armed forces of the other shall be fully respected;

4. The establishment of an armistice between the armed forces of the two Parties is accepted as an indispensable step toward the liquidation of armed conflict and the restoration of peace in Palestine.

342 JORDAN AND THE WEST BANK

Article II

With a specific view to the implementation of the resolution of the Security Council of 16 November 1948, the following principles and purposes are affirmed:

1. The principle that no military or political advantage should be gained under the truce ordered by the Security Council is recognized;

2. It is also recognized that no provision of this Agreement shall in any way prejudice the rights, claims and positions of either Party hereto in the ultimate peaceful settlement of the Palestine question, the provisions of this Agreement being dictated exclusively by military considerations.

Article VIII

1. A Special Committee, composed of two representatives of each Party designated by the respective Governments, shall be established for the purpose of formulating agreed plans and arrangements designed to enlarge the scope of this Agreement and to effect improvements in its application.

2. The Special Committee shall be organized immediately following the coming into effect of this Agreement and shall direct its attention to the formulation of agreed plans and arrangements for such matters as either Party may submit to it, which, in any case, shall include the following, on which agreement in principle already exists: free movement of traffic on vital roads, including the Bethlehem and Latrun-Jerusalem roads; resumption of the normal functioning of the cultural and humanitarian institutions on Mount Scopus and free access thereto; free access to the Holy Places and cultural institutions and use of the cemetery on the Mount of Olives; resumption of operation of the Latrun pumping station; provision of electricity for the Old City; and resumption of operation of the railroad to Jerusalem.

3. The Special Committee shall have exclusive competence over such matters as may be referred to it. Agreed plans and arrangements formulated by it may provide for the exercise of supervisory functions by the Mixed Armistice Commission established in article XI.

Signed at Rhodes, Island of Rhodes, Greece, on 3 April, 1949

The Constitution of the Hashemite Kingdom of Jordan

Passed on 7 November, 1951. Revised 1 January, 1952.
The following are excerpts from the Constitution's 131 articles:

Chapter One
The State and Form of Government

1. The Hashemite Kingdom of Jordan is an independent Arab State. It is indivisible and no part of it may be ceded. The people of Jordan form part of the Arab nation. The form of Government shall be parliamentary with hereditary monarchy.

2. Islam shall be the religion of the State and the Arabic Language shall be its official language.

3. The City of Amman shall be the capital of the Kingdom, The capital may be transferred to another place by special Law.

Chapter Two
Rights and Duties of Jordanians

5. The Jordanian nationality shall be defined by Law.

6. (i) Jordanians shall be equal before the Law, There shall be no discrimination between them as regards their rights and duties, on grounds of race, language or religion.

(ii) The Government shall ensure work and education, within the limits of its possibilities, and shall ensure a state of tranquility and equal opportunities, to all Jordanians.

7. Personal freedom shall be safeguarded.

9. (i) No Jordanian shall be exiled from the territory of the Kingdom.

(ii) No Jordanian shall be prevented from residing at any place, or be compelled to reside in any specified place, except in the circumstances prescribed by law.

14. The State shall safeguard the free exercise of all forms of worship and religious rites in accordance with the customs observed in the Kingdom, unless such exercise is inconsistent with public order or decorum.

15. (i) The State shall guarantee freedom of opinion. Every Jordanian shall be free to express his opinion by words of mouth, in writing, or by means of photographic representation and other forms of expression, within the limits of the law.

(ii) Freedom of the press and publications shall be ensured within the limits of the law.

The above is the official English translation of the Constitution as published by the Government of the Hashemite Kingdom of Jordan.

(iii) Newspapers shall not be suspended from publication nor their permits be withdrawn except in accordance with the provisions of the law.

(iv) In the event of the declaration of martial law or a state of emergency, a limited censorship on newspapers, pamphlets, books and broadcasts in matters affecting public safety or national defence may be imposed by law.

(v) Control of the resources of newspapers shall be regulated by law.

16. (i) Jordanians shall have the right to hold meetings within the limits of the law.

(ii) Jordanians are entitled to establish societies and political parties provided that the objects of such societies and parties are legitimate, their methods are peaceful, and their Bye-Laws are not inconsistent with the provisions of this Constitution.

(iii) The establishment of societies and political parties and control of their resources shall be regulated by law.

19. Congregations shall have the right to establish and maintain their own schools for the education of their own members provided that they will comply with the general provisions of the law and submit to the control of government in matters relating to their curricula and tendency.

20. Elementary education shall be compulsory for Jordanians and free of charge in government schools.

22. (i) Every Jordanian shall be entitled to be appointed to public offices under such conditions as are prescribed by law or regulations.

(ii) Appointment to any government office or to any institution attached to the Government, or to any municipal office, whether such appointment is permanent or temporary, shall be made on the basis of merits and qualifications.

23. (f) Free Trade unions shall be formed within the limits of law.

Chapter Three
Powers of the State—General Provisions

24. (i) The nation is the source of all powers.

(ii) The nation shall exercise its powers in the manner prescribed by this Constitution.

25. The Legislative Power shall be vested in the National Assembly and the King. The National Assembly shall consist of a Senate and a House of Deputies.

26. The Executive Power shall be vested in the King who shall exercise His powers through His Ministers in accordance with the provisions of this Constitution.

27. The Judicial Power shall be exercised by the different courts of law, and all judgments shall be given in accordance with the law and pronounced in the name of the King.

Chapter Four

The Executive Power

Part I

The King and His Prerogatives

28. The throne of the Hashemite Kingdom is limited by inheritance to the dynasty of king Abdullah Ibn Al-Hussein in a direct line through his male heirs . . .

(e) No person shall ascend the Throne unless he is a moslem, mentally sound and born by a legitimate wife and of moslem parents.

(g) The King attains his age of majority upon the completion of his eighteenth year, according to the lunar calendar. If the Throne devolves upon a person who is under this age, the powers of the King shall be exercised by a regent or council of regency, who shall be appointed by a Royal Decree by the reigning King, but if the King dies without making such nomination, the Council of Ministers shall appoint the Regent or Council of Regency.

30. The King is the head of the State and is immune from any liability and responsibility.

31. The King approves all Acts of Parliament and promulgates them. He shall direct the enactment of such regulations as may be necessary for the enforcement of such Acts, provided that such Regulations are not inconsistent with the provisions thereof.

32. The King is the Supreme Commander of the Army, Naval and Air Forces.

33. *(i)** The King declares war, concludes peace and confirms treaties and agreements.

(ii) Treaties and agreements which involve financial commitments to the treasury or affect the general or personal rights of Jordanians shall not be enforceable unless they are sanctioned by the National Assembly. In no circumstances shall any secret conditions contained in any treaty or agreement be contradictory to the openly declared conditions.

34. (ii) The King convenes the House of Deputies, opens it, adjourns it, and prorogues it in accordance with the provisions of the Constitution.

(iii) The King may dissolve the House of Deputies.

35. The King appoints the Prime Minister, dismisses him or accepts his resignation. Ministers are appointed, dismissed and their resignations accepted by the king on the recommendation of the Prime Minister.

36. The King appoints members of the Senate, and appoints the Speaker from amongst them and accepts their resignation.

38. The King has the right to grant a special pardon or remit any sentence, but any general pardon shall be determined by special law.

39. No death sentence shall be executed except after confirmation by the King. Every such sentence shall be placed before the King by the Council of Ministers accompanied by their opinion thereon,

* As amended in Official Gazette No. 1380 date 4/5/1956.
** As amended in Official Gazette No. 1396 date 1/9/1958.

40. The King shall exercise the powers vested in Him by Royal Decrees. Any such Decree shall be signed by the Prime Minister and the Minister or Ministers concerned. The King expresses his concurrence by placing his signature above the signatures of the other ministers.

Part Two
Ministers

41. There shall be constituted a Council of Ministers consisting of the Prime Minister, who shall be the President, and such number of Ministers as may be needed and as the public interest may require.

42. No person shall be appointed as a minister unless he is a Jordanian.

45. *(i) The Council of Ministers shall be entrusted with the responsibility of administering all affairs of the State, internal and external, with the exception of such matters which are or may be entrusted by this Constitution **or by any other legislation to any person or any other body.

(ii) The duties of the Prime Minister, the Ministers and the Council of Ministers shall be prescribed by Regulations made by the Council of Ministers and confirmed by the King.

48. The Prime Minister and Ministers shall sign all decisions taken by the Council of Ministers which shall be submitted to the King for approval where this Constitution, or any law, or Regulations enacted thereunder, so require. Such decisions shall be executed by the Minister and Ministers each within the limits of his jurisdiction.

49. Verbal or written orders of the King shall not release the Ministers from their responsibility.

50. In the event of the resignation or release of the Prime Minister from his office, all Ministers shall be considered to have automatically resigned or released from their offices, as the case may be.

54. (iii)** Every newly formed Council of Ministers shall, within one month of its formation, in cases where the House of Deputies is in session, place before the House of Deputies a statement of its policy and ask for a vote of confidence on the basis of that statement. If the House of Deputies was not in session, at the time, or was dissolved, the Speech from the Throne shall be considered a statement of its policy for the purposes of this Article.

* As amended in the Official Gazette No. 1380 of 4/5/1958.
** As amended in the Official Gazette No. 1396 of 1/9/1958.

Chapter Five
The Legislative Power
The National Assembly

62. The National Assembly shall consist of two Houses:—
The Senate and the House of Deputies.

Part I
The Senate

63. The Senate, including the Speaker, shall consist of not more than one-half of the number of the members of the House of Deputies.

65. *(i) The term of office of Senators shall be for four years, and their appointment shall be renewed every four years. Senators whose term of office had expired may be reappointed for a further term.

Part II
The House of Deputies.

68. (i)** The term of office of the House of Deputies shall be for four calendar years commencing from the date of the announcement of the results of the general elections in the official Gazette. The King may, by a Royal Decree, prolong the term of the House for a period of not less than one year and not more than two years.

* As amended in Official Gazette No. 1243 of 16/10/1955.
** As amended in Official Gazette No. 1380 of 4/5/1958.

Part III
Provisions Governing both Houses of Parliament

75. **(i) No person shall become a Senator or Deputy:
(a) Who is not a Jordanian,
(b) Who claims foreign nationality or protection,
(h) Who is related to the King within a degree of consanguinity to be prescribed by special law.

82. (i) The King may, whenever necessary, convene the National Assembly to meet in an extraordinary session for an unspecified period for the purpose of deciding matters to be specified in the Royal Decree, when the summons is issued. An extraordinary session shall be dissolved by a Royal Decree.

** As amended in Official Gazette No. 1476 of 16/2/1960.

Chapter Six
The Judiciary

99. The courts shall be divided into three categories:—
(i) Civil Courts
(ii) Religious Courts
(iii) Special Courts

103. (ii) Matters of personal status are those matters which are defined by law and are within the exclusive jurisdiction of the Sharia Courts where the parties are Moslems.

104. The Religious Courts shall be divided into:—
(i) The Sharia Courts.
(ii) The tribunals of other Religious Communities.

105. The Sharia Courts shall have exclusive jurisdiction in the following matters in accordance with its special laws:—

(i) Matters of Personal status of Moslems.

(ii) Cases concerning blood money (diyeh) where the two parties are Moslems or where one of the parties is not a Moslem and the two parties consent to the jurisdiction of the Sharia Courts.

106. The Sharia Courts shall apply in its proceedings the provisions of the Sharia Law.

109.(i) Tribunals of Religious Communities shall be established in accordance with a law to be enacted concerning them. Such law shall define the jurisdiction of such tribunals in matters of personal status and trusts (wakfs) constituted for the benefit of the community concerned. Matters of personal status of any such community shall be the same matters as are, in the case of Moslems, within the jurisdiction of the Sharia Courts.

(ii) Such laws shall determine the procedure to be followed by the tribunals of the Religious Communities.

124. In the event of an emergency necessitating the defence of the realm, a law which shall be cited as the Defence law shall be enacted giving power to any person, specified therein, to take such actions and measures, as may be necessary, including the suspension of the operation of the ordinary laws of the State, with a view to ensuring the defence of the Realm. The Defence law shall come into force upon its proclamation by a Royal Decree based on a decision of the Council of Ministers.

125. (i) In the event of an emergency of a serious nature to the extent that action under the preceding Article of this Constitution would be considered insufficient for the defence of the Kingdom, the King may, by a Royal Decree, based on a decision of the Council of Ministers, declare martial law in all or any part of the Kingdom.

1/1/1952   TALAL

Summary of Resolutions of Arab Summit Conference, Khartoum, Sudan, 1 September 1967

The eight Arab Heads of State who attended the Conference were from the UAR, Saudi Arabia, Sudan, Jordan, Lebanon, Kuwait, Iraq and Yemen. Morocco, Libya, Tunisia and Algeria were represented by their Prime Ministers. Syria, who did not attend, was represented by her Foreign Minister, Dr. Ibrahim Makhous, at the Foreign Ministers' Conference which preceded the Summit and drew up its agenda.

First, the Conference affirmed Arab solidarity and the unification of Arab joint action is a cordial atmosphere of coordination and conciliation.

Source: Arab News and Views, No. 13 (Sept. 1967), reprinted in 2 New York University Journal of International Law and Politics 209-10 (1969). Reprinted by permission.

The Heads of State reaffirmed their commitment to the Charter of Arab Solidarity issued at the Third Arab Summit Conference in Casablanca.

Second, the Conference affirmed the necessity of concerted joint efforts in the elimination of all traces of aggression on the basis that the recovery of all occupied Arab territory is the joint responsibility of all Arab countries.

Third, the Arab Heads of State agreed on unifying their efforts in joint political and diplomatic action at the international level to ensure the withdrawal of Israeli forces from the occupied Arab territory. This is within the framework of the basic Arab commitment, which entails non-recognition of Israel, no conciliation nor negotiation with her and the upholding of the rights of the Palestinian people to their land.

Fourth, the Minister of Finance, Economy and Oil recommended the possibility of using oil as a weapon in the struggle. The Summit Conference, after careful study, sees that oil export could be used as a positive weapon which would be directed toward the strengthening of the economies of the Arab countries that suffered directly from the aggression.

Fifth, the Conference approved the proposal submitted by Kuwait to establish an Arab Economic and Social Development Bank in accordance with the recommendations of the Arab Finance, Economy and Oil Ministers' Conference which met in Baghdad.

Sixth, the Conference decided that it is necessary to take all steps to consolidate military preparedness to face the consequences of the situation.

Seventh, the Conference decided to speed up the liquidation of foreign bases in the Arab countries.

Security Council Resolution 242 of 22 November 1967

The Security Council,

Expressing its continuing concern with the grave situation in the Middle East,

Emphasizing the inadmissibility of the acquisition of territory by war and the need to work for a just and lasting peace in which every State in the area can live in security,

Emphasizing further that all Member States in their acceptance of the Charter of the United Nations have undertaken a commitment to act in accordance with Article 2 of the Charter,

1. Affirms that the fulfillment of Charter principles requires the establishment of a just and lasting peace in the Middle East which should include the application of both the following principles:

(i) Withdrawal of Israeli armed forces from territories occupied in the recent conflict;

(ii) Termination of all claims or states of belligerency and respect for and acknowledgment of the sovereignty, territorial integrity and political independence of every State in the area and their right to live in peace within secure and recognized boundaries free from threats or acts of force;

2. Affirms further the necessity

(a) For guaranteeing freedom of navigation through international waterways in the area;

(b) For achieving a just settlement of the refugee problem;

(c) For guaranteeing the territorial inviolability and political independence of every State in the area, through measures including the establishment of demilitarized zones;

3. Requests the Secretary-General to designate a Special Representative to proceed to the Middle East to establish and maintain contacts with the States concerned in order to promote agreement and assist efforts to achieve a peaceful and accepted settlement in accordance with the provisions and principles in this resolution;

4. Requests the Secretary-General to report to the Security Council on the progress of the efforts of the Special Representative as soon as possible.

Rabat Conference Resolution of 29 October 1974

"The Conference: -

"A) Affirms the Palestinian people's right to its homeland and its right to self-determination.

"B) Affirms the right of the Palestinian people to set up an independent national authority under the leadership of the PLO, as the sole legitimate representative of the Palestinian people, on any liberated Palestinian land. The Arab countries will support such an authority once it is established in all spheres.

"C) Support for the PLO in exercising its national and international responsibilities within the framework of Arab commitments.

"D) Calls upon the Hashemite Kingdom of Jordan, Syria and the PLO to outline a joint formula for the coordination of their relations in the light of these decisions, and for their implementation.

"E) All the Arab countries undertake to consolidate the national Palestinian unity and avoid intervention in the internal affairs of the Palestinian action."

The Attitude of King Hussein Following the
Rabat Conference Resolution

Q: Many Arab heads of state reportedly told you privately before the summit that they believed only Jordan could obtain the return of the West Bank in negotiations with Israel. Then they went to Rabat and decided to turn responsibility for the West Bank over to the Palestine Liberation Organization. What happened?

Hussein: It is the Arab conviction that a Palestinian entity is an imperative necessity, Israel has been doing its best to wipe out the very name of Palestine. The decision will compel Israel—if not today, sometime in the future—to recognize the Palestinian reality.

Q: And you decided to acquiesce?

Hussein: There is an Arab verse which says, in effect, where my tribe goes, I go. I was able to present my convictions to all responsible Arabs. As a part of the Arab nation, ever seeking its unity, I go with the general consensus—regardless of any previous feelings.

Q: But you often said you would never agree to prejudge the future of the West Bank without a referendum to allow the Palestinians living there to exercise their right of self-determination. Now, the PLO has the automatic right to take over any liberated part of the West Bank. What changed your mind?

Hussein: We didn't change our mind. We have always said we would be willing to give our support to either option—our way, or the PLO way. The collective Arab will was to choose the PLO option. And we support it, regardless of the consequences. But there will be no change in our attitude toward all Palestinians on the West Bank. For as long as is needed, we shall honor our obligations to help them in every way.

. . .

Q: Does Jordan now consider itself relieved of any further responsibility for the liberation of the West Bank?

Hussein: If Israel refuses to negotiate with Jordan on the ground that whatever Palestinian territory is returned will be turned over to the PLO, then there won't be much we can do about it. An entirely new situation exists now.

Israel Knesset Statement Delivered on 5 November 1974 by the Prime Minister, Mr. Yitzhak Rabin, Following the Rabat Conference

Excerpts:

. . . The meaning of [the Rabat] Resolutions is clear. The Rabat Conference decided to charge the organizations of murderers with the establishment of a Palestinian State, and the Arab countries gave the organizations a free hand to decide on their mode of operations. The Arab countries themselves will refrain, as stated in the Resolution, from intervening in the "internal affairs" of this action.

We are not fully aware of the significance of the fourth Resolution, which refers to "outlining a formula" for the coordination of relations between Jordan, Syria, Egypt and the PLO. It is by no means impossible that it is also intended to bring about closer military relations between them.

The significance of these Resolutions is extremely grave. The aim of the terrorist organizations is well known and clear. The Palestine National Covenant speaks bluntly and openly about the liquidation of the State of Israel by means of armed struggle, and the Arab States committed themselves at Rabat to support this struggle. Any attempt to implement them will be accompanied by at least attempts to carry out terrorist operations on a larger scale with the support of the Arab countries.

The decisions of the Rabat Conference are merely a continuation of the resolutions adopted at Khartoum. Only, further to the "no's" of Khartoum, the roof organization of the terrorists has attained the status conferred upon it by the presidents and kings at Rabat. Throughout this conference not a voice was raised expressing readiness for peace. The recurring theme of this conference was the aspiration to destroy a member-state of the United Nations. The content of this gathering has nothing whatsoever in common with social progress or the advancement of humanity among the Arab nations or in the relations with the peoples in the region and throughout the world.

There is no indication of any deviation from the goal and policy of the terrorist organizations, so let us not delude ourselves on this score. The terrorist organizations had no successes in the administered territories, but the successes they achieved at the U.N. General Assembly and at Rabat are encouraging them to believe that the targets they had so confidently set themselves are now within reach.

The policy laid down in Khartoum and Rabat shall not be executed. We have the power to prevent its implementation. The position of the government of Israel in the face of these resolutions of the Rabat Conference is unequivocal:

A) The government of Israel categorically rejects the conclusions of the Rabat Conference, which are designed to disrupt any progress towards peace, to encourage the terrorist elements, and to foil any step which might lead to peaceful coexistence with Israel.

B) In accordance with the Knesset's resolutions, the government of Israel will not negotiate with terrorist organizations whose avowed policy is to strive for Israel's destruction and whose method is terrorist violence.

C) We warn the Arab leaders against making the mistake of thinking that threats or even the active employment of the weapon of violence or of military force will lead to a political solution. This is a dangerous illusion. The aims of the Palestinian National Charter will not be achieved, either by terrorist acts or by limited or total warfare.

The Rabat Conference Resolutions do not justify the adoption of other resolutions, and merely add force to our determination. To anyone who recommends negotiations with the terrorist organizations, I have to say that there is no basis for negotiation with the terrorist organizations. It does not enter our minds to negotiate with a body that denies our existence as a State and follows a course of violence and terrorism for the destruction of our State.

Negotiations with such a body would lend legitimacy and encouragement to its policy and its criminal acts. The U.N. General Assembly's decision to invite this body to its debates is a serious error from the moral and political standpoints, but it has no substance so long as Israel denounces this body, its policies and its deeds, as incompatible with the very existence of the State of Israel. Israel will grant no recognition to those who conspire against her existence.

Rabat is not a surprising innovation, but our policy will not be determined by its decisions. We shall carefully watch the steps the Arab States will take in the wake of this conference and, in particular, we shall watch the moves of those States with whom we were about to embark on negotiations on stages of progress towards peace. Above all, we shall see whether Egypt is in fact ready for this, or whether she has committed herself to the ban on reaching a separate agreement with Israel. We shall be watching Jordan's moves, too, to see whether she surrenders to Arafat.

In the face of this development, we believe that the strength and stability of the State of Israel, and the Israel defense forces, powerful and prepared for any test, are the guarantee for our safety. As long as we are strong and follow a wise and courageous policy, the chances will increase that our neighbors will be ready to seek ways of coming to terms with us.

Security Council Resolution 338 of 22 October 1973

The Security Council

1. *Calls upon* all parties to the present fighting to cease all firing and terminate all military activity immediately, no later than 12 hours after the moment of the adoption of this decision, in the positions they now occupy;

2. *Calls upon* the parties concerned to start immediately after the cease-fire the implementation of Security Council resolution 242 (1967) in all of its parts;

3. *Decides* that, immediately and concurrently with the cease-fire, negotiations shall start between the parties concerned under appropriate auspices aimed at establishing a just and durable peace in the Middle East.

Adopted at the 1747th meeting by 14 votes to none.

Israel Government Decision Concerning Settlement in the Israel-Administered Areas

1. The Government will act to increase settlement on both sides of the "Green Line" (the 1949-1967 armistice lines between Israel and the neighboring Arab States), in accordance with decisions to be adopted by the Cabinet, on the basis of the Government's Basic Policy Principles, as approved by the Knesset.

2. The Government will prevent settlement attempts without its approval and decision, as contrary to law and contrary to Israel's security and peace policy.

3. The procedure governing the adoption of decisions concerning settlement will be continued by means of the Ministerial Settlement Committee and the Ministerial Committee on Jerusalem, subject to Cabinet approval.

4. No settlement shall be established at Kaddoum. At a date in the near future, to be determined by the Cabinet, the Kaddoum nucleus will be transferred to a permanent place of settlement that will be offered it within the framework of the Government's approved program. Until such time, nothing shall be done at Kaddoum that could transform it into a permanent settlement.

Adopted by the Government of Israel,
9 May 1976.

Assassination Attempts Against King Hussein

November 10, 1958: Two MIGS intercepted a plane carrying King Hussein and his uncle, Sherif Nasser Ben Jamil, over Syrian territory. The King, headed for a vacation in Switzerland, had informed the Syrian authorities that he would be flying over Syria and had received authorization. The pilot succeeded in eluding his pursuers and returned to Jordan.

The incident aggravated tension between Jordan, Damascus and Cairo. Jordan had opposed the February 1958 creation of the United Arab Republic (of Syria and Egypt). King Hussein viewed the Union as directed against Jordan.

August 29, 1960: Time bombs in the building housing the Prime Minister's offices killed Prime Minister Hazza Majali and 11 others. Jordan placed responsibility for the act on the Syrian Secret Service. An unconfirmed but widespread theory held that the explosions were meant to kill King Hussein, who was expected in the building.

August 7, 1962: The Moroccan police uncovered a plot to kill King Hussein during his private visit to Rabat. Jordan accused Egypt of having supplied the false Saudi passports enabling the two Palestinian conspirators to enter Morocco.

September 2, 1970: According to Radio Amman, a convoy including King Hussein was fired upon by ''armed elements.'' The attack occurred on the road to the airport, near Ain Ghazaleh. Palestinian commandos were suspected. The Jordanian civil war began on September 17.

November 18, 1972: Talal Khatib, a Jordanian air force pilot, allegedly fired a rocket from his plane at a helicopter being boarded by King Hussein. The King was wounded in the leg and hospitalized. Loyal pilots shot down the assailant's plane. The attempt was never officially confirmed. King Hussein was said to have entered the hospital for a routine medical check-up.

There have been rumors of other assassination attempts but these have never been verified.

The Palestine Liberation Organization: Factions

Al Fatah: is an acronym derived from the Arabic initials of the words "Palestine Liberation Organization" read backwards which also means "victory." Has been the dominant voice in the PLO since 1969. Started by Egypt, its first recruits were from Gaza and Kuwait who received their initial training in Algeria in 1962 before moving on to camps in Jordan and Syria. Its origins lie in the *Muslim Brotherhood,* an extremist nationalist and fundamentalist Islamic movement. It is headed by Yasser Arafat. Other prominent leaders are Salah Khalaf (Abu Iyyad) and Farouk Kaddoumi, generally regarded as the PLO's political spokesman.

Popular Front for the Liberation of Palestine: emerged shortly after the 1967 war, when the former *Movement of Arab Nationalists* reconstituted itself as a guerrilla organization *(al Tha'r)* and joined forces with a group led by Ahmad Jibril. Headed by Dr. George Habbash, it professes to be Marxist-Leninist in ideology. Leila Khaled, the woman hijacker, is one of its members. It is allied with the *Japanese Red Army* whose members have been responsible for terrorist acts in Japan and participated in the attack on passengers at Israel's Lod international airport on May 30, 1972.

Popular Democratic Front for the Liberation of Palestine: is headed by Nayef Hawatmeh. It broke away from the PFLP, accusing Habbash of "bourgeois tendencies."

Popular Front for the Liberation of Palestine-General Command: is another splinter group which separated itself from the PFLP. Its commander is Ahmad Jibril, a former Syrian army officer who believes that "actions speak louder than words."

Al Saiqa: (Thunderbolt) was started by Syria in 1967 and has Syrian forces in its ranks. Its head is Zuhair Mukhsan. In line with Syrian policy, it is hostile to Arafat.

Arab Liberation Front: is the Iraqi equivalent of the Syrian *Saiqa.*

Black September: is the military overseas terrorist wing of *al fatah,* created during the Jordan civil war and directly controlled by Arafat.

Black June: is headed by Abu Nidal, a former *fatah* member and operates out of Iraq. With Abu Daoud, Nidal was one of the organizers of *Black September* and responsible for the 1972 massacre of Israeli athletes at the Munich Olympics. Abu Nidal calls Syria the "apostate regime" and says that country is the main target of his terrorist operations. Nidal has been condemned to death by the Arafat-led PLO leadership, which he terms "fascist." He trains Palestinian "suicide squads" at a camp near Baghdad. Although he does not officially claim responsibility for such operations as the seizure by four terrorists of the Semiramus Hotel in Damascus in 1976, he displays posters commemorating this "Tel al-Zaatar Operation" (a reference to Syria's siege of the refugee camp in Lebanon during the civil war there) in his headquarters. He does not openly claim the attack on the Intercontinental Hotel in Amman in November 1976 so as not to embarrass his Iraqi hosts. Shown a list of terrorist acts by Nidal's organization, David Hirst, in *The Manchester Guardian Weekly* (Vol. 115, No. 25, week ending December 19, 1976) reported:

If accurate, it is an impressive one. There certainly was an explosion in the Damascus Air Ministry about three months ago. Abu Nidal . . . says that President Assad left the building five minutes before . . . This Palestinian ultra sees an Arab world tottering on the brink of revolutionary chaos and civil war. "We are not a Red Cross Society," he says. Arabs seizing Arab hostages—public relations terrorism at its most shocking—is his way of trying to push it over.

NOTE: The PLO has periodically denied any connection with hijackings, murders and other atrocities carried out by the groups under its umbrella and has maintained that its own policies are moderate and that it cannot be held responsible for the acts of others. It has little or no control over these affiliated groups. It has also denied responsibility, on occasion, for acts carried out by Arafat-directed groups.

Since mid-December 1976, some 100 functionaries, training personnel and terror experts of the *Popular Front for the Liberation of Palestine* have set up their headquarters in Baghdad, Iraq and Aden, South Yemen, moving from Beirut. The organization is financed by Libya, but no longer receives aid from the more moderate Arab governments. The new Iraqi-PFLP alliance rejects a negotiated settlement with Israel; has threatened to execute any Arab state or PLO leader who recognizes Israel or declares his willingness to accept a West Bank state; has intensified terrorist and subversive activities against Arab governments such as Saudi Arabia, Kuwait and the Gulf Emirates and has declared that any means is justified in order to overthrow President Assad of Syria.

The "Rejection Front" (the PFLP, the PDFLP and the PFLP-General Command) is violently opposed to Arafat and his private militia *al fatah* organization, while *al Saiqa's* leader, Zuhair Mukhsan, is in competition with Arafat for the PLO leadership. The struggle for power between all the groups has been accompanied by constant shootings and terrorist acts.

▼

DISTRIBUTION OF REFUGEES AND DISPLACED PERSONS BEFORE AND AFTER THE 1967 WAR

(East and West Banks)

Location	Refugees	Displaced Persons	Total Refugees and Displaced Persons		Total Population
			Number	Percent of Population	
Before 1967 war:					
West Bank	390,000	—	390,000	42	930,000
East Bank	332,000	—	332,000	28	1,200,000
Total Jordan	722,000	—	722,000	34	2,130,000
As of 9-1-68					
East Bank	494,000	201,000	696,000	46	1,513,000
West Bank	245,000	—	245,000	38	650,000
As of 12-31-72					
East Bank	558,000	[1]208,000	266,000	46	[2]669,000
West Bank	281,000	—	281,000	41	[2]679,000

1. Receiving rations from Jordan.
2. Population figures for 1971.
Source: U.S. Mission to Amman, Jordan, and UNRWA report.

The composition of refugees and displaced persons on the East Bank as of September 1, 1968, and December 31, 1972, is shown in the following two tables, respectively.

East Bank Refugees and Displaced Persons as of 9-1-68

Source	Refugees	Displaced Persons	Total
In East Bank before 1967	332,000	—	332,000
From West Bank after 1967	145,000	135,000	280,000
From Gaza Strip after 1967	17,000	16,000	33,000
From East Bank (note 1)	—	50,000	50,000
Total	494,000	201,000	695,000

1. East Bankers who fled their homes in the areas of intensive fighting—principally the Jordan River Valley. Many stayed away during the period of fighting along the river between the *fedayeen* and Israel during 1968-70. By late 1972 these displaced persons had begun returning to the valley.

Source: U.S. Mission in Amman, Jordan.

East Bank Refugees and Displaced Persons as of 12-31-72

Source	Refugees	Displaced Persons	Total
In East Bank before 1967	319,000	—	319,000
From West Bank after 1967	205,000	187,000	392,000
From Gaza Strip after 1967	34,000	21,000	55,000
From East Bank	—	—	—
Total	558,000	[1]208,000	766,000

1. Receiving rations from Jordan.
Source: UNRWA report.

The two previous tables show one of the basic problems facing both UNRWA and the Jordan Government—the continuous growth of the registered refugee population. Many factors contributed to the growth—a continuous trickle of people from the Israeli-occupied sectors (Gaza Strip and the West Bank), a high birth rate, and some unreported refugee deaths. This happens particularly if the deceased had a ration card—the card is passed on to family or friends.)

* All the data in this section (p. 358-9), is excerpted from: Summary of United States Assistance to Jordan, Department of State Agency for International Development, Report to Congress by the Comptroller General of the United States, B-179001, Washington, D.C. 20548.

TOTAL NUMBER OF PALESTINIAN ARAB REFUGEES ACCORDING TO UNRWA RECORDS 1 July 1975 — 30 June 1976

Distribution by place of registration of total registered refugee population and of camp population

	Total registered population	Number of camps Established	Number of camps Emergency	Number of persons officially registered in established camps[1]	Number of persons actually living in camps Established[2]	Number of persons actually living in camps Emergency[3]
East Jordan	644,669	4	6	72,265	89,214	127,031
West Bank	296,628	20	—	74,120	74,941	—
Gaza Strip	339,824	8	—	191,96	201,960	—
Lebanon	198,637	15	—	96,815	102,136	—
Syrian Arab Republic	188,447	6	4	30,160	35,550	19,406
Total	1,668,205	53	10	463,316	505,299	146,437

651,736

1. Persons officially registered in these camps are refugees registered with UNRWA who are shown in UNRWA records as living in camps, irrespective of their category of registration (RSN), although some may have moved to villages, towns or cities in other parts of the country and their removal has yet to be reported to the Agency. The figures do not include refugees in camps who are not given shelter by UNRWA but benefit from sanitation services.

2. Of the 505,299 persons actually living in these camps, 498,570 are UNRWA-registered refugees and their unregistered dependants. The balance of 6,729 are not UNRWA-registerd refugees and are thus not eligible for UNRWA assistance.

3. Persons actually living in these camps comprise 103,610 UNRWA-registered refugees and 42,827 other persons displaced as a result of the June 1967 hostilities or subsequent fighting in the Jordan Valley in early 1968.

SOURCE: Report of the Commissioner-General of the United Nations Relief and Works Agency for Palestinian Refugees in the Near East, 1 July 1975—30 June, 1976. General Assembly Official Records: Thirty-First Session. Supplement No. 13 (A/31/13). United Nations. Table 4, p. 76.

BIBLIOGRAPHY

'Abdallah, King. *My Memoirs Completed (al-Takmilah)*. Translated by Harold Glidden. Washington, D.C.: American Council of Learned Societies, 1954.

'Abdullah, King. *Memoirs of King 'Abdullah of Transjordan*. New York: Philosophical Library, 1950.

Abidi, Aqil. *Jordan: A Political Study, 1948-57*. London: Asia Publishing House, 1965.

Abu Jaber, Kamel S. "The Legislature of the Hashemite Kingdom of Jordan: A Study in Political Development." *The Muslim World*, Vol. 59, Nos. 3 & 4 (July-October 1969): 211-233.

Agha, Hussein J. "What State for the Palestinians?" *Journal of Palestine Studies*. Vol. VI, No. 1 (Autumn 1976): 3-38.

Antonius, George. *The Arab Awakening: The Story of the Arab National Movement*. New York: Capricorn Books, 1965.

Antoun, Richard T. *Arab Village: A Social Structural Study of a Transjordanian Peasant Community*. Bloomington: Indiana University Press, 1972.

Aresvik, Oddvar. *The Agricultural Development of Jordan*. Praeger Special Studies in International Economics and Development. New York: Praeger Publishers, 1976.

Aruri, Naseer H. *Jordan: A Study in Political Development (1921-1965)*. The Hague: Martinus Mijhoff, 1972.

Azm, Sadik, al-. "The Palestinian Resistance Movement Reconsidered," in *The Arabs Today: Alternatives for Tomorrow*, edited by Said, Edward and Suleiman, Fuad. Columbus, Ohio: Forum Associates, Inc., 1973.

Bernadotte, Count Folk. *To Jerusalem*. London: Hodder-Stoughton, 1951.

Brecher, Michael. *Decisions in Israel's Foreign Policy*. New Haven: Yale University Press, 1975.

Campbell, John C. *Defense of the Middle East: Problems of American Policy*. Published for the Council on Foreign Relations. New York: Harper & Brothers, 1960.

Cohen, Amnon. "The Jordanian Communist Party in the West Bank, 1950-1960," in *The U.S.S.R. And The Middle East*, edited by Confino, Michael and Shamir, Shimon. New Brunswick: Transaction Books, 1973.

Dann, Uriel. "The Beginnings of the Arab Legion." *Middle Eastern Studies*, Vol. 5, No. 3 (October 1969): 181-191.

———. "The Political Confrontation of Summer 1924 in Transjordan." *Middle Eastern Studies*, Vol. 12, No. 2 (May 1976): 159-168.

Dayan, Moshe. *Story of My Life: An Autobiography*. New York: William Morrow and Company, Inc., 1976.

Dearden, Ann. *Jordan*. London: Robert Hale, 1958.

Dodd, Peter, and Barakat, Halim. *River Without Bridges: A Study of the Exodus of the 1967 Palestinian Arab Refugees.* (Monograph Series No. 10.) Beirut: Institute for Palestine Studies, 1969.

Efrat, Elisha. "Changes in the Patterns of Settlement in Judea and Samaria, 1947-1967." (In Hebrew, with English summary.) *Hamizrah Hehadash,* Vol. XXIII, No. 3 (91), (1973): 283-295.

Fabian, Larry and Schiff, Zeev, eds. *Israelis Speak: About Themselves and the Palestinians.* Washington, D.C.: Carnegie Endowment for International Peace, 1977.

Faddah, Mohammad Ibrahim. *The Middle East in Transition: A Study of Jordan's Foreign Policy.* New York: Asia Publishing House, 1974.

Friedman, Isaiah. *The Question of Palestine, 1914-1918: British-Jewish-Arab Relations.* London: Routledge and Keegan Paul, 1973.

Furlonge, Sir Geoffrey. "Jordan Today." *Royal Central Asian Journal,* Vol. LIII, Part III (October 1966): 277-285.

Gerber, Haim. "The Ottoman Administration of the Sanjaq of Jerusalem, 1890-1908." (In Hebrew, with English summary.) *Hamizrah Hehadash,* Vol. XXIV, Nos. 1-2 (93-94), (1974): 1-33.

Glubb, Sir John Bagot. *A Soldier With the Arabs.* New York: Harper & Brothers, 1957.

———. *Syria, Lebanon, Jordan.* New York: Walker & Company, 1967.

———. *The Story of the Arab Legion.* London: Hodder & Stoughton, 1952.

Gosenfeld, Norman. "Changes in the Business Community of East Jerusalem." (In Hebrew, with English summary.) *Hamizrah Hehadash,* Vol. XXIV, No. 4 (96), (1974): 261-279.

Gubser, Peter. *Politics and Change in Al-Karak, Jordan.* London: Oxford University Press, 1973.

Hanna, Paul L. *British Policy in Palestine.* Washington, D.C.: American Council on Public Affairs, 1942.

Hourani, Albert H. *Great Britain and the Arab World.* London: John Murray, 1945.

———. *Minorities in the Arab World.* London: Oxford University Press, 1947.

Howard, Norman F. "Jordan: The Price of Moderation." *Current History,* Vol. 68, No. 402 (February 1975): 61-65.

———. "The Uncertain Kingdom of Jordan." *Current History,* Vol. 66, No. 390 (February 1974): 62-65.

Hurewitz, J.C. *Diplomacy in the Near and Middle East.* Volume 2. Princeton: Van Nostrand, 1956.

———. *Middle East Dilemmas: The Background of United States Policy.* New York: Russel & Russel, 1973.

———. *Middle East Politics: The Military Dimension.* New York: Octagon Books, 1974.

———. *The Struggle for Palestine*. New York: Schocken Books, 1976.

Hussein, King. *My War With Israel*. As told to and with additional material by Vick Vance and Pierre Lauer. New York: William Morrow and Co., Inc., 1969.

———. *Uneasy Lies the Head: The Autobiography of His Majesty King Hussein I of the Hashemite Kingdom of Jordan*. New York: Bernard Geis Associates, 1962.

Isaac, Rael Jean. *Israel Divided: Ideological Politics in the Jewish State*. Baltimore and London: The Johns Hopkins University Press, 1976.

Jarvis, Claude Scudamore. *Arab Command: The Biography of F.G. Peak Pasha*. London: Hutchinson & Co., 1943.

Johnston, Charles. *The Brink of Jordan*. London: Hamish Hamilton, 1972.

Kanovsky, Eliyahu. *Economic Development of Jordan*. Tel Aviv: University Publishing Projects, 1976.

Kaplan, Stephen S. "United States Aid and Regime Maintenance in Jordan, 1957-1973." *Public Policy*, Vol. 23, No. 2 (Spring 1975): 189-217.

Kedourie, Eli. *In the Anglo-Arab Labyrinth: The McMahon- Husayn Correspondence and Its Interpretations, 1914-1939*. New York: Cambridge University Press, 1976.

Khaddouri, Majid. "Fertile Crescent Unity," in *The Near East and the Great Powers*, edited by Frye, R.N. Cambridge, Mass.: Harvard University Press, 1955.

Kirkbride, Sir Alec. *From the Wings: Amman Memoirs 1947-1951*. London: Frank Cass, 1976.

Klieman, Aaron S. *Foundations of British Policy In The Arab World: The Cairo Conference of 1921*. Baltimore and London: The Johns Hopkins University Press, 1970.

Lias, Godfrey. *Glubb's Legion*. London: Evans Brothers, 1956.

Mazur, Michael P. "Economic Development in Jordan," in *Economic Development and Population Growth in the Middle East*, edited by Cooper, Charles A. and Alexander, Sidney Y. New York: American Elsevier, 1972.

Meinertzhagen, Colonel Richard. *Middle East Diary: 1917-1956*. New York: Thomas Yoseloff, 1959.

Meir, Golda. *My Life*. New York: Dell Publishing Co., 1975.

Milson, Menahem, ed. *Society and Political Structure in the Arab World*. New York: Humanities Press, 1973.

Mogannam, E. Theodore. "Development in the Legal System of Jordan." *Middle East Journal*, Vol. 6, No. 2 (Spring 1952): 194-206.

Monroe, Elizabeth. *Britain's Moment in the Middle East, 1914-1956*. Baltimore: The Johns Hopkins University Press, 1963.

Morris, James. *The Hashemite Kings*. London: Faber and Faber, 1959.

Nevakiki, Jukka. *Britain, France and the Arab Middle East, 1914-1920*. London: The Athlone Press, 1969.

Nuseibeh, Hazem Zaki. *The Ideas of Arab Nationalism*. Port Washington, N.Y.: Kennikat Press, 1972.

Nyrop, Richard F., et. al. *Area Handbook for the Hashemite Kingdom of Jordan*. Washington, D.C.: U.S. Government Printing Office, 1974.

O'Ballance, Edgar. *Arab Guerilla Power, 1967-1972*. Hamden, Conn.: Archon Books, 1973.

————. *The Electronic War in the Middle East*. Hamden, Conn.: Archon Books, 1974.

————. *The Third Arab-Israeli War*. Hamden, Conn.: Archon Books, 1972.

Patai, Raphael. *The Kingdom of Jordan*. Princeton: Princeton University Press, 1958.

————, ed. *Jordan*. New Haven: Human Relations Area Files, 1957.

Peake, Frederick G. *History and Tribes of Jordan*. Coral Gables, Florida: University of Miami Press, 1958.

Remba, Oded. "Why Jordan Can Survive." *New Middle East*, No. 6 (March 1969): 24-30.

Riebenfeld, Paul. "Israel, Jordan, Palestine." *Midstream*, Vol. XXII, No. 3, (March, 1976): 30-44.

Seton, C.R.W., ed. *Legislation of Transjordan, 1918-1930*. London: Crown Agents for the Colonies, 1931.

Shwadran, Benjamin. *Jordan: A State of Tension*. New York: Council for Middle Eastern Affairs, 1959.

————. "Jordan Annexes Arab Palestine." *Middle Eastern Affairs*, Vol. 1, No. 4 (April 1950): 99-111.

————. "Union of Jordan With Iraq and Recoil." *Middle Eastern Affairs*, Vol. IX, No. 12 (December 1958): 370-392.

Simon, Reeva S. "The Hashemite 'Conspiracy': Hashemite Unity Attempts, 1921-1958." *International Journal of Middle East Studies*, Vol. 5, No. 3 (1974): 314-327.

Snow, Peter. *Hussein, A Biography*. Washington and New York: Robert B. Luce, Inc., 1972.

Sofer, Na'im. "The Integration of Arab Palestine in the Jordan Kingdom." (In Hebrew, with English summary.) *Hamizrah Hehadash*, VI (1955): 189-196.

————. "The Political Status of Jerusalem in the Hashemite Kingdom of Jordan, 1948-1967." *Middle Eastern Studies*, Vol. 12, No. 1 (January 1976): 73-94.

Sparrow, Gerald. *Modern Jordan*. London: Allen & Unwin, 1961.

Stein, Leonard. *The Balfour Declaration*. New York: Simon and Schuster, 1961.

Stevens, Georgiana. *Jordan River Partition*. Stanford: Stanford University Press, 1965.

Stookey, Robert W. *America and the Arab States: An Uneasy Encounter*. New York: John Wiley & Sons, Inc., 1975.

Sutcliffe, Claud R. "The East Ghor Canal Project: A Case Study of Refugee Resettlement, 1961-1966." *Middle East Journal*, Vol. 27, No. 4 (Autumn 1973): 471-482.

Syrkin, Marie. *Golda Meir, Israel's Leader*. New York: G.P. Putnam's Sons, 1969.

Van Arkadie, Brian. *Benefits and Burdens: A Report On The West Bank and Gaza Strip Economies Since 1967*. Washington, D.C.: Carnegie Endowment for International Peace, 1977.

Vatikiotis, P.J. *Politics and the Military in Jordan: A Study of the Arab Legion, 1921-1957*. New York: Praeger Publishers, 1967.

Woodward, E.L. and Butler, Rohan, eds. *Documents on British Foreign Policy, 1919-1939*. Volume 13. London: Her Majesty's Stationary Office, 1963.

Wright, Esmond. "Abdallah's Jordan: 1947-1951." *Middle East Journal*, Vol. 5, No. 4 (Autumn 1951): 439-460.

Young, Peter. *Bedouin Command With the Arab Legion, 1953-1956*. London: W. Kimber, 1956.

Index

'Abdallah, King, 24, 28, 40, 89, 94, 144-5, 176, 323, 326; and Britain, 23, 38-9, 93, 125, 323, 328; and Greater Syria, 139, 148-9, 160, 214, 323; and Israel, 27, 107, 160, 213; and Palestine, 25, 40; and the Arab states, 24, 26, 93-4, 324; and the Palestinian Arabs, 13, 25-6, 42, 93, 103, 105, 107, 130, 144-5, 160, 212, 215, 325; and the Palestinian Jews, 26, 125-6, 323-4; and the West Bank, 27-8, 42, 91, 93-4, 102, 105, 131, 212, 247-8; as a Hashemite, 143, 147, 330; as Emir of Transjordan, 11, 23, 26, 37, 90, 101, 159, 327-8

Ahmed, Abdul Azzia Haj, 298

Akashah, Saba al-, 104

Alami, Musa al-, 106

Alia, Queen, 330

Allenby, General, 22, 36, 39, 326

All-Palestine Government in Gaza, the, 212, 214

Amru, Dr. Subhi Amin, 105

Anabtawi family, the, 110

Anglo-Jordanian Treaties, the, 24-6, 29, 39-41, 129, 150, 159, 161, 176, 178

Arab-Israel War of 1948, the, 11-12, 40, 42, 108, 115, 125, 159, 176, 203-4, 211, 221, 275, 279

Arab-Israel War of 1967, (also, Six Day War), the, 13, 32, 45, 115, 130, 163, 165, 175, 177, 180, 202-3, 205, 259, 305; and Israel, 206, 247, 252, 260; and the Palestinians, 202, 205, 211, 215; effects on Jordan, 75, 82-3, 99, 106, 132, 163; Hussein's role in, 152-3

Arab-Israel War of October 1973, (also, Yom Kippur War), the, 34, 47, 153, 166, 178, 282

Arab League, the, 11, 26-7, 31, 51, 59, 145, 148-9, 207, 252

Arab Legion, the, 11, 26-7, 29, 38-9, 41-2, 92, 125-30, 143-4, 161, 177, 179, 191, 294, 324, 329

Arab Liberation Front, the, 55, 57, 286, 356

Arab Revolt, the, 22, 139-41, 144, 147, 323, 326, 330

Arab Solidarity Pact, the, 150

Arab Summit Conference in Algiers, the, 218

Arab Summit Conference, the first, 31, 108, 152, 163, 213

Arab Summit Conference, the second, 31

Arab Summit Conference at Khartoum, the, 32, 106, 109, 164, 348

Arab Summit Conference at Rabat, the, 14, 35, 104, 106, 165, 183, 215, 218, 264, 279-82, 284-5, 293, 350

Arab Union, the, 162

Arafat, Yasser, 34, 36, 184, 254, 264, 288, 290, 294; and the West Bank, 293, 295-6; as head of *fatah*, 31, 356; on a Palestinian entity, 288, 290, 292; role in Jordan civil war, 13, 33, 46-7, 55, 57, 59-60

Assad, President Hafez al-, 13, 47, 49, 139, 153, 185-6, 291

Atasi, President, 182

Auster, Daniel, 318

Awdah, Adnan Abu, 107

Azzam, 'Abd al-Rahman, 145

Badran, Mudar, 103, 113, 282

Baghdad Pact, the, 28, 41, 95, 105, 108, 110, 125, 150, 161, 178

Bakr, Ibrahim, 60

Balfour Declaration, the, 22-3, 37, 134, 176, 327, 329

Bedouin, the, 18-20, 23, 42, 89-91, 104, 115, 160, 191, 200; in army, 29, 38, 92, 97, 101, 107, 111

Ben Gurion, David, 129, 326

Bevin, Ernest, 126, 128

Black June, 356

Black September, 33, 61, 177-8, 183, 286, 291, 356

Brezhnev, Leonid, 182

British Mandate for Palestine, the, 11, 22-3, 25, 27, 36, 40, 69, 159, 176, 228, 317, 337; and the West Bank, 205; and Transjordan, 37-8, 125, 273; population during, 201-4; Zionist provisions of, 328

Bunche, Dr. Ralph, 27

Cairo Conference of 1921, the, 327-8

Chechens, the, 26, 90, 100, 115